High-Performance Data Stores for Markets

Applied Techniques with kdb+ and ClickHouse

Thomas V. Trex

Published by NobleTrex Press

For permissions and other inquiries, write to:
P.O. Box 3132, Framingham, MA 01701, USA

Contents

Introduction

Markets speak in time-stamped facts. Quotes arrive, orders revise, trades print, clocks advance-and in each nanosecond lies information that is valuable only if it can be captured, organized, and queried before the next event renders it stale. This book is about building data stores that keep pace with that conversation. It pairs the pragmatism of production systems with the clarity of first principles, using two complementary platforms-kdb+ and ClickHouse-to show how to achieve ultra-low-latency ingest, fast analytical scans, and reliable operations at scale.

Our premise is simple: performance is a property of the entire stack. Database behavior is inseparable from CPU caches, memory hierarchies, NVMe queues, NIC ring buffers, and clock discipline. Likewise, correctness in market analytics is inseparable from temporal semantics, session calendars, and microstructure rules. The opening chapter on systems and market foundations establishes this substrate: Linux kernel scheduling and I/O paths; cache-aware compute and SIMD; low-latency networking; time representation; microstructure semantics; and the modeling, compression, and concurrency patterns that will reappear in every design that follows.

With that substrate in place, we develop cross-platform columnar principles. We explain why column orientation, late materialization, and vectorized operators win on analytic workloads; how partitioning, sorting, and data-skipping indices reduce I/O; what snapshot isolation really guarantees in high-throughput systems; how engine-level caches interact with the OS page cache; and how to measure performance credibly, with distributions-especially tails-rather than averages. Throughout, we emphasize workload specificity and repeatable experiments: the only benchmark that matters is the one that resembles your production job.

Market data pipelines receive their own treatment because ingestion is where many designs succeed or fail. We dissect exchange protocols and feed handlers, normalization and schema mapping, order book reconstruction, time alignment across venues and sessions, data-quality controls, and streaming ETL patterns. These chapters are written to be directly translatable into your runbooks: they favor idempotence, replay, and gap detection over cleverness.

Two platform-focused parts then dive deep. kdb+ architecture and the q language are presented as they are used in practice: types and IPC; table attributes and HDB layout; asof joins and temporal windows; tick pipelines; deployment, NUMA pinning, gateways, and integration patterns. ClickHouse is treated with equal specificity: SQL dialect fit for time-series; MergeTree internals and part lifecycle; partition and ORDER BY design; replication and Keeper; sharding and distributed queries; materialized views and streaming ingest; temporal windows and ASOF JOIN; indices, codecs, and storage policies. We aim to teach each system on its own terms while illuminating the common ideas that make them fast.

Performance engineering is separated from platform chapters to sharpen your diagnostic habits. You will learn to tune for vectorization and locality, manage NUMA and memory mapping, optimize Linux and network stacks, and profile with intent before changing code. We pair this with guidance on benchmarking methodology and regression guards so that improvements persist beyond the lab.

Operations matter as much as algorithms. An operations part provides patterns for Kafka/Redpanda ingestion at scale, backfill and late-data strategy, kdb+ - ClickHouse bridges, backup and disaster recovery, security and lineage, deployment topologies, capacity planning, automation, upgrades, and cost governance. The goal is not merely to reach performance once, but to keep it through growth, failure, audits, and change.

The book closes with applied designs: limit order book analytics, transaction cost analysis, historical backtesting, real-time risk, and hybrid architectures that combine kdb+ front ends with ClickHouse back ends.

Each study is end-to-end-ingest, storage, and query-so that you can adapt it to your own constraints.

This book is for engineers, quants, SREs, and architects who care about both speed and truth. We assume comfort with Linux, SQL, and at least one programming language; everything else we build from the ground up. Code examples use q and ClickHouse SQL; timestamps are UTC with nanosecond precision unless stated; schemas prefer explicit types and composite keys grounded in market semantics.

What this book is not: it is not a survey of every database, a generic SQL tutorial, or a substitute for exchange rule books. It is a field manual for two proven systems and the ideas that make them sing. If you read linearly, you will gain a coherent mental model from hardware to analytics; if you are on a deadline, you can jump to the platform chapters and return to foundations as needed.

Ultimately, we want you to leave with a bias for measurement over folklore, for temporal correctness over approximate speed, and for designs that degrade gracefully under stress. The markets will not slow down. Your systems do not have to either.

Chapter 1

Systems and Market Foundations

Databases in markets do not run in the abstract-they run on concrete hardware, under a specific kernel, against unforgiving clocks, and in the middle of a chaotic limit order book. This chapter strips away the magic and gives you a trader's view of systems: how Linux decides which task runs next; why a single cache miss can wipe out a day's worth of micro-optimizations; how NIC queues and kernel bypass change what "real time" means; why timestamps are never as simple as "nanoseconds since epoch"; and how the fine print of market microstructure leaks all the way into your table layouts and encoding choices. You will learn to read performance symptoms-spikes in latency, dropped packets, strange gaps in timestamps-as signals about interactions between these layers, and to design data structures and ingestion pipelines that behave predictably when markets are least forgiving.

1.1 Linux Kernel and I/O Fundamentals

In the previous chapter we treated the operating system mostly as a black box: a place where processes run and data is read from and written to disks. For high-performance market data systems, that abstraction is too coarse. The Linux kernel is directly in the critical path between a multicast packet on the wire and a row appended to a kdb+ table or a ClickHouse MergeTree part.

In this section we will open that black box just enough to explain why two queries that look “the same” at the database level can have radically different runtimes in production. We will connect three kernel subsystems to the behavior you observe:

- **Scheduling:** which cores your processes run on, how often they are preempted, and how that interacts with feed bursts.
- **Virtual memory:** how address spaces, page tables, and the page cache create the illusion of large, fast memory while hiding page faults.
- **Filesystem and storage I/O:** how buffered I/O, direct I/O, and write-back policy translate into latency spikes, even on NVMe.

Once you see how a single packet travels through these layers, it becomes much easier to reason about:

- Why the same time-range query is sub-millisecond in one run and tens of milliseconds the next.
- Why the first query after a quiet period is always slower.
- Why a market-open burst can stall ingest even when CPU and disks look only partially utilized.

From packet to disk: the ingest path

Let us start with a simplified but realistic narrative: a quote update for a liquid equity arrives on a multicast feed and ends up durable in your tick store.

1. The network interface card (NIC) receives the Ethernet frame and writes the packet into a receive (RX) ring in main memory using DMA (direct memory access).

2. The NIC signals the CPU (by interrupt or polling). The kernel's networking stack runs, parses the packet, identifies the UDP socket, and copies the payload into a kernel socket buffer.

3. Your feed-handler process, blocked in recvfrom or using non-blocking I/O, is scheduled on a core. It copies the data from the kernel buffer into user-space, decodes the market protocol, and writes a normalized record into an in-memory structure or directly into the database process.

4. The database process appends this record to an in-memory buffer and, at some point, makes a write call: perhaps appending to an on-disk log segment or flushing a columnar part.

5. The kernel translates that write into one or more page cache updates and, later, into actual I/O operations against the filesystem and NVMe device.

At each of these steps, the kernel and hardware make decisions that affect latency: which core will run the handler, whether the memory access hits in cache, whether the data is already in the page cache, and when the write is pushed to physical media.

Right after we outline this path, it is helpful to anchor it visually.

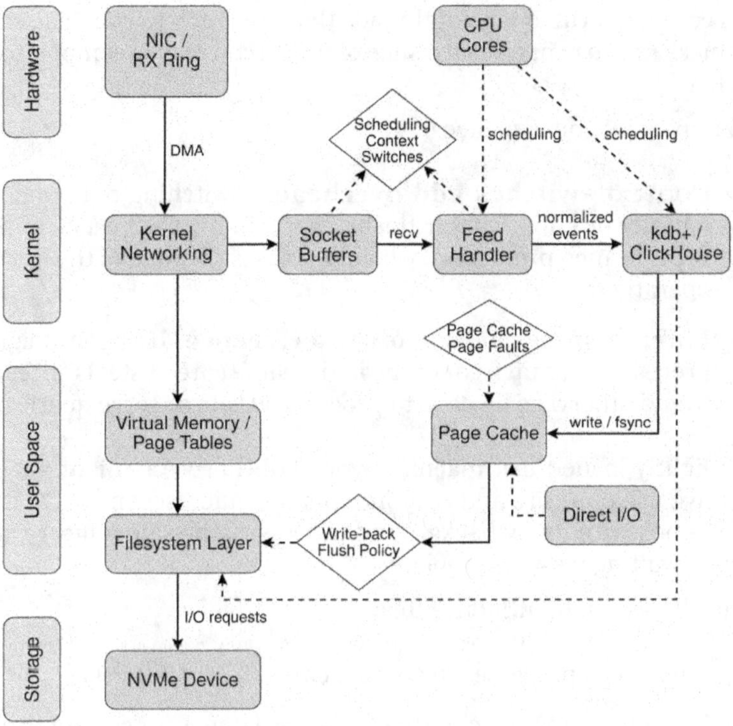

Scheduling: who runs, when, and where

Linux runs multiple runnable threads on each core by time-sharing them. For a market data system, you typically have at least:

- One or more feed-handler processes or threads.
- One or more database processes or threads for ingest and queries.
- Background services: monitoring agents, log shippers, system daemons.

Run queues and priorities

Each core has a run queue of threads that are ready to run. The scheduler picks one to run, gives it a slice of time, then may preempt it to run another.

Two important consequences:

- **Context switches add overhead.** Switching out your feed-handler or kdb+ worker flushes parts of the CPU cache and disrupts branch prediction, which increases the time of the next few operations.
- **Latency spikes arise from interference.** If a noisy neighbor process wakes up frequently on the same core, it steals slices that would otherwise be used to process packets or serve queries.

On a lightly loaded test machine, your kdb+ process might get near exclusive use of a core and respond in a few microseconds. On a production box with many background processes, the same query can be delayed waiting in the run queue.

Linux allows you to influence this:

- Pin critical processes to specific cores (CPU affinity).
- Use scheduling policies that favor low latency for certain threads.
- Move noisy, non-critical daemons away from your hot cores.

In a market data pipeline, it is common to dedicate a small set of cores to feed handlers and another set to database ingest and queries, ensuring that a burst of monitoring activity does not preempt your most latency-sensitive paths.

Core locality and per-core queues

Modern NICs and Linux networking stacks can deliver packets to specific cores (for example, with RX queue affinity). If your feed handler is pinned to core 2, but the kernel delivers most packets to a handler on core 5, then incoming packets will bounce between cores, causing additional cache misses and context switches.

To keep latency predictable, you want alignment:

- NIC RX queue → kernel soft-IRQ handler → feed-handler thread all on the same core or at least the same NUMA node.
- kdb+ or ClickHouse ingest threads pinned to cores that own the hot memory and disk queues they use most frequently.

When this alignment is off, you often see behavior like: average latency is fine, but the 99.9th percentile is bad, because a small fraction of packets always end up on the "wrong" core and are delayed while the scheduler shuffles threads around.

Virtual memory: the illusion of a huge, uniform RAM

Virtual memory is a layer that lets each process pretend it has a large, continuous address space. The kernel maps these virtual addresses to physical memory pages and, when necessary, to disk.

Pages, page tables, and TLBs

A *page* is a fixed-size block of memory, typically 4KB or 2MB (for huge pages). The kernel tracks, for each page of virtual memory, where it is in physical memory or on disk.

The CPU keeps a small cache of recent address translations called the TLB (translation lookaside buffer). If your kdb+ scan walks a big column in a smooth, sequential way, the kernel and hardware can set up page mappings and TLB entries in a very predictable pattern. Latency is low and stable.

If your access pattern jumps around – for example, following sparse pointers or doing random symbol lookups – the TLB may miss often, forcing the CPU to walk the page tables in memory. This adds extra memory accesses and contributes to slower, more variable runtimes.

Page cache and page faults

The page cache is a region of memory that stores copies of disk pages. When your database reads from a file with normal buffered I/O, the kernel:

- Checks if the requested page is in the page cache. If it is, the read completes quickly without touching the disk.

- If it is not, the kernel issues a disk read, waits for the data, stores it in the page cache, then passes it to your process.

A *page fault* happens when your process touches a memory address whose underlying page is not yet in RAM. For file-backed mappings (for example, a memory-mapped column file), that means the kernel must load the page from disk.

The impact on query latency is direct:

- A query that walks only pages already in the page cache can run entirely from memory and CPU caches. On a modern NVMe system this might be microseconds to low milliseconds.
- The same logical query that happens to touch a cold symbol or an older partition will incur page faults and disk reads. Latency now includes the time to fetch data from NVMe, plus any queuing delay in the storage stack.

This is one of the main reasons you see a faster "second run" of the same query: the first run pulled the relevant pages into the page cache; the second run finds them already resident. In benchmarks that clear the page cache between runs, this "caching effect" disappears and the raw I/O cost becomes visible.

Major faults, swap, and catastrophic pauses

Not all page faults are equal. Roughly:

- A **minor fault** can be satisfied from memory without I/O (for example, setting up a mapping to a page already loaded).
- A **major fault** requires disk I/O because the page is not in memory.

Major faults are the ones that cause obvious latency spikes. If your system is also under memory pressure and begins to swap (writing anonymous pages out to a swap device), latency can become unpredictable and extreme. A kdb+ process whose working set no longer fits in RAM may cause major faults in the middle of a query, introducing tens of milliseconds or more of delay on each access.

For a production market data store, best practice is to:

- Size RAM so that the hot working set of current-day data fits comfortably.
- Avoid swapping for latency-critical processes, either by system configuration or by monitoring and alerting.
- Use huge pages for large, frequently accessed structures (where compatible) to reduce TLB pressure.

Filesystem and storage I/O: buffered vs direct, read-ahead and write-back

At the bottom of the stack, the kernel translates logical file operations into I/O commands for storage devices such as SATA SSDs or NVMe. The behavior here determines not just absolute latency but also how predictable your system is.

Buffered I/O and read-ahead

By default, reads and writes go through the page cache (buffered I/O). For reads:

- When your process reads a range of bytes, the kernel loads the corresponding page(s) from disk into the page cache and returns the data.
- The kernel also performs *read-ahead*: if it observes sequential access, it proactively loads subsequent pages into the cache.

For a columnar engine like ClickHouse or a kdb+ process reading a contiguous column, read-ahead can be a big win: by the time your query asks for the next page, it is already in memory. Latency per row appears much lower than the raw disk latency.

However, this behavior also introduces variability:

- If your access pattern is slightly non-sequential, the kernel may mispredict, reading pages you never use and failing to load the ones you need in time.
- Different queries may interfere in the page cache, evicting each other's working sets and causing sudden page faults.

This is why two similar-looking queries — say, scanning the same time range but with different symbol filters — can behave differently. One might fully benefit from read-ahead on a hot partition; the other might touch a sparser set of pages, defeating read-ahead and causing additional I/O.

Write-back caching and durability

When your database process writes data using buffered I/O, the kernel usually:

- Copies the data into page cache pages and marks them as "dirty".
- Returns control to the process quickly, often before the data is actually written to disk.
- Flushes dirty pages to disk later, either periodically or when memory pressure is high.

From a throughput perspective this is excellent: many small writes are merged into larger, more efficient I/O operations. But for latency and durability:

- You may see bursts of disk activity when the kernel decides to flush many dirty pages, competing with your read I/O and slowing down queries.
- If you depend on data being durable at a particular point (for example, end-of-day checkpoints), you must use fsync or similar mechanisms, which force the kernel to push dirty pages to disk and wait for completion. These calls can cause noticeable stalls.

A common pattern in market data systems is:

- Use append-only logs or WALs written with buffered I/O for high ingest speed.
- Use explicit, batched fsyncs or group commits to amortize the cost of forced flushes.
- Run periodic compaction processes that transform write-optimized files into read-optimized columnar parts, scheduled to avoid peak trading periods.

Direct I/O and log-structured designs

Direct I/O bypasses the page cache and reads or writes directly to and from user buffers. This removes double-buffering and gives the database more explicit control over when data hits disk and what is kept in memory.

kdb+ and ClickHouse both can be configured, directly or indirectly, to use patterns that resemble direct I/O for certain paths:

- Append-only partitions or log segments where the access pattern is strictly sequential.
- Large, infrequently accessed historical partitions where you want to avoid polluting the page cache.

Direct I/O has trade-offs:

- It tends to make latency more predictable, since you no longer have surprise page cache evictions or read-ahead artifacts.
- It shifts more responsibility to the database: scheduling its own read-ahead, managing its in-memory caches, and aligning I/O to device block sizes.

In log-structured designs — heavily used for market data because of their natural fit with appends — these trade-offs are often acceptable. An ingest process can append to large, well-aligned segments, while query workers rely on their own cached structures (such as kdb+'s in-memory tables or ClickHouse's mark ranges) instead of the kernel's generic heuristics.

Storage hardware: SATA SSD vs NVMe and queue depth

Underneath the filesystem, the storage device itself has a major impact on latency profiles.

- **SATA SSDs** offer substantial improvement over spinning disks, but they are relatively limited in parallelism and often exhibit higher and more variable latency under load.
- **NVMe** devices connect directly to the PCIe bus and support many parallel queues and deep command queues, allowing much higher IOPS and lower tail latency when used correctly.

The key concept is *queue depth*: how many outstanding I/O operations you have at once. For throughput, you typically want a moderate queue depth so the device can reorder and pipeline operations. For per-operation latency, especially tail latency, you want to avoid very deep queues where an unlucky read can get stuck behind many others.

Market data workloads combine:

- Many small writes (trade and quote updates).
- Periodic large writes (compaction and checkpointing).
- Concurrent reads (research and monitoring queries).

If compaction jobs submit large, long-running writes at high queue depth, small, latency-sensitive reads for hot symbols may suffer. This manifests as sudden spikes in query latency that correlate with background maintenance tasks.

Practical mitigation strategies include:

- Throttling background compaction and checkpointing so they do not saturate the I/O queues during market hours.
- Using separate physical devices or NVMe namespaces for hot partitions versus cold history, so they do not compete for the same queues.

- Tuning the filesystem and I/O scheduler for low-latency, random I/O patterns rather than maximum bulk throughput.

Putting it together: explaining divergent query runtimes

We can now revisit our central question: why do ostensibly similar queries behave so differently in practice?

Consider two queries run at 10:01:00:

- Both scan the last 30 minutes of trades for a set of 500 symbols.
- Both compute volume-weighted average price (VWAP) per symbol.

Yet you observe:

- Query A completes in 3 milliseconds.
- Query B, run seconds later with a slightly different symbol list, takes 45 milliseconds and shows a long tail in latency.

Using the concepts from this section, a plausible explanation might look like:

1. **Scheduling differences:** Query B runs at the moment a logging daemon wakes up and competes for the same core, causing extra context switches and cache disruption.
2. **Page cache state:** The symbols in Query A are heavily traded and their recent partitions are already in page cache. Query B touches a less active symbol whose data has not been accessed recently, triggering major page faults and disk reads.
3. **Filesystem and I/O contention:** At the same time, a background compaction process begins flushing a large set of dirty pages for previous-day partitions, filling the NVMe queues. The read I/O for Query B must wait behind these writes.

4. **Storage characteristics:** The NVMe device is operating at high queue depth, so a few unlucky read operations suffer much higher latency than the average, stretching the tail for Query B.

To an end user, both queries "do the same thing." To you, as the system designer, they exercise different parts of the kernel and hardware stack under different transient conditions.

In the rest of this book, when we discuss specific kdb+ and ClickHouse designs — choices of partitioning, file layout, compression, and ingest pipelines — we will keep referring back to these Linux fundamentals. The goal is not to turn you into a kernel developer, but to give you enough mental models to connect an observed latency profile to concrete mechanisms:

- Run queue congestion versus application bugs.
- Page cache thrash versus bad schema or partitioning.
- NVMe queue saturation versus "the database is slow."

With that foundation, you can reason systematically about performance, rather than treating it as a mysterious property of the database engine.

1.2 CPU Caches, SIMD, and Memory Architecture

In the previous section we treated the Linux kernel and storage stack as the environment in which our market data systems live. We saw how scheduling, virtual memory, and filesystem behavior can make two similar queries exhibit very different latency profiles.

In this section we move one layer deeper, into the CPU and memory fabric itself. Even when the kernel behaves perfectly and data is in RAM, performance can still vary by orders of magnitude depending on how your data is laid out and accessed. The difference between a cache-friendly column scan and a pointer-chasing join is often the difference between microseconds and milliseconds.

Our goal is to build a clear mental model of three closely related ideas:

- **Cache hierarchy:** multiple levels of small, fast memory close to each core.
- **Memory bandwidth and access patterns:** how contiguous versus scattered access can fully utilize or completely waste available bandwidth.
- **SIMD / vector units:** how the CPU can operate on many values at once when they are aligned and packed appropriately.

With these tools, you should be able to look at a kdb+ or ClickHouse query plan and make an informed prediction: *this will be cache-friendly* or *this will be disastrous*, even before running a benchmark.

A tour of the cache hierarchy

Modern CPUs are built on the assumption that most data you want next is either what you just used or sits near it. Caches exploit this by keeping small, fast copies of recently accessed data close to the core.

Although exact structures vary by vendor and generation, a typical server used for market data will have:

- **L1 cache:** tiny but extremely fast, private to each core.
- **L2 cache:** larger and slightly slower, also private to each core.
- **L3 cache:** even larger, shared among cores on a socket.
- **DRAM:** main memory, hundreds of times slower than L1 in terms of access latency.

Think of it as a nesting set of boxes around each core: the innermost box (L1) is the smallest and fastest; the outer ones are bigger and slower.

When a core needs a value (for example, the next price in a column):

- It first checks L1. If the data is there, the cost is minimal.

- If not, it checks L2, then L3, and finally main memory.
- On a miss, the data is fetched from the lower level into the higher level, often bringing along neighboring bytes.

Two observations are crucial for database work:

- Caches operate on *cache lines*, not individual values. A cache line is a small block (often 64 bytes). Accessing one value brings in the whole line, so data packed contiguously benefits from this.
- Every miss to a lower level costs time. Hitting DRAM instead of L1 is not a small penalty; it can be hundreds of extra cycles. Those penalties quickly add up in a scan over billions of rows.

Spatial and temporal locality

The core principle governing cache performance is *locality*: how predictable your access pattern is in space and time.

Spatial locality. If you read one byte, how likely are you to read nearby bytes soon?

- A columnar layout, such as a contiguous array of trade prices, has excellent spatial locality when you scan it from start to finish. Each cache line you load will likely be used fully, as you move neatly from one group of prices to the next.
- A row-oriented layout with many fields and pointers can have poor spatial locality, especially if you only care about one or two fields; many bytes in each cache line are wasted.

Temporal locality. If you read one value, how likely are you to read it again soon?

- A hot working set of symbols referenced repeatedly in sliding-window analytics exhibits temporal locality: the same cache lines are reused across nearby queries.

- A one-off pass through a large historical partition has low temporal locality: once a cache line is used, it may not be needed again for hours.

Columnar databases like kdb+ and ClickHouse are designed to maximize spatial locality for typical analytic queries: when a query needs only time, symbol, and price, it efficiently streams those three columns, ignoring the rest. Good schema and sort-order choices further align hot query patterns with favorable locality.

When locality is strong, the CPU can treat main memory almost like an extended cache; when locality is poor, even a large DRAM system becomes a bottleneck.

Relating cache levels to perceived latency

To make this more concrete, it is useful to think in relative terms. You do not need exact numbers, but you should appreciate the ratios.

Imagine that accessing L1 cache is like walking to a file cabinet in your office. Accessing L2 is like walking down the hallway. Accessing L3 is like taking the elevator to another floor. Accessing DRAM is like leaving the building to fetch something from another office a few streets away. Each step adds time, and if you have to do the "walk out of the building" thousands of times per query, overall latency explodes.

Markets amplify this effect because you are often working under strict time budgets: a few hundred microseconds in a low-latency trading engine, a few milliseconds in a tick query on a shared research cluster. In that budget, just a handful of DRAM-level misses can dominate all arithmetic and logic work.

From the perspective of a columnar engine:

- A scan that mostly hits in L1 and L2 feels almost free.
- A scan that streams from DRAM but with good prefetching can still be satisfactory.
- A scan that degenerates into a sequence of unpredictable DRAM accesses, with little prefetching, often becomes catastrophically slow.

The multi-core landscape

On a modern server, you do not have just one core; you have many. Each has its own L1 and L2 caches, and they share a larger L3 and the DRAM channels. This layout matters because:

- Multiple query workers can run in parallel, but they also compete for shared resources.
- Data may move between cores if ownership of a cache line changes (for example, when different threads update the same structure).

To set the stage before we talk about how a columnar scan versus pointer-chasing behaves, it is helpful to visualize this structure.

This schematic highlights two contrasting patterns we will now examine in detail: a smooth, predictable column scan that moves neatly through memory, and a jagged, unpredictable path characteristic of pointer-chasing across scattered structures.

Columnar scans: the "happy path"

Consider a typical analytic in kdb+ or ClickHouse: compute the volume-weighted average price over the last hour for a set of symbols. Conceptually, this involves:

- Scanning the time, symbol, price, and size columns over a time range.
- Applying simple filters (time window, symbol set).
- Accumulating per-symbol totals.

In a well-designed column store, these columns are stored contiguously on disk and in memory for each partition. When the query executes:

- The engine reads sequential chunks of each column.

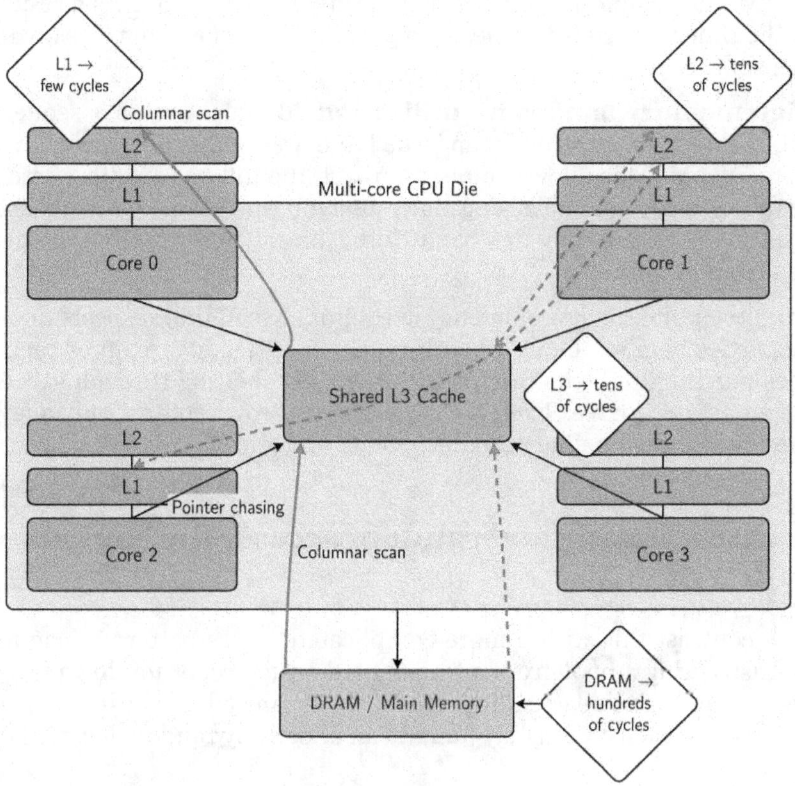

- Each chunk is processed in tight loops that walk linearly through arrays of values.

This has several positive consequences:

Efficient cache line use. Each cache line fetched contains several consecutive values that you will soon use. For example, one line might hold eight or more price values. As your scan proceeds, you naturally consume these values without wasted bytes.

Hardware prefetching. CPUs are good at detecting simple patterns, such as "keep accessing the next cache line." Hardware prefetchers watch your access stream and pull in subsequent lines from L3 or

DRAM into L2 and L1 before you explicitly request them. As a result, by the time your code touches an address, the data is often already in a closer cache.

High memory bandwidth utilization. Because access is sequential, the memory controller can issue large, well-aligned bursts of traffic to DRAM. This allows you to approach the full bandwidth offered by the memory channels. For many analytic workloads, performance is ultimately limited by this bandwidth; linear scans are how you get close to that limit.

From the point of view of latency, a columnar scan that respects these properties behaves like a smooth pipeline: a steady stream of cache lines moving up the hierarchy, with the CPU chewing through values as fast as they arrive. Even if each individual row requires only a few operations, the pipeline remains full and efficient.

Pointer chasing and random access: the "unhappy path"

Now contrast this with a more complicated access pattern: imagine reconstructing a book from a fragmented structure, or joining a large trade table with a sparse dimension table organized as a hash map. In these cases, each access may jump to an effectively random location in memory.

Typical behaviors include:

- Following pointers or indices deep into nested structures.
- Accessing small records scattered throughout a large heap.
- Jumping between partitions or symbol groups in a non-contiguous order.

This pattern undermines the mechanisms that made the columnar scan so fast:

Poor cache line utilization. Every pointer hop may land you on a new cache line. Even if that line carries 64 bytes, you might only use a small fraction before jumping away again. The rest of the bytes are effectively wasted.

Prefetching breaks down. The hardware prefetcher relies on simple, regular strides. When addresses jump unpredictably, it cannot guess where you are going next. Each new access becomes a surprise miss, forcing the core to stall while waiting for the data to be fetched from L3 or DRAM.

Underutilized bandwidth. Because each access is small and scattered, the memory system cannot aggregate them into efficient bursts. Total bandwidth may remain underused, even though latency per access is high. The CPU spends more time waiting than computing.

At the query level, this manifests as:

- Longer runtimes for joins and group-bys that rely on poorly organized lookup structures.
- Large differences between cold and warm cache behavior, since scattered accesses stress the entire hierarchy.
- High sensitivity to the size of working sets: once the set of touched addresses exceeds cache capacity, thrashing ensues.

This is why, in columnar engines, considerable effort goes into arranging data to minimize pointer chasing in the hot path. Dimension tables are often encoded as compact arrays; dictionary encoding turns string symbols into small integers; and join strategies are chosen to make inner loops as contiguous as possible.

Bandwidth: how much data can you move per unit time?

So far we have focused on latency (how long it takes to access one value). Another key factor is bandwidth: how much data you can push through the memory system per unit time.

A useful mental model is this:

- The CPU can do a huge number of simple arithmetic operations per second.

- Often, the limiting factor is not computation but how fast you can feed data to the cores.

Columnar engines like kdb+ and ClickHouse are designed to be *scan-bound*: they try to keep each core busy by streaming data at high bandwidth. A scan that processes tens or hundreds of millions of rows per second per core may be close to the memory bandwidth limit; at that point, optimizing arithmetic has limited effect.

Two main patterns emerge:

Bandwidth-bound scans. Operations like computing a simple aggregate over a contiguous column are limited by how fast you can move cache lines through the hierarchy. Performance here is largely a function of:

- How many bytes you need to read (which you can influence via compression and encoding).
- How well your access pattern allows hardware prefetching and avoids cache thrash.

Latency-bound random access. Operations dominated by pointer chasing are often limited by per-access latency rather than overall bandwidth. Even if the total volume of data is small, many individual cache misses can add up to significant stall time.

Understanding whether a given query is likely to be bandwidth-bound or latency-bound helps you decide which optimization levers matter most: column selection and compression for the former, data structure layout and join keys for the latter.

SIMD and vector units: doing more per memory access

So far we have assumed that the CPU processes one value at a time. In reality, modern cores have vector units that can operate on several values in parallel using Single Instruction, Multiple Data (SIMD) instructions.

At a high level:

- Instead of adding one pair of numbers, the CPU can add many pairs at once, as long as they are laid out consecutively in memory and packed into a vector register.
- Similarly, comparisons, multiplications, and simple functions can be done over multiple values per instruction.

This matters for columnar engines because:

- Columns are naturally aligned arrays of values; they are ideal candidates for vectorization.
- Filters and aggregations often apply the same operation to many rows, exactly the scenario SIMD was designed for.

For example, a filter such as "price greater than threshold" over a price column can be implemented as:

- Load a chunk of consecutive prices into a vector register.
- Compare them all to the threshold in one SIMD instruction.
- Produce a mask indicating which entries passed.

The potential speedup is significant, but only if the underlying memory pattern cooperates:

- Data must be reasonably aligned and contiguous so it can be loaded efficiently into vector registers.
- The control flow inside the loop must be simple; heavy branching or data-dependent decisions can prevent effective vectorization.

kdb+ and ClickHouse both exploit these ideas, albeit in different ways and with different toolchains. As a designer or user, you do not usually write SIMD instructions by hand, but your schema and query patterns either help or hinder the engine's ability to use them.

Bringing it together: predicting query cost from structure

We can now tie these concepts back to core database operations you use daily: scans, joins, and aggregations.

Scans. A range query over a time-sorted partition that touches a small set of columns and applies simple filters is the ideal case:

- Sequential access, good spatial locality.
- Strong hardware prefetching.
- High bandwidth utilization.
- Effective SIMD on filters and arithmetic.

You should expect such operations to scale linearly with the number of rows and to exhibit tight latency distributions.

Joins. A join can be implemented in many ways; performance depends heavily on layout:

- Hash joins that probe a dense, cache-friendly hash table built over a small dimension often behave well, especially if probing keys are contiguous.
- Joins that require pointer chasing into large, scattered structures or that repeatedly traverse long chains of collisions will suffer from cache misses and poor branch prediction.

From your mental model:

- If the join key is well-clustered and the dimension is small enough to fit in L3, you can expect good performance.
- If the join key is high-cardinality with no locality, and the dimension is wide and sparse, expect a latency-bound, pointer-chasing regime.

Aggregations and group-bys. Group-by operations maintain per-group state. Performance depends on:

- The number of groups (cardinality).
- How group keys are distributed over the input.
- How the per-group state is stored in memory.

A low-cardinality group-by over a column with good locality can often be implemented using small, contiguous arrays that fit entirely in cache. A high-cardinality group-by over a hash of symbol and venue may require accessing large state structures in DRAM, with scattered patterns.

Once again, your cache and bandwidth intuition applies:

- Small, hot state → cache-resident, vectorizable, bandwidth-efficient.
- Large, cold state → random access, latency-bound, sensitive to working-set size.

Practical implications for schema and query design

Armed with this understanding, several practical guidelines emerge for designing kdb+ and ClickHouse schemas and queries for market data:

- **Favor columnar access patterns.** Design tables and queries so that the hot path is dominated by sequential scans of a few columns, rather than repeated random lookups.
- **Choose sort orders that align with queries.** Sorting by time within symbol (or symbol within time, depending on the workload) can dramatically improve locality for common filters.
- **Control working set size.** Partitioning by date or session, and sometimes by symbol, keeps hot data subsets small enough to fit into cache hierarchies during intensive analysis.
- **Simplify hot loops.** Avoid unnecessary branching and complex expressions in the inner loops of frequent queries; this encourages better vectorization and prefetching.

- **Beware of hidden pointer chasing.** High-level abstractions like nested arrays or maps may hide scattered memory access. Understand how these logical structures map to physical layout.

In later chapters, when we look at specific kdb+ and ClickHouse implementations—for example, how ClickHouse's MergeTree structures marks and granules, or how kdb+ lays out columns in memory—we will keep referring back to this section. The overarching theme is simple: *structure your data so that the CPU sees long, predictable runs of contiguous values, and avoid forcing it into random walks through memory.*

When you can mentally trace where a query will move through L1, L2, L3, and DRAM, you are well on your way to understanding and controlling performance in high-frequency market data systems.

1.3 Low-Latency Networking Essentials

In the previous sections we worked from the inside out: first the Linux kernel and storage stack, then the CPU and memory hierarchy. We now move one step further outward to the network, where market data first enters the system and where replication and cross-site streaming keep clusters consistent.

For most trading organizations, the network is both the starting point of the data pipeline and an ever-present source of tail latency. At market open, when feeds spike and every microburst matters, details of packet delivery, protocol choice, and network interface card (NIC) configuration directly determine how smoothly your kdb+ or ClickHouse ingest and query paths behave.

Our aim in this section is not to turn you into a network engineer, but to give you enough intuition about:

- How packets move from publisher to your processes.
- How UDP and TCP behave under load and why markets lean heavily on multicast.

- How NICs, queues, and interrupts interact with cores and scheduling.
- How kernel versus user-space networking trade off reliability, latency, and complexity.

With that, you will be able to reason about network-related latency issues in your data stores and make informed design decisions for ingestion, replication, and cross-site links.

Packets and protocols in a market data context

At the physical and link layers, the picture is straightforward: exchanges and vendors send Ethernet frames over fiber to your co-located racks or to your data centers. Inside those frames, however, several protocol choices shape performance.

UDP versus TCP: different tools for different jobs

Two transport protocols dominate in trading systems:

UDP (User Datagram Protocol). UDP is connectionless and unreliable: the sender emits packets, and the network does its best to deliver them, but there are no built-in acknowledgments, retransmissions, or ordering guarantees.

While that may sound unattractive, it has key advantages:

- Very low overhead per packet.
- No per-connection state to maintain in the kernel.
- Natural fit for multicast, where one sender transmits to many receivers at once.

For *market data dissemination*, these benefits dominate. Exchanges push continuous streams of quotes and trades; receivers must keep up with the firehose and can recover lost information out-of-band using gap-fill mechanisms. UDP multicast is therefore the standard choice for primary feeds.

TCP (Transmission Control Protocol). TCP is connection-oriented and reliable: it provides ordered delivery, retransmissions on loss, and flow control. This simplifies application logic but adds latency and variability:

- Each connection maintains a state machine, sequence numbers, and buffers.
- When loss occurs, the sender must retransmit; the receiver waits for missing data to arrive in order.
- Flow control can throttle the sender if the receiver cannot keep up.

TCP is usually used for:

- Recovery channels: re-sending missed packets when sequence gaps are detected on the UDP feed.
- Point-to-point links between internal services, including replication between database nodes.
- Cross-site replication and disaster-recovery streams, where reliability is more important than single-digit microsecond latency.

A key design pattern in feed handling and distributed storage is therefore:

- Use UDP multicast for high-fanout, low-latency dissemination.
- Use TCP for targeted, reliable delivery where timing is less extreme but correctness is non-negotiable.

Multicast groups and subscription patterns

With multicast, a sender transmits a single packet that is replicated in the network and delivered to all subscribed receivers. Receivers join specific multicast groups, often one per feed or per partition of instruments.

This has important consequences:

- **Fanout efficiency.** Adding more subscribers does not increase bandwidth on the publisher's link; the network takes care of duplication.
- **Per-group tuning.** You can subscribe different servers to different subsets of feeds based on their roles (strategy servers, recorders, analytics clusters).
- **Misconfiguration risk.** Overly broad subscriptions (for example, "just join all groups") can overwhelm NIC queues and kernel buffers on a host that never intended to process that much data.

Under market-open conditions, when auctions and opening prints produce extremely bursty traffic, subscription choices can mean the difference between smooth processing and sustained packet loss.

The practical message: treat multicast group design and host subscriptions as part of your capacity planning and latency engineering, not as an afterthought.

From wire to core: NIC internals and host queues

Once packets arrive on your network interface card, the NIC and kernel networking stack take over. Understanding this path is essential for diagnosing where latency is added or packets are dropped.

RX rings, DMA, and interrupts

Modern NICs use the following pattern for receive (RX) processing:

- The NIC maintains one or more RX queues (rings), which are circular buffers in main memory.
- For each queue, the NIC writes incoming packets directly into memory using DMA (direct memory access), without involving the CPU for every byte.
- When one or more packets have been placed into a queue, the NIC notifies the CPU, commonly via an interrupt. In low-latency setups, polling may partially or fully replace interrupts.

The kernel then:

- Runs a handler (often in a soft interrupt context) that processes packets from the RX queue.
- Parses headers, identifies the associated socket, and enqueues the payload into a socket buffer for user-space consumption.

Two things are immediately clear:

- RX queues have finite depth. If they fill up because the CPU is too slow to drain them, inbound packets are dropped at the NIC.
- Each notification (interrupt or poll cycle) carries overhead. If configured poorly, the system may enter a regime where it spends too much time handling interrupts relative to actual application work.

At market open, when bursts of packets arrive faster than steady-state, these two factors are critical. A feed that looks stable in average packets per second may still produce microbursts that temporarily overflow RX queues.

Receive Side Scaling (RSS) and per-core queues

To spread load across cores, NICs support Receive Side Scaling (RSS):

- Incoming packets are hashed (based on headers) into different RX queues.
- Each queue can be associated with a specific CPU core or a set of cores.

This allows multiple cores to process packets in parallel. For market data:

- You might dedicate one RX queue per feed-handler thread and pin each handler to the corresponding core.
- Or, you might group related feeds on the same queue to preserve per-feed ordering while still achieving parallelism across feeds.

Misalignment here creates avoidable latency:

- If RSS maps packets to cores where your application threads do not run, processing will involve cross-core handoffs, adding cache misses and scheduling delay.
- If many heavy feeds collide onto one RX queue, that queue may overflow while others remain underutilized.

The design goal is a balanced mapping:

- Heavy feeds split across queues and cores that can keep up.
- Feed-handler and ingest threads pinned to cores that own the queues they care about.
- Minimal cross-core traffic for hot paths, aligning with the cache and NUMA principles from the previous section.

Interrupt coalescing: smoothing bursts versus hiding latency

NICs also support interrupt coalescing, where they delay notifying the CPU until either:

- A certain number of packets have arrived, or
- A short timer expires.

This reduces interrupt overhead and can improve throughput. However, it introduces additional per-packet latency: each packet may wait in the NIC for the coalescing window to close.

In low-latency trading, coalescing parameters must be chosen carefully:

- Aggressive coalescing (waiting longer or for many packets) reduces CPU load but increases tail latency.
- Conservative coalescing (minimal delay) keeps latency low at the cost of higher CPU usage, especially during bursts.

For raw tick ingestion and trading paths, it is common to favor lower latency, accepting that some cores will be heavily utilized at market open. For replication and cross-site links, a more throughput-oriented configuration may be appropriate.

Socket buffers, kernel limits, and back pressure

After leaving the NIC and kernel networking layer, packets are delivered to socket buffers associated with your processes.

Socket receive buffers and overflow

Each socket has a receive buffer of limited size. As packets are delivered:

- The kernel appends data to the socket buffer.
- Your application reads data (for example, via recvfrom in a feed handler).

If the application does not read fast enough, the buffer fills up:

- New packets for that socket are dropped once the buffer is full.
- For TCP, flow control signals the sender to slow down; for UDP, packets are simply lost.

At market open, several factors can cause socket buffers to overflow temporarily:

- Application threads preempted by the scheduler (as discussed in the Linux kernel section).
- Garbage collection or spurts of CPU activity in the database process.
- Contention with other network-heavy tasks on the same host (for example, log shipping).

Practical mitigations include:

- Increasing socket buffer sizes where appropriate.
- Ensuring feed handler threads are pinned and have sufficient CPU priority.
- Isolating ingest paths from unrelated workloads using cgroups or dedicated hosts.

System-wide limits and cgroup constraints

Beyond per-socket settings, the kernel enforces global limits on the total amount of memory reserved for socket buffers. In containerized environments or shared hosts, cgroups may further restrict the memory and CPU available to your processes.

Under sustained market-open load:

- If cgroup memory limits are tight, the kernel may be forced to shrink sockets' buffers or reject buffer growth, increasing drop likelihood.
- CPU limits can prevent feed handlers from keeping up with packet arrival, even when there are idle cores elsewhere on the machine.

From the perspective of a kdb+ or ClickHouse operator, this can appear simply as sporadic packet loss or ingest lag. But the underlying causes sit at the boundary between networking and resource management, reinforcing the theme that low-latency behavior is an end-to-end property of the system, not of the database alone.

Kernel versus user-space networking

The traditional model—and the one most readers will rely on initially—is kernel networking with sockets. However, for extreme low latency, some systems use kernel-bypass or user space stacks.

Traditional sockets: simplicity with hidden costs

Using standard sockets:

- The kernel manages RX queues, protocol parsing, and socket buffers.
- Applications block on recv or use non-blocking I/O with select/epoll.

Advantages include:

- Mature, well-understood APIs and tooling.
- Good enough performance for many analytics and storage use cases.
- Automatic support for many features (routing, firewalls, congestion control).

Costs include:

- Extra data copies between kernel and user space.
- Context switches between user threads and kernel handlers.
- Less predictable latency under heavy load due to shared resources in the kernel.

For feed ingestion into kdb+ or ClickHouse, well-tuned socket-based setups are usually adequate and far simpler to operate than kernel-bypass alternatives.

Kernel bypass and user-space stacks: shaving the tail

Technologies such as DPDK, RDMA, and various user-space TCP/UDP implementations allow applications to:

- Access NIC queues directly from user space.
- Poll for packets in tight loops without interrupts.
- Manage their own memory pools and protocols.

This reduces latency and jitter by eliminating several kernel transitions and data copies. However, it comes at a cost:

- Significantly higher engineering complexity.
- Additional operational burden: custom tooling, careful isolation from non-bypass traffic.
- Often, a need for dedicated cores that busy-poll, which may sit near 100% CPU even when traffic is low.

In practice:

- Matching engines and ultra-low-latency strategies are the typical consumers of kernel bypass.
- Tick stores and analytic databases often remain on traditional sockets, benefiting more from careful kernel and NIC tuning than from bypass.

For cross-site replication, which typically runs at lower packet rates but higher throughput per connection, the gains from bypass are rarely worth the added complexity.

Networking patterns in distributed market data stores

With the mechanics in hand, we can now connect networking behavior to three common patterns in market data architectures: feed ingestion, replication, and cross-site streaming.

Feed ingestion: surviving the open

Feed handlers sit closest to the network. Their responsibilities include:

- Joining relevant multicast groups and managing subscriptions.
- Receiving and decoding vendor or exchange protocols.
- Handing normalized events off to kdb+ or ClickHouse ingest paths.

Under market-open load, critical success factors are:

- **Sufficient headroom** in NIC RX queues and socket buffers to absorb microbursts.
- **Pinned, high-priority threads** aligned with RSS queues and CPU cores.
- **Predictable handoff mechanisms** to database processes, avoiding long queues or blocking between handler and storage.

When tuning these systems, you will often see a direct trade-off:

- Larger buffers and more aggressive interrupt coalescing make it easier to survive bursts without drops but add latency.
- Smaller buffers and minimal coalescing reduce latency but increase the risk of overflow during bursts.

For most tick storage pipelines, the priority is to *not lose data* while keeping latency low enough that downstream consumers (such as strategy engines or risk systems) receive information in a timely fashion. Ultra-tight single-digit microsecond targets typical of matching engines are usually not required for the storage path.

Replication within a data center

Inside one site, replication between database nodes is commonly done over TCP:

- Leader or primary nodes send change streams or merged parts to secondaries.
- Followers replay changes or attach new partitions as they arrive.

Key trade-offs here include:

- **Reliability versus lag.** TCP ensures ordered, reliable delivery, but if a follower cannot keep up, its replication lag grows. Flow control may eventually slow the primary if buffers fill.
- **Burstiness versus smoothing.** Replication might be designed to stream changes continuously or to send them in larger batches. Batching improves throughput but can create visible stepwise lag.

From the network perspective:

- Replication links should be sized and isolated such that they handle worst-case market days without saturating.
- NIC and kernel tuning for replication paths can prioritize steady throughput and robustness over absolute minimum latency.

The main connection back to query behavior is that replication lag, combined with network hiccups, determines how "fresh" data appears on secondary nodes servicing read-only workloads.

Cross-site streaming and disaster recovery

For cross-site links between, say, a colocation site and a regional data center, or between regions, the network characteristics differ:

- Higher base latency due to distance and routing.
- Potentially lower bandwidth and stricter bandwidth management policies.
- More variability in round-trip time and occasional congestion or packet loss.

Cross-site streaming patterns therefore:

- Rely heavily on TCP with tuned congestion control and buffering to maximize throughput without overwhelming intermediate links.
- Often transfer compressed, batched data (for example, archive partitions or compacted parts) rather than individual tick events.

Here, the key trade-off is between:

- **RPO (Recovery Point Objective)**: how much data you can afford to lose in a disaster.
- **RTO (Recovery Time Objective)**: how quickly you can bring up a secondary site.

Networking choices—buffer sizes, congestion control algorithms, compression strategies—translate directly into how quickly new data arrives at the DR site and how far behind it may be during stress.

For the purposes of this book, the important point is that your kdb+ and ClickHouse designs must be aware of these realities when planning replication strategies. A schema and partition strategy that works nicely inside one rack may look very different when you account for a high-latency cross-ocean link.

Connecting networking behavior back to latency profiles

We can now revisit common phenomena you will see when operating market data stores and interpret them in networking terms:

- **Sudden ingest gaps at market open** can result from RX queue overflow, socket buffer exhaustion, or feed handlers not keeping up due to scheduling.
- **Increased tail latency on certain queries** during specific times may correlate with replication bursts saturating NICs or kernel I/O paths, causing queueing not only in storage but also in network buffers.
- **Intermittent packet loss on specific feeds** may be traced to poor RSS configuration, with hot feeds congesting one queue while others are idle.

Because you now understand the journey of packets:

1. From wire to NIC RX queue.
2. From RX queue to kernel networking and socket buffers.
3. From socket buffers to feed handlers and on into the database.

you can systematically map observed behavior (drops, spikes, lag) to concrete mechanisms. Instead of attributing problems generically to “the network” or “the database,” you can ask:

- Which queue or buffer is overflowing?
- Which core is struggling to keep up?
- Is the bottleneck in the NIC, the kernel, or the application?

This systems-level view completes the foundation for the rest of the book. In subsequent sections, as we talk about time semantics, microstructure, and modeling, we will assume that you can mentally place each trade or quote event not just in logical market time, but also along the physical path from exchange matching engine, through network and kernel, into your kdb+ or ClickHouse store. That full path is where latency, reliability, and throughput are actually determined.

1.4 Time Representation and Calendars

By this point in the chapter we have followed a trade or quote from the exchange, across the network, through the kernel, and into the CPU and memory hierarchy. We have focused on latency and throughput in a physical sense: packets, queues, caches, and disks.

In practice, however, almost everything you do with a market data store is expressed in terms of *time*: "last five minutes", "session high", "VWAP for yesterday's close". If your notion of time is even slightly wrong, your calculations may be precise but meaningless.

This section builds the conceptual foundations you need to reason about time in trading systems. We will concentrate on four areas:

- Different notions of time in a market data pipeline.
- How kdb+ and ClickHouse encode timestamps and why precision matters.
- How trading calendars and sessions really work across venues and time zones.
- How to design resampling and bucketing logic that stays correct under holidays, half-days, and daylight-saving shifts.

The goal is not to catalog every calendar exception, but to give you a mental model that prevents the common, painful mistakes: duplicated bars, missing minutes, misaligned sessions, and silent drift between front-office and research metrics.

Three notions of time in a trading system

When you look at a row in a tick table, the column named `time` or `ts` looks deceptively simple. But behind that single value there are at least three distinct clocks:

- **Exchange event time.** When the event happened in the matching engine: when a trade executed or an order book level changed.
- **Arrival time.** When the corresponding message arrived at your infrastructure, for example at your gateway in a colo.
- **Processing or insert time.** When your feed handler or database process actually handled and recorded the event.

For a perfectly synchronized, lossless system under no load, these might be separated by only a few microseconds. In real environments:

- Network jitter and path asymmetries skew arrival times.
- Congestion, scheduling, and GC pauses introduce variation in processing times.
- Recovery and replay paths can insert historical events into the store long after they occurred.

Different analyses require different notions of time:

- If you are studying microstructure or building a trading strategy, *exchange event time* is usually the right axis: it reflects the sequence of events as seen by the market.
- If you are investigating slippage between signal and execution, *arrival time* at your edge is often more relevant.

- If you are diagnosing system behavior (for example, why your store lagged during an auction), *processing time* within your stack matters.

The crucial design point is: *do not collapse these three concepts into one column*. In a high-quality market data schema, you typically reserve:

- A primary timestamp representing exchange event time (normalized to a common scale).
- An optional secondary timestamp for arrival or gateway time.
- A separate field (sometimes implicit) for recording or ingest time, often used for operational metrics and audit trails.

Keeping these distinct lets you answer questions like "Was this quote stale when we saw it?" or "Did we process events out of order during this burst?"

Timestamp encodings: picking the right representation

Once you decide which times you care about, you need to decide how to encode them.

kdb+ time types

kdb+ offers a family of temporal types with nanosecond resolution, all represented internally as integers counting units from an epoch. Common ones include:

- timestamp: date and time with nanosecond precision relative to a base date.
- time: time of day with millisecond or microsecond resolution.

This representation has several advantages:

- Arithmetic is simple and precise: differences are integer operations.
- Ordering and comparison are cheap: you compare integers, not strings.
- Memory layout is dense and cache-friendly: a column of timestamps is just a column of integers.

For tick data and order books, the usual practice is to store *event time* as a nanosecond timestamp, often combined with a separate date or partition key for performance.

ClickHouse time types

ClickHouse also provides several temporal types:

- Date, Date32: days since epoch.
- DateTime, DateTime64: seconds or fractional seconds since epoch, with optional time-zone awareness.

DateTime64 with a scale of 6 or 9 (microsecond or nanosecond) is often chosen for market data. Again, under the hood this is an integer count of subsecond units since a fixed epoch.

In both systems, what matters for performance is that:

- Timestamps are stored as fixed-width integer columns.
- Sorting by time is cheap; range scans over time partitions are natural.
- Compression can exploit smoothness or regularity (for example, deltas between adjacent timestamps in a high-frequency stream).

What matters for correctness is that:

- You choose a single epoch and scale for each timestamp column and document it.

- You convert all event times into a consistent reference time zone (*usually UTC*) before storage.
- You reserve separate fields or columns for local clock interpretations if needed for reporting.

Time zones and daylight saving: where intuition fails

Most painful time bugs emerge when local civil time and UTC diverge, especially around daylight-saving transitions and across regions.

UTC as the backbone

To keep your mental model clean, adopt one simple rule: *all internal event times are stored and compared in UTC*. This means:

- Exchange timestamps are normalized to UTC as early as possible in the pipeline.
- Partitions and primary sort keys use UTC dates and times.
- Any conversion to local time is done at the edges, for example in reports or user interfaces.

UTC is not subject to daylight-saving jumps, and it is globally unambiguous. This removes an entire class of errors.

Daylight-saving transitions

Consider a venue in New York. On the day clocks "spring forward", one hour is skipped in local time. On the day clocks "fall back", one hour is repeated. If you naively:

- Partition data by local date, and
- Resample by local wall-clock minute,

you will see:

- Missing bars for the skipped hour in spring.
- Duplicate local times in autumn, where you cannot tell which occurrence of 1:30 a.m. you are aggregating.

By keeping storage and aggregation in UTC, you avoid this. You still need to be aware that:

- Session start and end times in UTC change when local daylight-saving rules change.
- Maintaining a correct mapping from local session hours to UTC requires an up-to-date calendar library or feed.

The usual pattern is:

- Maintain session definitions in the exchange's local time zone (for example, "regular trading hours: 9:30 to 16:00 America/New_York").
- Precompute or look up, for each trading date, the corresponding UTC open and close times.
- Use these UTC times in your schemas (for example, storing session identifiers and UTC ranges), then only convert back to local time for display.

Trading calendars and sessions

Unlike retail calendars, trading calendars are full of exceptions:

- Regular holidays.
- Ad-hoc closures (for example, national days of mourning).
- Half-days and early closes.
- Venue-specific pre- and post-market sessions.

If your database treats every weekday as a trading day and every day as 24 hours long, your analytics will subtly diverge from the front office's.

Venue-specific calendars

Each exchange or venue has its own calendar. For example:

- The primary U.S. equity exchange calendar differs from the main Japanese equity calendar.
- Futures and options on the same underlying may follow different session rules.
- Some dark pools mirror primary sessions; others have their own hours.

For a multi-asset or multi-venue tick store, you therefore need:

- A representation of trading days per venue: a list of dates when the venue is open.
- For each open date, a description of sessions: regular hours, pre-open, auctions, after-hours, and any special sessions (for example, extended trading during an event).

This information is often maintained outside the database itself, in a calendar service or configuration repository. But the database schema should be designed to *consume* it:

- Include fields for *venue* and *session* in your fact tables.
- Partition or index by trading date and venue where appropriate.
- Ensure that resampling and aggregation functions are session-aware, not just naive by UTC day.

Sessions as first-class citizens

Treating sessions as first-class concepts pays off. A "session" here is an interval of time during which a coherent set of trading rules applies. For example:

- Pre-open auction period.

- Continuous regular trading hours.
- Auction close.
- Post-market trading.

For each event, you can attach:

- A session identifier (string or small integer).
- A session type (for example, auction, continuous, extended).

This enables:

- Fast filtering: "only regular session trades".
- Correct bar construction: starting and ending aggregations exactly at session boundaries.
- Robustness to future changes: if the exchange extends or shifts regular hours, you can simply update the calendar; existing data with attached session IDs remains meaningful.

From a performance perspective, encoding sessions as small integers is important. Whether in kdb+ enumerations or ClickHouse low-cardinality types, compact session IDs:

- Compress well.
- Are cheap to filter and group by.
- Fit naturally alongside timestamps in columnar layouts.

Resampling and bucketing: from ticks to bars

Most users of a tick store do not work directly on every event; instead, they analyze time-bucketed aggregates such as 1-second or 1-minute bars. Turning irregular tick streams into regular bars sounds trivial but is rich in traps.

Defining the time grid

Start by defining your time grid precisely in UTC:

- For a given bar interval (for example, 1 second), define boundaries as half-open intervals: $[t, t + 1s)$.
- Ensure that your bar construction logic consistently assigns each event to exactly one interval.

If you use UTC, these intervals are uniform and unaffected by local daylight-saving transitions. Session rules then determine which of these buckets are considered part of a given trading session.

In practice:

- You may generate a fixed sequence of bar boundaries covering 24 hours for each day in UTC.
- You then flag which buckets fall within each venue's sessions for that day.

This separation avoids complex branching in the hot path of bar aggregation: the engine only needs to check bucket IDs and session flags, not reason about calendars on the fly.

Dealing with empty intervals

In illiquid instruments or at fine resolutions (for example, 1 millisecond bars), many intervals contain no trades. How you handle these empty intervals can significantly affect downstream analytics:

- For prices, you may wish to forward-fill the last known trade or quote to avoid artificial gaps in charts and indicators.
- For volumes or counts, you typically leave zeros to indicate no activity.

The key is consistency:

- Decide per measure whether you forward-fill, back-fill, or leave missing.
- Ensure that your bar builders and query templates respect this convention across all instruments and venues.

In kdb+, this often manifests as well-defined aggregation pipelines that first group ticks into time windows, then apply per-column fill rules. In ClickHouse, similar behavior is implemented with a combination of window functions, join with a template time grid, and explicit fill expressions.

Aligning across venues and instruments

Cross-sectional analytics require bars for many instruments or venues on a common time grid. Misalignment can create subtle biases:

- If you build bars separately per symbol and later join on timestamp, floating-point rounding or inconsistent offset rules can produce slightly different bucket boundaries.
- If you use local times per venue, cross-venue comparisons at the same UTC time may accidentally combine pre-market activity in one venue with regular hours in another.

To avoid this:

- Use a single, canonical UTC grid per bar interval.
- Build or normalize all venue-specific bars onto this grid.
- Store both the raw bar and its session metadata, so queries can choose to compare only regular hours, or include extended sessions as needed.

Schema patterns for time and calendars

We can now synthesize these ideas into concrete schema patterns for kdb+ and ClickHouse.

Partitioning and sort orders

For high-frequency data, common choices include:

- Partitioning by trading date (often as UTC date) and sometimes by venue.
- Sorting within each partition by primary time, then by symbol or instrument ID.

This aligns well with:

- Time-range scans per symbol: a single, mostly contiguous run of rows.
- Session-level filtering: session IDs changing slowly within a time-sorted partition.
- Compression: time deltas and dictionary-encoded sessions compress effectively.

The choice of partition key must, however, respect venue calendars:

- For globally traded instruments, you may need to define trading "dates" per venue or by region rather than using calendar UTC days.
- For products that trade across what would be two calendar days in UTC (for example, Asian markets relative to UTC), you might partition by local trading date but still store primary timestamps in UTC.

Storing session and calendar attributes

To make your database calendar-aware, you typically:

- Maintain reference tables that map (venue, local date) to trading sessions, with their UTC open and close times and session IDs.

- Enrich fact tables (ticks, trades, quotes, bars) with venue and session columns, either at ingest time or via joins in query paths.

In kdb+, reference tables are often kept in memory and joined on demand or at load. In ClickHouse, they can be stored as dimension tables, joined via foreign keys or dictionary lookups.

The important point is to avoid baking local time calculations into every query. Instead, precompute and store:

- A small integer session identifier per row.
- A trading date per venue, which may differ from the UTC date.

This makes it easy to pose precise questions like:

- "Give me regular-session VWAP per symbol on its local trading date, across all venues."
- "Compare pre-open auction behavior across two exchanges, normalized to their local clocks, but aggregated and stored in UTC."

Avoiding common pitfalls

To close the section, it is useful to list a few recurring mistakes that this framework helps you avoid:

- **Using local time as a primary key.** This leads to ambiguities around daylight-saving transitions and complicates cross-venue analysis.
- **Ignoring session rules in bar construction.** This can mix pre-market and regular-session activity or misclassify auction prints, leading to bars that do not match front-office definitions.
- **Assuming every weekday is a trading day.** This can produce empty bars that are treated as zeros, or cause rolling window calculations to include non-trading days unintentionally.

- **Not distinguishing event time from processing time.** This prevents correct reconstruction of the market state and hides system-induced delays.

By instead:

- Storing all event times in UTC with clear precision and epoch.
- Treating sessions and calendars as first-class entities.
- Designing bar grids and resampling logic explicitly with these constraints in mind.

you create a foundation where subsequent modeling, strategy backtests, and risk calculations rest on a sound temporal footing.

In the next section, when we dive into market microstructure and data semantics, we will build on this temporal understanding. Every order, quote, and trade is not just an event with a price and size, but an event at a precise point along the time axis we have just carefully constructed.

1.5 Market Microstructure and Data Semantics

In earlier sections we treated trades and quotes largely as generic "events" arriving over the network and flowing through kernels, caches, and disks. We focused on how quickly and reliably those events move. In this section we turn to what the events *mean*.

A high-performance market data store is not just a fast bucket of rows. Every row encodes a small piece of market microstructure: an order submitted to a limit order book, a quote update, a trade, a cancellation or correction. If you do not respect the underlying mechanics of the book, your database may be syntactically valid but semantically wrong: spreads go negative, depth disappears, or prices jump without explanation.

Our goals here are to:

- Define a clear vocabulary for trades, quotes, orders, and book updates.
- Introduce the basic invariants a central limit order book must satisfy.
- Show how these semantics shape schema design in kdb+ and ClickHouse.
- Explain how to build validation rules that catch errors at ingest, not in research.

Once you internalize these concepts, you will look at each stored row not as an isolated fact, but as a state transition in a well-defined dynamical system: the order book.

Core event types: trades, quotes, and order-book updates

At the finest level, a modern electronic market is a stream of messages. Different feeds and venues use different encodings, but most messages fall into a small number of conceptual types.

Orders and order instructions

An *order* is an instruction from a participant to buy or sell a quantity of an instrument under certain conditions. In a limit order book, the most important fields are:

- **Instrument identifier:** symbol, ISIN, or another product code.
- **Side:** buy (bid) or sell (ask).
- **Price:** a limit price for limit orders, or a special indicator for market orders.
- **Quantity (size):** number of shares, contracts, or units.
- **Order ID:** a unique identifier assigned by the participant or the venue.

- **Time and venue:** when and where the order entered the book.
- **Flags and attributes:** time-in-force, hidden/iceberg, special handling instructions, and so on.

Orders can be introduced, modified, and cancelled. Feeds may report these as:

- *Add / enter order*
- *Modify / replace order*
- *Cancel order*

Each such message changes the state of the order book.

Quotes and book snapshots

A *quote* is an aggregate view of supply and demand at or near the best prices. Top-of-book quotes show:

- Best bid price and size (highest buy interest).
- Best ask price and size (lowest sell interest).

Depth-of-book quotes extend this to multiple levels, for example showing the top 5 or 10 price levels on each side, with aggregated sizes at each level.

Depending on the feed, quote messages may be:

- *Incremental updates* that adjust individual price levels.
- *Full snapshots* of the top N levels, replacing prior state.

From a storage perspective, a quote record typically includes:

- Instrument identifier and venue.
- Bid and ask prices and sizes (possibly arrays for multiple levels).
- Timestamp(s) and sequence information.

- Flags indicating whether the quote is firm, indicative, or subject to special conditions.

Trades and executions

A *trade* occurs when compatible buy and sell instructions meet in the book and are executed. Trade events typically report:

- Instrument and venue.
- Trade price and executed quantity.
- Aggressor side (which side initiated the trade, when available).
- Trade conditions and flags (for example, auction print, off-exchange, odd lot, late report).
- One or more order IDs involved in the execution (if available).

You can think of each trade as:

- Decreasing available depth on one or both sides of the book.
- Reflecting a change in ownership and possibly in informational content (trade direction and size).

In a consolidated feed, the same underlying trade may appear multiple times with different normalizations or under different reporting rules.

Central limit order book mechanics

To understand how these events fit together, we need a minimal model of a central limit order book (CLOB), which is the dominant structure for modern equities, futures, and many other instruments.

Bids, asks, and price-time priority

The book is conceptually two sorted lists of standing limit orders:

- **Bid side:** buy orders, sorted by descending price (highest bid first) and, within a price level, by arrival time.

- **Ask side:** sell orders, sorted by ascending price (lowest ask first) and, within a price level, by arrival time.

Key invariants:

- *No crossed book:* best bid price must be strictly less than or equal to best ask price. If a new order would cross, it trades immediately.
- *Price-time priority:* at a given price, older resting orders are filled before newer ones.
- *Non-negative depth:* aggregate size at each price level is the sum of outstanding orders; it cannot become negative through legitimate operations.

Market orders do not rest in the book. They execute immediately against the best available counterparties until either the order is fully filled or the book is exhausted at compatible prices.

Events as state transitions

Every message from the exchange can be viewed as a transition function on the book:

- *Add order:* inserts a new order at the appropriate place in the bid or ask ladder. Depth at that price level increases.
- *Cancel order:* removes an existing order, reducing depth.
- *Modify order:* often represented as a cancel followed by an add (depending on protocol).
- *Trade:* matches one or more resting orders against incoming orders, reducing depth and possibly changing best prices.

This is the lens through which your database must interpret each row: as a small, well-defined transformation of an evolving state.

From messages to a visual book

Before we dive into schema implications, it is helpful to visualize a simple order book and a short sequence of events.

Imagine an instrument with the following initial book:

- Bids: 99.0 (100 units), 98.5 (200 units)
- Asks: 100.5 (150 units), 101.0 (100 units)

We then apply:

1. A new buy order at 99.5 for 50 units.
2. A cancel of 50 units from the 98.5 bid.
3. A market sell for 120 units that trades at the best bid(s).

The following diagram captures the ladder and these transitions.

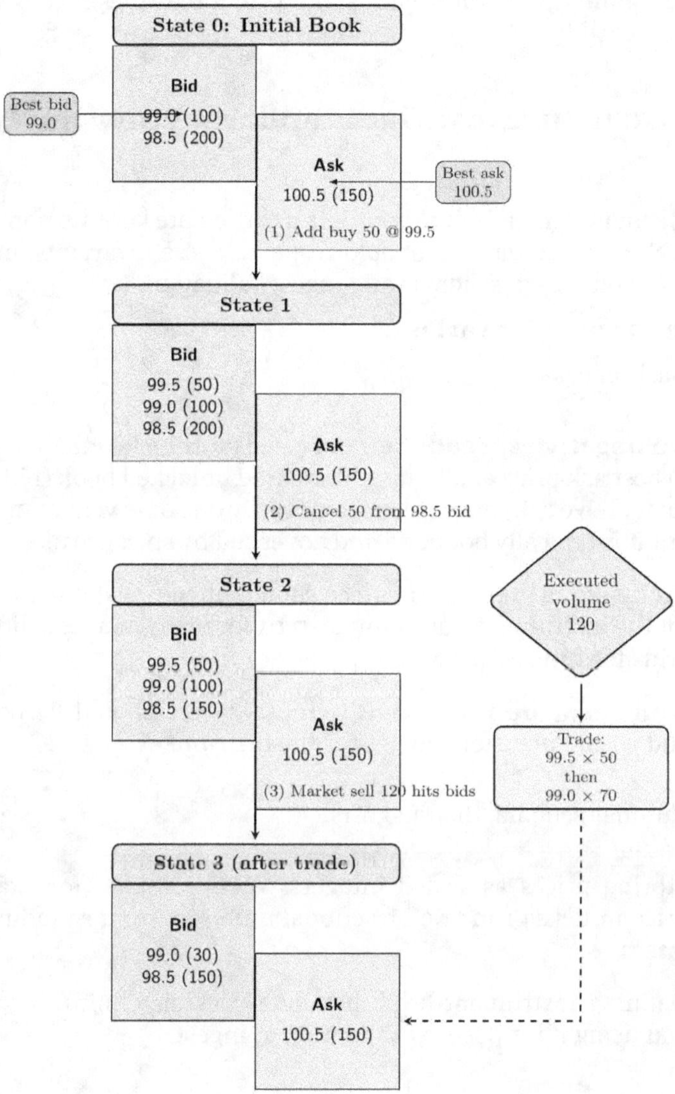

This ladder view emphasizes that each message type corresponds to specific, checkable changes in depth and prices. Your database schemas and validation logic should enforce these constraints wherever feasible.

Microstructure invariants and what they imply for data

Having a mental model of the book lets us articulate key invariants that every well-behaved data set should respect. These invariants, in turn, drive how you design schemas and ingest validation.

Price and spread invariants

Some basic checks:

- **No negative spread:** best bid price must be less than or equal to best ask price at all times. A crossed or locked book (bid equal to or above ask) may occur temporarily on some venues or feeds, but it is typically bounded and governed by specific rules.
- **Tick size adherence:** prices should align to valid increments for the instrument (for example, 0.01 for many equities, different grids for futures or FX).
- **Non-zero, non-negative prices:** prices should be positive and within plausible ranges for the instrument.

In a columnar schema, this suggests:

- Storing prices as scaled integers when possible (for example, price in ticks or in fixed fractional units) to avoid rounding surprises.
- Defining instrument-level metadata (tick size, min/max price) and using it for per-row validation at ingest.

Depth and quantity invariants

For any given instrument, venue, and side:

- Aggregate depth at each price level must be non-negative.

- Cancellations and trades must not remove more size from a level than is resting there (unless the feed uses aggregated updates without individual order IDs, in which case checks are approximate).
- Total executed volume over time must not exceed the sum of all entered sizes, accounting for cancels.

From a storage perspective, this motivates:

- Keeping separate columns for event type and side, encoded as small integers or enums.
- For full depth feeds, storing sufficient identifiers (order IDs or exchange references) to reconstruct and sanity-check per-order depth.
- For aggregated depth feeds, designing update semantics carefully: are changes deltas, replacements, or absolute levels?

Sequence and ordering invariants

The temporal structure is just as important:

- Within a single venue feed, message sequence numbers should be strictly increasing, with no unexplained gaps or reversals.
- Within a specific book (instrument and venue), order IDs should exhibit consistent lifecycle: created, possibly modified, then cancelled or fully filled.
- For multi-venue consolidated feeds, per-venue order must be preserved, even if global interleaving is arbitrary.

Schema implications include:

- Always storing the exchange-provided sequence number for each message where available.
- Having clear keys: at minimum (venue, instrument, event time, sequence) for uniqueness; often extended with channel or partition identifiers.

- Considering partitioning or clustering strategies that keep per-venue sequences close together on disk to facilitate gap detection and replay.

Schema design: encoding semantics explicitly

Armed with vocabulary and invariants, we can discuss how to reflect them in table layouts in kdb+ and ClickHouse.

Fact tables as streams of normalized events

The core of most market data stores is a set of *fact tables* that capture events in normalized form. Typical patterns:

Trade fact table.

Columns might include:

- Time fields: event time, possibly arrival time.
- Instrument and venue identifiers.
- Price and size.
- Aggressor side.
- Trade condition flags (auction, off-book, dark, etc.).
- Sequence number and source channel.

Normalization choices:

- Store instrument and venue as foreign keys (enums or dictionaries) pointing to dimension tables with static metadata.
- Encode side and condition as compact integer codes, with a well-documented dictionary.

Order-book event table.

For full-depth feeds, you might have:

- Time, instrument, venue.

- Event type (add, modify, cancel, trade).
- Side, price, size.
- Order ID or quote ID.
- Sequence number and channel.

This table is append-only and represents the raw building blocks for reconstructing the book state at any time.

Snapshots versus events

Some systems store snapshots of the book at a fixed frequency (for example, once per second) instead of or in addition to full event streams. Each snapshot row might include:

- Time, instrument, venue.
- Arrays or repeated fields of bid and ask prices and sizes at each depth level.
- Derived fields such as spread, mid price, and total depth.

Snapshots trade detail for volume: they are cheaper to store and query for many analytics, but lossy. You cannot reconstruct intra-second microstructure or exact execution paths from snapshots alone.

A robust architecture often includes:

- High-fidelity event tables for core instruments and venues, used for strategies and sensitive research.
- Derived snapshot or bar tables for broader coverage and easier daily analytics.

Designing the schema to make the derivation explicit (for example, with provenance fields or view definitions) helps maintain consistency.

Handling corrections and cancels

Real feeds are messy. Trades can be:

- Cancelled after publication (for example, error trades).
- Corrected with new price or size.
- Marked as late or out-of-sequence.

To maintain semantic integrity, you need to represent these operations explicitly. Common patterns:

- Include a *trade action* field (new, cancel, correct) and a reference to the original trade ID when applicable.
- When building derived tables (for example, daily volume or VWAP), apply corrections and cancels in sequence order to adjust aggregates.
- Preserve the original feed messages in raw tables, even if views or materialized tables present a corrected, "official" history.

This is a classic case where microstructure semantics dictate storage: without a place to store references between original and correcting messages, you cannot reliably maintain adjusted analytics.

Validation logic: catching anomalies at ingest

Given the complexity of real-world feeds, your ingestion pipeline should include checks that enforce or at least monitor the invariants discussed earlier.

Syntactic and range checks

Simple but essential:

- Validate that required fields are present and uncorrupted.
- Check that prices, sizes, and IDs fall within reasonable ranges.
- Reject or flag clearly invalid records (negative sizes, nonsensical prices).

These can often be done cheaply as part of parsing and initial normalization.

Stateful consistency checks

More interesting are checks that require state:

- Detect sequence gaps or reversals per channel and venue.
- Ensure that cancellations reference known live orders (when order IDs are provided).
- Monitor for persistent crossed books or impossible depth changes.

Ingest pipelines for kdb+ frequently maintain in-memory state per instrument and venue to perform such checks in real time, logging anomalies and optionally quarantining suspect data. ClickHouse, which is more batch-oriented, may incorporate these checks in upstream processing stages before data lands in MergeTree tables.

Soft versus hard failures

Not every anomaly should cause ingest to stop. You will encounter:

- Temporary data quality issues from a vendor.
- Inconsistent behaviors across venues and product types.

Define clear policies:

- *Hard* violations: structurally corrupt records, missing essential keys, or clearly impossible values should be rejected.
- *Soft* violations: unusual but plausible conditions (brief crossed markets, anomalous spreads) may be ingested but flagged for downstream awareness.

Storing flags directly in your fact tables—for example, a small integer "quality" or "anomaly" code—allows queries and backtests to include or exclude suspect data explicitly, rather than silently mixing it in.

Interpreting stored rows: from bits to book

With these semantics in hand, you can now look at any row in your market database and ask:

- What kind of event is this (order add, cancel, trade, snapshot)?
- Which instrument and venue does it affect?
- Which side and price level of the book changes as a result?
- How should book depth, spread, and mid-price evolve when this row is applied?

This is a powerful shift in perspective. Rather than treating your database as a set of flat tables, you see it as a recorded history of state transitions governed by well-defined rules. This enables:

- Faithful reconstruction of historical books for backtesting.
- Robust computed metrics (spreads, liquidity measures, impact estimates) that reflect true microstructure.
- Meaningful anomaly detection, where deviations from invariants are signals, not just noise.

It also explains why different storage designs in kdb+ and ClickHouse look the way they do. Choices about partitioning, column types, and normalization are all downstream of the core requirement: to preserve and expose the semantics of an evolving order book.

In the next and final section of this chapter, we will connect these semantic considerations back to modeling, compression, and concurrency. You will see how microstructure fields and invariants influence table width, encoding choices, and parallel execution strategies in real kdb+ and ClickHouse deployments.

1.6 Modeling, Compression, and Concurrency Basics

By now we have built up three complementary views of a market data system:

- The *systems view*: Linux scheduling, virtual memory, filesystems, and networking, all of which control how quickly bytes move.
- The *hardware view*: CPU caches, memory bandwidth, and SIMD units, which determine how quickly we can process those bytes once they are in RAM.
- The *market view*: time semantics and microstructure, which give each row of data a precise meaning in terms of sessions and order-book state.

In this section we synthesize those perspectives into concrete design patterns for:

- Modeling tick and order-book data in tables.
- Encoding and compressing columns so they are both compact and fast to scan.
- Structuring concurrency so that ingest and queries can exploit parallel hardware without stepping on each other.

The focus is conceptual rather than product-specific: we will point to kdb+ and ClickHouse, but the intent is to give you a reusable set of mental templates. When you later see particular kdb+ schema idioms or ClickHouse MergeTree configurations, they should feel like natural consequences of these underlying principles.

Foundational modeling choices: facts, dimensions, and table shape

The first step is to choose how you represent your data in tables. For market data this usually means deciding:

- What counts as a *fact*.
- What attributes are stable and shared across many facts (dimensions).
- How wide or narrow each fact table should be.

Facts: events and derived aggregates

At the core of most designs are two broad categories of fact tables:

- **Event facts:** individual ticks, order-book updates, or trades. Each row represents a single microstructure event with fields like event time, instrument, venue, side, price, size, and event type.
- **Aggregate facts:** regularized data such as 1-second bars, depth snapshots, or daily OHLCV. Each row rolls up many events into a coarser time bucket and set of measures.

From a modeling standpoint, you want:

- Event tables that are as close to the feed semantics as possible, with minimal interpretation.
- Aggregate tables that are explicitly derived from events, with clear rules for resampling, session treatment, and corporate-action adjustments.

This separation lets you:

- Use event tables for microstructure studies and forensic work.
- Use aggregates for most strategy backtests and risk analytics.

Dimensions: instruments, venues, calendars

Many columns in your fact tables will take values from small, slowly changing sets. Examples include:

- Instrument identifiers (symbols, ISINs).
- Venue codes (exchange, dark pool, trading platform).
- Session identifiers (pre-open, regular, auction).
- Trade conditions and flags.

In both kdb+ and ClickHouse, you typically model these as *dimensions*:

- A separate small table or dictionary that maps a compact code to human-readable attributes (for example, symbol code to full name, tick size, currency).
- A compact representation (usually an integer or enumeration) in the fact tables.

This has three benefits:

- Saves space: codes are much smaller than verbose strings.
- Improves scan speed: integers compare and group more efficiently than text.
- Localizes schema evolution: when attributes change (for example, tick size or sector classification), you update the dimension, not all historical facts.

Wide versus narrow tables

You must also decide whether to use:

- **Wide tables:** each row contains many columns, capturing all aspects of an event (for example, price, size, side, all flags, and possibly multiple levels of the book).
- **Narrow tables:** each row contains a small, fixed set of fields, often representing one measure, with additional columns to describe what that measure is.

For most tick and book data, *moderately wide* tables work best:

- Market events naturally bundle multiple attributes (price, size, side, venue, event type).
- Columnar storage means you can still scan a subset of columns efficiently, even if the logical table is wide.

However, there are cases for narrower layouts:

- Storing many book levels (for example, top 50) as a set of repeated rows per level rather than 50 pairs of bid_px_n, bid_sz_n columns.
- Time-series of derived indicators where the set of metrics is large and sparse across instruments.

The key is to align table shape with likely access patterns. A wide table with many unused columns in most queries is acceptable in a columnar system, as long as you avoid complex, nested structures that destroy locality.

Partitioning and sort order: respecting time and microstructure

Once you know what each table represents, the next question is how to break it into physical chunks (partitions, shards) and how to sort rows within each chunk. These choices directly drive performance on the hardware and OS we have discussed.

Partitioning keys: date, instrument, venue

In high-frequency data, the cardinality of rows is huge. You rarely keep all ticks for all instruments in a single monolithic file or table; instead, you partition along one or more keys. Common patterns:

- **By trading date (UTC) or local trading day:** natural for most tick and bar tables; aligns well with operational tasks like daily loading and archiving.

- **By instrument or instrument group:** useful for extremely active instruments or when you want to isolate hot symbols on faster storage.
- **By venue:** helpful in multi-venue setups where each venue's feed and calendar differ.

Partition design must reflect both:

- *Query patterns:* what time ranges and instrument sets you typically access.
- *Operational patterns:* how you load, backfill, and archive.

For example:

- If most research queries are "last N days by symbol set", daily partitions per venue and instrument group work well.
- If you frequently perform cross-sectional snapshots at specific times, you may treat time as the primary key and instruments as secondary.

Within-partition sort order

Within each partition, you typically choose a primary sort order such as:

- time $\rightarrow$ symbol, or
- symbol $\rightarrow$ time.

Each has pros and cons:

Time-then-symbol. This layout:

- Keeps events in exact time order, which simplifies full-market replays and book reconstruction.

- Makes contiguous slices for time-range scans across many instruments easy.
- May scatter all ticks for a single symbol across the partition, which is less ideal for symbol-specific scans.

Symbol-then-time. This layout:

- Keeps each symbol's time series in a contiguous block; scans per symbol are extremely cache-friendly.
- Can still support cross-sectional snapshots with careful indexing, but may require more random access.

In practice, many designs pick one dominant order based on the most important workload and use indexes or secondary data structures for less common patterns. For example:

- A kdb+ historical tick store might partition by date and sort by symbol-then-time, while intraday capture processes maintain additional structures for global time-ordered replay.
- A ClickHouse MergeTree might use a compound primary key of (trading_date, symbol, event_time), achieving a compromise between both orderings.

Your earlier understanding of CPU caches and sequential scans should guide this choice: ask yourself which scans you want to be pure linear sweeps versus ones that can tolerate some randomness.

Compression and encoding: trading CPU for I/O and memory

After modeling and layout, compression and encoding are your main levers for controlling the cost of I/O and the effective size of your caches. The goal is not just to shrink data on disk, but to do so in a way that *helps* the CPU execute vectorized scans.

Dictionary encoding for symbols and venues

Symbols, venues, session IDs, and many flags are naturally dictionary-encoded:

- Build a mapping from a set of distinct values (for example, all symbols) to small integer codes.
- Store the codes in the fact tables.

Benefits:

- Reduces space: a 2- or 4-byte integer instead of a longer string.
- Improves cache behavior: arrays of integers are much denser and more predictable.
- Enables SIMD: comparisons and filters on integers can be vectorized easily.

kdb+ does this implicitly with enumerated symbol types; ClickHouse provides low-cardinality and dictionary codecs to achieve a similar effect.

Run-length encoding for repeated values

Many market data fields change slowly:

- Session identifiers: constant within a long time interval.
- Venue or feed identifiers: constant per partition or file.
- Certain flags (for example, "is auction" is usually false except at a few points).

Run-length encoding (RLE) compresses sequences of repeated values as (value, run length) pairs. This is especially powerful when:

- Partitions are defined to keep values constant or slowly changing.

- Queries often filter or group by these fields.

Importantly, RLE interacts well with SIMD:

- If a run covers many rows, the engine can apply a single decision for the entire run, skipping or including whole blocks at once.
- This reduces branching and can dramatically cut down work per row.

Designing schemas so that "slow" fields vary mostly across partitions or large spans of rows is therefore not just a modeling decision, but a performance optimization.

Delta and frame-of-reference encoding for time and price

Timestamps and prices often evolve smoothly:

- Event times increment monotonically with relatively small gaps between adjacent events.
- Prices move in discrete ticks and rarely jump by huge amounts between consecutive trades in a liquid instrument.

Delta encoding stores:

- A base value for a block (for example, start time or price).
- Small differences (deltas) for each subsequent row.

Frame-of-reference encoding is similar but normalizes all values in a block against a reference, often allowing them to fit in fewer bits.

The advantages:

- Better compression: small deltas need fewer bits.

- Faster scans: deltas can often be decoded with simple integer additions that vectorize well.

Both kdb+ and ClickHouse exploit such patterns implicitly or via configuration. As a schema designer, you help by:

- Ensuring time and price columns are sorted and grouped so that adjacent rows are correlated.
- Avoiding arbitrary re-ordering that would enlarge deltas and reduce compressibility.

Concurrency and parallelism: structuring work with partitions and shards

So far we have optimized the *sequential* path for one core. Real systems must also exploit multiple cores and multiple machines.

Partition-level parallelism

Partitioning, which we introduced for modeling and I/O convenience, is also a natural unit of parallelism:

- Different partitions (for example, different trading days or instrument groups) can be processed by different threads or processes independently.
- Ingest jobs can write to one partition while queries scan others, reducing contention.

This is the essence of a *shared-nothing* approach at the partition level:

- Each partition is mostly self-contained.
- Operations like compaction, re-encoding, or reindexing can run in parallel across partitions.

In kdb+, this may manifest as one process per day or per symbol shard. In ClickHouse, MergeTree tables often have many parts spread across disks and can be merged or queried in parallel.

Sharding across nodes

When a single machine cannot hold all data or serve all queries, you shard across multiple nodes. Common sharding keys include:

- Date or date ranges.
- Instrument ranges or hash buckets of symbols.
- Venue or region.

Each shard:

- Owns a subset of the data.
- Receives relevant ingest streams.
- Serves queries whose filters map to its shard key.

From a concurrency standpoint, sharding:

- Converts global bottlenecks into many smaller, parallel tasks.
- Reduces synchronization needs between nodes for most read queries.

However, it also requires:

- A routing layer or query planner that knows where data lives.
- Replication strategies to ensure durability and availability when one shard fails.

Shared-memory concurrency and contention points

Within a single node, you still need to manage concurrent threads:

- Ingest threads parsing feeds and writing to append-only logs or in-memory buffers.

- Background workers compacting and re-encoding partitions.
- Query threads scanning and aggregating columns.

Naive shared-memory concurrency can lead to contention at:

- Locking points protecting shared data structures.
- Memory allocators when many threads allocate and free small objects.
- Cache lines that are written by multiple threads (false sharing).

Well-designed systems reduce these by:

- Sharing as little mutable state as possible across threads.
- Using per-thread or per-core buffers and queues.
- Choosing lock-free or low-contention data structures for critical paths.

Partitioned execution helps here too: if each thread primarily works on disjoint partitions or shards, they naturally avoid stepping on the same cache lines or locks.

End-to-end patterns: from ingest to query

We can now describe some recurring architectural patterns that naturally emerge from the combination of modeling, compression, and concurrency strategies we have discussed.

Append-only fact tables with periodic compaction

Event streams are naturally append-only: new data arrives and is only rarely corrected or cancelled. A common pattern is therefore:

- Ingest threads append events to write-optimized files or segments, one per partition or shard.

- These raw segments may be lightly encoded but are optimized for sequential writes and low latency.
- Background jobs periodically compact many small segments into larger, read-optimized partitions, applying heavier compression and reordering if needed.

Benefits:

- Separates low-latency ingest from heavy optimization work.
- Keeps read paths simple and predictable: queries mostly touch compacted segments.
- Allows flexible trade-offs between how fresh data is and how compressed it is.

kdb+ often implements this pattern via intraday logs rolled into end-of-day hdb partitions. ClickHouse's MergeTree family embodies a similar idea with parts that are merged in the background.

Immutable columnar partitions

Once data is compacted into a partition, it is typically treated as immutable:

- No in-place updates; corrections are applied by adding new segments or overlay tables.
- Partitions may be replaced wholesale by a new, re-encoded copy.

Immutability simplifies concurrency:

- Readers never contend with writers for locks on existing partitions.
- Background merges can produce new partitions without disturbing ongoing queries.

It also plays well with compression:

- Encodings that benefit from global ordering, such as RLE and delta encoding, are easier to apply when you can reorder freely at compaction time.
- There is no need to keep space or metadata for in-place modifications.

Write-optimized ingest feeding read-optimized stores

Bringing it together:

- **Ingest layer:** write-optimized, often row-oriented or lightly columnar, minimal compression, focused on low latency and resilience to bursts.
- **Storage layer:** read-optimized, fully columnar, heavily compressed, sorted and partitioned to favor common queries.
- **Query layer:** uses parallel scans and aggregations over these read-optimized structures.

Your earlier knowledge about Linux I/O, NICs, and CPU caches informs the tuning of each layer:

- Ingest paths use larger buffers and careful scheduling to survive microbursts without drops.
- Storage paths use direct or buffered I/O, aligned with NVMe capabilities and filesystem behavior.
- Query paths are engineered to be cache-friendly and vectorizable, with minimal pointer chasing.

Putting it all together: why designs look the way they do

We can now answer the question posed at the beginning of the chapter: why do kdb+ and ClickHouse schemas and storage layouts look the way they do in real trading organizations?

Because they are the natural outcome of reconciling:

- **Systems constraints:** cores, caches, page caches, NICs, disks, and their quirks.
- **Market semantics:** microsecond event times, venue calendars, order-book invariants.
- **Operational realities:** 24/6 trading, market-open bursts, regulatory retention, backtesting workloads.

When you see:

- Daily partitions by symbol in a kdb+ hdb, you can recognize the interplay between session calendars, time-based queries, and cache-friendly symbol scans.
- A ClickHouse MergeTree with primary key (date, symbol, time) and codecs for low-cardinality and delta encoding, you can see a deliberate attempt to align encoding with access patterns and hardware.
- Separate tables for raw ticks, corrected trades, and derived bars, you can infer an architecture that respects both feed semantics and downstream analytical needs.

The purpose of this section is not to prescribe one "correct" design, but to give you the intellectual tools to reason about trade-offs. As your instruments, venues, and workloads evolve, you will adjust partitioning schemes, encodings, and concurrency models. With the foundations from this chapter, those adjustments can be principled and predictive rather than ad hoc.

In the rest of the book we will use these patterns as the backdrop for concrete kdb+ and ClickHouse implementations, walking through real schemas, ingest pipelines, and query plans. Each concrete design will be an instance of the general ideas you have now seen: model the market cleanly, compress with the CPU in mind, and structure concurrency so that hardware and kernel details work *with* you, not against you.

Chapter 2

Columnar Database Fundamentals

Most trading teams know that columnar databases are fast; far fewer can explain why. This chapter peels back the layers-from on-disk layout to CPU pipelines and isolation models-to show how columnar engines turn raw ticks into millisecond answers. Rather than focusing on vendor quirks, we isolate the core ideas: how columns compress into memory-sized shards, how vectorized operators ride the CPU's SIMD units, how partitions and indexes keep the disk cold, and how transactional guarantees are right-sized for real-world analytics. By the end, you will be able to read a query plan, reason about its performance, and deliberately shape your schemas and workloads for sustained intraday speed.

2.1 Columnar Storage Principles

In the previous chapter we looked at why modern market data workloads stress traditional databases: huge volumes of ticks and orders, relatively simple aggregations, and a constant tug-of-war between ingest speed and analytic latency. We now turn to the core architectural answer that systems like kdb+ and ClickHouse provide: columnar storage.

This section explains how columnar tables are physically and logically laid out, and how three ideas work together:

- **Column orientation**: storing data column-by-column instead of row-by-row.
- **Late materialization**: delaying the assembly of full rows until it is absolutely necessary.
- **Compression**: exploiting patterns in each column to reduce space and I/O.

We will focus relentlessly on market data examples: trades, quotes, and intraday analytics. By the end of the section, you should be able to look at a query such as "compute VWAP for the last hour for a basket of symbols" and mentally trace which columns are read, how they are compressed, and why the engine avoids most of the bytes on disk.

Row-Oriented vs Column-Oriented Layout

Consider a simple equity trade table with four fields:

- time: event time
- sym: instrument symbol
- price: last traded price
- size: traded quantity

Logically, both a row store and a column store present the same table to the user. What differs is the physical arrangement of bytes on disk and in memory.

Row-Oriented Layout

In a row-oriented database (for example, a classic OLTP system), the engine stores each trade as a *record* containing all fields, and then places records back-to-back:

[time_1, sym_1, price_1, size_1]
[time_2, sym_2, price_2, size_2]
[time_3, sym_3, price_3, size_3]
⋮

Physically, the file (or page in memory) looks like:

time_1 sym_1 price_1 size_1 time_2 sym_2 price_2 size_2 ...

This layout is excellent if most queries need *all* fields of a single trade at once. For example, an order management system might frequently fetch a specific order by ID and then display every attribute of that order.

However, analytic queries on market data usually behave differently:

- A VWAP query needs price, size, and maybe time, but not other infrequently used attributes.
- A liquidity heatmap might only need sym, price, size.
- A factor model might read dozens of numeric columns from a bar or factor table, but ignore many others.

In a row store, reading any of these fields means reading *all* fields in the row, because they are interleaved. Even if you discard half of the columns at the query engine level, you still pay the I/O and memory bandwidth to move them.

Column-Oriented Layout

In a column-oriented database, each column is stored separately as a contiguous array of values:

- Column time: [time_1, time_2, time_3, ...]
- Column sym: [sym_1, sym_2, sym_3, ...]
- Column price: [price_1, price_2, price_3, ...]

- Column size: [size_1, size_2, size_3, ...]

Physically, a file or set of files might look conceptually like:

```
time: time_1 time_2 time_3 ...
 sym: sym_1 sym_2 sym_3 ...
price: price_1 price_2 price_3 ...
 size: size_1 size_2 size_3 ...
```

In kdb+, this is visible when you inspect a column in memory: it is literally a vector of values. In ClickHouse, a MergeTree table persists each column in its own set of data files and marks.

The key benefit is that a query can read only the columns it needs:

- A VWAP query scanning price, size, and time touches just those three arrays; other columns are never read.

- A count of trades per symbol might only need sym.

Instead of dragging along irrelevant data, the engine limits both *logical* work (operations performed) and *physical* work (bytes fetched from disk and memory) to exactly what the query references.

Right after this conceptual contrast, it is helpful to visualize the physical difference between row and column layouts.

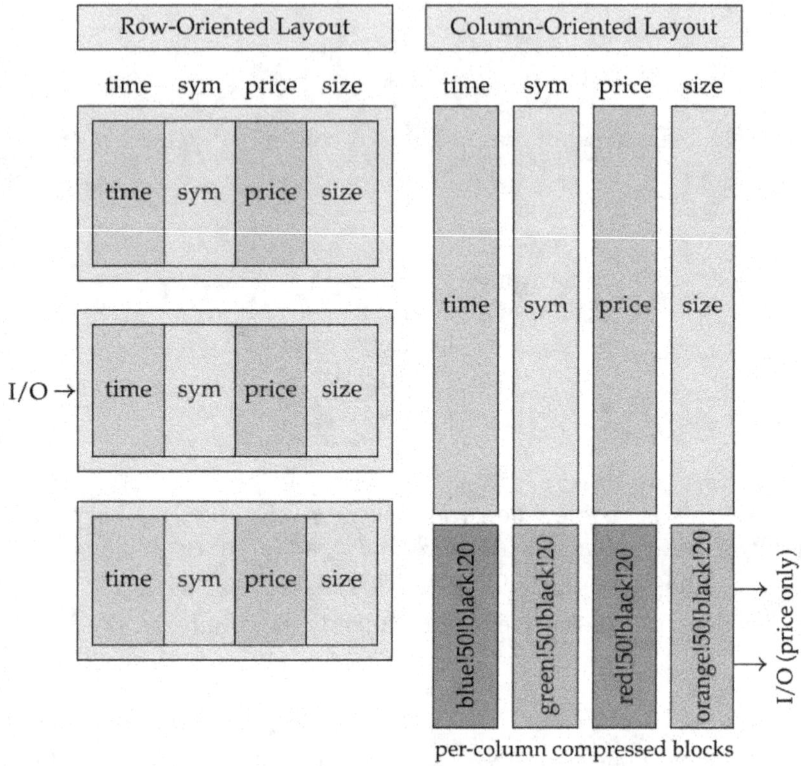

On the left, the row store must read through every field to get to the ones you care about. On the right, the column store pulls exactly the compressed blocks for the referenced columns.

Storage Units: Segments, Stripes, Parts, and Blocks

Real-world columnar engines do not store one giant array per column. Instead, they break each column into manageable chunks. The terminology varies:

- In ClickHouse MergeTree tables, you will encounter *parts* and *marks*: each part holds a range of rows, and each mark indexes a group of rows within a part.
- In kdb+, a table in memory is conceptually a single vector per column, but on disk, splayed tables use one file per column, often naturally grouped by date.
- In the literature, you will also see terms like *segments*, *stripes*, or *blocks*.

Even though names differ, the core ideas are similar:

1. **Group rows into blocks.** For example, 8 192 rows per block.
2. **For each column, store the values for that block contiguously.**
3. **Attach metadata to each block.** For instance, minimum and maximum values, counts, and offsets into the file.

This structure matters for performance:

- The engine can skip entire blocks when a filter condition does not overlap the block's min/max range. A query for trades on AAPL can avoid reading blocks whose sym min and max are between other tickers.
- Reading is done in large, sequential chunks, which align well with how disks and SSDs prefer to operate.
- Compression can be applied independently per block, making it easier to tune for different parts of the data.

For market data, these blocks are often aligned with time. For instance, you might have one part per day and internal blocks that correspond to small time slices. This makes it natural to prune data when you query for a specific trading session or intraday window.

Why Columnar Layout Helps Market Analytics

Column orientation is not just a stylistic choice. It directly reduces both I/O and CPU work for typical analytic queries.

Reading Only What You Need

Suppose you want the last traded price for each symbol at the close of the day. Conceptually, this might scan through all trades for the session, grouped by symbol and time. The query needs:

- sym
- time
- price

It does not need:

- size
- Trade conditions, venue codes, or feed IDs
- Various flags (auction, dark pool, odd lot, and so on) unless you are doing a more sophisticated selection

In a row store, scanning the table means reading everything. Even if the engine discards unnecessary fields early, the bytes still travelled from disk to memory and through the CPU caches. In a column store, the engine simply never reads those columns' blocks. The result is:

- Fewer bytes from disk or the networked storage system.
- Less pressure on CPU caches and memory bandwidth.
- Faster query completion, especially when repeated many times.

This effect scales with table width. As your schema grows—common in research environments where you keep adding fields—the advantage of ignoring cold columns becomes more pronounced.

Aligning with Vectorized Execution

In later sections we will discuss vectorized execution in detail, but the connection to storage is intuitive. In a column store, price is stored as a dense array of numbers. This is exactly the shape that the CPU prefers to process:

- Branch prediction is easier because you are doing similar operations on consecutive elements.
- SIMD instructions can operate on several prices in parallel.
- The hardware prefetcher can anticipate future accesses, because you move linearly through memory.

Row stores, by contrast, often mix different types and sizes in each record, which leads to more irregular access patterns and more cache misses.

Late Materialization: Postponing Row Assembly

So far we have talked about where the bytes live. Late materialization is about *when* the engine assembles them into rows, or whether it needs to at all.

Early vs Late Materialization

Imagine a query that filters trades by symbol and time, then computes an aggregation over price and size. There are two conceptual strategies:

- **Early materialization:** Read all referenced columns, immediately stitch together full rows for each matching trade, then pass rows through the rest of the query plan.
- **Late materialization:** Operate on column vectors and row identifiers as long as possible, only assembling full rows if the final result or operator absolutely requires them.

Columnar engines usually favor the second approach.

Working with Positions Instead of Rows

Internally, when you filter a column—say, sym = 'AAPL'—you can represent the result as a list of positions (row numbers) where the condition holds. You can then use those positions to select corresponding entries from other columns:

- Filter sym to get positions where sym = 'AAPL'.
- Use those positions to pick the relevant time, price, and size entries.
- Aggregate directly on these filtered vectors.

At no point do you need to allocate row objects. This keeps memory usage compact and lets the CPU work with simple, predictable data structures.

In kdb+, this style aligns naturally with q's vector operations: you filter one column and use the resulting boolean mask or indices to slice other columns. In ClickHouse, the query engine uses similar concepts internally when it operates on blocks of column data.

Benefits for Market Workloads

Late materialization offers several advantages that are particularly relevant to trading analytics:

- **Less memory traffic:** You often avoid touching columns that are not needed for filters or final output, even if they are present in the table.
- **Fewer cache misses:** The CPU keeps small, tight vectors hot in cache rather than larger, more complex row structures.
- **Cheaper intermediate results:** Many analytic queries build up temporary structures. If those are column-oriented or index-based instead of row-based, they consume less memory and are faster to process.

Consider a surveillance query that:

- Filters trades for a watchlist of symbols.
- Applies multiple conditions on price movements and trade sizes.
- Outputs a small set of suspicious events with full detail.

Most of the data is thrown away after each filter. Late materialization ensures that heavy row assembly work happens only for the small fraction of records that survive all filters, not for all candidate rows.

Compression: Matching Encodings to Market Data

Column orientation unlocks powerful compression techniques. The more similar and predictable consecutive values are within a column, the more you can shrink them without losing information. Trading data is full of such patterns:

- Symbols from a limited universe.
- Prices that move in small ticks.
- Timestamps that are strictly increasing within a feed.
- Flags that remain constant over long stretches.

Columnar engines exploit these patterns by choosing encodings tailored to each column type.

Dictionary Encoding for Symbols and Venues

Symbol and venue columns are natural candidates for dictionary encoding:

- Build a dictionary that maps each unique symbol (e.g., "AAPL", "MSFT") to a small integer.
- Store the column as a vector of integers instead of strings.

If your symbol universe has a few thousand entries, each symbol can often be represented as a 16-bit or 32-bit integer, which is much smaller than the original string. The dictionary itself is small and heavily reused across blocks.

Benefits:

- **Space savings:** Fewer bytes per row.
- **Faster comparisons:** Comparing integers is much cheaper than comparing strings.
- **Better cache behavior:** Compact codes mean more values fit into CPU caches.

For filters like "sym IN watchlist", the engine can translate the watchlist symbols into integer codes once and then compare against the encoded column very efficiently.

Run-Length Encoding for Flags and Slowly Changing Values

Run-length encoding (RLE) represents repeated values as "(value, count)" pairs. If your data looks like:

$$\text{OFF, OFF, OFF, ON, ON, OFF, OFF, OFF, OFF, ...}$$

An RLE representation is much smaller:

$$\text{(OFF, 3), (ON, 2), (OFF, 4), ...}$$

Market data has many columns that change infrequently or in bursts:

- Trading status flags.
- Halt indicators.
- Auction phases.

- Exchange codes for a particular feed.

Applied to such columns, RLE can dramatically reduce storage. Even better, filters can sometimes operate directly on the runs:

- To find all rows with status ON, you can skip entire runs with value OFF.
- Aggregations can multiply the contribution of a run by its count instead of iterating row by row.

Delta and Frame-of-Reference Encoding for Timestamps and Prices

Timestamps and prices in trading data are often:

- Increasing (or nearly so) within a feed.
- Close together in value from one row to the next.

Instead of storing each absolute value, we can store:

- A base value for the block (for example, the first timestamp or a reference price).
- Small deltas from that base for each subsequent row.

This is known as delta encoding or frame-of-reference encoding. Because the deltas are smaller than the absolute values, they can often fit into fewer bits and compress better with generic techniques.

For example:

- If trades are microseconds apart, the difference between consecutive timestamps is small.
- If prices move in ticks, the differences between prices are often one or a few ticks.

Delta encoding pairs naturally with other compressions such as bit-packing and generic algorithms. When the engine scans a block, it reconstructs values on the fly, typically with simple additions that are cheap for the CPU.

Combining Compression with Late Materialization

Compression and late materialization reinforce each other:

- If you read only a subset of columns, you only decompress those specific compressed streams.
- If a filter excludes many rows, you avoid decompressing the corresponding values in other columns.
- If block-level metadata (e.g., min/max timestamps or symbols) shows that an entire block cannot satisfy a predicate, the engine can skip decompressing that block entirely.

For instance, a query for trades in a time interval $[t\_start, t\_end]$ might proceed as follows:

1. Inspect timestamp block metadata to find blocks whose ranges intersect the interval.
2. Read and decompress only those timestamp blocks.
3. Apply the time filter to determine relevant positions.
4. Using those positions, read and decompress only the needed slices of price and size.

Each step narrows the amount of data that needs to be touched.

Interaction with Filesystem I/O

Columnar layout also changes how the database interacts with the underlying filesystem or storage layer.

Large Sequential Reads

Disk and SSDs are much faster at reading large, contiguous regions than at seeking to many small random locations. Columnar stores design their formats so that:

- Each block of a column is stored contiguously.
- Blocks are grouped so that common access patterns (e.g., scanning by time) translate into mostly sequential reads.

When you run a query that scans trades for a particular day, the engine can issue a small number of large reads per referenced column. This makes heavy use of the available bandwidth and minimizes seek overhead.

Column-Wise Prefetch

Because access patterns are more predictable—you usually read blocks in increasing row order—the engine or the OS can prefetch upcoming blocks. The hardware then has more time to bring data into memory and caches before the CPU needs it, smoothing out latency spikes.

In contrast, row stores serving analytic workloads may issue more scattered reads, especially when only a subset of columns is ultimately used, because the useful data is interleaved with irrelevant fields.

Wide Tables vs Vertical Partitioning

One practical design tension in market schemas is:

- **Wide tables:** Many columns in a single logical table.
- **Vertical partitioning:** Splitting rarely used columns into separate tables or projections.

Columnar storage mitigates some of the cost of wide tables because unused columns are not read. However, there are still trade-offs:

- Metadata overhead per column (indexes, statistics, encoders).
- Complexity of managing extremely wide schemas.
- Edge cases where some engines perform less optimally on very wide tables.

Vertical partitioning (e.g., separating core trade fields from exotic annotations used only in research) can further reduce I/O for common operational queries. But it comes at a cost: you may need joins to recombine data, and you must keep partitions consistent.

kdb+ and ClickHouse approach this differently in detail, but the principles hold in both systems: start by putting frequently joined and frequently scanned columns together, use columnar benefits to avoid waste, and split rarely used or bulky columns only when measurements justify the added complexity.

Schema Design Guidelines for Trading Data

All of these pieces—column orientation, late materialization, compression, and I/O patterns—come together when you design schemas for real trading systems. Some practical guidelines:

- **Separate facts from dimensions.** Keep fast-moving fact tables (ticks, trades, orders, quotes, bars) separate from slowly changing dimensions (instruments, venues, corporate actions). Fact tables benefit most from columnar compression and time-based partitioning; dimensions are smaller and can be cached entirely.
- **Align types with statistical properties.** Choose column types and encodings based on how the values behave: dictionary encoding for symbols and venues, delta or frame-of-reference for timestamps and prices, RLE for flags and statuses.
- **Design for dominant access paths.** If most queries filter by time and symbol, store and partition data so that time and symbol columns are easy to prune and efficient to scan. This will influence how you group rows into blocks and how you sort within partitions (discussed more in the partitioning chapter).

- **Keep frequently used columns narrow and clean.** Paying attention to how you represent prices (scaled integers vs floating point), sizes, and timestamps helps both compression and correctness.
- **Let compression and layout do the work.** Before adding secondary indexes or complex summary tables, make sure you are fully exploiting columnar benefits: selective scans, block-level pruning, and efficient encodings.

Well-designed columnar storage turns high-volume market data from a liability into an advantage. The structure of the data—repetitive symbols, incremental timestamps, small price steps—is exactly what columnar engines need to shrink storage, increase scan speed, and keep latency low under load.

In the next section, we will move one level up, from *where* data is stored to *how* queries execute on top of it. We will see how vectorized execution engines in kdb+ and ClickHouse turn these columnar arrays into high-throughput analytic pipelines.

2.2 Vectorized Query Execution

In the previous section we focused on *where* columnar engines store data: one vector per column, compressed and laid out in blocks. We now move up one level and ask: given that the data is physically stored as vectors, *how* should the engine run your queries?

Row-oriented systems traditionally think in terms of one row at a time: fetch a row, apply predicates, update aggregates, then move on. Columnar systems like kdb+ and ClickHouse take a very different approach. They operate on *batches* of column values at once, using tight loops that exploit the CPU's caches and SIMD (single instruction, multiple data) instructions.

This section explains:

- What vectorized execution means and how it differs from row-at-a-time processing.

- How this model fits the CPU's cache hierarchy and SIMD units.
- How scans, filters, and aggregations over market data benefit from vectorization.
- How joins and skewed symbol distributions are handled in a vectorized world.
- How to reason about whether a query will be CPU-bound, memory-bound, or I/O-bound on your hardware.

From Rows to Batches of Column Vectors

Row-at-a-Time Execution

In a traditional row store, query execution often looks like this conceptually:

1. Fetch the next row from the table.
2. For that row, evaluate each predicate (for example, time >= t_-start, sym IN basket, price > 0).
3. If the row passes all filters, update your aggregates (for example, sum of price * size, sum of size).
4. Repeat until there are no more rows.

Each loop iteration handles one row. The CPU is constantly bouncing between different columns and between operators (scan, filter, aggregate). Function calls and virtual method calls may be involved at each step, which adds overhead and makes it harder for the CPU to predict control flow.

Batch-at-a-Time Vectorized Execution

Columnar systems invert this pattern. Instead of rows, they process *batches* of column values at a time. Conceptually:

1. Read a batch of values from each referenced column: for example, the next 4,096 or 65,536 entries of time, sym, price, size.

2. Apply predicates to entire vectors: compute a mask or index set of rows that pass each filter.
3. Use that mask to filter other vectors.
4. Aggregate over the resulting vectors.

Each step is now a tight loop over an array of homogeneous values, which is exactly what the CPU is good at.

In kdb+, this style is visible to the user: q primitives operate on entire vectors, and queries are naturally expressed as operations over columns rather than individual rows. In ClickHouse, SQL queries are translated into an internal pipeline that passes blocks of columnar data between operators.

Right after introducing this core idea of batch-at-a-time processing, it is helpful to see a visual pipeline of how vectors flow through operators.

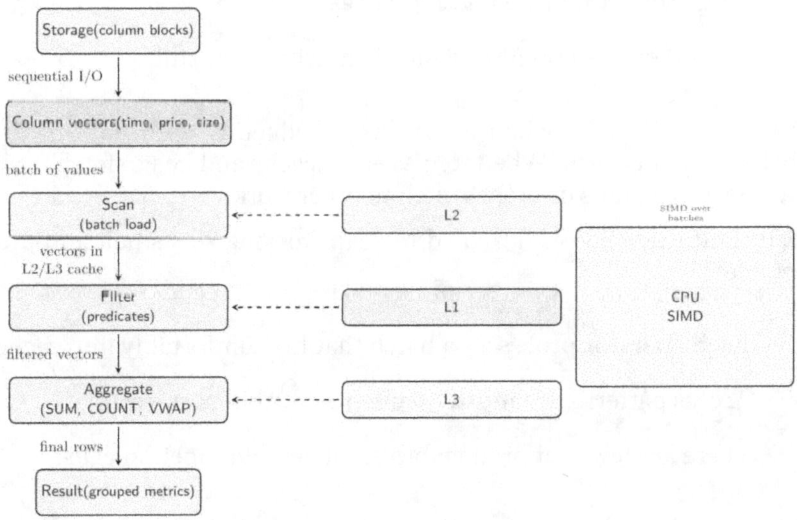

This diagram highlights three key features:

- Data flows horizontally in batches.

- Operators act on entire vectors.
- The CPU and caches sit above the pipeline, working on these vectors efficiently.

Why Vectorization Fits Modern CPUs

To understand why vectorized execution is so effective, it helps to recall a few basic facts about CPU and memory architecture, without going into low-level detail.

Cache Hierarchy and Latency Gap

Modern CPUs are much faster than main memory. To bridge this gap, they use a hierarchy of caches:

- Very small, very fast L1 caches closest to the execution units.
- Larger but slower L2 and L3 caches.
- Main memory (DRAM), which is much slower still.

The CPU works best when it can keep frequently used data in the smaller, faster caches. When it misses the cache and has to fetch from lower levels, it stalls or must switch to other work.

Vectorized execution is designed to keep working sets small and predictable:

- Each operator processes a batch that fits comfortably into cache.
- Access patterns are mostly sequential within each vector.
- There are fewer unpredictable branches and function calls.

This is particularly important in market analytics, where scans over millions or billions of rows are common. Without careful attention to cache locality, the CPU spends more time waiting for data than actually computing.

SIMD: One Instruction, Many Data Elements

Modern CPUs also have SIMD instructions. These allow the CPU to apply the same operation to multiple elements in a vector at once. For example:

- Add four or eight prices in one instruction.
- Compare several prices against a threshold in parallel.

Compilers and query engines can map vector operations onto these SIMD instructions. When the engine loops over a column of prices to apply a filter or sum values, it can pack several values into one register and process them together.

Row-at-a-time execution makes it hard to use SIMD efficiently, because it jumps between fields of different types and sizes. Columnar, vectorized execution makes it natural: you are already operating on a homogeneous array of numbers.

Scanning and Filtering Market Data in Batches

Let us consider a simple but ubiquitous example: scanning a trade table and filtering by time and symbol.

The Workload

Suppose you have a trade table with the familiar columns:

- time
- sym
- price
- size

You want to compute the total traded volume and VWAP over a time interval for a basket of symbols. Logically, the query looks like:

1. Filter by time in the desired interval.
2. Filter by sym in the basket.

3. For matching rows, aggregate price and size.

Vectorized Scan and Filter

In a vectorized engine, this might happen in the following stages:

1. **Scan stage.** Read a batch of time, sym, price, size for, say, 16,384 rows. These come in as four column vectors.
2. **Time filter.** Create a boolean mask (or an array of row positions) by applying the time predicate to the time vector in one tight loop.
3. **Symbol filter.** Apply the symbol predicate. If sym is dictionary-encoded, this becomes a set of integer comparisons against pre-computed codes.
4. **Combined filter.** Combine the masks (for example, logical "and") to get the rows that satisfy both conditions.
5. **Selection.** Use the final mask to select the matching entries of price and size into new, smaller vectors.

All these steps operate over vectors. For example, applying the time filter involves a loop that looks conceptually like "for each element in the time vector, set mask[i] to true if time[i] is in the interval". In practice, the engine uses SIMD and other tricks to make this loop very fast.

Benefits for Market Queries

This style of execution is a natural fit for market workloads:

- Time and symbol predicates are often simple comparisons that map well to SIMD.
- Most analytic queries have simple control flow but large amounts of data, which is where vectorization shines.
- Filters tend to drop many rows early, leaving smaller vectors for later operators to work on.

For example, a query focused on a dozen symbols out of several thousand will quickly reduce the working set after the symbol filter. Later stages have less work and better cache behaviour.

Vectorized Aggregations: From Sums to VWAPs

Once you have filtered vectors of price and size, you can aggregate them in a vectorized fashion.

Basic Aggregates

Consider basic aggregates like sum, count, min, and max. In a vectorized engine:

- The engine keeps a small number of accumulator variables in registers.
- It iterates over the vector, updating these accumulators for each element.
- The loop is simple, branch-free, and often unrolled by the compiler.

When SIMD is applied, each iteration processes several elements at once. This is much more efficient than updating aggregates per row, especially when coupled with late materialization (only rows that pass filters ever reach this stage).

Group-By Aggregations

Most market queries need grouped aggregates: volume per symbol, VWAP per symbol, or risk measures per bucket. Vectorized engines handle these with slightly more complex data structures, but still in a batched style.

Conceptually, for a *group by symbol* aggregation:

1. Maintain a hash table (or other grouping structure) mapping each symbol (or its dictionary code) to an aggregation state (for example, sum of price * size, sum of size).
2. Process the input in batches. For each batch:
   - Take the vector of symbols and derive hash table positions in a tight loop.
   - Update the aggregation state for each group using vectorized additions and multiplications.

Because symbols are encoded as small integers and repeated heavily, hash table operations can be optimized. Many real-world symbol distributions are also skewed: a small subset of very liquid names accounts for a large fraction of trades. Vectorized engines can structure their hash tables and caches to keep hot groups in very fast memory.

VWAP as a Running Example

VWAP (volume-weighted average price) is particularly amenable to vectorization. It requires:

- Sum of price * size per group.
- Sum of size per group.

Both are simple arithmetic on numeric vectors. The engine can multiply entire segments of the price and size vectors together using SIMD, then add the products into group states. Division to form the final VWAP happens once per group at the end, which is negligible compared to the bulk of the work.

For intraday research where you compute VWAPs across many symbols and many time windows, this vectorized approach turns what could be an expensive operation into a routine one.

Joins in a Vectorized World

Joins are central to market analytics: you join trades to instrument metadata, quotes to reference prices, and factor tables to position books. Columnar engines perform joins in a way that preserves the benefits of vectorization.

Hash Joins Over Column Vectors

The dominant join strategy in analytic systems is the hash join. In vectorized execution, a hash join typically proceeds in two phases:

- **Build phase:** For the smaller input (for example, an instrument dimension table), build a hash table from join keys (such as symbol, or symbol plus date) to the corresponding rows or projected columns.

- **Probe phase:** For the larger input (for example, trades), process it in batches. For each batch:
  - Extract the join key vector from the batch (for example, symbols).
  - Compute hash values for all keys in a single vectorized pass.
  - Probe the hash table in a tight loop, looking up matches and forming result rows or vectors.

Throughout this process, the engine is working on column vectors and small, cache-resident hash table data structures. It avoids materializing full rows until the last moment, if at all.

Compressed Keys and Dictionary Encoding

As discussed in the storage section, dictionary encoding of symbols and venues means join keys are often compact integers instead of strings. This is precisely why vectorized hash joins are efficient:

- Hashing integers is faster and more regular than hashing strings.
- Equality checks are cheaper and more SIMD-friendly.
- The hash table itself can be more compact, improving cache locality.

In ClickHouse, many joins are explicitly designed around such encoded keys, and kdb+ users often achieve similar benefits by using enumerated types or integer IDs for symbols and instruments.

Handling Skewed Distributions

Market data is famously skewed: a small set of very active symbols dominates traffic. This skew can affect joins:

- Some keys are probed far more often than others.
- Poorly designed hash tables might degenerate when many keys map to similar buckets.

Vectorized engines mitigate this in several ways:

- Designing hash tables to perform well under skew (for example, with open addressing schemes tuned for typical loads).
- Keeping frequently accessed entries hot in cache by virtue of repeated probes within a batch.
- Sometimes using special-case optimizations when a key distribution is extremely skewed.

In practice, this means joins between large trade tables and much smaller dimension or factor tables remain efficient even on very active names.

Operator-at-a-Time vs Pipelines

Not all vectorized engines organize their work in exactly the same way. Two conceptual models are worth distinguishing:

- **Operator-at-a-time:** Each operator consumes an entire input, produces its full output vectors, and then hands those vectors to the next operator. Think "scan everything, then filter, then aggregate".
- **Pipeline (chunked) model:** Operators are linked in a pipeline, and data flows through in chunks. A batch is scanned, filtered, partially aggregated, and so on before the next batch arrives.

In practice, high-performance systems blend these ideas. The key is that data always moves in *batches* of column vectors, not individual rows.

For market workloads, pipelines are particularly appealing because:

- They allow streaming of large datasets without needing to materialize full intermediate results.
- They align well with append-only ingestion: new batches can flow into the pipeline as they arrive.

- They mesh neatly with time-based partitioning, where each partition or block can be processed as a series of batches.

kdb+'s execution engine is deeply vector-oriented and often fuses operations over columns. ClickHouse builds explicit pipelines where each stage processes blocks of data, with backpressure and parallelism controls.

CPU-Bound, Memory-Bound, or I/O-Bound?

Understanding vectorized execution also helps you reason about where the bottlenecks in a query might be. Broadly:

- A query is **I/O-bound** if the engine spends most of its time waiting for data from disk or network storage.
- It is **memory-bound** if the main limitation is moving data between memory and CPU caches.
- It is **CPU-bound** if the CPU's arithmetic and control units are fully utilized.

Vectorized execution is so efficient at using the CPU that many analytic queries become memory-bound or I/O-bound instead. For market systems, you will commonly see:

- **I/O-bound scans** when you read cold historical data that is not in OS cache and that must be fetched from storage.
- **Memory-bound scans** when working sets fit in RAM but not in the faster CPU caches.
- **CPU-bound computations** when you perform complex calculations per row or heavy joins and group-bys over already-hot data.

This classification is not just academic. It guides tuning:

- If a query is I/O-bound, you look at partitioning, indexing, and compression, not at micro-optimizing arithmetic.

- If it is memory-bound, you consider schema changes that reduce column width or improve locality.
- If it is CPU-bound even after vectorization, you may need to reduce complexity, precompute more, or scale out to more cores.

Vectorized engines like kdb+ and ClickHouse give you a strong baseline: simple scans, filters, and aggregates are already very close to hardware limits. Most further gains come from smart layout and from avoiding unnecessary work, not from hand-tuning loops.

Putting It All Together for Market Workloads

We can now combine storage and execution to form a mental model for how a typical analytic query runs in a columnar engine:

1. **Partition pruning and block selection.** Based on time and other predicates, the engine chooses which partitions and blocks to scan.
2. **Columnar scan.** For each selected block, the engine reads only the needed columns, as compressed data.
3. **Decompression to vectors.** It decompresses those columns into in-memory vectors for a batch of rows.
4. **Vectorized filters.** It applies predicates to produce masks or position lists.
5. **Vectorized joins.** If necessary, it probes dimension or factor tables using batched hash join logic.
6. **Vectorized aggregations.** It updates per-group aggregations using tight loops and SIMD operations.
7. **Final materialization.** Only at the end, and only if the client needs row-oriented output, does it assemble rows from the aggregated or filtered vectors.

At every stage, the engine is choosing data structures and access patterns that:

- Keep caches hot.
- Exploit SIMD instructions.
- Avoid touching irrelevant columns or rows.

For trading and investment analytics, where you may need to recompute complex metrics over large datasets many times during the day, this model is what makes columnar engines viable. Harnessing vectorized execution is not about clever tricks; it is about consistently presenting the CPU with the kind of work it is built to do.

In the next section, we will build on this execution model and study how partitioning, sorting, and indexing can further reduce the amount of data that needs to be scanned in the first place. Together, layout and vectorized execution form the foundation of high-performance market data systems in both kdb+ and ClickHouse.

2.3 Partitioning, Sorting, and Indexing

So far we have focused on two pillars of columnar performance:

- *Storage layout*: storing data column-by-column with compression.
- *Execution*: processing queries in vectorized batches that align with CPU caches and SIMD units.

Even with these in place, blindly scanning entire tables is rarely acceptable in production market systems. A typical historical trade store can hold trillions of rows. No amount of vectorization will save you if every query has to read all of them.

The third pillar is *I/O avoidance* through clever data layout. In this section we will see how three techniques work together:

- **Time-based partitioning**: physically splitting a table into manageable chunks, usually by date or session.

- **Sorting within partitions**: arranging rows so that access patterns match how queries filter the data.
- **Lightweight indexes**: small pieces of metadata (like min/max values) that tell the engine which blocks it can safely skip.

The goal is simple: when a user asks a question about a narrow time range and a small set of instruments, the engine should touch only a tiny fraction of the bytes in the full dataset, and it should do so in predictable, scalable ways.

Why Time-Based Partitioning Is Natural for Markets

Most trading data has an obvious primary dimension: time. Trades, quotes, orders, and bars all arrive in chronological order. Queries almost always specify a time window:

- "Last 5 minutes of trades for this symbol."
- "Full session yesterday for all FX pairs."
- "First hour after a macro announcement across all futures."

If we store all years of data in a single physical chunk, every query must wade past a lot of irrelevant history. Instead, columnar engines typically *partition* tables by time: they create one physical unit (file set, directory, shard, or part) per day, per hour, or per session.

Logical vs Physical Partitioning

It is useful to distinguish two perspectives:

- **Logical partitioning** is what the user sees. For example, a kdb+ database might expose a single trade table with a date column, or a ClickHouse MergeTree table might have a partition key on trade date.

- **Physical partitioning** is how the engine stores data on disk and across nodes. For example, a directory per date in kdb+ or a set of parts per partition in ClickHouse.

From the user's point of view, the table is continuous. Under the hood, the engine can restrict a query to just the partitions whose time ranges overlap the requested interval.

Partition Granularity: Day, Hour, or Session?

Choosing how fine-grained your partitions should be is an important design decision.

Daily partitions. Many equity and futures systems choose one partition per trade date. This usually works well because:

- Most historical queries are day-based (e.g., "all of 2024-04-17").
- Exchanges operate in daily sessions, and many reports are session-scoped.
- Maintenance tasks (backups, rcindcxcs, drops) naturally run at the day level.

Hourly or sub-daily partitions. Some high-frequency or 24/5 FX/crypto systems use smaller partitions, such as one per hour. This can be helpful when:

- You often query narrow intraday windows across many days.
- Individual days are so large that they become unwieldy units for maintenance.

However, very fine partitions increase metadata and small-file overhead, and they complicate lifecycle management.

Session-based partitions. For markets with well-defined sessions (e.g., pre-open, regular, after-hours), you might align partitions with these sessions, especially if your users care about them directly.

In practice, most organizations start with daily partitions, then consider finer granularity only if measurements show clear benefits.

Right after introducing time-based partitioning, it is helpful to make the physical picture concrete.

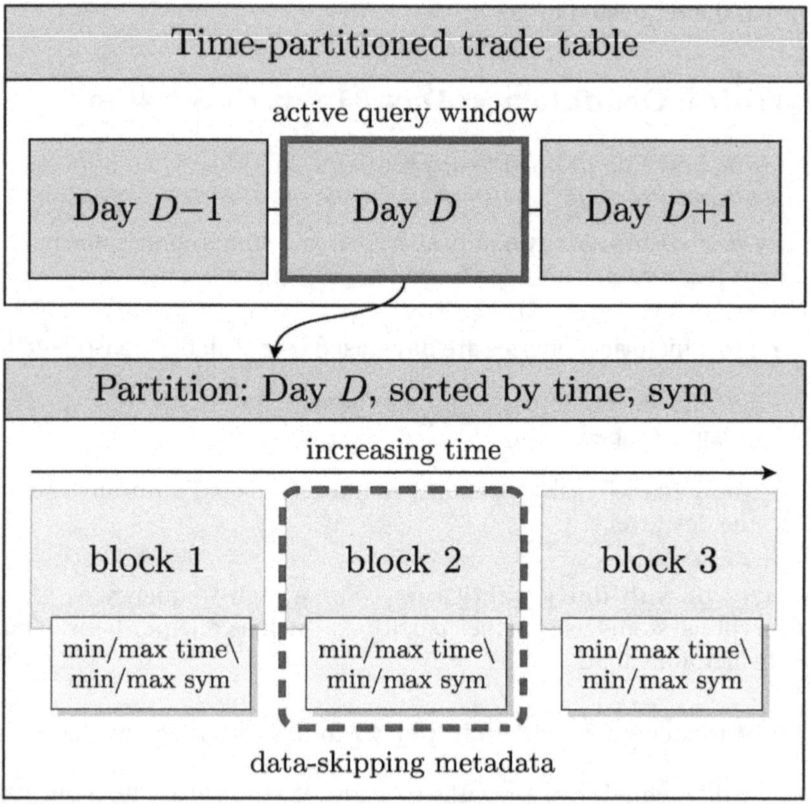

At the top, the table is split into daily partitions. Only the relevant day(s) are examined for a query. Within the active partition, data is further organized into sorted blocks, each with small index cards containing min/max metadata. We will build up to this full picture step by step.

Sorting Within Partitions

Partitioning limits how many large units (days, hours, sessions) a query must visit. Sorting within each partition controls how many *blocks* inside those units must actually be read.

Ordering Keys

Inside a single partition, the engine will typically maintain a specific sort order. For market data, a common choice is:

- Primary: time (within the partition's date or session).
- Secondary: symbol (or a bucketed form of symbol).
- Tertiary: venue or other fields, if needed.

This is sometimes called the *ordering key*. In ClickHouse, you explicitly define an ORDER BY key for MergeTree tables. In kdb+, you often achieve a similar effect by inserting data in time order and, if needed, periodically sorting tables by time and symbol when writing to disk.

How Sorting Helps

Sorting brings three intertwined benefits:

Efficient range scans. If your rows are ordered by time, then any time interval corresponds to one or a few contiguous regions within a partition. The engine can seek to the start of the interval and then scan sequentially until the end, avoiding random I/O.

Better compression. Sorted data often shows more regular patterns:

- Timestamps increase monotonically, helping delta and frame-of-reference compression.
- Symbols cluster, improving dictionary and run-length encoding.

This shrinks stored data and speeds scans, as seen in the storage section.

More selective indexing. When blocks are sorted, the min/max metadata for each block becomes more informative. For example, a symbol-concentrated block might have sym_min = sym_max = 'AAPL', so a filter for another symbol can skip it entirely.

Practical Ordering Strategies

You do not need to pick a perfect ordering; you need one that aligns with your dominant access patterns.

Common choices for trade and quote tables include:

- **time only**: simple and good for workloads dominated by pure time filtering.
- **time, sym**: excellent for queries that filter by both time and symbol, such as per-name analytics.
- **sym, time**: useful if symbol-centric queries dominate and you often scan entire symbol histories.

In multi-asset environments you may also consider symbol buckets or instrument IDs that cluster related instruments together (for example, futures of the same underlying).

The key is to choose a small number of ordering keys and keep them consistent across fact tables. That consistency simplifies reasoning about performance and makes join patterns more predictable.

Lightweight Indexes and Data-Skipping

Once you have partitioned by time and sorted within partitions, you can add a thin layer of indexing to avoid reading irrelevant blocks entirely.

Columnar engines typically favor *lightweight*, block-level indexes rather than heavy, per-row structures. The idea is to store just enough metadata per block to answer the question: "Is it even possible that this block contains rows matching the query?"

Min/Max and Zone Maps

The simplest and most widely used index form is a set of min/max statistics per column per block. For each block, the engine records:

- Minimum time and maximum time.
- Minimum symbol and maximum symbol.
- Sometimes additional fields such as price or other hot predicates.

Given a query predicate, the engine compares its constraints to a block's metadata:

- If the query's time range does not overlap the block's time [min, max], the block can be skipped.
- If the query targets a symbol outside the block's [sym_min, sym_max], the block can be skipped.

This pattern is sometimes called a *zone map* or *data-skipping index*. It is extremely cheap to maintain and to consult:

- The metadata is tiny compared to the data.
- It can be kept in memory even when the underlying blocks live on disk.
- It is updated naturally as part of block creation and merges (for example, when ClickHouse compacts parts).

Combining Multiple Predicates

Data-skipping is particularly powerful when you combine several predicates. Imagine a query:

- Time between 09:30 and 10:00 on a given day.
- Symbol in {AAPL, MSFT}.

The engine might:

- Restrict to the partition(s) that contain the desired date.
- Within each partition, consult block-level min/max for time to restrict to blocks that intersect the 30-minute window.
- Within those blocks, consult symbol min/max to restrict to blocks whose symbol range includes the desired names.

Only then does it actually read and decompress the candidate blocks, at which point vectorized filters and aggregations take over.

Misaligned partitioning or sorting can dramatically weaken this effect. For example, if each block contains a random mix of times and symbols, the min/max ranges will be wide and unhelpful, forcing the engine to read far more blocks than necessary.

Sparse Secondary Indexes

In addition to min/max statistics, some engines offer *sparse secondary indexes*. These are more explicit index structures, but still coarser and lighter than traditional B-trees.

Examples include:

- Bitmaps identifying blocks or row ranges where a condition holds.
- Sampled value-to-position maps for specific columns.
- Bloom filters that tell you probabilistically whether a value *might* be present in a block.

For market data, sparse indexes can help with:

- Narrow symbol filters in very wide symbol universes.

- Rare event detection, such as specific flags or error codes.

However, their benefits must be weighed against the maintenance cost during ingestion. Because fact tables like ticks and trades are write-heavy, many practitioners start with min/max zone maps and add more sophisticated indexes only when profiling shows they are necessary.

How Partitioning, Sorting, and Indexing Work Together

It is helpful to walk through a concrete example that shows all three techniques cooperating to prune data.

Example Query

Suppose a researcher issues this query against a multi-year trade history:

> Compute the 1-minute bar series (open, high, low, close, volume) for AAPL and MSFT between 2024-04-10 09:30 and 2024-04-10 10:00.

Conceptually, this involves:

- Filtering by trade date = 2024-04-10.
- Filtering by time between 09:30 and 10:00.
- Filtering by symbol in {AAPL, MSFT}.
- Aggregating trades into 1-minute buckets and computing OHLCV.

Step 1: Partition Pruning

If the trade table is partitioned by date, the engine can restrict its attention to the partition for 2024-04-10. All other partitions (other days, months, years) are simply not opened.

On a multi-node cluster, this may also reduce network traffic: only the node(s) holding the relevant partition participate in the query.

Step 2: Block-Level Time Pruning

Within the 2024-04-10 partition, suppose data is sorted by time and symbol, and each block holds a contiguous time slice. For each block, the engine has recorded min/max time.

The query's time window (09:30-10:00) overlaps only a small fraction of the day. The engine scans the metadata and finds, say, that only blocks 5 through 9 have time ranges overlapping this interval. Blocks 1-4 (early pre-open) and 10+ (later in the day) are skipped.

Step 3: Block-Level Symbol Pruning

Of blocks 5-9, not all may hold AAPL or MSFT trades. Because rows are sorted by time and symbol, some blocks might contain only other names.

For each candidate block, the engine checks symbol min/max:

- If a block's symbol range does not include AAPL or MSFT, skip it.
- Otherwise, mark it as needing a detailed scan.

After this step, perhaps only blocks 6 and 7 remain.

Step 4: Vectorized Scan and Filter

The engine now reads only the needed columns (time, sym, price, size) from blocks 6 and 7. It decompresses them into vectors and applies vectorized filters:

- A time predicate, to enforce the exact 09:30-10:00 range.
- A symbol predicate, to keep only AAPL and MSFT.

Because the heavy pruning has already occurred at the partition and block level, only a few tens of thousands of rows might survive, out of millions for the full day.

Step 5: Vectorized Aggregation

Finally, the engine bins the filtered trades into 1-minute buckets and computes OHLCV per symbol, using the vectorized aggregation techniques covered in the previous section.

From the user's perspective, this entire process is just a single query. Behind the scenes, partitioning, sorting, and indexing have cooperated to reduce the work from "scan everything in the table" to "touch only a few carefully chosen blocks".

Practical Design Patterns for Market Systems

Designing effective partitioning, sorting, and indexing strategies is as much about avoiding pitfalls as it is about cleverness. Some practical patterns and cautions:

Separate Hot and Cold Data

A common pattern is to keep *hot* recent data in one set of partitions and *cold* historical data in another:

- Hot partitions (today, this week) may live on faster storage, have more aggressive indexes, and be frequently updated.
- Cold partitions (previous months or years) may be compressed more heavily, placed on cheaper storage, and updated rarely.

This separation helps:

- Keep working sets small for intraday queries.
- Reduce contention between ingestion and historical analytics.

- Simplify retention policies (for example, drop partitions older than a certain date).

Align Partitioning with Operational Workflows

Partition boundaries should make operational tasks easier:

- Rebuilding or backfilling a single day's data should not disturb other days.
- Taking a snapshot or backup of a partition should align with report boundaries.
- Maintenance jobs (compaction, defragmentation) should run partition-by-partition.

Time-based partitioning fits this naturally. Misaligned designs—for instance, random hash partitioning by symbol in a system dominated by time-based queries—can complicate operations and hurt performance.

Choose a Small, Stable Set of Keys

Frequent changes to partitioning or ordering keys are painful. They trigger costly data reorganization and introduce complexity.
Instead:

- Choose partition keys that are unlikely to change: typically trade date or event time bucket.
- Choose ordering keys that match your core predicates: time, symbol, maybe venue.
- Document these choices and ensure application developers understand them.

kdb+ and ClickHouse both reward stability: once your partition and sort strategy is in place, many optimizations (vectorized execution, OS caching, statistics) accumulate on top of it.

Index Sparingly on Fact Tables

Because tick, trade, and order tables can see hundreds of thousands to millions of inserts per second, heavy per-row indexing is usually a bad idea. It can:

- Slow ingestion dramatically.
- Increase memory and disk overhead.
- Complicate backfills and corrections.

A better approach is:

- Rely on partitioning, sorting, and block-level statistics for most queries.
- Use sparse secondary indexes only where they show clear benefits.
- Push heavier indexing into smaller, derived tables (for example, factor or summary tables) where write rates are lower.

Measure and Iterate

Finally, design should be guided by measurement, not guesswork:

- Capture representative query logs for real trading days.
- Analyze which predicates are most common (time ranges, symbol sets, venues).
- Evaluate how many partitions and blocks are touched per query under your current design.
- Experiment with different partition and ordering strategies on a subset of data and compare.

Because kdb+ and ClickHouse expose plan and profiling tools, you can often see exactly how many parts, blocks, and rows each query scanned. Use that information to iteratively refine your layout.

Partitioning, sorting, and indexing are the structural tools that make columnar storage and vectorized execution practical at market scale:

- **Time-based partitioning** limits which large chunks of data a query must even consider.
- **Ordering keys** within partitions ensure that queries can access relevant rows with sequential scans and that compression is effective.
- **Lightweight indexes** such as min/max zone maps enable data skipping, so entire blocks are bypassed without reading or decompressing them.

When these elements are aligned with your market workloads—time windows, symbol filters, and typical reports—I/O shrinks to a manageable fraction of the full dataset, and performance becomes predictable and scalable.

In the next section we will step from data layout into concurrency and correctness, examining how columnar engines support transactional updates, backfills, and snapshot isolation in high-throughput market environments.

2.4 Transactions and Snapshot Isolation

Up to this point we have treated the columnar store as if it were static: data is neatly partitioned, sorted, and indexed; queries stream through in vectorized batches. Real trading systems are not static. New ticks arrive continuously, corrections dribble in late, and research users launch long-running queries while risk systems demand up-to-date positions.

This section explains how columnar analytics engines such as kdb+ and ClickHouse reconcile these conflicting pressures. We will focus on three tightly connected ideas:

- **Transactional models**: how the engine groups writes and ensures they are applied safely.
- **Snapshot isolation**: how readers see a consistent view of the data even as writes happen.
- **Concurrency and deduplication**: how high-throughput feeds, backfills, and corrections interact with partitions and metadata.

Our goal is not to reproduce a database theory textbook, but to give you an accurate, practical mental model for how these systems behave under load, and how to design market workflows that play to their strengths.

From OLTP Transactions to Analytic Snapshots

Traditional OLTP databases, such as those used for order entry, emphasize fine-grained transactions:

- Many small updates and inserts, often modifying a few rows at a time.
- Strict guarantees such as full serializable isolation.
- Heavy use of row-level locks and index maintenance.

Columnar analytic engines face a different environment:

- Very high write rates, usually in large batches (for example, appending tens of thousands of ticks per second).
- Mostly append-only behavior; updates and deletes are rarer and often handled in batches.
- Read-heavy workloads that scan large time ranges or symbol universes.

To support this, they typically relax some OLTP guarantees in favor of:

- **Snapshot isolation**: each query sees a stable picture of the data as of some point in time, even if writes are happening concurrently.
- **Multi-version or append-only data**: instead of overwriting rows in place, new versions are appended and old versions retired or compacted later.
- **Coarse-grained transactions**: transactions often correspond to batches of data (for example, one feed batch, one micro-batch, one backfill job) rather than individual rows.

Understanding this difference is crucial when you design ingestion, backfill, and correction workflows around kdb+ or ClickHouse.

Basic Concurrency Concepts in Columnar Context

Before diving into specific engine behaviors, let us recap a few concurrency terms in the context of columnar analytics.

Transactions

A *transaction* is a group of writes that the engine treats as an all-or-nothing unit:

- Either all the changes become visible to readers, or none of them do.
- Transactions usually correspond to a batch insert, a backfill patch, or a set of mutations.

In columnar engines, the content of a transaction is often stored as new partitions, new parts within a partition, or new column files. Commit means making pointers to these new structures visible.

Isolation Levels

Isolation levels describe how concurrent transactions interact. In analytic systems:

- Full serializable isolation (as in OLTP) is rare; it is expensive and unnecessary for many read-heavy workloads.
- Snapshot isolation is common: a query sees data as it existed at a specific point, without being disturbed by concurrent writes.

Snapshot isolation is strong enough to give analysts a consistent view while allowing continuous ingestion at scale.

Multi-Version Concurrency Control (MVCC)

MVCC is an approach where the database keeps multiple versions of data:

- When a transaction writes new data or changes existing data, it creates new versions instead of modifying old ones in place.
- Readers use a version timestamp (or transaction ID) to decide which versions they should see.

Not every columnar engine exposes MVCC in the same way, but most use the underlying idea: new partitions or parts represent newer versions; older ones remain accessible until no active query depends on them.

Append-Only Mutations and Commit Visibility

For market workloads, the dominant write pattern is *append-only*:

- New ticks, trades, and quotes are appended to the relevant partitions.
- Derived tables (bars, factors) are often created by appending new rows for recent time buckets.

Columnar engines are optimized for this pattern.

How Appends Commit

Conceptually, a batch append goes through the following steps:

1. The engine receives a batch of rows (for example, all trades for a short time interval).
2. It encodes and compresses them into column blocks and writes them to new files or parts, typically grouped by partition (for example, by date).
3. Once the physical data is safely written, it updates metadata to register the new parts as belonging to the table.
4. At the commit point, the engine publishes this metadata change so new queries see the new data.

Crucially, existing queries that started earlier continue using the metadata snapshot they saw at their start time:

- They do not see the newly committed parts.
- They are not disrupted or forced to restart.

This is snapshot isolation in action.

Readers and Writers in High-Throughput Feeds

Imagine a live environment:

- Trades stream in, batched every second into append transactions.
- A risk dashboard runs a query every minute, aggregating the last 15 minutes of data.
- Research users run long-running backtests over historical partitions.

The engine's behavior typically looks like this:

- Each dashboard query starts, takes a snapshot of the current partitions/parts, and executes against that snapshot. It may miss the last fraction of a second of data still in-flight, but it will see everything committed before it started.
- When a new batch of trades commits, it becomes immediately visible to queries that start afterwards, but not to queries that are already running.
- Historical backtests often operate exclusively on older, stable partitions that are never modified. They enjoy excellent cache behavior and minimal concurrency concerns.

This model allows very high ingest rates and steady query latency without complex locking.

Corrections, Backfills, and Late-Arriving Data

Real feeds are messy. You often have to:

- Ingest late trades that belong to earlier time windows or even previous days.
- Correct previously ingested data, such as bad prices or missing fields.
- Backfill newly sourced fields (for example, additional flags) for historical data.

Because columnar stores favor append-only operations, these actions are usually implemented as *addition then subtraction* rather than in-place updates.

Corrections via New Versions

A common pattern for handling corrections is:

1. Append corrected rows to the table, possibly with a higher "sequence" or "version" value.

2. Optionally mark original rows as obsolete using a logical delete flag or by moving them to a separate "quarantine" or "tombstone" structure.
3. Update queries and downstream logic to respect versions and delete markers, selecting the latest non-deleted version per key.

From the engine's perspective, this is still mostly append-only. Over time, background compaction can merge partitions and materialize the effect of deletions, dropping old versions from disk when safe.

Late-Arriving Data and Partition Windows

Late-arriving data raises two questions:

- *Where does it go?* Typically into the partition corresponding to its event date or time, even if that partition is older.
- *When is a partition "closed" for reporting?* Many organizations define a cut-off after which a day is considered final, and any subsequent corrections are handled through overlays or adjustments.

You can think of each partition as having life-cycle phases:

- **Hot/open**: Ingestion is ongoing; you welcome late arrivals; corrections are applied freely.
- **Warm/stable**: Writes are rare; the partition is mostly read-only; corrections are more controlled.
- **Cold/frozen**: The partition is immutable; any further corrections are handled via higher-level adjustments.

Columnar engines make it cheap to have many partitions, so you can align these phases with your operational SLAs. For example, you might freeze equity trade partitions two days after trade date, while keeping FX partitions open longer due to slower reference data.

Backfills and Bulk Loads

Backfills—for example, loading a new history from a different vendor—are usually done as bulk operations:

- Create new partitions or parts for the backfilled data.
- Optionally mark existing partitions as superseded.
- Re-point logical table metadata to include the new parts and exclude the old ones.

Because metadata changes are cheap, you can stage the backfill in a separate schema or test table, validate it, then atomically switch readers over by changing a view or metadata pointer. From the reader's perspective, the switch happens at a single moment in time; before that, they see the old history, after that, the new.

Deduplication in Overlapping Feeds

Market data platforms often ingest the same logical events through multiple feeds:

- A direct exchange feed plus a consolidated vendor feed.
- Multiple venues feeding the same OTC instrument.
- Replays or re-sends after a heartbeat loss.

This creates duplicate or overlapping rows. Deduplication is typically implemented at two levels:

- During ingestion, where possible.
- In periodic cleanup or compaction processes.

Ingest-Time Deduplication

If the ingestion process can reliably identify duplicates (for example, by a unique combination of trade ID, symbol, venue, and timestamp), it can:

- Drop known duplicates before writing to the columnar store.
- Or write them into a temporary staging area and run a fast dedup step that writes a cleaned version into the main table.

This keeps the main fact tables clean and minimizes wasted I/O.

Batch Deduplication Using Snapshot Isolation

Sometimes you cannot fully deduplicate at ingest time: you might only realize later that certain feeds overlap or that IDs were reused.

In such cases, you can perform dedup as a bulk operation that benefits from snapshot isolation:

1. Run a query that identifies duplicate groups in a stable snapshot of the data (for example, by grouping on trade ID and picking the best record per group).
2. Write out a new, deduplicated version of the affected partitions or symbol subsets.
3. Atomically swap the old and new partitions by updating metadata.

Readers during the dedup job see the old snapshot. Once the swap occurs, new queries see the cleaned data. The engine's append-plus-swap model makes this operation safe and predictable.

Distributed Execution and Commit Ordering

Modern analytic engines are usually distributed: data is sharded across nodes, and queries run in parallel. This introduces new questions:

- How do we ensure that a committed batch is visible everywhere it needs to be?
- How do we think about "time" and "freshness" when replicas may lag?

Replication and Eventual Consistency

For fault tolerance and load balancing, partitions or parts are commonly replicated across nodes. Replication can be:

- **Synchronous**: a write commits only after all replicas have acknowledged it.
- **Asynchronous**: a write commits on a primary node, and replicas catch up later.

Many analytic systems favor asynchronous replication for performance and availability. This introduces slight staleness:

- A query on one replica might see a recent batch that another replica has not received yet.
- Cross-node queries must either be pinned to a consistent view (for example, using a coordinator) or accept some replication lag.

For risk and reporting, firms usually define explicit SLAs: for example, "all risk queries must see data that is no more than 30 seconds behind the feed". You can enforce this by:

- Monitoring replication lag.
- Directing certain classes of queries only to replicas that meet the freshness requirement.
- Or using stronger consistency guarantees on the partitions that feed critical systems.

Global vs Local Snapshots

In a single-node engine, snapshot isolation is straightforward: a query sees the local set of committed parts at its start time.

In a distributed engine, we distinguish:

- **Local snapshots**: each node provides snapshot isolation with respect to its local data.
- **Global snapshots**: a coordinator, or a global commit log, defines a consistent cut across nodes. Queries tagged with a snapshot ID see data that is at least as fresh as that ID everywhere.

For many market analytics, local snapshots are sufficient: queries often run against data that is co-located on a single node or use replicated tables where slight timing differences are acceptable.

Where strict ordering matters—for example, for official end-of-day reports—it is common to run those jobs against a controlled environment (a specific cluster, a frozen snapshot) where data has been fully replicated and validated.

Designing Around Snapshot Isolation in Practice

Understanding snapshot isolation is particularly useful when you design user-facing analytics, correction workflows, and SLAs.

What "As-Of" Really Means

When a user asks for a report "as of 10:00:00", there are at least two interpretations:

- *Event-time as-of:* include all trades whose event time is less than or equal to 10:00:00, regardless of when they arrived.
- *System-time as-of:* include all trades that had arrived and been committed to the store by 10:00:00.

Snapshot isolation naturally supports system-time as-of semantics: you run the query at or shortly after 10:00:00, and it sees a consistent set of committed data.

Event-time as-of semantics require careful handling of late-arriving data:

- If you allow late trades to be inserted into earlier partitions, an "as of 10:00:00 event-time" query run at different wall-clock times may return different results.
- You can address this by defining a cutoff: after some delay, you treat a partition's data as frozen for event-time purposes and handle later arrivals with adjustments.

Being explicit about which semantics apply in which systems avoids confusion and misinterpretation of risk and P&L.

Long-Running Queries and Data Drift

A long-running backtest might take minutes or hours. Meanwhile, new data continues to arrive. Snapshot isolation ensures that:

- The backtest runs against a fixed snapshot; its results are reproducible.
- It is not disturbed by ongoing ingestion or schema changes (as long as backward compatibility is maintained).

However, this has two practical implications:

- The engine must retain old versions of partitions or parts until all queries that depend on them have finished.
- If you run many overlapping long queries, you may delay the reclamation of storage from compaction and version cleanup.

Operationally, you should:

- Monitor query lifetimes and avoid unboundedly long sessions on shared clusters.
- Schedule heavy backtests on dedicated resources or off-peak hours where their impact on version retention is acceptable.

Correction and Reprocessing Workflows

When you fix data, you often need to re-run downstream processes: factors, risk measures, or official reports. With snapshot isolation:

- You can run those recalculations against a controlled snapshot that includes the corrections.
- Old results (for example, yesterday's risk files) remain valid representations of what the system believed at that time.

This separation between "what we thought then" and "what we know now" is important for auditability. Columnar engines that version their data naturally support this, provided you manage snapshots and retention policies consciously.

Avoiding Contention in Shared Columnar Stores

Finally, let us address a common concern: what happens when many readers and writers share the same columnar store?

Because columnar engines lean on append-only writes, batch commits, and snapshot isolation, they largely avoid the classic row-level locking problems of OLTP systems. That said, you can still create contention if you are not careful.

Common Pitfalls

Some problematic patterns include:

- **Frequent small commits:** writing and committing tiny batches (for example, single-row inserts) at very high frequency. This stresses metadata, replication, and compaction.

- **Random in-place updates:** attempting to update single values in large fact tables instead of appending corrections. This breaks the columnar and append-only assumptions.
- **Overlapping heavy writes and reads on the same hot partitions:** for example, re-sorting or rebuilding today's partition in the middle of the trading session.

Practical Guidelines

Healthier patterns look like:

- **Micro-batching ingestion:** aggregate incoming ticks into reasonable batch sizes (e.g., thousands of rows) before committing. This amortizes overhead and keeps a steady, predictable flow of new parts.
- **Append then compact:** treat corrections as new data; let background jobs compact and merge partitions when the system is less busy.
- **Separate ingestion and analytics clusters when necessary:** in very high-throughput environments, you might ingest into one cluster and replicate to another dedicated to analytics, decoupling their performance characteristics.
- **Schedule heavy maintenance outside peak hours:** big resorts, backfills, or large-scale dedup jobs should run when query load is light.

By aligning your workflows with the columnar engine's transactional model, you can support continuous ingestion and rich analytics without stepping on your own toes.

Columnar analytics engines trade some of the fine-grained transactional guarantees of OLTP systems for scalability, simplicity, and performance in read-heavy, append-focused environments like market data. The key ideas to carry forward are:

- **Snapshot isolation** ensures that each query sees a consistent view of the data, even as high-throughput ingestion and corrections proceed in parallel.
- **Append-only and multi-version designs** avoid in-place updates, making it easier to scale writes, compact data, and manage late-arriving events.
- **Deduplication and corrections** are best handled as batch operations that create new versions of partitions or parts, then atomically switch readers to the cleaned data.
- **Distributed execution and replication** introduce freshness and ordering questions that must be addressed with clear SLAs and snapshot usage patterns.

With a clear understanding of these models, you can design ingestion, correction, and reporting workflows that make full use of kdb+ and ClickHouse without compromising correctness or overcomplicating your architecture. In the next section, we will connect these transactional and visibility models to the realities of memory and caching, and examine how to keep your hot market data close to the CPU for sustained low-latency analytics.

2.5 Caching and Hot-Set Management

In the previous sections we treated storage layout, vectorized execution, and transactional behavior largely in isolation. We saw how columnar layout cuts I/O, how vectorization squeezes more work out of each CPU cycle, and how snapshot isolation lets readers and writers coexist.

All of this performance, however, is modulated by a more basic question: *where is your data physically sitting when a query runs?* If the bytes you need are already near the CPU, even simple hardware can deliver excellent latency. If they live far away—on a slow disk tier or across the network—no amount of clever query planning will save you.

This section explains how to think about:

- The memory hierarchy: CPU caches, RAM, and storage.
- The interaction between the operating system's page cache and the database engine's own caches.
- What it means, concretely, for your market data "hot set" to fit in memory or, better yet, in CPU caches.
- Patterns and anti-patterns for keeping hot market data close to the CPU under real workloads.

Our goal is to give you a practical, intuitive model that connects the theory of columnar databases with the realities of hardware performance.

The Memory Hierarchy: From CPU to Disk

Modern servers are built on a pronounced hierarchy of memory-like resources. You do not have to memorize every latency number, but you should internalize the *shape*:

- **CPU registers**: tiny, extremely fast storage directly inside the CPU cores. This is where arithmetic actually happens.
- **L1 cache**: very small (tens of kilobytes per core), very fast. Often just a few CPU cycles away.
- **L2 and L3 caches**: larger, somewhat slower caches shared between cores to varying degrees. Still much faster than main memory.
- **RAM (DRAM)**: main memory. Orders of magnitude slower than L1 but far larger (dozens or hundreds of gigabytes).
- **Persistent storage**: SSDs, NVMe, or network-attached storage. Much larger but far slower again than RAM.

Moving data down the hierarchy towards the CPU—say, from disk to RAM to L3 to L1—takes time and bandwidth. The less often you have to move data, and the more you can reuse what is already nearby, the better your performance.

Columnar databases and vectorized execution are designed to exploit this hierarchy:

- They store columns as contiguous, compressible arrays that map naturally into cache lines.
- They operate on batches of data that comfortably fit in L1/L2 caches.
- They encourage sequential scans, which allow hardware prefetchers to pull data into caches ahead of time.

But there is another key player between the database and the hardware: the operating system.

OS Page Cache vs Engine-Level Caches

On most trading servers, the OS (typically Linux) manages a *page cache*. This is memory the OS uses to keep frequently accessed file pages in RAM:

- When a process reads from a file, the OS copies the data into pages in RAM.
- If the same part of the file is read again, the OS can satisfy the request from this cache instead of going to disk.
- When memory pressure grows, the OS evicts less-recently used pages to make room for new ones.

Columnar engines often add their own caches or buffer pools on top:

- **kdb+** keeps tables in memory by default; on-disk splayed tables are loaded into memory-mapped regions and then heavily reused.
- **ClickHouse** uses a combination of OS page cache (via direct file reads) and its own structures, such as uncompressed cache and mark caches for MergeTree tables.

Understanding the division of labor is important:

- The **OS page cache** is *generic*: it sees file paths, offsets, and access patterns, but knows nothing about tables, columns, or queries.
- The **database engine** is *semantic*: it knows that a particular file region corresponds to trades.price for today's partition, and that this column is hot.

A healthy design lets the engine's knowledge guide access patterns and workload shape, while allowing the OS to perform generic caching and prefetching efficiently.

What Is the "Hot Set"?

The *hot set* is the subset of your data that is touched frequently enough that it is worth keeping close to the CPU:

- Typically includes today's or this week's fact partitions (trades, quotes, orders).
- Often includes small dimension tables (instruments, venues, calendars).
- May include a handful of narrow factor tables used intensively in intraday research.

A useful way to think about the hot set is in layers:

- **Disk-hot**: Data that is on persistent storage but frequently loaded into RAM via the page cache; access is I/O-bound.
- **RAM-hot**: Data resident in RAM, either as cached file pages or as in-memory tables; access is limited by RAM-to-cache bandwidth.
- **Cache-hot**: Data so frequently reused that it tends to stay in L3/L2/L1 caches across queries; access approaches pure CPU speed.

For low-latency market analytics under load, you ideally want:

- The working set for your critical queries to be RAM-hot most of the time.
- The *narrow core* of columns those queries use to be cache-hot during bursts of activity.

Achieving this is not just a matter of turning on a "cache" setting. It emerges from the combination of schema design, partitioning, query patterns, and operational discipline.

How Columnar Layout Interacts with Caching

Columnar storage has two main advantages for caching:

- **Selective loading**: queries only touch the columns they actually use, so the OS and engine spend memory on relevant pages.
- **Dense packing**: consecutive values of a column are stored contiguously, maximizing useful information per cache line.

Consider a typical intraday query:

> Compute rolling 5-minute realized volatility and VWAP for a basket of 50 symbols over today's session.

The engine will:

- Restrict to today's partition (or partitions).
- Scan mostly time, sym, price, and size.
- Possibly join with small instrument or factor tables.

If you run such queries repeatedly:

- The OS page cache learns that the relevant parts of the trade table's column files are hot and keeps those file pages in RAM.

- The database's internal structures (e.g., dictionary tables for symbols, uncompressed chunks for today's partition) stay in memory.
- Within a single query, vectorized execution ensures that hot vectors are revisited many times while they reside in CPU caches.

The reverse is also true: if you scan many wide, rarely-used columns "just in case", you pollute both OS and CPU caches with data that provides little analytical value.

Patterns for Keeping the Hot Set in Memory

In practice, keeping the hot set RAM-hot and cache-friendly comes down to a few structural patterns.

Separate Hot and Cold Partitions

As discussed earlier, partitioning by date or session is natural for market data. It also helps with caching:

- Today's partition(s) tend to be accessed the most; they are likely to stay in RAM and caches.
- Older partitions may be large and rarely accessed; they drift out of RAM and down to storage.

You can formalize this separation:

- Place hot partitions on faster storage (e.g., NVMe) and cold ones on cheaper media, if available.
- Configure separate clusters or server roles: one group for real-time and intraday analytics, another for deep historical jobs.
- Use routing logic (in applications or via gateways) to send latency-sensitive queries only to the hot-data cluster.

Narrow Core Tables and Projections

Another pattern is to distinguish between:

- **Core fields**: a small set of columns used by most intraday queries (e.g., time, symbol, price, size, a few flags).
- **Extended fields**: dozens or hundreds of auxiliary columns used only by infrequent research queries (e.g., vendor-specific flags, microstructure metrics, trace information).

In a columnar engine, wide tables are less harmful than in row stores because irrelevant columns are not read. Still, you can amplify cache effectiveness by:

- Designing schemas where core columns are physically co-located and frequently scanned together.
- In ClickHouse, using projections or vertical partitioning for heavy, rarely used columns.
- In kdb+, placing auxiliary data into separate tables keyed by time and symbol when appropriate.

The less unnecessary data your hot queries even *have the option* to touch, the cleaner your caches will be.

Prewarming Before Market Open

On many desks, there is a predictable surge of queries around market open:

- Dashboards start refreshing.
- Risk systems recompute exposures as liquidity returns.
- Traders run "sanity checks" on overnight fills and pre-open indications.

You can leverage this predictability by prewarming:

- Shortly before the open, run a controlled set of representative queries (or explicit scan jobs) that touch the key partitions and columns you know will be needed.

- This pulls the relevant file pages into the OS page cache and, in some engines, populates internal caches.

The first queries during live trading then hit warmed caches rather than paying the cost of cold storage access. This reduces latency spikes at precisely the time when users are most sensitive to performance.

How Queries Shape Cache Behavior

Caching is not just about static configuration; it is heavily shaped by actual query patterns.

Repeated Vectorized Scans

When you run the same or similar vectorized scans repeatedly over a window of data:

- The column vectors involved are loaded into RAM and reused many times.
- CPU caches repeatedly see the same memory ranges, promoting them from L3 into L2 and L1.
- Branch predictors and hardware prefetchers learn the patterns, improving pipeline efficiency.

This is why many analytic teams:

- Design standard query templates for dashboards and risk reports.
- Encourage reuse of common aggregations and factors instead of ad hoc queries that constantly randomize access patterns.

The more coherent your workload, the more likely the system is to keep a tight hot set in cache.

Ad Hoc Exploration vs Production Workloads

Research users naturally issue more varied, exploratory queries:

- They might scan unusual time ranges, exotic instruments, or rarely used columns.
- Their queries may evict hot pages from the OS cache or push other data out of CPU caches.

This is not necessarily bad—after all, the system exists to support research—but it suggests:

- Separating interactive research clusters from production risk and reporting clusters when possible.
- Applying resource controls (e.g., query concurrency limits, memory caps) so that ad hoc workloads cannot starve hot production queries.
- Educating power users about the cost of certain operations, such as full-history scans over all symbols.

The more you can segregate workloads with different cache profiles, the easier it is to maintain predictable performance where it matters most.

Anti-Patterns: How to Thrash Your Caches

Several common practices work directly against effective hot-set management.

Scanning Too Many Rarely Used Columns

Even in columnar systems, you can still write queries that request more columns than necessary. Problems include:

- Loading large, mostly unused columns into RAM and CPU caches.
- Increasing memory bandwidth consumption, which can make otherwise CPU-bound queries become memory-bound.
- Causing the OS to evict genuinely hot pages to make space for one-off reads.

Disciplined query design helps:

- Only select columns that are needed for filters, joins, and output.
- Use narrow projections or views tailored to common analytics.

Overfitting Cache Settings to Synthetic Benchmarks

It is tempting to tune cache-related settings (such as buffer sizes or prefetch windows) based on synthetic benchmarks. That is risky:

- Synthetic workloads are often too simple and too regular compared with real trading days.
- Settings that look optimal in a benchmark may behave poorly when mixed workloads with concurrent ingestion are introduced.

A better approach is:

- Start with reasonable defaults.
- Profile performance on real, captured query traces from busy trading days.
- Make small, incremental adjustments while monitoring out-of-sample behavior.

Confusing Filesystem Caching with Engine Performance

Sometimes an engineer runs a query twice, observes that the second run is much faster, and concludes that the database engine is "optimizing" the query. Often, the improvement is simply due to OS page cache warming.

If you then:

- Compare two engines or two configurations using only warmed-cache runs,
- Or extrapolate latency numbers from warm-cache micro-benchmarks to production,

you may delude yourself. In production:

- Queries compete for cache with many other processes.
- Some partitions are cold; some are hot.

You must design tests and metrics that distinguish:

- Cold-cache behavior: first-time access to a partition or after a long idle period.
- Warm-cache behavior: steady-state performance under representative load.

Both matter in market environments: cold-cache spikes can coincide with infrequent but business-critical queries (for example, regulatory reports), while warm-cache behavior dominates daily operational analytics.

Monitoring and Diagnosing Hot-Set Issues

To manage the hot set deliberately, you need visibility into how memory and caches are being used.

Key Metrics

Some useful indicators include:

- **OS-level:**

- Total page cache size and hit rate.
- Disk or SSD read throughput and latency.
- Swap usage (ideally zero for servers running databases).

- **Engine-level:**

- Cache hit rates for any internal caches (e.g., mark cache, uncompressed cache in ClickHouse).

- Per-query statistics on bytes read from disk vs bytes read from memory.
- Number of parts / blocks scanned per query.

- **Hardware-level:**

- CPU utilization vs memory bandwidth utilization.
- Cache miss rates (if you use performance counters or observability tools).

Trends in these metrics can flag hot-set problems:

- Sudden increases in disk reads during the trading day may indicate queries hitting cold partitions unexpectedly.
- Rising memory bandwidth utilization without corresponding CPU utilization can suggest inefficient wide scans.

Correlating with Schema and Workload Changes

Cache behavior is sensitive to changes in:

- Partitioning and sorting schemes.
- Table widths and encodings.
- Query mixes (new dashboards, new risk jobs).

When you roll out such changes, you should:

- Compare pre- and post-change cache-related metrics under similar market conditions.
- Inspect a few representative queries with profiling tools to see whether they now touch more partitions or more columns.
- Check that the hot set you assumed in design (e.g., "today's trades for these products") actually fits into the memory budget of the servers in practice.

Hot-Set Management as an Emergent Property

A central message of this chapter bears repeating in the context of caching: *performance emerges from the interaction of design choices and workload, not from any single configuration knob.*

For caching and hot-set management:

- Schema design (columnar layout, partitioning, sorting) determines how compact and well-aligned your data is with hardware.
- Transaction and ingestion patterns determine how often hot partitions are updated and how much churn they experience.
- Query patterns determine which parts of the data are exercised heavily and which remain cold.
- Hardware characteristics (cache sizes, memory bandwidth, storage) set the physical limits.

If you design these elements in isolation, you will likely underuse your caches or thrash them. If you design them together, with a clear picture of the hot set, you can often achieve near-OLTP latencies for complex analytic queries on recent market data.

Caching and hot-set management are where the abstractions of columnar databases meet the realities of silicon and spinning disks. In this section we have seen that:

- The memory hierarchy imposes strong constraints; keeping hot data in RAM and CPU caches is critical for low-latency analytics.
- The OS page cache and engine-level caches cooperate: the OS provides generic file caching, while the engine shapes access patterns based on table semantics.
- The hot set consists of the subsets of partitions and columns that are repeatedly accessed; effective design and workload shaping help keep this set close to the CPU.
- Patterns such as separate hot/cold partitions, narrow core tables, and prewarming before market open improve cache efficiency.

- Anti-patterns—overly wide scans, synthetic-only tuning, and misinterpreting warm-cache benchmarks—can easily lead to cache thrashing and misleading conclusions.

Armed with this understanding, you can approach performance tuning of kdb+ and ClickHouse deployments with a more holistic view, treating caches as shared, finite resources shaped by schema, workload, and hardware. In the final section of this chapter, we will turn to measurement and observability: how to capture the right metrics and design experiments that reveal whether your columnar system is truly operating near its potential.

2.6 Performance Measurement and Observability

By now we have a conceptual model of how columnar engines like kdb+ and ClickHouse store, execute, and cache market workloads. The final piece is learning how to *observe* these systems in production, and how to make performance decisions without fooling yourself.

This section develops a disciplined approach to:

- Characterizing market workloads in measurable terms.
- Measuring latency, throughput, and resource usage in ways that capture real user experience.
- Designing benchmarks and experiments that reflect production conditions.
- Instrumenting systems so that performance regressions and bottlenecks can be understood and fixed.

The emphasis is on habits of thought: how to avoid the common traps that lead engineers to optimize the wrong things or to overfit designs to artificial tests.

Describing Your Workload Precisely

Any performance discussion must begin with a crisp definition of the workload. For market systems, relevant characteristics include:

Data Arrival Rates

You should quantify:

- **Ingestion rates**: trades, quotes, orders, and derived rows per second, broken down by source and table.
- **Bursts**: peak rates during volatility spikes or market open, which can be several times higher than mid-day averages.

Understanding arrival patterns is essential for sizing ingestion pipelines and for planning when compaction or backfills can safely run.

Query Mix

Next, categorize queries by function and frequency:

- **Operational dashboards**: short, repeated queries (e.g., every few seconds) over hot intraday data.
- **Risk and P&L**: scheduled jobs (e.g., every few minutes or hourly) that may touch larger windows and multiple systems.
- **Research and backtesting**: long-running, less frequent queries scanning deep history and many symbols.
- **Ad hoc diagnostics**: one-off queries by support or developers, often under time pressure.

Each class has different latency expectations and resource footprints.

Concurrency Levels

You also need a picture of how queries overlap:

- How many queries run concurrently at market open, mid-day, and close?

- How many concurrent ingestion streams do you maintain?
- Are high-cost research jobs allowed to run during peak periods, or are they throttled?

Concurrency strongly influences cache behavior and perceived performance.

Service-Level Targets

Finally, performance targets should be written down and quantified, not left as vague notions of "fast enough". Examples:

- "95% of dashboard queries for today's data should complete within 200 ms."
- "End-of-day risk reports must be available within 15 minutes of market close."
- "Ad hoc research queries may take minutes, but they must not cause operational queries to exceed their targets."

These targets become the lens through which you interpret all subsequent measurements.

Latencies: Averages Are Not Enough

In market environments, it is rarely acceptable to describe performance using only average latency. Users and downstream systems care about *distributions*, not means.

Latency Percentiles

Instead of a single number, consider:

- The median (50th percentile): what a typical query sees.
- The 95th percentile: what "slow but still acceptable" feels like.
- The 99th percentile and beyond: how bad the worst experiences are.

Analytically, the median tells you whether your optimizations help "most of the time". The tail percentiles tell you whether your system is robust under stress and whether rare but important queries (e.g., during market shocks) will complete in time.

Tail Behavior and User Experience

Consider a risk dashboard that refreshes every 5 seconds:

- If the median latency is 50 ms but 5% of queries take 3 seconds, users will perceive the system as laggy and untrustworthy.
- If the median is 150 ms, but 99% of queries are under 300 ms, the dashboard will appear smooth and predictable.

For end-of-day reports, the tail may matter less on a per-query basis but more in aggregate: you care when the last report finishes, not just an average. Percentile-based metrics make these distinctions visible.

Cold vs Warm Cache Latency

Latency also depends heavily on whether the relevant data is hot in cache:

- **Cold-start latency**: the first time a partition is queried after a long idle period, or immediately after a process restart. Here, disk I/O often dominates.
- **Steady-state latency**: when queries repeatedly hit the same hot set of partitions and columns. Here, CPU and memory bandwidth dominate.

Your measurement framework should explicitly distinguish:

- Performance expectations for cold vs warm scenarios.
- Benchmark phases that measure each regime separately.

For example:

- You might tolerate higher latency for the first query of the day on a rarely used symbol, but not for the 100th query on today's trades for a key index future.

- During testing, you should measure both first-run latencies and latencies after running a realistic warmup sequence.

Throughput and Capacity

Latency is one side of the coin; the other is *throughput*: how much work the system can do per unit time without violating latency targets.

Ingestion Capacity

For ingestion, you should measure:

- Maximum sustained event rates per table while keeping ingest latency (from wire to committed) within requirements.
- Sensitivity to bursts and micro-batches: does performance degrade gracefully when bursts exceed average rates?

In analytic columnar systems, ingestion is often batched:

- Larger batches reduce overhead per row but increase latency for individual events.
- Smaller batches reduce individual latency but stress metadata and commit paths.

Your throughput measurements should explore this trade-off and identify a batch size that fits your SLAs.

Query Throughput and Contention

For queries, meaningful throughput metrics include:

- Maximum number of concurrent dashboard queries before median and tail latencies drift out of spec.
- How many long-running research queries can be tolerated while keeping operational jobs within bounds.
- Sensitivity to mixed workloads: combinations of light and heavy queries running at the same time.

These measurements should be framed in terms of *capacity planning*: how many users and how many scheduled jobs a cluster can support during peak market conditions.

Benchmarking Methodology: Avoiding Self-Deception

It is easy to produce attractive numbers from a benchmark that has little to do with real-world behavior. To avoid this, structure your benchmarking approach around a few principles.

Use Realistic Query Traces

Rather than inventing synthetic queries, capture:

- Real queries from production logs, anonymized as needed.
- Representative time windows (quiet days, volatile days, special events).
- Mixes of query types (dashboards, risk, research).

You can then replay these traces against test clusters. This ensures that peculiarities of the production workload-such as peculiar filters, odd joins, and skewed symbols-are represented in evaluation.

Control Variables Carefully

Best practice is to vary only one factor at a time:

- Fix hardware (CPU, memory size, storage configuration).
- Fix software versions and OS tuning, or change them explicitly as the subject of a test.
- Fix dataset samples (e.g., one month of trades, one year of bars).

When you compare two configurations-say, different partitioning schemes or different ClickHouse MergeTree settings-ensure everything else is held constant. Document the differences so you can later interpret results.

Separate Cold-Start and Steady-State Phases

A robust benchmark should include:

- Cold-start phase: restart the engines or flush caches, then run a set of queries that exercise key paths. Measure latency and resource usage.
- Warm-up phase: run a realistic workload for long enough that OS and engine caches stabilize.
- Steady-state phase: measure latency, throughput, and resource usage during this stabilized period.

Reporting these phases separately helps you understand:

- How the system behaves early in the trading day or after failover.
- How it behaves during typical hours-long sessions.

Inspect Plans, Not Just Timings

Database engines often expose query plans and operator-level statistics. During benchmarking, you should:

- Examine how many partitions and parts are read, how many rows are scanned, and which indexes are used.
- Verify that vectorized execution is actually applied and that filters are pushed down early.
- Check for regressions in plan shape when schema or configuration changes.

This prevents situations where timing appears acceptable but underlying behavior has degraded (for example, a query accidentally scanning 10x more data than before due to a schema change).

Observability: Seeing Inside the Engine

Beyond one-off benchmarks, you need continuous observability in production. That means instrumenting the system at multiple levels.

Per-Query Metrics

For each query (or at least for a sampled subset), useful metrics include:

- Start time, end time, and total latency.
- Number of rows read vs number of rows returned.
- Bytes read from disk vs bytes read from cache.
- Number of partitions, parts, and blocks touched.
- Main operators used (scans, joins, aggregates) and their individual timings.

Such metrics can typically be collected via:

- Built-in system tables (e.g., system.query_log in ClickHouse).
- Logging and tracing hooks in your application's query layer.
- Custom instrumentation in kdb+ scripts or gateways.

Resource Utilization

At the node level, monitor:

- CPU utilization, by core and by process.
- Memory usage, including page cache and any engine-level caches.
- Disk and network I/O: throughput, latency, queue depth.
- Context switches and run queue lengths, for signs of oversubscription.

At the cluster level, track:

- Load distribution across nodes.
- Replication lag and the consistency of snapshots.
- Health of coordination services (if any) that manage metadata.

Correlating these metrics with query-level data illuminates whether a slow query is CPU-bound, memory-bound, or I/O-bound, as discussed earlier.

Schema and Partition Changes

Observability should extend to structural metadata:

- When new partitions are created or old ones are dropped.
- When MergeTree parts are merged or compacted.
- When kdb+ tables are re-sorted, re-partitioned, or backfilled.

Logging such events with timestamps allows you to correlate performance shifts with layout changes. For example:

- A sudden increase in scan cost might coincide with a misconfigured partitioning for a new product line.
- Unexplained spikes in disk I/O might correspond to large compaction jobs running during peak hours.

Interpreting Regressions and Anomalies

Even with good metrics, interpreting performance shifts requires discipline.

Distinguish Workload Changes from Engine Changes

When performance degrades, first ask:

- Has the workload changed? New users, new dashboards, new products?

- Has the data distribution shifted? For example, trading volume has moved to new venues or symbols.
- Or have we changed the engine? New version, different configuration, new partitioning or encodings?

It is easy to blame the database for slowdowns that actually stem from a sudden spike in research usage, an unplanned backfill, or a new, expensive query pattern.

Look for Structural Breaks

Plot metrics over time-latency percentiles, bytes scanned per query, cache hit rates-and look for structural breaks:

- Changes that align with deployments or schema migrations suggest regressions in engine behavior.
- Changes that align with business events (e.g., new product launch, volatility episodes) suggest legitimate load increases that may require scaling out.

Being able to answer "what changed when this started?" is half of performance engineering.

Avoid Overreacting to Outliers

Columnar databases processing large datasets will occasionally produce very slow outlier queries, especially under stress. Before rearchitecting:

- Check whether the outliers correspond to clearly abnormal events: massive one-off backfills, rare bug-hunting queries, or system maintenance.
- Evaluate whether tail behavior is getting systematically worse over days or weeks, or whether incidents are isolated.

The goal is to improve systemic behavior, not to chase every single outlier.

Common Pitfalls in Performance Work

Finally, let us summarize a few frequent mistakes specific to columnar market systems.

Micro-Benchmarking in Isolation

Engineers sometimes focus on micro-benchmarks, such as:

- Summing a single column over a synthetic table.
- Running a single query repeatedly on an idle system.

While these tests can help understand raw engine capabilities, they are poor predictors of production behavior because they ignore:

- Mixed workloads and concurrency.
- Continuous ingestion and background jobs.
- Interaction with OS caches and the network.

Use micro-benchmarks for sanity checks and for understanding hardware scaling, but base capacity planning and tuning decisions on realistic workloads.

Ignoring Background Ingestion and Maintenance

Backfills, compactions, and snapshot creations all consume I/O, CPU, and memory. If you benchmark without them and then enable them in production, you will see surprising slowdowns.

In your experiments:

- Include representative background tasks when measuring query performance.
- Stagger maintenance jobs to avoid coinciding with the busiest query periods.
- Monitor the resource footprint of these jobs and budget capacity for them explicitly.

Overfitting to One Trading Day

It is tempting to tune configurations based on a single, interesting day's workload. But markets evolve:

- Volume and volatility shift across instruments and venues.
- New strategies and products change access patterns.
- Regulatory requirements drive new reports and audits.

To ensure robustness:

- Benchmark and observe across multiple days, including both quiet and volatile periods.
- Periodically revalidate that your partitioning, indexing, and caching strategies still align with current usage.

A Practical Checklist

To close this chapter, here is a concise checklist you can use when designing performance measurement and observability for kdb+ and ClickHouse in market environments:

- **Workload definition**
  - Document arrival rates, query mixes, and concurrency targets.
  - Define explicit latency and freshness SLAs for each query class.
- **Latency and throughput metrics**
  - Track latency percentiles, not just averages.
  - Measure cold-start and steady-state behavior separately.
  - Quantify ingestion and query throughput under realistic load.
- **Benchmarking practice**

  - Use real or realistic query traces.
  - Control variables and document configuration differences.
  - Include background ingestion and maintenance tasks.

- **Observability**
  - Collect per-query statistics (rows, bytes, operators, parts scanned).
  - Monitor CPU, memory, disk, and network utilization.
  - Log schema, partition, and engine-version changes with timestamps.

- **Analysis habits**
  - Differentiate between workload-driven and engine-driven regressions.
  - Focus on distribution and tail behavior, not just central tendencies.
  - Revalidate tuning decisions periodically as markets and usage evolve.

With such a disciplined approach, you can confidently evolve your columnar data stores-optimizing schemas, queries, and infrastructure-while maintaining the trust of traders, researchers, and risk managers who depend on fast, predictable analytics.

Chapter 3

Market Data Pipelines

Every trading idea lives or dies on the quality of its data pipeline. In this chapter we peel back the layers from raw exchange packets to time-aligned, replayable order books-showing how protocol quirks, schema design, and streaming ETL choices quietly shape your back-tests, your risk, and ultimately your P&L.

3.1 Market Data Protocols

In the previous chapter we worked from the outside in: we discussed why market data matters, what a high-performance store needs to provide, and how kdb+ and ClickHouse fit into a broader trading stack. In this section we move one level closer to the wire.

Before we can design tables, queries, or analytics, we have to understand what actually arrives from an exchange: the network transports, the feed topologies, and the message formats themselves. Only then can we make sensible choices about feed handlers, logging, and storage schemas.

This section will:

- Outline how market data travels over the network (unicast vs.

multicast, TCP vs. UDP).

- Describe common feed topologies and what they imply for scaling and failure modes.
- Introduce three key protocol families: FIX, FAST, and ITCH.
- Tie specific protocol features (sequence numbers, compression, message catalogs) to design decisions in your ingestion and storage layers.

From Raw Packets to Handler Outputs

At the lowest level, market data is just a sequence of network packets. Your colocation cage or data center receives Ethernet frames on one or more network interfaces. Each frame carries an IP packet, which in turn carries UDP or TCP, which finally contains bytes that conform to a particular exchange protocol.

From the point of view of a data platform, the journey looks like this:

- **Network interface** captures packets for one or more feeds.
- **Transport layer** (UDP or TCP) provides delivery semantics.
- **Protocol decoder** reassembles packets into application messages and validates ordering.
- **Feed handler** parses messages into structured events (trades, quotes, reference data).
- **Normalization layer** maps those events onto your canonical schema, ready for kdb+ or ClickHouse.

It is tempting to skip straight from "we have packets" to "we have a trades table," but all of the tricky edge cases live in the middle steps: gaps, duplicates, out-of-order packets, protocol upgrades, and so on. The concrete choices an exchange makes for transport and message format will determine *what* you must log, *how* you detect problems, and *how* you design your storage keys.

Right after this conceptual overview, it is helpful to ground the discussion with a visual pipeline from exchange to normalized events.

Diagrammatic representation:

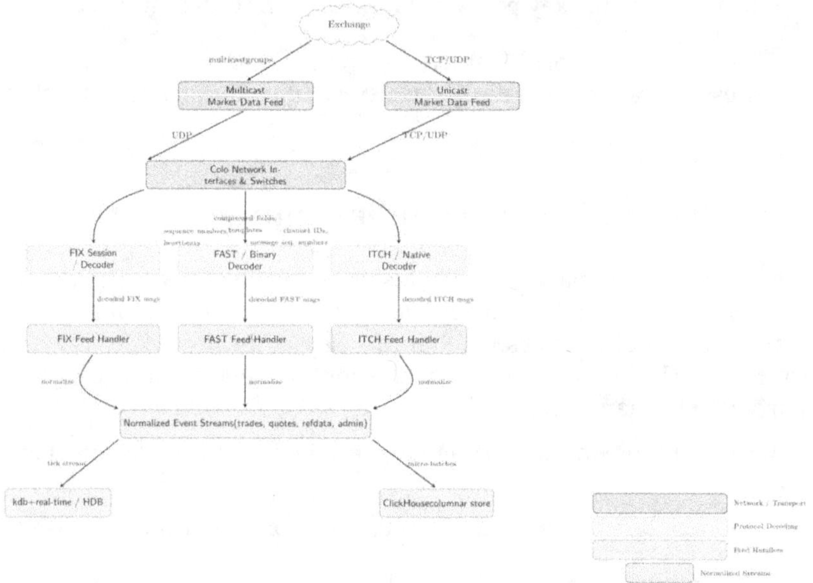

This diagram highlights three important ideas that will recur throughout the chapter:

- You often have *separate* feeds and handlers for different protocols.
- You want a *single* normalized event model feeding kdb+ and ClickHouse.
- To get there, you must understand both the transport and the protocol structure.

We now unpack each layer in turn.

Network Transport: TCP vs. UDP, Unicast vs. Multicast

UDP Multicast: Broadcast At Scale

Many exchanges distribute market data over UDP multicast. The idea is simple: send each packet once, and let the network replicate it to all subscribers that have joined a particular multicast group.

- **Pros:**
  - Very efficient when many consumers need the same data.
  - Low protocol overhead; packets are small and simple.
  - Natural fit for "firehose" style data such as depth-of-book updates.
- **Cons:**
  - No built-in retransmission or congestion control.
  - Packets can be lost or reordered without notification.
  - You must implement gap detection and recovery in your handler.

Conceptually, think of multicast as a television broadcast: if your antenna misses a frame, the broadcaster does not resend it for you. Your receiver just has to live with the gap, or buffer and recover from another source.

For your data platform, UDP multicast implies:

- You *must* track per-channel sequence numbers to detect gaps.
- You likely need a separate *retransmission* or *snapshot* channel (often TCP or a reliable unicast) to repair gaps.
- Your storage design should log enough to diagnose these issues later: channel ID, sequence number, and possibly network metadata.

TCP Unicast: Reliability For Fewer Consumers

Some feeds — particularly order entry, but also certain incremental or replay feeds — use TCP unicast. Here, the exchange maintains a separate logical connection to each client.

- **Pros:**
  - Built-in delivery guarantees: in-order, reliable byte stream.
  - Simpler handler logic: no gap detection at the packet level.
  - Easier debugging: clear notion of a "session" with logs.
- **Cons:**
  - Scaling is harder when many clients need the same data.
  - Retransmissions and congestion control can add jitter.
  - Per-connection state overhead on both sides.

For your purposes, TCP gives you a more reliable channel for feeds where correctness matters more than absolute minimal latency, or where the number of consumers is inherently limited (for example, a private drop copy of your own orders and trades).

Feed Topology and Failure Modes

Exchanges rarely offer just one feed. More commonly you will see a topology such as:

- **Incremental multicast feeds:** real-time updates to the order book, often split across multiple channels by symbol range or instrument type.
- **Snapshot or refresh feeds:** point-in-time full books, often over TCP or a separate multicast channel.
- **Replay or historical feeds:** slower streams used to backfill or reproduce events.

From a pipeline design perspective, you should always ask:

- Which feeds define the *authoritative* ordering of events?
- Where do sequence numbers live, and how are they reset?
- How are gaps detected and repaired?

Once you know this, you can design your feed handlers to emit not just trades and quotes, but also metadata events such as "gap detected," "recovery started," and "recovery complete." In kdb+ and ClickHouse, those can live in technical tables that track data quality alongside the business data.

FIX: Text-Based, Session-Oriented Protocol

The Financial Information eXchange (FIX) protocol was originally designed for order routing and trade execution. Many venues also use FIX, or FIX-like formats, for streaming market data.

FIX On The Wire

On the wire, FIX is a sequence of tag=value pairs separated by delimiters. Each message has:

- A **header**, including:
  - Message type (e.g. market data snapshot, incremental refresh).
  - Sender and target identifiers.
  - Sequence number.
  - Sending time.
- A **body**, with fields specific to the message type.
- A **trailer**, typically including a checksum.

FIX sessions run over TCP. The combination of message sequence numbers and TCP delivery gives a robust ordering discipline: if you receive message 101, you know that 100 either has already arrived or will arrive before any higher number. If 100 never arrives, session-level gap detection kicks in and the protocol defines how to request resends.

FIX Market Data Messages

For market data, the most common message types are:

- **Market Data Snapshot** (full book for one instrument).
- **Market Data Incremental Refresh** (changes since last update).

These messages often carry:

- **Instrument identifiers**: symbols, security IDs, or both.
- **Entry type**: bid, offer, trade, index value, and so on.
- **Price and size**: usually decimal quantities represented as text.
- **Quote conditions**: flags for indicative quotes, auctions, etc.

Because FIX uses textual encoding, messages are relatively verbose. Latency-sensitive venues often combine FIX semantics with binary encodings (for example, FAST) to reduce size. We will discuss that next.

Implications For Feed Handlers and Storage

For FIX-based feeds:

- **Session state:** Your handler must maintain session state: sequence numbers, heartbeats, logon/logoff, and resend logic. This state should be reflected in monitoring tables, because lost or stalled sessions are a root cause of missing data.
- **Parsing overhead:** Text parsing is CPU-intensive. You may choose to parse only relevant tags, skipping fields you do not need for your normalized schema.
- **Field naming:** FIX tags have numeric IDs (e.g. 55 for symbol, 48 for security ID). Decide early how you map these to stable column names (for example, sym, secid). That mapping becomes part of your data contract.

- **Precision handling:** Prices and sizes may come as strings with implied decimals. Your handler must convert them to fixed-precision numeric types, mindful of precision requirements in kdb+ or ClickHouse.

A practical rule of thumb: treat your FIX-to-normalized mapping as a small specification, not as ad hoc code. Keep it versioned and testable. When the exchange adds or deprecates tags, your storage schema and handler both should evolve in a controlled way.

FAST: Compressed FIX For High Throughput

FIX Adapted for STreaming (FAST) is a way to encode FIX-style data in a much more compact binary form. The key idea is that market data messages often repeat the same structure and many field values change slowly. FAST exploits this by sending only differences from a shared template and a running state.

Templates and State

Instead of sending full tag=value pairs for every message, FAST uses:

- **Templates:** predefined message layouts that specify which fields appear and how they are encoded.
- **Field operators:** rules for each field (for example, copy the previous value, increment, use a default) so that the sender can omit unchanged fields.
- **Session state:** shared between sender and receiver, holding the last known values of fields for each template.

On the wire, a FAST message is a bitstream: a series of bits packed together that indicate presence or absence of fields and then the encoded field values. To interpret this, your decoder must already know the template and the previous state.

Failure Modes And Recovery

This design is extremely efficient but fragile if you lose synchronization:

- If you lose one FAST packet, you may decode subsequent messages incorrectly because your state is wrong.
- If you decode using the wrong template, every field will be misinterpreted.

To mitigate this, exchanges typically provide:

- **Reset points:** messages or snapshots that reset the template state.
- **Out-of-band templates:** distributed over a reliable channel so you can reinitialize decoders.

Your feed handler should log enough information to diagnose and repair such issues:

- Template identifiers and versions for each message.
- Any reset or state-initializing messages.
- Checksums or sequence numbers that help detect misalignment early.

Implications For Storage

From a storage viewpoint, FAST is "just" a more compressed way to ship FIX-like messages, but it has some specific consequences:

- **Decoder correctness is critical:** A bug in your FAST decoder will silently corrupt many fields at once. You therefore want offline validation tables in kdb+ or ClickHouse that compare derived aggregates (for example, daily volume per symbol) against reference sources.

- **Template-aware mapping:** Different templates may represent different message types, even if they share many fields. Your normalized schema should reflect the semantic message type, not the template number, but your technical logs should preserve the template metadata.
- **Versioning pressure:** When templates change, the mapping from encoded fields to columns may also change. You may need schema version columns or partitioning by protocol version to keep old and new data interpretable.

A healthy practice is to store not only the normalized rows but also a lightweight representation of the decoded message — for example, a compact JSON or key-value view in a technical table — so that you can inspect and debug decoding issues without re-reading the entire binary stream.

ITCH and Native Binary Feeds: Event Catalogs

Many equities and derivatives venues expose "native" binary market data feeds rather than FIX-based ones. NASDAQ's ITCH family is the most widely known example. These protocols are designed from the ground up to represent the order book and trades as a sequence of small, fixed-format messages.

Message Catalogs and Sequence Numbers

A typical ITCH-like protocol defines:

- A **message catalog**: a finite list of message types, each with a one-character or small numeric type code and a fixed set of fields.
- A **stream per channel**: each channel carries a sequence of messages with monotonically increasing sequence numbers.
- **Order IDs**: long-lived identifiers that tie together order additions, modifications, cancellations, and executions.

Examples of message types include:

- **Add order**: a new limit order enters the book.
- **Modify / replace order**: changes price or size.
- **Cancel order**: reduces or removes remaining quantity.
- **Trade**: executes against a resting order.
- **Cross trade**: auction or opening/closing cross.
- **System events**: start of day, end of day, halts.

Unlike FIX, which can be used for many different functions, ITCH-style protocols are tightly focused: they are a precise log of how the order book evolves.

Order Book Reconstruction Implications

Because the protocol exposes order IDs and explicit add/modify/-cancel/trade messages, you can reconstruct an order-level order book. This has important implications:

- **Stateful handlers:** your feed handler is essentially an event-sourced engine. It consumes the ITCH stream and maintains in-memory state representing the book.
- **Snapshot strategies:** to avoid replaying from the start of the day every time, you will want to build and store periodic snapshots of the book state. Later sections will detail snapshot design, but the key point here is that the protocol supports it.
- **Rich derived metrics:** with order-level events, you can compute order lifetimes, queue positions, and many microstructure metrics that are invisible in trade-only feeds.

From a storage design perspective, these protocols encourage a layered schema:

- **Raw events table:** one row per raw protocol message with fields such as message type, channel ID, sequence number, order ID, price, size, and flags.

- **Derived trades and quotes tables:** normalized views that present the familiar trade and quote abstractions.
- **Book snapshots or ladders:** periodic representations of the book at various depths and aggregation levels.

Both kdb+ and ClickHouse are well suited to storing these layers. Kdb+ might hold the raw events and near-real-time snapshots in an intraday database; ClickHouse might store larger histories of derived metrics and snapshots for backtesting.

Designing Feed Handlers With Storage In Mind

With the main protocol families described, we can now tie them back to handler and storage design. A feed handler should not only decode messages and update in-memory state but also act as the "front door contract" for your data stores.

What To Log For Replay and Audit

Regardless of protocol, you want to be able to rebuild downstream tables from a log of inputs. Practically, this means logging:

- **A lossless representation of the decoded messages**: either raw binary blobs plus protocol version metadata, or a structured form that preserves every field.
- **Ordering metadata**: sequence numbers, channel IDs, and timestamps (both exchange and receipt).
- **Session and quality events**: disconnects, gap detections, recoveries, and protocol errors.

In kdb+, this might take the form of a narrow append-only table partitioned by date and channel. In ClickHouse, it might be a MergeTree table keyed by date and channel with ordering on sequence numbers. The key is that the combination of keys uniquely defines the order of messages for replay.

Choosing What To Normalize Early

Protocols expose many fields that you may not need for every analysis. There is a trade-off between normalizing aggressively at the feed handler stage and deferring some interpretation to later ETL stages.

Guiding principles:

- **Normalize identifiers and timestamps early:** map exchange-specific instrument codes to your internal instrument keys; convert timestamps to a common representation (usually UTC at nanosecond precision where available).
- **Preserve raw flags and conditions:** do not over-interpret protocol flags such as trade conditions or quote qualifiers. Instead, map them to stable, well-named columns and document their semantics.
- **Defer heavy aggregations:** things like bar construction or feature engineering can be performed downstream, using the normalized event stream as input.

For kdb+, normalization often feeds directly into real-time tables that act as sources for analytics. For ClickHouse, normalization may produce micro-batches of columnar data written into staging tables, later merged into long-term storage.

Handling Protocol Evolution

Protocols are not static. Exchanges add new message types, deprecate fields, change enumerations, or split channels. A robust design anticipates change.

You can make this concrete by:

- **Versioning schema mappings:** maintain explicit versions of your protocol-to-schema mapping. Each version corresponds to a known exchange protocol version.

- **Tagging data with protocol version:** include a version column in your raw or normalized tables so that downstream queries can adapt if needed.
- **Testing against sample captures:** keep example packet captures and raw message logs for each protocol version. Use them in automated tests when you change handlers or schemas.

For both kdb+ and ClickHouse, schema evolution tools are available, but you should minimize disruptive changes. It is often better to add a new column and backfill gradually than to rename or remove an existing one.

Market data protocols are not an implementation detail to be hidden away in a black box. They determine:

- How you detect and repair gaps (UDP multicast vs. TCP unicast).
- How you maintain session and template state (FIX vs. FAST).
- How detailed your order book reconstruction can be (ITCH-style native feeds).
- What keys you need in kdb+ and ClickHouse to support replay, audit, and efficient queries.

By treating the on-the-wire reality as a first-class design input, you can build feed handlers that cooperate with your storage layer rather than fight it. The next sections of this chapter will build on this foundation: we will design normalization and schema mappings that turn these diverse message families into a coherent, analysis-ready dataset.

3.2 Normalization and Schema Mapping

In the previous section we treated market data as it appears "on the wire": UDP versus TCP, multicast versus unicast, and concrete protocol families such as FIX, FAST, and ITCH. We ended with protocol-specific feed handlers emitting decoded messages and basic events.

We now take the next step: turning those protocol-specific events into a single, coherent dataset that analysts, quants, and risk systems can use without constantly thinking about which venue or protocol a record came from.

This translation layer is what we will call *normalization and schema mapping*. It sits between the protocol handlers and your storage engines (kdb+ and ClickHouse). Done well, it makes downstream work dramatically simpler and safer. Done poorly, it leads to fragile research, duplicated logic, and subtle bugs in production models.

Our goals in this section are:

- To define what "normalized" market data actually means in practice.
- To show how to derive a canonical event model from heterogeneous protocol catalogs.
- To design concrete trade, quote, and instrument schemas that work well in kdb+ and ClickHouse.
- To discuss how to keep this mapping robust as protocols and business requirements evolve.

Why Normalization Matters

Recall that each protocol family brings its own naming, typing, and structural conventions:

- FIX uses tag numbers and text values; symbol might be tag 55, security ID tag 48, and so on.
- FAST compresses those FIX tags according to templates, but semantically they are still FIX fields.
- ITCH-style feeds use compact binary messages with short type codes and fixed layouts; order IDs and instrument identifiers may use entirely different encodings from FIX.

If you simply dump each feed into its own schema with its own conventions, every downstream query becomes a maze of conditional logic: "If this is ITCH, use field X; if this is FIX, use field Y; but for venue Z, use field Z1 except on half-days." This is not sustainable.

Normalization solves this by giving you:

- **Stable column names**: for example, every trade has ts, sym, price, and size, no matter which venue it came from.
- **Consistent data types**: prices are always numeric with known precision; timestamps are always in UTC with clear resolution; flags are well-defined enumerations.
- **Unified semantics**: a column called is_auction or trade_condition has the same meaning across venues, or at least a documented mapping.

You can think of normalization as building a *dictionary* between the outside world (protocols and venues) and your internal world (canonical events and schemas). The rest of this section is about how to design that dictionary so it is:

- explicit rather than implicit,
- testable rather than tribal knowledge, and
- friendly to kdb+ and ClickHouse rather than fighting them.

Defining a Canonical Event Model

The first step is to define the small set of event types that matter to you. For most equities and futures workflows, three families cover a large share of use cases:

- **Trades**: executions and related events such as corrections and cancellations.
- **Quotes**: order book state, at least top-of-book and often depth ladders.

- **Instruments**: reference data describing the securities you trade or track.

In addition, you will likely want technical or control events (system status, halts, session boundaries), but we focus here on the three core families.

A *canonical event model* is a language-neutral description of these families. It says, for example:

> "A trade event must include: a timestamp, an instrument identifier in internal form, a venue identifier in internal form, a price, a size, a side if available, and a small set of standardized condition flags."

This is intentionally independent of any particular database system. Only after we are clear about the event semantics do we design kdb+ tables or ClickHouse schemas.

Core Dimensions and Measures

When defining your event model, separate *dimensions* from *measures*:

- **Dimensions** describe the "who, what, where, when" of an event:
  - Timestamps (both exchange and receipt, if available).
  - Instrument identifiers (internal instrument_id, human-readable sym).
  - Venue identifiers (exchange code, MIC, internal venue key).
  - Trade or quote conditions and flags (e.g. auction, dark pool, odd lot).
- **Measures** are numeric values you typically aggregate:
  - Price and size.
  - Notional, volume, and other derived quantities.
  - Book depth metrics, imbalance, and similar.

This distinction matters because columnar systems like kdb+ and ClickHouse can often dictionary-encode dimensions very efficiently, while measures typically remain as raw numeric arrays that aggregates can scan quickly.

From Protocol Catalogs to Mapping Rules

Each exchange protocol specification contains a *message catalog*: a list of message types, the fields they contain, and the possible values of those fields. Your job is to translate that catalog into mapping rules for your canonical event model.

Conceptually, a mapping rule looks like:

- "For message type X from protocol Y, take field A, convert it to type T, and store it in canonical column C, possibly after applying transformation F."

For example:

- "In ITCH, message *Trade* contains a 64-bit integer *match number*; map it to trade_id as a string or unchanged 64-bit integer, depending on your internal convention."
- "In FIX, tag 55 (*symbol*) is mapped to sym, and tag 48 (*security ID*) is mapped to instrument_id, using a reference table to ensure stable internal IDs."

These rules can be written as configuration, code, or a combination. The important thing is that they are explicit and versioned.

Goals of Normalization

Before we dive into concrete designs, it is worth stating explicit goals. A good normalization layer should:

- **Hide protocol quirks** from most downstream code while preserving enough detail for microstructure research.

- **Preserve information**: mapping should be mostly one-to-one; discarding fields should be a conscious choice.
- **Be performant**: normalization should not become a bottleneck relative to decoding and disk I/O.
- **Support replay**: normalized events should be reproducible from raw protocol logs.
- **Evolve safely**: adding new protocols or message types should be a controlled extension, not a redesign.

Right after clarifying these goals, it is helpful to visualize how multiple heterogeneous message formats converge into a single normalized schema.

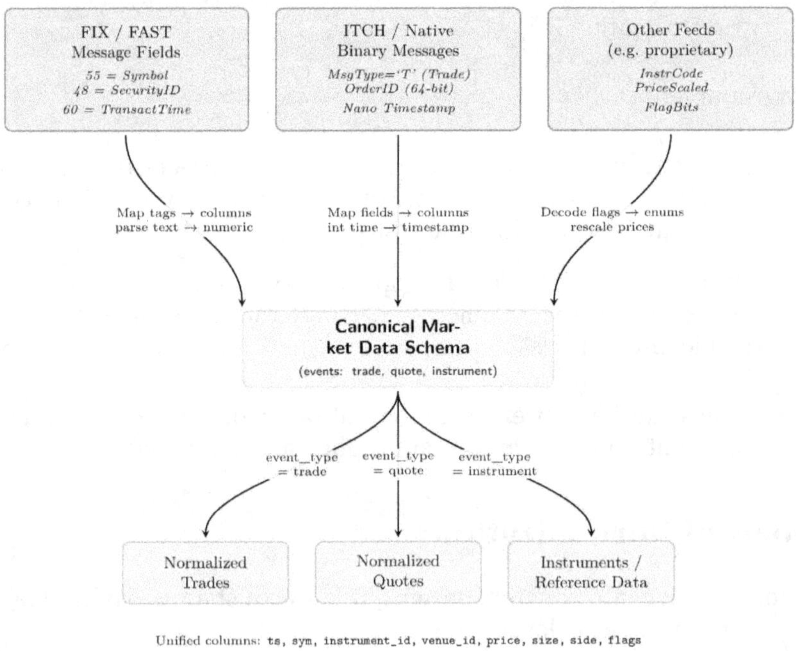

This figure captures the essence of normalization: different message formats flow through protocol-specific decoders into a central mapping layer, which in turn feeds a small set of well-defined tables.

We now turn this picture into concrete designs, first at the conceptual level, then in the context of kdb+ and ClickHouse.

Designing Normalized Trade Tables

Trades are often the first dataset quants want, and they are also the simplest to normalize compared to full order book state.

At the conceptual level, a normalized trade event should include:

- **Time**: a primary exchange timestamp, plus optional receipt time.
- **Instrument**: an internal instrument key and, optionally, a symbol string.
- **Venue**: internal venue identifier, and possibly the native exchange code.
- **Price and size**: numeric, with clear precision rules.
- **Side**: if exposed by the protocol, or inferred where appropriate.
- **Conditions**: standardized flags for trade type, auction involvement, corrections, and so on.
- **Technical identifiers**: trade ID, order IDs where available, and sequence numbers.

Mapping Examples

Consider three simplified examples:

- In a FIX trade capture message, tags might include: 55 (symbol), 31 (last price), 32 (last quantity), 60 (transact time), and 150 (execution type). Your mapping would:

  - Map 55 to sym, then resolve instrument_id via a reference table.
  - Convert 31 and 32 from strings to numeric price and size, applying any implied decimal rules.
  - Parse 60 into a UTC timestamp ts_exchange.
  - Map 150 and related tags to a small set of trade condition flags.

- In an ITCH *Trade* message, the feed gives you: timestamp (integer counts), order ID, match number, executed shares, and price as an integer. Your mapping would:
  - Convert timestamp to a real-time value ts_exchange, using the exchange's documented epoch and scale.
  - Map the integer price to a floating-point price or keep it as an integer plus a known scale; in both cases the normalized table has a clearly defined unit.
  - Keep order_id and trade_id as technical identifiers for later joins to order book tables.

- In a proprietary dark-pool feed, you might only see aggregated execution reports with limited instrument detail. Your mapping might:
  - Resolve a venue-specific instrument code to your internal instrument_id.
  - Set is_dark_pool to true and leave certain other fields as null or a special value indicating unavailability.

Across all these cases, the normalized trade table presents a unified structure, and the differences are captured in the values of flags and condition fields rather than in the shape of the schema.

Designing Normalized Quote and Book Tables

Quotes and order books are more complex because protocols expose different levels of detail:

- Some feeds provide only best bid and offer (top-of-book).
- Others provide full depth-of-book, with per-order detail.
- Some feeds mix both quote and trade information in the same stream.

Rather than attempting to hide all these differences, a practical approach is to define a few standardized quote-oriented tables, for example:

- **Top-of-book quotes**: each row represents the best bid and best offer at a point in time.
- **Price-level depth**: each row represents a price level on one side of the book, possibly with aggregated size.
- **Order-level book** (optional): each row represents a distinct order with quantity and price.

Normalization here means:

- Mapping protocol-specific messages (add, modify, cancel, refresh) into changes in these standardized views.
- Defining consistent keys: instrument, side, price (for price-level), or order ID (for order-level).
- Handling missing information gracefully: for example, representing unknown sides or sizes explicitly rather than inferring incorrectly.

Later in the chapter, the order book reconstruction section will go into more detail. For now, the key concept is that your schema should make microstructure concepts visible (bids, offers, depths, imbalances) in a way that is independent of which protocol supplied the raw events.

Designing Instrument and Reference Data Tables

Instrument and reference data binds everything together. Without a robust instrument schema, normalized trades and quotes float around without context.

At minimum, your instrument table should include:

- **Internal instrument identifier**: a stable key used across your entire system.
- **Human-readable symbol**: for inspection and reporting.
- **Venue-specific codes**: exchange symbols, local IDs, ISINs, CUSIPs, or other identifiers necessary to decode protocol messages.
- **Static attributes**: asset class, currency, tick size, lot size, corporate action flags, listings status, and so on.

Normalization in this context means resolving multiple external identifiers into a single internal ID and storing the mapping in one place. Feed handlers then only need to know how to look up that mapping; they do not hard-code instrument logic.

This design is particularly important when you store data in both kdb+ and ClickHouse:

- Kdb+ often acts as the fast-changing view of instrument state (for example, intraday listings changes).
- ClickHouse can store longer histories of instrument attributes for backtesting and historical analysis.

A shared internal identifier makes cross-database joins and comparisons straightforward.

kdb+ Table Design Considerations

Kdb+ is often used as the primary store for real-time and recent historical tick data. Normalization should therefore produce tables that play to kdb+'s strengths:

- **Partitioning by date**: most kdb+ installations partition trades and quotes by trading day.
- **Time-ordered inserts**: intraday tables are typically append-only in time order.
- **Columnar access patterns**: frequent queries filter by instrument and time, then aggregate numeric measures.

For normalized trades in kdb+, a common pattern is:

- Use a primary time column (e.g. a timestamp) that includes date and time.
- Store internal instrument ID as a symbol or integer that can be used as a key for joins.
- Keep venue, side, and condition flags as enumerated values that compress well.
- Avoid excessively wide rows in the hot path; consider splitting rarely used attributes into separate tables.

Normalization influences these choices directly. For example, if you decide at the mapping stage that every trade must carry both instrument and venue identifiers, you might keep those as separate columns in the main trade table or store venue in a dimension table and reference it by key, depending on your query patterns.

ClickHouse Table Design Considerations

ClickHouse shines as a scalable, distributed columnar store for large histories and heavier analytics workloads. The normalized events produced by your mapping layer can be streamed or batch-loaded into ClickHouse.

When designing ClickHouse schemas for normalized trades and quotes, consider:

- **Primary key and order by**: typically a combination of date, instrument, and time or sequence number, to support efficient range scans.
- **Partitioning**: often by date or month, aligning with trading calendars.
- **Data types**: using the most compact types that still preserve full precision, such as 64-bit integers with explicit scaling for prices when appropriate.
- **Encoding and compression**: leverage low-cardinality encodings for dimension fields (instrument IDs, venues, flags).

A well-thought-out normalization layer helps by:

- Ensuring that all events use the same internal instrument ID type, simplifying joins across tables.
- Constraining the variety of flags and condition values, making them highly compressible.
- Providing clean, typed fields, so ClickHouse does not have to parse text or handle irregular formats.

Because ClickHouse often ingests data in micro-batches, the mapping layer may also be responsible for grouping normalized events into chunks aligned with your partitioning strategy.

Keeping Mapping Logic a First-Class Artifact

One of the most common failure modes in market data platforms is allowing protocol-specific knowledge to leak into ad hoc research code, dashboards, or downstream microservices. This happens when the normalization mapping is not treated as a first-class artifact.

To avoid this, adopt the following practices:

- **Centralize mappings**: maintain one place where protocol fields are mapped to canonical columns, ideally in a readable, version-controlled form.

- **Document semantics**: for every canonical column, describe its meaning, units, and how it is derived from source fields.
- **Provide utilities**: expose small helper libraries or views that make it easy to work with normalized data without re-implementing mappings.
- **Test with real captures**: validate mapping changes against recorded sessions from each protocol version, and compare high-level metrics (e.g. daily volume) against reference data.

For example, a change in an exchange protocol that introduces a new trade condition flag should result in:

- A mapping update from the new raw value to your standardized condition column.
- A schema or enumeration update in kdb+ and ClickHouse if the set of possible values expands.
- Regression tests that confirm old queries behave as expected and that new conditions are visible where needed.

Versioning and Evolution

Finally, normalization is not a one-time task. Protocols change, business needs evolve, and new venues come online. Your schema and mapping must evolve without breaking existing data or queries.

Practical tools for this include:

- **Schema version columns**: attach a version identifier to each row or batch of rows, indicating which mapping version was applied.
- **Backward-compatible changes**: prefer adding new columns over renaming or removing existing ones. Use default values for old data where necessary.
- **Migration and backfill processes**: when you must change semantics, plan explicit backfill jobs that rewrite affected data, using deterministic replay from raw logs when possible.

Because both kdb+ and ClickHouse handle append-only workloads well, you can often stage new versions of tables side by side with old ones, then gradually migrate consumers.

Normalization and schema mapping turn the messy, heterogeneous world of market data protocols into a coherent internal language of trades, quotes, and instruments. By:

- defining a clear canonical event model,
- systematically mapping protocol fields into that model,
- designing schemas that fit the strengths of kdb+ and ClickHouse, and
- treating mappings as explicit, versioned artifacts,

you give your organization a stable foundation for analytics, backtesting, and real-time decision-making. In the next section, we will build on this foundation to reconstruct full limit order books from normalized incremental events, and to persist that state efficiently for both intraday and historical workloads.

3.3 Order Book Reconstruction

In the previous sections we moved from raw network packets to decoded protocol messages, and then from protocol-specific fields to a normalized event model: trades, quotes, and instruments with stable column names and consistent types.

We now focus on what is, for many strategies, the core deliverable of a market data platform: a reliable reconstruction of the limit order book over time.

Market feeds rarely send you full order books on every tick. Instead, they stream *incremental* updates: new orders arriving, existing orders being modified or canceled, and trades executing against resting liquidity. Your job is to:

- Consume normalized incremental events in strict order.

- Maintain an in-memory representation of the order book.
- Periodically materialize this state into snapshots suitable for storage in kdb+ and ClickHouse.
- Handle missing, duplicated, or out-of-order messages without silently corrupting the book.

This section explains how to design such a pipeline, starting from the event types exposed by your normalized schema and ending with concrete storage patterns.

From Normalized Events to Book Operations

Normalization has already reduced protocol diversity to a small set of canonical event types. For order book reconstruction, four are fundamental:

- **New** (or *Add*): a resting order is added to the book at a price level and size.
- **Modify** (or *Replace*): an existing order changes its price or remaining size.
- **Cancel**: an existing order is partially or fully removed without a trade.
- **Trade** (or *Execute*): one or more resting orders are matched and reduced, possibly removed.

Each normalized event should include, at a minimum:

- An instrument identifier and side (bid or ask).
- Either an order identifier (for order-level books) or a price level identifier (for price-level books).
- A size (quantity) and possibly a price change.
- A timestamp and sequence number that define event ordering within a venue and channel.

Your reconstruction engine transforms these events into changes in an internal data structure that represents the current book state. Conceptually, this is an event-sourced system: the state is the cumulative effect of all prior events.

Order-Level vs. Price-Level Books

Before designing the engine, you must decide whether you want to maintain an *order-level* book, a *price-level* book, or both.

Order-Level Book

An order-level book tracks each visible order separately:

- Keys: instrument_id, order_id.
- Attributes: side, price, remaining size, and possibly owner or participant identifiers, if exposed.

Pros:

- Maximum detail; you can derive queue position, order lifetimes, and fine-grained microstructure measures.
- Straightforward mapping from ITCH-style messages, which are already order-centric.

Cons:

- Higher memory footprint; many more rows than a price-level view.
- More work at query time if you frequently want aggregated price-level views.

Price-Level Book

A price-level book aggregates all resting orders at the same price and side into a single record:

- Keys: instrument_id, side, price.
- Attributes: total size, number of orders, and possibly additional aggregates such as number of participants.

Pros:

- Much smaller state; easy to store and query.
- Directly aligned with common analytics: top-of-book, depth ladders, spreads, and imbalance.

Cons:

- Loses individual order information; queue modeling must be approximate.
- Some exchange messages are order-centric and must be aggregated carefully.

In practice, a common design is:

- Maintain an order-level book in memory, driven directly by normalized events.
- Derive a price-level view on the fly or periodically, and store that in kdb+ and ClickHouse as snapshots.

We will describe reconstruction in order-level terms, with the understanding that price-level views are aggregations over that state.

Stateful Reconstruction Engine

The reconstruction engine is typically a long-running process per feed or per instrument group. It:

- Receives a strictly ordered stream of normalized events for a given instrument universe and venue.
- Applies those events to an in-memory data structure representing the order book.
- Emits derived outputs: snapshots, incremental book updates, and monitoring signals.

The in-memory state for each instrument usually consists of:

- Two sorted collections: one for bids (descending by price), one for asks (ascending by price).
- Within each price level, a collection of orders (often a queue) with remaining sizes and order IDs.
- Optional indexes: maps from order ID to its position in the book for fast lookup.

Each incoming event triggers a state transition. At a high level:

- **New**: insert an order at the appropriate side and price level; update aggregate sizes.
- **Modify**: find the existing order; adjust its price and/or size; maintain ordering and aggregates.
- **Cancel**: find the existing order; reduce or remove its size; adjust aggregates.
- **Trade**: find the resting order(s) being executed; reduce sizes; remove when fully filled; optionally emit trade records.

To make this more concrete, it helps to visualize the state transitions along a time axis.

This state-transition view emphasizes two aspects:

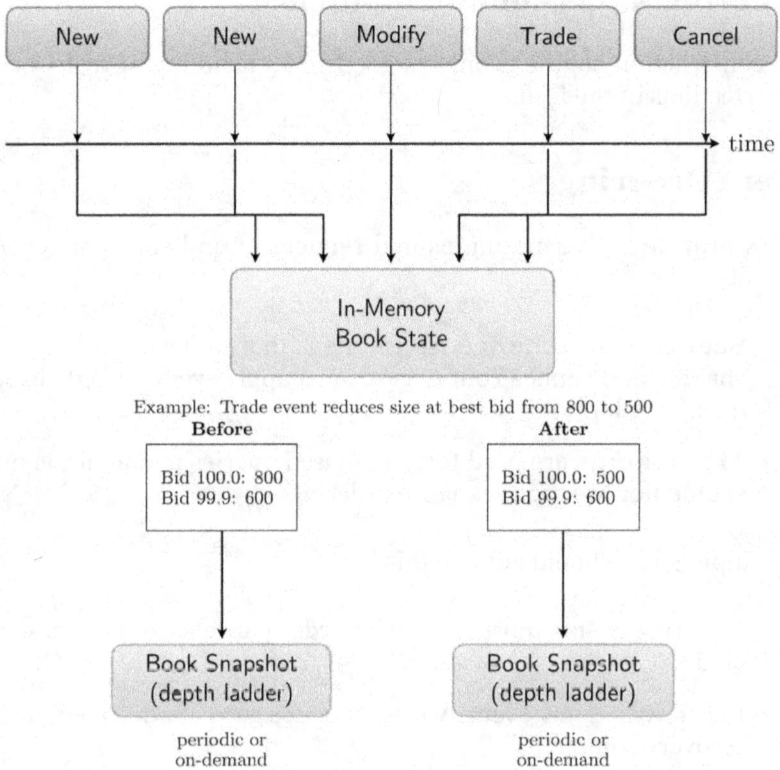

- A continuous stream of events drives a single evolving book state.

- Snapshots are secondary products, extracted at chosen points along the timeline.

With this picture in mind, we now address some practical challenges: ordering, handling missing events, and merging snapshot and incremental feeds.

Ordering, Gaps, and Idempotence

A reconstruction engine is only as good as its handling of real-world imperfections in the feed.

Event Ordering

Feeds provide both timestamps and sequence numbers. For reconstruction:

- **Sequence numbers** establish the authoritative order within a channel and venue. Your engine must apply events strictly in sequence order.
- **Timestamps** are used for time-based queries and analysis but should not override sequence ordering.

Your input stage should enforce this by:

- Buffering events until any out-of-order packets can be reassembled.
- Refusing to apply events when sequence gaps are detected, until recovery completes.

Gap Detection and Recovery

Gaps occur when one or more messages are lost. If you apply events beyond a gap, your book drifts away from the true state.

Typical strategies:

- **Short gaps**: request retransmissions from the exchange, then resume.
- **Long or unrecoverable gaps**: mark the book as stale and wait for a fresh snapshot or end-of-day reset.

Your engine should:

- Track the last applied sequence number per channel and instrument universe.
- Emit technical events into a monitoring or quality table when gaps are detected and when they are resolved.
- Avoid applying any incremental events that arrive *after* an unrecoverable gap until you have reset from a known good snapshot.

Idempotence and Duplicates

Duplicate events can appear due to retransmissions or upstream issues. To prevent double-application:

- Use the combination of channel ID and sequence number as a unique key for events.
- Keep a small window of recently applied sequence numbers per channel; ignore exact duplicates.

Idempotent processing is also important when replaying data from logs into a reconstruction engine for backfill or testing. You want to guarantee that reprocessing the same raw events yields the same sequence of book states.

Snapshots and Incremental Feeds

Many exchanges offer both:

- **Incremental feeds**: continuous streams of adds, modifies, cancels, and trades.
- **Snapshot feeds**: full-depth pictures of the book at a point in time, often on request or at a scheduled cadence.

Your reconstruction pipeline must define how these interact.

Cold Start and Periodic Resync

When the engine starts, or after a major gap, you need an initial state:

- Request or load a full snapshot of the current book state.
- Determine the sequence number or timestamp associated with that snapshot.
- Begin applying incremental events from just after that point.

Periodic resync strategies include:

- **Fixed-interval snapshots**: for example, take a fresh full-depth snapshot every few minutes and discard events older than a certain horizon in memory.
- **Event-count-based**: trigger snapshots every N_{iter} events or after a certain volume of updates.

The choice depends on the trade-off between CPU and memory usage, restart times, and your need for granular history.

Rolling Snapshots

Instead of treating snapshots as rare, heavy operations, you can think of them as a continuous process:

- Maintain the in-memory book as usual.
- On a separate cadence, serialize the current state of selected price levels or the entire book into a snapshot record and write it to kdb+ or ClickHouse.

For example:

- Every second, persist the top 10 levels on each side for active instruments.

- Every minute, persist deeper ladders or full depth for a narrower universe.

In kdb+, these snapshots may land in intraday tables partitioned by time and instrument. In ClickHouse, they might be batch-inserted as micro-batches, keyed by timestamp and instrument, providing an efficient base for historical depth analysis.

Persisting Book State in kdb+ and ClickHouse

Once you have a reliable in-memory reconstruction, you must decide what to store and how.

Tick-Level vs. Snapshot-Level Storage

There are two complementary approaches:

- **Tick-level storage**: store every normalized event (add, modify, cancel, trade) in an event table. This is compact and lossless with respect to the feed; you can always replay to reconstruct the book.
- **Snapshot-level storage**: store periodic snapshots of the book (for example, top 10 levels per side). This is easier to query directly for many analytics without replay.

A robust system does both:

- The tick table is the canonical source of truth for deterministic replay and fine-grained microstructure research.
- The snapshot tables provide direct access for common queries (spreads, depth, imbalance) without re-running the engine.

kdb+ Patterns

In kdb+, a typical design might be:

- **Event table**: partitioned by date, keyed by instrument and maybe by venue; columns include sequence number, event type, side, price, size, and identifiers.
- **Snapshot table**: partitioned by date and time bucket (for example, per second), keyed by instrument and depth level; columns include bid/ask prices and sizes at each level.

Because kdb+ excels at handling time-ordered append-only data, you can:

- Append normalized events in real time as they arrive.
- Append snapshots at regular intervals, possibly generated by the same process that maintains the in-memory book.

Resilience comes from the ability to rebuild snapshot tables from event tables, using deterministic replay, when you change your snapshot design or discover a bug.

ClickHouse Patterns

In ClickHouse, you emphasize scalability and efficient historical queries:

- **Event table**: implemented as a MergeTree-derived engine, partitioned by date and sharded by instrument range; primary key might be (date, instrument, sequence number).
- **Snapshot table**: similar partitioning, with keys (date, instrument, snapshot_time, level, side).

ClickHouse's strengths include:

- Fast scans over large histories to compute, for example, the distribution of spreads over months.
- On-the-fly aggregation of snapshots to coarser intervals (minute, hour).

A common approach is:

- Stream normalized events to ClickHouse either directly from the feed handler or via an intermediate log system.
- Derive and materialize snapshot tables using background jobs or materialized views that consume the event table.

Because ClickHouse is not usually in the ultra-low-latency path, you can afford a small delay between live events and stored snapshots.

Debuggability and Auditability

Reconstructing the order book is operationally sensitive. Bugs can be subtle and expensive, especially if models or risk systems rely on incorrect book states.

You improve debuggability and auditability by:

- **Logging technical events**: track when snapshots are taken, when gaps are detected, when recoveries start and end, and when sequence anomalies occur.
- **Capturing inputs**: store lossless raw or decoded events alongside normalized ones; this allows cross-checking against exchange reference data.
- **Instrument-level diagnostics**: maintain simple per-instrument counters (number of adds, cancels, trades, current depth) that can be monitored for anomalies.

When a discrepancy is reported (for example, your recorded best bid does not match exchange records at a given time), you should be able to:

- Query kdb+ or ClickHouse for the raw events for that instrument and time window.
- Replay those events through the reconstruction logic in a controlled test environment.

- Inspect intermediate states and snapshots to isolate the cause.

This workflow depends on the deterministic nature of your reconstruction engine and the completeness of your stored events.

Handling Tricky Protocol Cases

Not all feeds expose full order IDs or clean event semantics. Some challenges include:

- **Price-level-only feeds**: some protocols only give you aggregate changes at price levels, without individual order IDs. In that case, your state is inherently price-level, and you must infer order-level behavior only probabilistically.
- **Implied orders and synthetic liquidity**: in some derivatives markets, implied orders (constructed from spreads and legs) may appear and disappear based on calculations rather than explicit messages. Your book representation should either model these explicitly or clearly distinguish them from "real" orders.
- **Hidden and iceberg orders**: visible book state is only a partial view of true liquidity. Your engine should not attempt to guess hidden volume; instead, represent what is explicitly in the feed and allow models to incorporate execution outcomes.

Normalization helps by standardizing how you represent these nuances:

- Use flags or condition fields to indicate implied, synthetic, or hidden-related events when the protocol exposes them.
- Keep the internal semantics of book state tightly bound to what the feed guarantees, not what you wish it provided.

Order book reconstruction turns a normalized stream of incremental events into a living, evolving view of market liquidity. A robust design:

- Defines clear event types (new, modify, cancel, trade) at the normalized layer.
- Maintains an in-memory order-level or price-level book per instrument and venue.
- Handles sequence ordering, gaps, and duplicates carefully to avoid silent drift.
- Integrates snapshot and incremental feeds to support cold start and periodic resynchronization.
- Persists both tick-level events and snapshot-level views into kdb+ and ClickHouse, enabling replay, backtesting, and efficient analytics.
- Treats reconstruction logic as a deterministic, testable component with strong observability.

With this machinery in place, you can trust that the depth-of-book you query from your databases is a faithful representation of what the exchange actually published. In the next section we will tackle another subtle dimension: aligning time and trading sessions across venues so that these reconstructed books can be compared and analyzed consistently in multi-venue and multi-asset workflows.

3.4 Time Alignment and Session Handling

Up to this point, we have focused on *what* happens in the market: protocol messages, normalized events, and reconstructed order books. In this section we address an equally important question: *when* things happen, and how to make "when" consistent across venues, instruments, and databases.

Time sounds simple–it is just a timestamp column–but, in real pipelines, it is one of the main sources of subtle errors. Misaligned clocks, daylight saving transitions, irregular sessions, and different time conventions across venues can all lead to incorrect comparisons and misleading analytics if they are not handled explicitly.

Our goal here is to design a time representation and session model that:

- allows you to merge events from multiple venues in a meaningful order,
- survives daylight saving changes and calendar quirks,
- supports common queries such as "first five minutes after the open" or "closing auction" without custom logic in every query, and
- fits naturally with kdb+ and ClickHouse partitioning and indexing.

Timestamps: Exchange Time vs. Receipt Time

The first conceptual distinction to make is between *exchange timestamps* and *receipt timestamps.*

Exchange Timestamps

An exchange timestamp is attached to an event by the matching engine or the market data system at the venue. It is the best available record of when, according to the exchange's own clock, an order was added, canceled, or traded.

Characteristics:

- Often very fine-grained (microsecond or nanosecond resolution).
- Usually expressed in the exchange's local time zone, but sometimes already in UTC.
- Shared across all subscribers to that feed.

Receipt Timestamps

A receipt timestamp is attached by your own systems when a packet or message arrives at your network interface or feed handler.

Characteristics:

- Captured by your hardware timestamps or software clock.
- Reflects network delays, queuing, and internal processing time.
- Can differ slightly between systems and colos, even for the same message.

Both are valuable:

- Exchange timestamps are ideal for reconstructing the sequence of market events and comparing behavior across participants.
- Receipt timestamps are essential for measuring your own latency and diagnosing infrastructure issues.

In your normalized schema, you should therefore plan for *at least two* time columns:

- A canonical ts_exchange, representing the exchange's view of time, converted to a common representation (for example, UTC with sub-millisecond resolution).
- A ts_receipt, representing when you observed the event.

Downstream code can then be explicit about which notion of time it uses.

Time Zones and UTC as the Common Denominator

Each venue operates in a particular local time zone, often with its own daylight saving rules. For storage and cross-venue comparisons, it is almost always best to convert all timestamps to a single time scale—typically UTC—as early as possible in the pipeline.

Why Store in UTC?

Storing in UTC offers several advantages:

- It removes ambiguity around daylight saving changes: every instant in time maps to a unique UTC value.

- It simplifies cross-venue joins: events from New York, London, and Tokyo can be aligned on a single timeline.
- It provides a stable basis for partitioning and ordering in kdb+ and ClickHouse.

Venue-local times are still important—for example, for reporting to clients in local time—but they can be derived at query time by formatting UTC according to the relevant time zone rules.

Converting Exchange Time to UTC

When decoding protocol messages, you must be precise about:

- The time zone and calendar the exchange uses for its timestamps.
- The units (seconds, milliseconds, microseconds, nanoseconds) and any epoch (for example, seconds since midnight, nanoseconds since some fixed date).

Your feed handler or normalization layer should:

- Parse the raw exchange timestamp and convert it to a full-date UTC timestamp.
- Preserve the original raw value in a technical column if you anticipate needing to debug conversions later.

The same applies to receipt timestamps: synchronize your systems' clocks carefully, ideally via a high-quality time source, and convert to UTC consistently.

Ordering Events Across Venues

Once times are in UTC, it is tempting to simply sort by timestamp and declare victory. Unfortunately, there are edge cases:

- Different venues may timestamp at slightly different layers of their internal pipeline.

- Clocks can be off by microseconds or more.
- Two or more events may share exactly the same exchange timestamp.

For *single-venue* analysis, exchange sequence numbers define ordering within a channel. For *cross-venue* analysis, there is no perfect total order that respects all venues' sequences and timestamps, but we can get close.

A practical approach:

- Use **venue, channel, and sequence number** to define ordering within each feed.
- Use **UTC exchange timestamp** as the primary coordinate for aligning feeds on a common axis.
- Break ties deterministically when timestamps are identical, using a stable tie-breaker such as venue ID or an internal sequence.

The key idea is that alignment for analytics usually does not require a strict global order of individual ticks; rather, it requires that events are attributed to the correct time intervals and sessions in a consistent way.

Trading Sessions and Calendars

Time alignment becomes especially delicate around session boundaries. Each venue has:

- **Regular trading hours**: the main continuous trading session.
- **Pre-market and post-market sessions**: often with different rules or lower liquidity.
- **Auctions**: opening, closing, and intraday auctions, sometimes overlapping with continuous trading.
- **Holidays and half-days**: full closures or shortened sessions.

- **Unscheduled events**: halts, circuit breakers, technical outages.

A *trading calendar* describes all of this for a particular venue: which dates are trading days, which hours are regular trading, which are pre/-post, and which exceptions apply.

To build robust pipelines, you should:

- Maintain explicit trading calendars per venue (and sometimes per instrument group).
- Use these calendars at ingestion time to tag each event with a *session identifier*.

Session Keys

A session key is a label that groups events that belong to the same logical trading session, for example:

- session_date: the date associated with the session in the venue's local calendar.
- session_type: pre-market, regular, post-market, auction, etc.
- session_id: a combined key such as "venue + session_date + session_type".

Attaching these keys early has important benefits:

- Queries like "first five minutes after the open" can simply filter on session_type = regular and a small offset after the session start, instead of re-deriving the open time every time.
- Cross-venue comparisons (for example, "closing auction across venues") can use session keys rather than hard-coded clocks.

Daylight Saving Time and Edge Cases

Daylight saving time (DST) introduces two classic problems:

- **Spring forward**: an hour is skipped; local times jump forward.
- **Fall back**: an hour is repeated; local times between, say, 1:00 and 2:00 appear twice.

If you rely on naive local timestamps, you can:

- Lose events that fall into the "skipped" period.
- Misorder events or double-count periods that occur twice.

Using UTC for storage largely avoids these issues: UTC does not have DST jumps. However, session boundaries are usually defined in local time, so you still must be explicit about:

- How local session times map to UTC on DST transition days.
- Whether the exchange changes its session hours or simply shifts them relative to UTC.

This is another reason to treat trading calendars as code or configuration rather than as loose documentation. You should:

- Encode DST rules and exceptions in your calendar definitions.
- Precompute, for each session, the UTC start and end times.
- Use those precomputed ranges to tag and partition events.

Session-Aware Partitioning and Storage

Both kdb+ and ClickHouse benefit from thoughtful partitioning. So far we have talked primarily about partitioning by date. When you introduce sessions, you gain another useful organizing principle.

In kdb+

In kdb+, a common pattern is:

- Partition by `date` (often aligned with the local session date of the primary venue).

- Within each partition, use a time or timestamp column for ordering.

To incorporate sessions:

- Ensure that partition dates correspond to session dates, not necessarily to UTC dates, for markets that trade overnight relative to UTC.
- Add a session_id or session_type column to your normalized tables.
- Provide helper views or tables that express session-relative time, such as seconds since session open.

This makes queries such as "all trades in the first ten minutes of the regular session over the last six months" both simple to write and efficient to run.

In ClickHouse

ClickHouse often uses MergeTree tables with partitions by day or month and primary keys that include date, instrument, and a time or sequence field.

To align this with sessions:

- Partition by a session_date column that reflects the venue's trading day, particularly for markets that straddle UTC midnight.
- Include session_id or session_type in your primary key or as a low-cardinality dimension column.
- Create materialized views that precompute session-relative aggregates, such as per-session volume profiles or VWAPs.

The important design choice is that session information becomes a first-class dimension in your schema, not something re-derived on the fly from hard-coded time ranges in queries.

Aligning Multiple Venues

With timestamps in UTC and sessions explicitly labeled, you can now tackle multi-venue alignment.

Common Use Cases

Examples include:

- Comparing spreads and depth between primary and alternative trading venues at the same moment.
- Studying lead-lag relationships: does venue A tend to move slightly before venue B?
- Aggregating volume across venues by session or time-of-day bucket.

To support these, design your schemas and pipelines so that:

- All venues share a common ts_exchange_utc column for alignment in time.
- A unified instrument identifier links equivalent instruments across venues.
- Venue identifiers are consistent and low-cardinality, enabling efficient grouping.

Watermarking and Late Data

In streaming systems, late or out-of-order data can complicate alignment. For instance, one venue's feed might temporarily lag another. To manage this:

- Use per-venue *watermarks*: a notion of "we have seen all data up to time T" for a given venue.
- For cross-venue computations (for example, joining books at time T), choose a cutoff where all relevant venues' watermarks have passed T.

In kdb+, this may correspond to waiting for a certain delay before treating recent data as stable. In ClickHouse, it may mean running periodic batch jobs that aggregate only up to the latest safe watermark across sources.

Session-Relative Time and Common Queries

Many analytics are naturally expressed relative to session boundaries rather than in absolute time. Typical examples:

- "First five minutes after the open."
- "Last ten minutes before the close."
- "Volume profile across the regular session, normalized to [0, 1] in session progress."

You can support such queries efficiently by precomputing:

- **Session-relative timestamps**: for each event, the offset from session start (for example, in seconds).
- **Session progress**: the fraction of the session elapsed at the event time.

These derived columns can be added during normalization or as lightweight transformations before writing into kdb+ and ClickHouse. Once they exist, queries become much simpler and more uniform across venues:

- Filter on session_type = 'regular' and session_offset in a fixed range.
- Group by session_progress buckets to compare volume curves day over day.

Handling Irregular Sessions and Halts

Not all sessions are regular and predictable. Markets may:

- Open late or close early due to technical issues.
- Enter trading halts for individual instruments or the whole market.
- Trigger circuit breakers that pause or limit trading.

A robust design incorporates such irregularities into the session model:

- For planned changes (half-days, special holidays), encode them explicitly in the trading calendar.
- For unplanned events (halts, outages), capture them as *session events* in a dedicated table, with start and end times and affected instruments or venues.

During normalization or downstream processing, you can then:

- Annotate events that fall inside a halt or outage window with special flags.
- Exclude or treat differently data around these periods when computing statistics.

From a storage perspective, both kdb+ and ClickHouse can hold a "session events" table that is joined or referenced in analytics. This makes irregularities visible and queryable rather than hidden in external logs.

Putting It All Together

Time alignment and session handling are cross-cutting concerns that influence every part of the market data pipeline:

- **At the protocol and normalization layer**, you parse raw timestamps, convert them to UTC, and attach venue-aware session keys.

- **In the reconstruction engine**, you rely on timestamps and sequence numbers to maintain correct ordering and to decide when sessions start and end.
- **In kdb+ and ClickHouse**, you partition and index by dates and sessions, store both exchange and receipt times, and precompute session-relative derivatives where useful.
- **In downstream models and analytics**, you use these standardized time and session fields to write simple, robust queries that compare like with like across venues and calendars.

By treating time and sessions as explicit design elements rather than afterthoughts, you greatly reduce the risk of silent misalignments and inconsistent analytics. The remaining sections of this chapter will leverage these concepts when we discuss data quality, validation, replay, and streaming ETL patterns: all of them depend on a clear, consistent notion of "when" things happened in the market.

3.5 Data Quality, Validation, and Replay

By this point in the chapter, we have defined how raw packets become decoded protocol messages, how those messages are normalized into a coherent schema, and how we reconstruct order books over time with careful attention to time alignment and sessions. In this section we turn to a different, but equally critical, question:

How do we know we can trust the data we have stored, today and ten years from now?

High-performance stores like kdb+ and ClickHouse can handle enormous volumes of market data. But scale without discipline can leave you with fast queries over inaccurate data. The purpose of this section is to design the controls and feedback loops that turn a best-effort pipeline into an auditable system:

- gap detection and repair,
- deduplication and idempotent processing, and

- deterministic replay from raw inputs to downstream tables.

Together, these capabilities let you detect problems early, correct them safely, and credibly answer questions like "What did we know at that time?" and "If we change our processing logic, what would have happened?"

Common Data Quality Problems in Market Feeds

Before designing controls, it helps to name the failure modes you are defending against. In market data pipelines, the most common issues are:

- **Dropped messages** Packets or messages never arrive due to network loss, hardware faults, or feed handler issues.
- **Duplicates** The same message is delivered multiple times, for example due to retransmissions.
- **Out-of-order delivery** Messages arrive in a different order than they were sent, especially over multicast or when multiple paths are involved.
- **Corrupted fields** Parts of a message are malformed or fail validation (for example, a negative size or impossible timestamp).
- **Protocol mismatches** The handler assumes one version of the protocol while the exchange is sending another, leading to misinterpreted fields.
- **Clock errors** Bad timestamps, from either the exchange or your own systems, that distort ordering or session assignment.

Some of these are detected at the protocol level (for example, checksums, sequence numbers). Others only show up when you look at the data in aggregate (for example, daily volume that is clearly too low).

The controls we discuss next operate at three layers:

- *Online*, in the feed handler and reconstruction engine.

- *Near-line*, in the immediate ingestion and normalization stages into kdb+ and ClickHouse.
- *Offline*, in batch audits and cross-checks over historical data.

Gap Detection and Monitoring

Sequence numbers and channel IDs are your primary tools for detecting dropped or out-of-order messages.

Per-Channel Sequence Tracking

For each venue and channel, maintain state that records:

- last successfully applied sequence number,
- expected next sequence number, and
- status flags (healthy, gap_suspected, recovering, stalled).

Whenever a new message arrives:

- If its sequence number equals the expected next, apply it and increment the expected value.
- If it is higher than expected, you have a gap: record the missing range and trigger recovery logic.
- If it is lower than or equal to the last applied, treat it as a duplicate or out-of-order and handle accordingly.

This logic lives in the feed handler or just above it, but its decisions should be *recorded* in your data stores. A small kdb+ table or ClickHouse log that tracks per-channel sequence state over time becomes invaluable for operational visibility and historical audits.

Gap Recovery Strategies

Gap recovery depends on what the exchange offers:

- **Resend / replay channels**: you can request the missing range and then apply it in order.
- **Snapshot feeds**: you can discard events after the gap, load a fresh snapshot, and resume from the associated sequence number or timestamp.
- **No recovery**: for some feeds, you may have to accept occasional irrecoverable gaps and mark the data accordingly.

In all cases:

- Mark gaps as events in their own right: record start time, end time, affected channels and instruments, and how they were resolved.
- Annotate the affected period in downstream tables, for example with a data-quality flag at the session or day level.

Doing this systematically allows you, months later, to answer questions such as "Why is depth missing for this symbol at 10:03:15?" without forensic guesswork.

Deduplication and Idempotent Processing

Once you are aware of gaps, the next challenge is duplicates. Many infrastructure layers (retransmission, at-least-once messaging, replay) can introduce duplicate messages. Your processing should be *idempotent*: applying the same input twice should not change the outcome.

Identifying Duplicates

The most robust way to identify duplicates is to define a unique key per event that is stable across deliveries. Common components include:

- venue or source ID,
- feed or channel ID,
- sequence number, and
- possibly a per-session or per-day identifier if sequence numbers reset.

When writing normalized events into kdb+ or ClickHouse:

- Ensure this key is either enforced as unique or checked in ingest logic.
- Put in place cheap lookups (for example, in-memory caches for the most recent keys) for online deduplication.

In some cases, the protocol includes an explicit unique ID for certain message types (for example, trade IDs). These can be added as additional safeguards, but sequence-based keys remain the basic layer.

Idempotence by Design

Beyond detecting duplicates, design pipeline stages so that they are naturally idempotent. Examples:

- **Append-only writes**: treat normalized event tables as append-only logs keyed by (session, channel, sequence). Ignore attempts to append a row with a key that already exists.
- **Deterministic transformations**: ensure that any aggregation or enrichment of events depends only on event content and stable reference data, not on external mutable state.
- **Side-effect isolation**: keep side effects (alerts, downstream triggers) separate from core data writes so they can be controlled or deduplicated independently.

The goal is that if, for any reason, you rerun part of the ingestion process over the same raw input, the resulting normalized tables in kdb+ and ClickHouse remain identical.

Schema Validation and Business-Rule Checks

Even if every message arrives exactly once and in the right order, its content may still be wrong or inconsistent. Two complementary types of validation help catch this:

- **Schema validation**: basic structural checks on types, ranges, and required fields.
- **Business-rule validation**: higher-level checks based on market logic or historical behavior.

Schema Validation

When mapping from protocol fields to normalized columns, verify that:

- required fields are present and non-null,
- numeric values fall within reasonable ranges (for example, prices are positive, sizes are non-negative),
- enumerated fields take on allowed values only.

Messages that fail schema validation should not silently disappear. Instead:

- Route them to a "quarantine" or "rejects" table with a reason code.
- Count them and surface metrics per feed and per instrument.

This allows you to distinguish between irrecoverable protocol issues (for example, upstream bugs) and internal mapping mistakes.

Business-Rule Validation

Business-rule checks go beyond formal protocol correctness. Examples:

- A trade price should not be wildly outside recent best bid/offer for the same instrument, unless flagged as a special type (e.g. off-book, auction).
- A best bid should not exceed the best ask on a lit market (except within well-understood edge cases).
- Daily aggregated volume from your tick data should roughly match independent reference sources.

These checks can be run:

- **Online**, in a simplified form, to catch gross anomalies quickly (for example, negative prices).
- **Offline**, in richer audits, comparing your stored data against alternative sources or summaries.

Violations should generate alerts and result in investigations, but they should also be logged in machine-readable form so you can track trends and spot systemic issues.

Cross-Venue and Cross-Source Sanity Checks

Some of the strongest validation signals come from *comparing* data across venues or sources.

Examples:

- If you receive trades for the same instrument from multiple venues, aggregated daily volume and notional should be consistent with known benchmarks.
- Reference data (such as instrument attributes) obtained from multiple providers can be cross-checked for mismatches.
- Derived measures like closing prices can be compared against official close or benchmark values.

Implementing these checks typically involves:

- Building summary tables in kdb+ or ClickHouse (for example, daily per-instrument aggregates).
- Joining these against external benchmark datasets.
- Logging discrepancies above a threshold and, where appropriate, flagging affected periods or instruments.

This cross-validation strengthens confidence that your feed handlers, normalization logic, and reconstruction engines are functioning correctly across the board, not only in unit-level tests.

Deterministic Replay: Concept and Requirements

Detection is only half of data quality; the other half is *correction*. To fix historical data, or to reprocess it with new business logic, you need deterministic replay: the ability to rerun the pipeline from a chosen point in time and obtain the same results every time.

Conceptually, think of your pipeline as a function:

> raw events + configuration → normalized and derived tables

Deterministic replay means that, given the same raw events and configuration, the function yields the *same* outputs.

To achieve this in practice, you need:

- **A durable log of inputs**: raw protocol messages or fully decoded-but-unmapped events.
- **A frozen mapping and configuration snapshot**: the exact versions of code and configuration used at the time.
- **An execution mode that is side-effect free**: replay should not double-trigger alerts or overwrite production data unless explicitly directed.

Capturing Raw and Normalized Streams

The first prerequisite is capturing inputs in a replayable form.

Raw Protocol Capture

For each feed, consider storing:

- Either the original binary messages (for example, FAST or ITCH packets) along with sufficient metadata (time, channel, sequence, protocol version), or
- A fully decoded but still protocol-shaped representation (for example, all fields extracted but not yet normalized).

Raw captures are typically stored outside the hot query path, for example:

- As compressed files or object storage blobs, partitioned by date and channel.
- With small index tables in kdb+ or ClickHouse that point into those blobs for discovery.

Normalized Streams

In addition to raw captures, your normalized event tables in kdb+ and ClickHouse can also act as a source for many replay scenarios, as long as you have preserved:

- all fields necessary for downstream computations, and
- ordering metadata (exchange time, sequence numbers, channel IDs).

When heavier changes are needed (for example, new decoding logic for a protocol bug), you will replay from raw. When changes only touch later pipeline steps (for example, new aggregation definitions), you can replay from normalized events.

Replay Harness and Modes

A replay harness is a controlled environment where you feed historical data through your processing logic. It can operate at multiple levels:

- **Unit-level replay** Reprocessing a small set of messages to test a mapping or reconstruction change.
- **Instrument- or day-level replay** Rebuilding all trades and books for a given instrument over one day.
- **System-level replay** Recomputing large portions of the historical database after a major change.

Key design points:

- **Isolation**: replay writes go to separate kdb+ partitions or ClickHouse tables (for example, with a run identifier), so they do not disturb production data.
- **Configurability**: you can specify which date ranges, instruments, and venues to replay, and which version of mapping or reconstruction logic to use.
- **Comparison**: tools to compare old and new outputs at both the row level (for small tests) and the aggregate level (for large replays).

Once you are satisfied with a replay run, you can:

- Promote the new data to production tables, via renames or controlled merges.
- Archive or delete superseded versions, keeping enough lineage information to explain what changed and why.

Exactly-Once Semantics at the Application Level

Infrastructure like message brokers, disks, and networks generally provide at-least-once or at-most-once guarantees. True exactly-once delivery is hard at the system level, but you can approximate *exactly-once processing* at the application level with the techniques discussed:

- Use unique keys (venue, channel, sequence) to detect duplicates.
- Make writes idempotent: multiple attempts to apply the same event are harmless.
- Keep processing deterministic: given the same set of events, results are the same.

For storage engines:

- In kdb+, append-only logs and careful keying can ensure that applying a batch twice does not double count.
- In ClickHouse, MergeTree tables and deduplication mechanisms (for example, replacing or collapsing variants, or external deduplication at ingest time) can help you enforce uniqueness on your chosen keys.

The objective is not to make duplicates impossible, but to make them *visible* and *harmless*.

Feedback Loops and Governance

Controls are only effective if they are part of a feedback loop: they must inform people and processes that can act on them.

Practical steps include:

- **Operational dashboards**: summarize gap events, validation failures, and unusual patterns by feed and day.
- **Data quality scores**: assign quantitative scores to days or sessions (for example, fraction of data passing all checks) and store them alongside market data for query filtering.
- **Change management**: whenever you roll out new mapping or reconstruction logic, couple it with a playback test, a data quality comparison, and a documented decision.

From a governance standpoint, it is valuable to be able to answer:

- What version of the pipeline created this data?
- What known issues or gaps affect this period?
- How and when was this data last reprocessed?

Maintaining small "lineage" or "run metadata" tables in kdb+ and ClickHouse, keyed by date ranges and output tables, gives concrete structure to these answers.

Data quality is not an afterthought to be bolted on once the pipeline "works." In a market data context, it is woven through every layer:

- Sequence tracking and gap detection ensure that your reconstructed books never drift silently from the exchange's published state.
- Deduplication and idempotent processing make ingestion robust to real-world infrastructure behavior.
- Schema and business-rule validation catch both structural and economic anomalies in incoming data.
- Cross-venue and cross-source checks provide external reference points for confidence.
- Deterministic replay, backed by durable raw and normalized logs, allows you to correct historical issues and evolve your pipeline safely.

With these controls and feedback loops in place, your kdb+ and ClickHouse systems become not just fast, but *trustworthy* over the long life of a trading business. In the final section of this chapter, we will connect these ideas into streaming ETL patterns, showing how to build end-to-end architectures that are both low-latency and resilient, from exchange feeds all the way to analysis-ready tables.

3.6 Streaming ETL Patterns

We now have all the building blocks of a robust market data platform:

- Protocol-aware feed handlers that understand FIX, FAST, ITCH and friends.
- A normalization layer that maps heterogeneous messages into a canonical event model.
- Order book reconstruction engines that turn incremental updates into consistent depth-of-book views.
- Time and session handling that make events comparable across venues.
- Data quality controls and deterministic replay that keep the history trustworthy.

In this final section of the chapter we focus on *how* to wire these components together in a continuous, low-latency way. The key idea is to treat the data pipeline as a series of streaming transformations rather than a sequence of isolated batch jobs.

We will:

- Introduce Kafka and Redpanda as the backbone of log-based ingestion.
- Describe common streaming ETL patterns for market data.
- Show how materialized views and stateful operators fit into the picture.
- Explain how to land these streams into kdb+ and ClickHouse while preserving ordering and replayability.
- Assemble a reference architecture that ties together all previous concepts.

Log-Based Ingestion with Kafka and Redpanda

At the heart of modern streaming architectures is a distributed log: an append-only sequence of records partitioned and replicated across a cluster. Kafka and Redpanda are widely used implementations of this idea.

You can think of the log as the *spine* of your market data system:

- Feed handlers publish decoded and normalized events into topics.
- Multiple consumers (order book builders, analytics pipelines, alerting systems) subscribe and process the same events at their own pace.
- The log retains data for some window, allowing replays and backfills.

This decouples ingestion from downstream processing:

- Feed handlers focus on correctness and low latency in decoding and normalization.
- Downstream consumers can be scaled, upgraded, or replayed independently, as long as they respect ordering guarantees within partitions.

Partitioning Strategies for Market Feeds

Choosing partition keys is central. For market data, two natural dimensions are:

- **Instrument**: all events for an instrument are in the same partition.
- **Venue or channel**: all events for a feed channel are in the same partition.

Trade-offs:

- Partitioning by *instrument* makes it easy to build per-instrument stateful consumers (for example, order book reconstruction) without cross-partition coordination. However, you may end up with many partitions and uneven load across them, as some instruments are much more active than others.

- Partitioning by *channel* mirrors the exchange feed structure and typically aligns with sequence numbers. This works well if your stateful consumers are also organized by channel, but they must then internally fan out by instrument.

Whichever strategy you choose, the invariant should be:

> All events that need to be processed in a strict order by a given consumer should land in the same partition.

This is critical for order book reconstruction, time-series aggregations, and exactly-once semantics at the application level.

Topic Design

It is often useful to split the pipeline into several topics that reflect logical stages, for example:

- **raw_protocol**: optional, containing decoded but not yet normalized events.
- **md_normalized**: canonical trades, quotes, and control events.
- **md_book_updates**: derived book deltas or snapshots.
- **md_bars_and_features**: higher-level aggregates such as bars and basic features.

This layered design keeps each topic relatively stable in schema and semantics, and allows consumers to attach at the appropriate level of abstraction.

Streaming ETL: From Normalized Events to Analytics-Ready Data

Streaming ETL (Extract-Transform-Load) is simply ETL done continuously instead of in large, infrequent batches. In our context:

- **Extract** happens when feed handlers put messages onto Kafka/Redpanda topics.
- **Transform** happens in consumers that normalize, enrich, aggregate, or reconstruct state.
- **Load** happens when results are written into kdb+ and ClickHouse tables.

We can identify several reusable patterns.

Pattern 1: Protocol-Specific Handlers to Normalized Topics

The first stage is the familiar one:

- Protocol-specific feed handlers read from network sockets.
- They decode FIX, FAST, ITCH, or other formats.
- They apply normalization and schema mapping to produce canonical events.
- They publish those events to a md_normalized topic.

This stage is where sequence numbers, timestamps, and basic validation are attached. Events should carry all metadata required for downstream ordering and replay: venue, channel, sequence, exchange and receipt timestamps, and session keys.

Pattern 2: Per-Instrument Streams for Order Book Reconstruction

Next, specialized consumers subscribe to normalized events and build order books:

- Each consumer instance is responsible for a subset of instruments or channels, aligned with topic partitioning.

- The consumer runs the order book reconstruction logic from the previous section: applying new, modify, cancel, and trade events to maintain in-memory book state.
- It emits:
  - incremental book deltas (for example, changes at the top 10 levels), and/or
  - periodic full or partial snapshots.

These outputs can be written to a md_book_updates topic or directly to kdb+ and ClickHouse, depending on latency requirements and degree of decoupling you want.

Pattern 3: Streaming Aggregation into Bars and Features

Another set of consumers focuses on aggregations:

- Subscribe to md_normalized trades and book updates.
- Maintain rolling windows per instrument and session: for example, 1-second, 5-second, or 1-minute windows.
- Emit bars (open, high, low, close, volume), microstructure metrics (spread, depth, imbalance), and simple features (returns, volatility proxies).

These consumers are inherently stateful: they maintain per-instrument, per-window accumulators. This is a natural place to use stateful user-defined functions (UDFs) or dedicated stream processing frameworks, but the same principles apply if you implement them directly on top of Kafka/Redpanda consumers.

Pattern 4: Quality and Monitoring Streams

Finally, quality and monitoring data - gaps, validation errors, latency measurements - can themselves be treated as streaming outputs:

- Feed handlers and reconstruction engines publish quality events into dedicated topics.
- Consumers aggregate these into dashboards, alerting systems, and quality summary tables in ClickHouse or kdb+.

This closes the feedback loop described in the previous section: the pipeline not only moves data, it continuously reports on its own health.

Materialized Views vs. Stateful Operators

When designing streaming ETL, you have two broad styles of implementation:

- **Materialized views**, where you define transformations declaratively and let a system maintain the results as new data arrives.
- **Stateful operators**, where you write code that explicitly manages per-key state and updates it as events flow through.

Both have roles to play in market data pipelines.

Materialized Views

A materialized view is a continuously updated table derived from another table or stream. In the streaming context, it might be:

- A view of the latest top-of-book per instrument.
- A view of the last trade per instrument and venue.
- A view of per-minute bars, updated as new ticks arrive.

Advantages:

- Simple to specify: you describe the desired result, not the update mechanics.

- Easy to query: the materialized view is just a table in kdb+ or ClickHouse.
- Often efficient: underlying systems optimize incremental maintenance.

In ClickHouse, for instance, materialized views can subscribe to input tables and compute derived tables (bars, aggregates) as inserts happen. In kdb+, similar behavior can be achieved with update functions attached to real-time tables.

Stateful Operators

Some transformations are too bespoke or too stateful for simple views, such as:

- Full order book reconstruction with apply/cancel/replace logic.
- Complex feature extraction that uses multiple rolling windows and cross-instrument relationships.
- Quality checks that depend on detailed protocol semantics.

Here, you write explicit operators - small services or functions - that:

- Subscribe to relevant topics.
- Maintain in-memory state keyed by instrument, venue, or other dimensions.
- Emit new events or write directly into kdb+ and ClickHouse as state changes.

The choice between materialized views and stateful operators is not either/or. A common pattern is:

- Use stateful operators for core microstructure tasks (book reconstruction, low-latency feature computation).
- Use materialized views for simpler aggregations and for "reshaping" data for consumers (for example, building wide bar tables or rollups).

Landing Streams into kdb+ and ClickHouse

The "L" in ETL is where streams meet storage. We want to achieve:

- low end-to-end latency,
- correct ordering and deduplication, and
- replayability.

Into kdb+

Kdb+ is often used as the real-time and near-term store, so latency matters. Two common approaches:

- **Direct subscription**: A process (for example, a tickerplant or gateway) subscribes to Kafka/Redpanda topics and writes normalized events directly into in-memory and on-disk tables, respecting partitioning and ordering.
- **Hybrid gateway**: The order book and feature operators themselves write into kdb+, while a thin gateway handles only routing and reconnections.

In either case, the design should:

- Preserve sequence numbers and timestamps so that table order reflects feed order.
- Use append-only, time-ordered feeds into intraday tables, with periodic flushes to historical storage.
- Maintain idempotence: if the gateway reconnects and replays a set of records, kdb+ should not double-count them.

Normalization and reconstruction logic can live either upstream (in Kafka consumers) or inside kdb+ processes, depending on your latency and operational requirements.

Into ClickHouse

ClickHouse excels at heavy analytics on larger horizons. It usually sits slightly downstream in terms of latency:

- Data is ingested in micro-batches - for example, every few seconds or minutes - from Kafka/Redpanda into staging tables.
- Materialized views or background merges reshape staging data into well-partitioned, query-optimized tables.

ClickHouse offers native Kafka engines that can subscribe to topics and batch-write into MergeTree tables. Regardless of the exact mechanism, you should:

- Ensure that ordering columns (time, sequence) and unique keys are preserved.
- Design partitions and primary keys around session dates, instruments, and time, as discussed earlier.
- Avoid heavy per-row transformation in the ingestion path; push complex logic upstream or into materialized views.

This split - kdb+ close to the wire, ClickHouse for deeper history and heavier rolls - allows you to align each system with what it does best.

Replay in a Streaming Architecture

Earlier, we treated replay primarily as a batch activity: take raw logs, run them through the pipeline, and rebuild tables. In a streaming architecture with Kafka/Redpanda, replay also has a natural expression:

- Topics act as logs that can be re-read from any offset.
- Consumers can be reset to earlier offsets to reprocess data, either into new tables or into test environments.

Key considerations:

- **Retention**: choose topic retention periods that are long enough to support operational replay needs (for example, days or weeks), while archival systems hold longer-term raw captures.
- **Isolation**: use separate consumer groups or dedicated clusters for replay so that you do not disturb live processing.
- **Versioning**: tie consumer configuration and code versions to replay runs, so you can attribute outputs to specific pipeline versions.

This streaming replay model complements the raw-capture-based model: Kafka/Redpanda give you convenient replay within a recent window, while raw captures plus offline tools cover deeper history and major logic changes.

Reference Architecture

We can now assemble a reference architecture that integrates all of these patterns. At a high level, it looks like a layered, left-to-right flow:

- **Exchange Feeds**: multicast/unicast feeds, decoded by protocol-specific handlers.
- **Log Backbone**: Kafka/Redpanda topics carrying normalized events and derived streams.
- **Streaming ETL Stages**: stateful operators and materialized-view-style components that reconstruct books, compute features, and produce aggregates.
- **Storage Layers**: kdb+ for real-time and near-term intraday data; ClickHouse for large-scale historical analytics.
- **Quality and Replay Infrastructure**: monitoring, quality tables, and replay harnesses attached throughout.

We capture this visually in the diagram below.

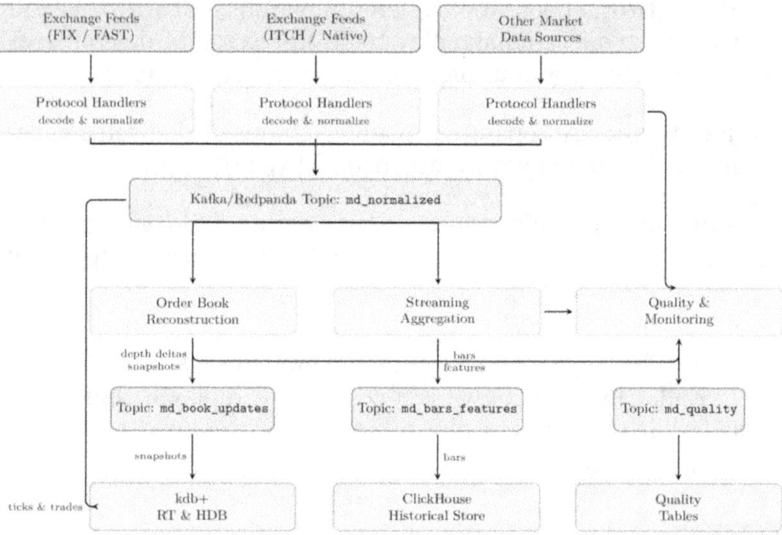

This reference architecture illustrates the main design principles:

- **Separation of concerns**: decoding, normalization, reconstruction, aggregation, storage, and quality monitoring are distinct stages.
- **Streaming by default**: data flows continuously through Kafka/Redpanda topics, not just in nightly batches.
- **Stateful where needed**: order book reconstruction and feature extraction are treated as stateful operators.
- **Materialization at the edges**: kdb+ and ClickHouse hold the analysis-ready tables, materialized views, and long-term history.
- **Replayable**: the log backbone and raw captures enable replay across all stages.

Streaming ETL patterns transform our earlier building blocks into an operational system:

- Feed handlers publish normalized events into a durable log.
- Stateful consumers reconstruct order books and compute features continuously.
- Materialized views and incremental aggregations create query-friendly tables.
- kdb+ and ClickHouse together provide low-latency access and scalable historical analytics.
- Quality events and replay capabilities are woven throughout, ensuring trust over time.

Designing your market data platform in this way - as a set of composable streaming transformations anchored by strong storage engines - gives you both performance and flexibility. You can add new consumers, change analytics, or onboard new protocols without redesigning the entire system, while keeping a clear, auditable path from on-the-wire market events to the data used in your trading and risk decisions.

Chapter 4

kdb+ Architecture and q Programming

kdb+ is deceptively small: a terse array language, a columnar database, and a real-time event engine all packed into one binary. What makes it the backbone of many trading desks is not a single killer feature, but how its language, storage layout, and process architecture interlock around time. In this chapter you will learn to "think in q": representing markets as vectors, composing temporal queries, and mapping those queries onto an architecture that can absorb millions of ticks per second while still answering sub-millisecond questions. By the end, you will understand both the code traders write and the topologies that keep it running when markets are at their noisiest.

4.1 q Language Fundamentals

In the rest of the book we will talk about kdb+ as a database, a time–series store, and a component in market data pipelines. Underneath all of that is a programming language: *q*. To design schemas, express queries, and tune performance, you need a working mental model of this language.

This section introduces q not as a general-purpose language, but as a tool shaped for market data. We will approach it with three questions in mind:

- How does its array-oriented style let us describe market problems without loops?
- How does its type system, especially around time, support intraday analytics?
- How does its inter-process communication (IPC) model move data between processes with minimal overhead?

By the end, q expressions should feel like short descriptions of market calculations on arrays of time, rather than procedural recipes that push values through loops.

Thinking in Arrays of Time

Most developers meet data as rows in tables: each row is a trade; each row is a quote. q takes a different starting point: everything is built on top of *arrays* (vectors). Tables are simply aligned collections of these vectors, one vector per column.

This sounds like a small distinction, but it changes how you think about problems:

- Instead of "loop over every trade and accumulate volume," you think "apply an operation to the entire vector of sizes, then reduce."
- Instead of "for each symbol, keep a running sum in a loop," you think "group the sizes by symbol and apply a sum to each group."
- Instead of "join each trade to a quote by scanning backwards in time," you think "take two time-ordered vectors and apply a temporal join primitive."

q was designed around the idea that the primitive unit of work is an operation on a whole vector. Modern CPUs are good at this: they can apply the same operation (for example, addition) to many values in parallel. The language exposes this directly.

For market data, this matches the shape of the problems we care about. We rarely ask "what is the value of this single trade?" in isolation. We ask about:

- distributions of prices,
- curves such as intraday volume,
- rolling or cumulative metrics across thousands or millions of ticks.

These are all properties of arrays.

Core Data Structures: Lists, Dictionaries, Tables

q builds complexity from a small number of core structures. Understanding them conceptually is more important than memorizing syntax.

Lists: Ordered Collections

A list in q is an ordered sequence of items. Conceptually, you can picture it as a column in a spreadsheet: every cell in that column is an item in the list.

In market terms, imagine:

- a list of trade prices across the day for one symbol,
- a list of timestamps for each quote update,
- a list of symbols in a portfolio.

Operationally, a list is stored contiguously in memory. This matters for performance:

- applying an operation like "add 1 tick to every price" touches consecutive memory,
- scanning the list is friendly to the CPU cache,
- sending the list across a socket can be done as a single block.

These features show up later when we look at IPC and serialization.

Dictionaries: Key–Value Mappings

On top of lists, q defines dictionaries: mappings from keys to values. Conceptually, they are like small hash maps or lookup tables.

In markets, you often want to map:

- a symbol to its last price,
- an exchange code to its time zone,
- a field name to a description or scale factor.

In q, the keys and values of a dictionary are themselves lists of equal length, kept aligned by position. This again preserves the "arrays first" philosophy. Looking up a value is still conceptually "find which index contains the key, then pick the value at that index."

This representation is compact, efficient to scan, and easy to serialize.

Tables: Columnar Collections of Records

A table in q is just a dictionary of lists, where each list (column) has the same length. Instead of thinking "a table is a set of rows," q defines:

- each column as a typed vector,
- the table as a bundle of these vectors that share an index.

In market data, a trade table might have:

- a vector of timestamps,
- a vector of symbols,
- a vector of prices,
- a vector of sizes.

The i-th trade is not a separate object; it is the collection of the i-th entries across these four vectors.

This columnar layout is central to kdb+ performance:

- queries that operate on a single column read contiguous memory; for example, computing the average price reads only the price vector, not the whole row structure,
- compression can be applied column-wise, which is especially effective for repeating or slowly changing values (such as symbols, venues, or side),
- when reading from disk, the engine can map only the columns used by the query.

Thus, even at the language level, q nudges you into patterns that align with efficient columnar computation.

Vector Operations Instead of Loops

Many developers come to q from languages where loops are the primary tool: a *for* or *while* construct that walks a list element by element. In q, explicit loops exist but are rarely the right tool for high-performance code.

The guiding idea is:

> Describe *what* you want done to each element or group, and let the language apply it to the entire vector.

There are two common patterns.

Elementwise Operations

Elementwise operations apply a function independently to each entry in a list or column. For example:

- converting a vector of prices from one currency to another by a fixed factor,
- clipping all spreads to a maximum cap,
- adding a small offset to all timestamps to account for a known clock skew.

Instead of looping over trades, you think of the entire price column as a single object and apply an operation to it. Behind the scenes, the interpreter can use vectorized CPU instructions or tight loops in C over contiguous memory.

Aggregation and Grouping

The second pattern is aggregation: reducing many values to a summary. Examples:

- total traded volume in a day,
- average trade size per symbol,
- maximum drawdown of a price series.

In q, aggregation is expressed as operations over whole lists, often after grouping. Grouping aligns naturally with market data: we almost always talk about measures "per symbol," "per venue," or "per minute."

Conceptually:

1. split a vector into sub-vectors by a key (for example, one sub-vector of prices per symbol),
2. apply an aggregation function, such as sum or average, to each sub-vector.

Because all of this is expressed in terms of vector operations, the implementation can avoid per-row overhead. This is one of the main reasons q code written in an idiomatic vector style is faster than equivalent loop-based code in other languages.

Functional Style: Projections, Composition, Adverbs

q supports a light functional style that makes vector operations easier to combine without plumbing boilerplate. There are three ideas worth understanding conceptually.

Projections: Fixing Some Arguments

Many calculations in trading reuse the same function structure with some arguments fixed. For example:

- scaling any price series by a constant volatility target,
- adjusting any timestamp by a fixed offset,
- applying the same slippage model across different strategies.

A *projection* in q is a partially applied function: you provide some arguments now, obtaining a new function that expects the remaining arguments later. This lets you define a generic transformation once, then specialize it cheaply and reuse it on many data sets.

Conceptually, you can think of it as pre-filling some fields in a template and leaving others blank to be filled when the data arrives.

Composition: Building Pipelines

Composition means creating a new function by chaining existing ones: the output of one becomes the input of the next. Market analytics often follow this shape:

1. clean or normalize raw prices (for example, remove outliers or adjust for splits),

2. compute a feature (for example, a rolling volatility),
3. aggregate the feature across a basket or time buckets,
4. feed the result into a risk or execution model.

Each of these steps can be a small function. Composition then creates a pipeline function, which you can apply to entire tables or columns. The benefits are:

- clarity: you see the logical stages of the computation,
- reuse: stages can be tested and reused independently,
- performance: the interpreter can avoid materializing unnecessary intermediate structures when possible.

Adverbs: Higher-Order Behavior Over Collections

Adverbs in q are modifiers that change how a function is applied to data. They are a concise way to express common iteration patterns over lists and groups without writing loops.

Three important patterns:

- **Apply to each element** of a list or each group in a table. For example, apply the same risk metric to each symbol's time series.
- **Fold (reduce) a list** with a binary operation. For example, repeatedly apply a profit-and-loss accumulation rule across trades.
- **Scan a list**, keeping intermediate results. For example, compute a running inventory after each trade.

In every case, you are not iterating manually. You specify the function and the pattern (*each*, *over*, *scan*), and q arranges the traversal.

This is not just syntactic sugar. It matters for performance because the interpreter knows in advance which pattern you intend, and can use specialized internal loops instead of per-iteration overhead.

Temporal Types: Time as a First-Class Citizen

Financial markets are about events in time: trades, quotes, orders, risk snapshots. Treating time as just another number leads to subtle errors, especially when you need nanosecond resolution, different time zones, or business versus calendar time.

q includes a rich set of temporal types, designed specifically for time-series work. This has three main implications for high-performance analytics.

Rich Temporal Domain

q distinguishes between:

- dates (days on a calendar),
- times (time-of-day),
- timestamps (a point in time, typically date plus time-of-day),
- timespans (durations between events).

Each of these has a fixed internal representation. In particular, q timestamps can represent nanoseconds, which is often required for modern market feeds.

Having dedicated temporal types helps in several ways:

- comparisons such as "before/after" or "within 5 milliseconds" are well-defined and do not rely on ad-hoc units,
- sorting by time respects the natural ordering without conversion,
- arithmetic on times and durations is available as primitives rather than hand-rolled.

Compact In-Memory Representation

Internally, q stores temporal values as integers (for example, a count of nanoseconds from a fixed epoch). This choice has important performance consequences:

- a column of timestamps is a contiguous vector of fixed-width integers,
- sorting by time is as efficient as sorting any integer vector,
- comparisons and arithmetic use simple integer operations on the CPU.

Compare this to an object-heavy representation where each timestamp is a separate struct or class. Integer vectors pack tightly, have predictable alignment, and are easy to move across the wire.

Temporal Semantics in Operations

Because temporal types are first-class, many vector operations and joins have time-aware semantics. Two examples that matter for markets:

- interpolating or aligning series by time (for example, filling in missing seconds in a time bar series),
- as-of joins, where a row in one table is matched to the most recent row in another table at or before a given time.

We will discuss these in more detail in the dedicated section on as-of joins and temporal windows. For now, the key idea is that by embedding time semantics into core operations, q avoids a lot of boilerplate and off-by-one logic that you might have to implement manually in other environments.

From In-Memory Types to IPC: Moving Vectors Between Processes

So far we have treated q as an in-process language manipulating vectors and tables. In a production kdb+ deployment, you almost never have a single process:

- feed handlers parse raw market data feeds,

- a tickerplant dispatches normalized ticks,
- real-time databases and historical databases serve queries,
- gateways orchestrate or route client requests.

All of these components communicate via IPC. A core design principle of q is that the in-memory representation of data is closely aligned with the on-the-wire representation. This minimizes serialization overhead.

Typed Serialization of Vectors

When a q process sends data to another, it does not walk each row and re-encode it as text. Instead:

1. it takes a vector or table as it exists in memory,
2. it writes a small header describing the type, length, and attributes,
3. it copies the underlying contiguous memory for each vector directly into the network buffer.

On the receiving side, the header is read, and the remaining bytes are mapped back into vectors of the appropriate type. Because the format is typed and structured, there is no need for parsing or type inference.

This has several consequences:

- **Low latency**: serialization cost is roughly proportional to the size of the data, with a small constant factor.
- **Predictability**: there are no hidden penalties from variable-length text encoding or schema mismatches.
- **Simplicity**: the same types and structures (lists, dictionaries, tables) work both in memory and on the wire.

For a market data pipeline, where millions of messages may flow per second, this efficiency is crucial.

Message Framing and Batching

q IPC uses a simple message framing format: each message has a header, including its length and a flag indicating whether it is synchronous (expects a reply) or asynchronous (fire-and-forget). The body is the serialized q value (often a table or a small list).

This framing fits well with common market patterns:

- feed handlers can batch multiple tick records into a single table message before sending, amortizing the fixed header cost,
- tickerplants can broadcast the same message to multiple subscribers without re-serializing it for each one,
- clients can send parameterized queries as a small message and receive large tabular results in a single response.

Because each message is self-contained and typed, components can remain loosely coupled: if you change the schema but keep types and field order consistent, intermediate systems need little or no adjustment.

IPC as an Extension of the Language

One subtle but powerful property of q is that the same expressions you use locally can be sent over IPC and evaluated remotely. For example, instead of requesting all trades for a symbol and then aggregating locally, a client can send:

- a reference to the remote table,
- plus a small function describing the aggregation.

The remote process then:

1. evaluates the function against its in-memory data,
2. sends back only the aggregated result.

This *push computation to the data* model is essential for performance:

- it minimizes data movement across the network,
- it makes use of the remote process's CPU and memory locality,
- it keeps client code simpler and less stateful.

In other words, q's functional style does not stop at process boundaries; it extends through IPC. The language and the communication layer are tightly integrated.

Putting It Together: A Market-Oriented Mental Model

We can now summarize the q language fundamentals in terms of market data work:

- You treat prices, sizes, and timestamps as *vectors* and *columns*, not as rows or objects.
- You combine small, composable functions into pipelines that transform these vectors, using adverbs to express standard iteration patterns without explicit loops.
- You rely on dedicated temporal types and semantics to handle time precisely, in nanoseconds, and to align events across series.
- You move data between processes using a binary, typed IPC mechanism that mirrors the in-memory layout, allowing whole vectors and tables to be sent and received with minimal overhead.

From this perspective, a query such as "compute per-symbol VWAP from today's trades and pass the result to a risk engine" is not a procedural program. It is:

- a set of vector transformations over columns (prices and sizes),
- grouped by symbol and time range,

- wrapped in a small function,
- invoked locally or remotely via IPC.

This is the style in which the rest of the book will express kdb+ operations. In the next sections, we will build on this foundation:

- first, by connecting these core structures to table design, attributes, and historical database layout,
- then, by exploring temporal joins and windowed analytics that rely heavily on q's time-aware types,
- and finally, by assembling these pieces into real-time pipelines, scaled deployments, and integrated feed handlers.

If you keep the "arrays of time" mental model in mind, q's often terse syntax becomes less mysterious. It is a thin layer over a few powerful ideas: arrays, functions, and time, all engineered to support time-critical market analytics.

4.2 Table Design, Attributes, and HDB Layout

In the previous section we treated q mainly as a language for manipulating arrays of time in memory. We focused on lists, dictionaries, tables, and on how vector operations let you describe market analytics without loops. In a production kdb+ system, however, you rarely work with a single in-memory table. You work with years of tick data spread across many files and processes.

This section makes the bridge from *logical* design to *physical* layout:

- how the way you define trade and quote tables in q determines their layout in memory and on disk,
- how table attributes guide the engine in choosing efficient access paths,

- how historical database (HDB) partitioning and compression affect query latency on real market workloads.

The goal is to give you an intuition for where each nanosecond goes when you ask a seemingly simple question such as "what was the per-symbol volume curve last month?"

From Logical Schema to Physical Representation

Recall that in q, a table is fundamentally a dictionary of columns, and each column is a typed vector. The logical schema answers questions such as:

- which columns exist, and in what types,
- which combinations of columns identify a record,
- how symbols, venues, and other keys are represented.

The physical representation is how these columns are laid out:

- in RAM inside a running process,
- and on disk inside an HDB partition.

kdb+ is deliberately simple in how it connects the two: there is very little abstraction between the in-memory column and the on-disk column file. The same columnar vector model appears in both places. This is excellent news from a performance perspective, but it also means your logical schema decisions have direct consequences.

Before introducing attributes and HDB layout, we will contrast two basic table forms that you will use constantly in market data: simple and keyed tables.

Simple vs. Keyed Tables

Conceptually, a *simple* table is "just rows." There is no notion of a primary key in the table itself. A *keyed* table embeds a key into its structure. Both are columnar, but they differ in how kdb+ stores and accesses them.

Simple Tables

Simple tables are well suited for:

- append-only data such as trades and quotes,
- situations where you mostly scan or aggregate whole columns or ranges (for example, all trades for a day),
- workloads dominated by streaming inserts and batch reads.

A typical trade table in this style might logically include:

- a timestamp,
- a symbol,
- a price,
- a size,
- possibly a venue, side, and trade condition.

Physically, each of these is a vector in memory and a separate column file on disk. The rows are implicitly numbered by position (row 0, row 1, and so on). To find "all trades for symbol A between two times," the engine typically:

1. identifies which date partitions and row ranges to scan,
2. reads (or memory-maps) the timestamp and symbol columns for those ranges,
3. applies a boolean filter to find the rows that match,
4. then reads the price and size for the matching rows.

Simple tables are particularly efficient when your queries naturally operate on large contiguous chunks of time and do not need random lookup by key.

Keyed Tables

Keyed tables bake a key directly into their structure. Conceptually, you can think of them as a dictionary:

- the key is one or more columns,
- the value is the remaining columns.

In markets, this is useful for:

- current state tables such as "latest quote per symbol",
- configuration or reference data such as instrument metadata keyed by symbol,
- small but frequently looked up structures where you want very fast key-based access.

If you define a keyed table keyed by *symbol* and *timestamp*, kdb+ stores the key columns together in a way that makes lookups and joins by that combination efficient. When you join a simple trade table against a keyed quote table, the engine can use the keyed structure as an index.

However, keyed tables come with trade-offs:

- inserts and updates can be more expensive than in a simple table, because the key structure needs to be maintained,
- they are typically used for smaller, more random-access workloads, not for huge tick histories,
- physical layout on disk is different: keyed tables are stored more like indexed maps, whereas large append-only histories are usually left as simple tables in the HDB.

In practice, most kdb+ market data systems:

- store large trade and quote histories as simple tables in the HDB,

- maintain smaller keyed tables in memory for fast lookups (for example, last trade per symbol, instrument attributes).

With this background, we can now look at attributes, which act as hints to the engine about ordering and uniqueness.

Column Attributes: Telling the Engine What You Know

Attributes in q are small markers attached to columns that communicate invariants such as "this column is sorted" or "these values are unique." They do not change the logical content of the table; they merely tell kdb+ about properties you, as the designer, know to be true. The engine then exploits these properties to accelerate queries.

The most important attributes in market data schemas are:

- sorted,
- unique,
- parted.

Sorted Attribute

If you know that a column is stored in ascending order, you can mark it as sorted. In trade and quote tables, the classic example is the timestamp column in each date partition. Data is usually appended in increasing time order, so within a partition the times are non-decreasing.

By telling kdb+ the column is sorted, you enable:

- binary search instead of linear scan when filtering by time range,
- faster merges and as-of joins, which rely on ordered time columns,
- efficient "range restriction" where the engine narrows down a time slice before even touching other columns.

For a query such as "all trades between 10:00 and 11:00," a sorted timestamp column means the engine can:

1. use binary search on the timestamp vector to find the first and last rows in that interval,
2. then read just those rows instead of inspecting the entire day's data.

This dramatically reduces I/O, especially when your day contains tens of millions of rows.

Unique Attribute

A column marked unique tells kdb+ that no value appears more than once. In market data, uniqueness often arises in:

- instrument identifiers in a reference table,
- order identifiers in an order book snapshot (if designed that way),
- sequence numbers in some feed-normalization schemes.

When a column is unique, the engine can:

- use faster lookup structures or algorithms,
- shortcut parts of joins or groupings because it knows there is at most one match per key.

In the HDB, uniqueness is most often leveraged in dimension tables and keyed structures rather than the main fact tables of trades and quotes, which naturally contain many repeated symbols and times.

Parted Attribute

The parted attribute communicates that the table is partitioned by the values of a particular column. In an HDB, the most common partition key is the date. Each date partition is stored in a separate directory on disk, and marking the date column as parted aligns the logical partitioning with the physical layout.

The benefits are obvious for time-based queries:

- if you ask for one day's trades, the engine can restrict itself to that day's partition directory,
- if you ask for a month of data, it knows exactly which set of daily directories to scan.

On the other hand, applying parted incorrectly can lead to subtle bugs or missed optimizations: you must ensure that the partitioning in the file system truly matches the attribute in the table.

Attributes in Practice: Trade and Quote Tables

Putting this together, a typical logical schema for large historical trade and quote tables in an HDB might adopt the following conventions:

- tables are simple (not keyed), because they store large append-only histories,
- each date partition holds that day's trades or quotes,
- within each partition, the time column is sorted and the date column is parted,
- symbol and venue columns may carry attributes such as enumeration or internal encoding, but are generally not marked unique.

Why this combination?

- The parted date column matches the on-disk partition structure, so date filters are cheap.
- The sorted time column allows fast time-range restriction and efficient as-of joins.

- Keeping the table simple avoids overheads from maintaining a complex key structure at tick scale.

Before we dive into HDB directory layout and compression, it is useful to visualize how these layers relate.

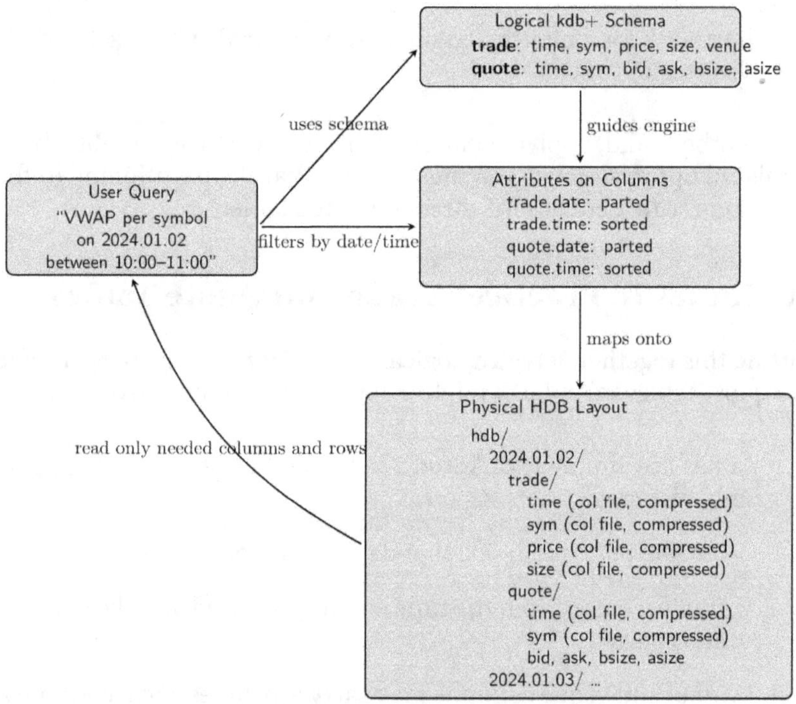

HDB Partitioning: Slicing Time on Disk

An HDB (historical database) in kdb+ is just a directory tree on disk, following a simple convention. Understanding this tree is essential for predicting query performance.

Date-Based Partitions

By default, each top-level directory under the HDB root represents a partition boundary. In market systems, the convention is:

- one directory per date, named with the calendar date,
- within each date directory, one subdirectory per table (for example, *trade*, *quote*),
- within each table directory, one file per column.

This layout mirrors your logical view of the data:

- the date column in the table is marked parted,
- each partition directory contains only rows with that date.

When a query specifies a date or a date range, kdb+ can translate that almost mechanically into:

- the set of partition directories to inspect,
- and the columns within those directories that are needed for the query.

For example, asking for trades on 2024-01-02 only requires:

- entering the 2024.01.02 directory,
- opening the *trade* subdirectory,
- mapping the relevant column files (for example, *time*, *sym*, *price*, *size*).

Other dates' directories are not touched at all, which is ideal for both spinning disks and SSDs: you avoid seeking through unrelated data.

Optional Secondary Partitioning

Some high-volume systems introduce a second layer of partitioning, for example by symbol or by symbol group, to spread load and improve locality for very hot names. In such designs, each date directory may contain further subdirectories by symbol range.

This kind of secondary partitioning can:

- reduce the size of each individual column file,
- increase the chance that queries for a subset of symbols touch only a smaller set of files,
- support parallel reads by different processes or threads.

The trade-off is added complexity:

- you must ensure that your logical schema and attributes (such as parted) accurately reflect the partitioning,
- your query routing logic must be aware of the secondary partitions so that it can target the right directories.

For many use cases, especially at modest scale, date-only partitioning is sufficient and simpler to operate.

Column-Oriented Storage and Memory Mapping

Within each table directory for a given date, columns are stored as separate files. This expression of the columnar model on disk has two main performance implications.

Reading Only the Columns You Need

Most analytical queries touch only a subset of columns. For example:

- computing VWAP uses prices and sizes, plus time and symbol as filters,

- computing spread statistics uses bid and ask, but not necessarily every other field in the quote table,
- counting trades by symbol may need only symbol and time.

Because each column is a file, kdb+ can:

- avoid opening or mapping irrelevant columns,
- limit disk and memory bandwidth to just the data you actually use.

This is especially powerful when combined with partitioning: a query on a single symbol over a few days might only need:

- a handful of date directories,
- within them, a handful of column files.

Memory-Mapped Access

Instead of reading column files into user-space buffers, kdb+ typically memory-maps them. This means:

- the operating system maps file contents directly into the process's virtual address space,
- when q code accesses a column element, it is effectively dereferencing a pointer into the mapped region,
- the OS lazily fetches pages from disk as needed and caches them.

The advantage of this approach is that:

- the same column file can be shared across multiple processes on the same host without duplicating pages in memory,
- you avoid copies between kernel and user space for large sequential scans,

- the engine can treat on-disk columns very similarly to in-memory vectors, simplifying the implementation.

In terms of query latency, memory mapping combined with attributes and partitioning means that:

- if your query touches data that the OS cache already holds, the response can be as fast as an in-memory scan,
- if it touches cold partitions or columns, the first access incurs I/O, but subsequent queries can benefit from warmed caches.

This is why kdb+ deployments often pay careful attention to which partitions and columns are "hot" and likely to be needed intraday.

Compression: Trading CPU for I/O

Market data volumes are large. Even with columnar layout, raw tick data can consume terabytes. kdb+ therefore supports compressing columns on disk. Compression sits on top of the columnar and partitioned layout: each column file may be stored compressed, and decompressed as needed when mapped.

Why Compression Helps

Compression can improve performance despite the extra CPU cost because:

- fewer bytes need to be read from disk or SSD,
- more data fits in OS page cache and RAM,
- sequential scans can process longer logical ranges per physical I/O.

These effects are strongest for:

- columns with low cardinality, such as symbol or venue codes,

- slowly changing fields, such as trade condition flags,
- numeric series with small deltas, where delta-based encodings are effective.

Where Compression Can Hurt

Compression is not free. It adds:

- CPU overhead for decompressing pages during reads,
- possible latency spikes when the first access to a compressed segment triggers decompression.

Compression can hurt when:

- queries are extremely latency-sensitive and touch only a tiny amount of data (for example, real-time quote lookups, which are usually served from in-memory RDBs anyway),
- the compressed size is not much smaller than the raw size, so you pay CPU cost without saving much I/O,
- hardware is constrained more by CPU than by I/O, which can be the case on some modern SSD-rich servers.

In practice, most production HDBs selectively compress:

- high-volume, less-latency-sensitive histories,
- columns where compression ratios are known to be good,
- while leaving some critical or frequently probed columns uncompressed.

Design Patterns for Trade and Quote Schemas

Let us now tie these pieces together with a concrete design pattern for production trade and quote tables.

Trade Table

A typical trade table might include:

- date and time as separate columns, with date parted and time sorted,
- symbol as a compact code type, mapped to human-readable names via a reference table,
- price and size as numeric columns,
- venue, side, and trade condition as additional dimensions.

Design choices that matter:

- **Simple, not keyed, in the HDB:** keeps appends cheap and supports fast scans for analytics.
- **Partitioned by date:** aligns with natural boundaries for reporting and risk.
- **Sorted by time within partition:** makes time slicing and as-of joins efficient.
- **Selective compression:** compress symbol, venue, and flags aggressively; consider compressing price and size if compression ratios are good and workloads are I/O bound.

Quote Table

A quote table is similar but includes bid and ask sides. It may contain:

- date and time (again parted and sorted),
- symbol,
- bid price and size,
- ask price and size,

- possibly depth levels if you store a multi-level book.

For many analytics, you only need top-of-book quotes:

- mid-price for a symbol at each tick,
- inside spread statistics,
- book liquidity at the best levels.

In those cases, designs often separate:

- a light, top-of-book quote table with high compression and efficient on-disk layout,
- deeper book data in separate structures, sometimes driven by specialized engines or stored at lower frequency.

How Schema and Layout Drive Query Latency

With all these elements in place, we can now reason about end-to-end latency for typical market queries.

Per-Symbol Volume Curves

To compute a per-symbol volume curve over a day or a month, the engine:

1. uses the parted date column to select relevant partitions,
2. uses the sorted time column to restrict to the intraday range (for example, regular trading hours),
3. reads the size column and, if needed, the price column,
4. groups by symbol and time bucket and aggregates.

If columns are compressed, the I/O reads fewer bytes, but the CPU must decompress them. For a workload dominated by scanning entire days or months for many symbols, the reduction in I/O often dominates, giving better end-to-end performance.

Intraday Liquidity Metrics

To compute intraday liquidity metrics such as average spread or depth per symbol and time bucket, the process is similar but with the quote table:

1. filter partitions by date,
2. filter rows by time range using sorted time,
3. read just the columns needed: bid, ask, sizes, symbol, and time,
4. aggregate by symbol and bucket.

If you have designed a separate top-of-book table with only these fields, queries avoid touching heavier structures and can run in predictable time even during peak hours.

In kdb+, table design is not just a logical exercise. Because the language and storage engine expose the same columnar model from RAM down to disk, your schema and attribute choices directly shape physical layout and query latency.

The main principles to carry forward are:

- Use simple tables for large, append-only tick histories in the HDB; reserve keyed tables for smaller, lookup-heavy structures.
- Attach attributes such as parted and sorted whenever you can justify them; they are promises to the engine that unlock more efficient access paths.
- Partition primarily by date, optionally by symbol or group when volumes justify it, and ensure the file-system structure mirrors your logical partitioning.
- Take advantage of columnar storage and memory mapping by designing schemas where common queries touch as few columns as possible.
- Apply compression selectively, focusing on columns and workloads where I/O dominates CPU.

With this foundation, we can now move on to temporal operations that exploit these layouts, in particular as-of joins and windowed analytics. There, you will see how sorted time columns, partitioning, and columnar access come together to support sophisticated intraday studies at interactive speeds.

4.3 As-Of Join and Temporal Windows

In the previous sections we treated q tables largely as static structures: columns with attributes, laid out across date partitions on disk. Real trading analytics, however, are rarely static. They ask questions such as:

- "What quote was in force when this trade happened?"
- "What was the last available price when we computed this risk snapshot?"
- "What is the rolling volatility of this symbol over the last five minutes?"

These questions all have two things in common:

- They respect the direction of time. You only look *backwards* when you search for reference data; you avoid peeking into the future.
- They summarize information over a time *window*, not just at a single instant.

In q, two constructs capture these patterns:

- the *as-of join*, which formalizes the idea of "nearest price in time" to the left,
- *windowed* operations, which formalize rolling and cumulative analytics.

This section explains both concepts and shows how they build directly on the sorted, columnar layouts discussed earlier.

Why Equality Joins Are Not Enough

Most relational databases are built around equality joins: you link rows when keys match exactly. This works well for things like joining an instrument table to a trade table on symbol. But time-series analysis rarely has exact matches in time.

Consider a simple example: you have two time-ordered tables for a given symbol.

- A quote table, with mid-prices at irregular times when quotes change.
- A trade table, with trades at their own irregular times.

You want to know, for each trade, what mid-price the market was quoting just before or at the moment of the trade. If you try to do a plain equality join on the timestamp, you will often get no match:

- quotes only update when something changes;
- trades may occur at times where there is no quote update.

Yet humans have no trouble interpreting the question. We implicitly say: "for each trade time, look back to the last quote time that is less than or equal to it." This is exactly what an as-of join expresses.

As-Of Join: "Nearest Price in Time"

An as-of join takes one table of "events we care about" and one table of "reference states that change over time". It attaches to each event row the most recent reference row at or before the event's timestamp.

In market terms:

- Event table: trades (or risk snapshots, or order arrivals).
- Reference table: quotes, prices, positions, or any stateful quantity updated over time.

The key idea is that matching is based on ordered time, not on equality.

Sorted Time Columns as the Foundation

As-of joins rely heavily on the sorted time columns and partitioning we introduced earlier:

- Both the event time column and the reference time column must be sorted in ascending order within the range being joined.
- In an HDB, this is usually enforced by design: each date partition contains rows in time order, with an attribute marking the time column as sorted.

Because the time columns are sorted, the join can be implemented with a linear or near-linear pass over both sides rather than with random lookups. Conceptually, the algorithm behaves like two fingers walking along two timelines:

- Start at the earliest time.
- Move along the quote times, tracking the "current" quote.
- When you hit a trade time, use the current quote as its match.
- Continue forward; you never have to go backwards in time.

This one-pass, forward-only structure is cache-friendly and well-suited to vectorized implementation.

Trades with Last Quote

The most common example is attaching quotes to trades. For one symbol, imagine:

- at 09:30:00, the quote mid is 100.00;
- at 09:30:05, it updates to 100.02;
- at 09:30:10, it updates to 100.05.

Trades occur at:

- 09:30:02 for 500 shares,
- 09:30:07 for 200 shares,
- 09:30:12 for 300 shares.

For each trade time, we look for the latest quote time that is at or before it:

- Trade at 09:30:02 uses the 09:30:00 quote.
- Trade at 09:30:07 uses the 09:30:05 quote.
- Trade at 09:30:12 uses the 09:30:10 quote.

There is no searching backward arbitrarily; we simply walk forward through time, always carrying the last known quote.

This pattern appears in:

- execution quality analysis (trade price versus prevailing quote),
- slippage measurement against mid-prices,
- labeling trades with microstructure state, such as spread or depth,
- constructing mid-price series from trades when you have only sparse quotes.

Immediately after this conceptual description is a visual timeline that makes the mechanics concrete.

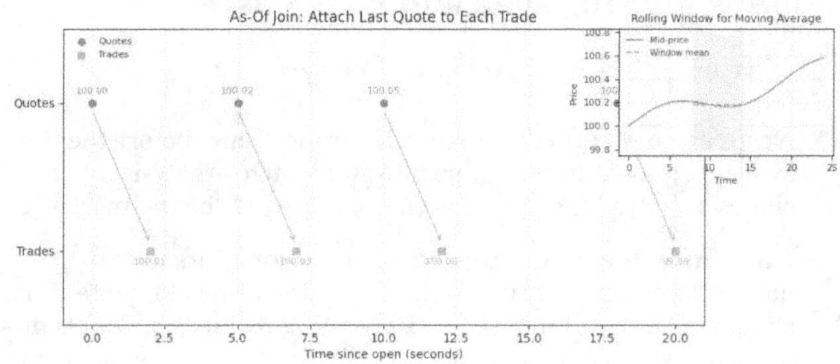

Multiple Symbols and Additional Keys

Real data almost always includes multiple symbols and possibly multiple venues. In that case, the as-of join works with a combination of equality and temporal matching:

- First, match rows where symbol (and optionally venue) are equal.
- Within each symbol (and venue) group, apply the as-of logic on the time columns.

Because symbol columns typically have many repeats, grouping by symbol partitions the work into smaller, cache-friendly segments. Within each segment, sorted times allow efficient forward-only traversals.

This pattern supports queries like:

- "For each trade in each symbol, attach the last quote for that symbol."
- "For each risk snapshot by symbol, attach the last mid-price on that symbol."

Handling Missing Data and Edge Cases

As-of joins must make explicit choices for edge cases:

- **No previous reference row:** if a trade occurs before the first available quote, there may be no valid match. Analysis often excludes such trades or treats them as occurring "before market".
- **Gaps in reference data:** if there are long intervals without quotes, large sets of trades may map to the same old quote. You should be aware of this when interpreting results; the join is doing what you asked, but the data may not be rich enough for meaningful microstructure inference.

These are data quality and modeling issues rather than language limitations, but q makes it explicit and relatively easy to detect when as-of matches are missing or stale.

As-Of Joins Beyond Trades and Quotes

Although the trade-versus-quote example is the most common, as-of joins are more general. Any time you have:

- a sequence of "events" you want to analyze,
- and one or more time-varying reference series,

an as-of join can attach the appropriate reference state.

Examples include:

- **Risk snapshots with last price:** compute portfolio risk every minute and attach the last price per instrument at or before that minute.
- **Orders with prevailing spread:** label each child order with the best bid and ask at the time it was sent.
- **Internal metrics:** link log messages or error events to the most recent configuration change or deployment event.

In each case, the sorted time columns and partitioned layout from the previous section underpin efficient evaluation.

Temporal Windows: Rolling and Cumulative Analytics

Where as-of joins answer "what was the last state when this event occurred?", temporal windows answer "what has been happening around this event, over some recent interval?"

Two broad classes of windows appear in intraday microstructure work:

- **Time-based windows**, where you consider a fixed amount of clock time (for example, the last five minutes).
- **Event-based windows**, where you consider a fixed number of past events (for example, the last 100 trades).

Both types of windows underlie common analytics:

- moving averages of prices or spreads,
- rolling volatility estimates,
- volume-weighted average prices (VWAP) over trailing intervals,
- measures of trading intensity or order flow imbalance.

q expresses these windows using its vector and functional machinery rather than explicit loops.

Rolling Windows in Market Time

Consider a simple time-based window: for each second of the day, you want the average mid-price over the last 60 seconds. Conceptually, you can imagine a sliding box of width 60 seconds moving along the time axis. At each position:

- the left edge is 60 seconds before now,

- the right edge is now,
- you average all points inside the box.

On the timeline figure, the inset panel illustrates such a window: a shaded box over a segment of the price series, and a horizontal line for the mean inside.

In q, you can think of this operation as:

- For each timestamp, determine the index range of all previous points within 60 seconds (sorted times make this efficient).
- Apply an aggregation such as mean or sum to the corresponding slice of the price vector.

Because q works with whole vectors, the engine can compute all these window summaries in batch, using array slices and efficient internal loops.

This kind of rolling window is central to:

- short-horizon volatility measures,
- moving averages in execution algorithms,
- intraday risk indicators that adapt to recent behavior.

Event-Based Windows: Last N Trades or Last N Quotes

Event-based windows ignore wall-clock time and instead look back over a fixed number of events. For example:

- last 100 trades per symbol,
- last 50 quote changes,
- last 10 order book updates.

These windows are useful when event frequency varies dramatically across the day or across symbols. A one-minute window might contain:

- dozens of trades for a highly liquid index future,
- zero trades for an illiquid small-cap stock.

If you instead ask for the last 100 trades, you always have the same number of observations, though they may span very different amounts of clock time.

In q, event-based windows are naturally expressed using cumulative scans and slicing over indices rather than time. For the last 100 trades, for instance, you can imagine:

- numbering trades from 0 to $N-1$,
- for each index, define a range from $\max(0, index-99)$ to index,
- aggregate over this index range.

Because the underlying data is stored as contiguous vectors, these range operations map directly to slicing operations on arrays.

Combining As-Of Joins with Windows

Many microstructure studies and execution analytics combine both as-of joins and windows. A typical pipeline might look like this:

- Start with a table of trades.
- Use an as-of join to attach the prevailing quote and derive features such as spread, depth, or imbalance at the trade time.
- Within each symbol, compute rolling features over trades: for example, rolling VWAP, rolling volatility, or cumulative volume since the open.

Because as-of joins and windows both rely on sorted time columns and vectorized operations, pipeline performance scales well:

- the as-of join is essentially a linear pass over time-sorted data,
- rolling analytics are implemented as vectorized scans and grouped aggregations.

There is no explicit row-by-row loop at the language level, and the implementation is free to exploit CPU caches and modern instruction sets.

Avoiding Look-Ahead Bias

Any time you process time-series data, you must be careful not to introduce “future information” into decisions or labels that are supposed to be based only on information available at the time.

q’s temporal constructs help you avoid look-ahead bias because:

- as-of joins only see reference rows at or *before* the event time,
- rolling windows are naturally backward-looking if you define them that way.

Still, it is easy to make mistakes. Common pitfalls include:

- using symmetric windows around an event (for example, 30 seconds before and 30 seconds after) when building features for predictive models,
- aggregating across a fixed time interval and then assigning that aggregate to all events within the interval, including those at the beginning,
- using end-of-interval outcomes (for example, close price) as features without careful alignment.

A disciplined approach is:

- always confirm that each feature is based on data at or before the timestamp it is attached to,

- prefer as-of and trailing window constructs over manual indexing.

Because kdb+ tables are naturally partitioned by date and sorted by time, you can enforce and inspect these properties more easily than in systems with looser time semantics.

Irregular Spacing and Business Time

Market events arrive at irregular times. Busy periods around the open or major news releases may see many events per second; quiet periods may see seconds or minutes without activity. This raises a practical question: what notion of time should a window use?

Two viewpoints are common:

- **Wall-clock time:** use actual clock duration (seconds, minutes) for windows. This is natural for risk and compliance metrics aligned with clock time.
- **Business time:** measure time in units of events or volume. For example, a "volume bar" might be defined as the time needed to accumulate a fixed traded volume, regardless of the clock time interval.

q can support both viewpoints:

- wall-clock windows use temporal differences between timestamps;
- business-time windows use differences in cumulative volume or event counts.

In both cases, the underlying operations are still vector-based: you compute cumulative sums or counts, then define windows in terms of these cumulative indices.

Understanding which notion of time your study uses is crucial. For example:

- rolling volatility in wall-clock time gives you a measure of absolute risk per unit of clock time,
- rolling volatility per fixed number of trades gives you a measure of risk per event.

Both are valid, but they answer different questions.

Performance Considerations

As-of joins and windowed operations can be heavy users of CPU and memory bandwidth, especially on large tick histories. However, their design in q makes good use of the storage and attribute choices discussed earlier:

- **Partitioning by date** ensures that joins and windows operate on manageable slices of data, often fitting into memory even for long histories.
- **Sorted time columns** enable single-pass algorithms and efficient time-range restriction before expensive work.
- **Columnar layout** means that only needed columns (time, price, size, etc.) drive the operations; unrelated fields remain untouched.
- **Compression** can reduce I/O when scanning long windows over cold data, though you must balance it against CPU cost.

For intraday, latency-sensitive analytics, you often:

- perform as-of joins and short rolling windows in a real-time database (RDB) held in memory for today's data,
- push longer-horizon studies and backtests to HDB processes where throughput rather than microsecond latency is the priority.

q's syntax does not change between these environments. The same expressions that run over today's in-memory RDB can usually be applied to years of historical data in the HDB, just with different performance characteristics.

As-of joins and temporal windows are the workhorses of intraday market microstructure analysis. They encode two intuitive but subtle ideas:

- "nearest price in time" — implemented as an as-of join that respects sorted time and avoids look-ahead,
- "recent history around an event" — implemented as rolling windows defined in clock time or business time.

q brings these ideas close to the surface:

- time is a first-class, precisely represented type,
- tables are partitioned and sorted so that forward-only passes are possible,
- vector and functional patterns replace explicit loops, allowing the engine to execute operations efficiently in C.

In the next section, we will place these language-level constructs into a wider architectural context: the kdb+tick real-time pipeline. There you will see how as-of joins and rolling features are used continuously on streaming data, powered by the same principles of sorted time columns, partitioning, and columnar access that we have developed so far.

4.4 kdb+tick Real-Time Pipeline

Up to this point we have focused on language and storage fundamentals in kdb+: how q treats data as arrays of time, how tables and attributes map to column files in an HDB, and how temporal joins and windows express market logic efficiently. We now turn from *what* queries do to *how* live data reaches those queries in the first place.

In production, kdb+ is rarely just a historical store. It is usually deployed as *kdb+tick*, a real-time pipeline that moves ticks from exchange feeds to in-memory analytics and finally to long-term storage. The classic pattern revolves around three core processes:

- a **tickerplant** (TP),
- a **real-time database** (RDB),
- a **historical database** (HDB).

You can think of these as three roles in a relay race:

- the tickerplant receives ticks from the wire and fans them out,
- the RDB holds today's data in memory for fast queries,
- the HDB maintains the full historical store on disk.

The details of how they interact—and how they take advantage of q's IPC and columnar layout—determine whether your tick plant runs with smooth, predictable latency or with stalls and dropped data.

The TP/RDB/HDB Trio at a Glance

At a high level, the kdb+tick pipeline looks like a left-to-right flow:

1. **Feed handlers** decode raw market data protocols and convert them into normalized q records.
2. They send these records to the **tickerplant**.
3. The tickerplant appends each record to an in-memory table, writes a compact log entry to disk, and distributes the update to any subscribers.
4. The main subscriber is the **RDB**, which maintains intraday tables in memory.
5. At certain intervals (typically end-of-day), the RDB flushes its tables out to the **HDB** as new date partitions.

6. Throughout the day, **client applications** subscribe directly to the tickerplant or query the RDB and HDB for analytics.

The diagram below summarizes this flow and highlights the TP log and replay loop.

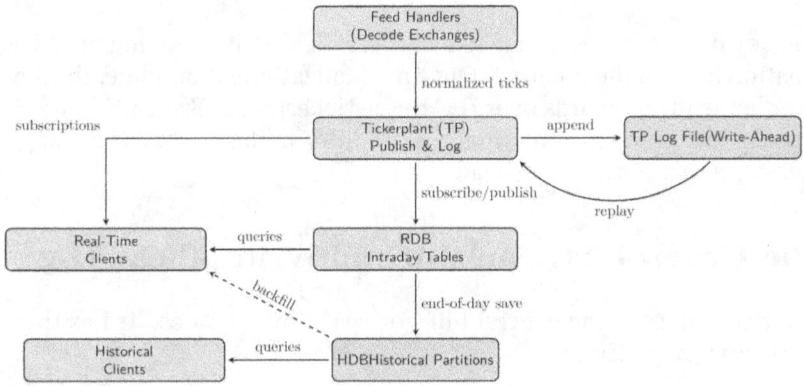

With this overall picture in mind, we now walk through each component and its rolc in controlling data copying and latency.

Feed Handlers: From Wire to q Records

The pipeline begins outside kdb+ itself. *Feed handlers* are processes that:

- consume raw exchange or vendor feeds (for example, binary multicast, TCP, or vendor APIs),
- decode wire formats into structured messages,
- normalize each message into a q-style record consistent with your schema (for example, fields matching your trade or quote tables).

Normalization is where you align the live feed with the table designs you created earlier:

- field names and types must match your RDB and HDB schemas,
- timestamps should be converted into the q temporal types you use everywhere else,
- symbols may be mapped into compact representations that match your historical data.

The key performance idea is to avoid per-field string parsing or object creation later in the pipeline. Once normalization is complete, the feed handler sends q records over IPC to the tickerplant. Typically, batches of ticks are grouped into small in-memory tables and sent as single messages to amortize overhead.

The Tickerplant: Fan-Out and Write-Ahead Log

The tickerplant is the central hub for real-time updates. It has three main responsibilities:

1. **Receive** normalized ticks from feed handlers.
2. **Distribute** those ticks to interested subscribers, especially the RDB.
3. **Persist** a compact log of every update, in order, for recovery and replay.

You can think of it as a small, specialized message broker designed specifically for q tables.

In-Memory Table of the Day

Internally, the tickerplant usually maintains:

- a small in-memory table for each stream (for example, *trade*, *quote*),
- these tables often hold just the current day's data or a rolling window of recent updates.

When the tickerplant receives an update message from a feed handler:

1. it appends the new rows to the appropriate in-memory table,
2. it writes a compact representation of the message to a sequential log file on disk,
3. it relays the update to all subscribers.

Append-only updates line up well with q's columnar vectors and with the sorted time attributes of your tables. As long as feed messages arrive in chronological order (or are normalized as such), each new row naturally extends the time-sorted sequence for that day.

Write-Ahead Log for Resilience

The tickerplant's log file is a *write-ahead log*: every update is recorded to disk as it passes through, before or at the same time as it is delivered to subscribers. The log has several uses:

- **Recovery**: if the RDB or another subscriber fails and restarts, it can request a replay from a given point in the log to reconstruct missed data.
- **Backfill**: you can use the log to feed other systems or regenerate intraday histories if needed.
- **Auditing**: the log is an authoritative record of what the system saw and when.

Because the log is written sequentially, the overhead per update is small: appending to a single file typically costs much less than random writes or complex transactional structures.

Minimal Copying via q IPC

Recall from the q fundamentals section that IPC sends typed vectors over the network closely aligned with their in-memory representation. The tickerplant leverages this by:

- receiving updates already in q table form from feed handlers,
- making minimal transformations (often just appending and stamping timestamps),
- forwarding those same structures to subscribers without re-encoding them as text or object graphs.

This approach keeps per-tick CPU cost predictable and low. The main overheads are:

- a small amount of q interpreter work to update in-memory tables,
- kernel work to append to the log,
- kernel and NIC work to send IPC messages out.

The RDB: Intraday In-Memory Store

The real-time database (RDB) is a kdb+ process that subscribes to the tickerplant and holds today's (or a recent intraday window of) data in memory. It is where most latency-sensitive analytics queries run.

Subscribing to the TP

When the RDB starts up, it connects to the tickerplant and issues subscriptions specifying:

- which tables it wants (for example, trades, quotes),
- and often which subset of symbols or venues, if you shard workloads.

From that point onward, the tickerplant sends every matching update as it arrives. If the RDB starts late or restarts, it can ask the TP to:

- replay the log from the beginning of the day or from a known point,

- then continue receiving live updates.

This sequence allows the RDB to reconstruct the intraday state even after a failure.

Maintaining Intraday Tables

The RDB maintains one or more in-memory tables for each subscribed stream. These tables mirror your HDB schemas:

- same column names and types,
- often the same attributes on time and symbol columns,
- sometimes additional intraday-only fields (for example, sequence numbers, processing timestamps).

As updates arrive from the tickerplant, the RDB:

1. appends them to the relevant in-memory tables,
2. may maintain some small derived structures, such as per-symbol last state or small rolling aggregates.

Because the tables grow throughout the day, you design queries and memory sizing so that a day's worth of data fits comfortably in RAM. For very high-velocity feeds, you might keep only a rolling window in the RDB and push older intraday data to the HDB sooner.

Serving Low-Latency Queries

Clients with tight latency requirements typically query the RDB directly for current-day data. This includes:

- execution algorithms needing current microstructure state,
- real-time risk dashboards,

- monitoring tools that track venue latencies, spreads, or order flow.

The advantages of querying the RDB are:

- all relevant data is in memory, avoiding disk I/O,
- time columns are sorted, enabling fast as-of joins and windows for intraday analytics,
- schemas mirror the HDB, so queries written for historical analysis can often be reused or lightly adapted.

In the context of performance, the RDB is where q's vector operations, as-of joins, and temporal windows operate at their fastest, benefiting from cached, contiguous columns.

The HDB: Long-Term Historical Store

At the far right of the pipeline sits the HDB, which we already examined from a storage perspective. Within the kdb+tick architecture, the HDB is the long-memory of the system.

End-of-Day Save from RDB to HDB

At a chosen boundary—commonly the end of the trading day—the RDB performs a *save* of its tables to the HDB. Conceptually, this involves:

1. stopping or pausing updates long enough to get a consistent snapshot of each intraday table,
2. writing those tables into a new date partition in the HDB on disk,
3. optionally applying compression and ensuring attributes (such as parted and sorted) are correct.

Because the RDB's in-memory tables were already designed with the HDB schema in mind, this save operation is mostly a matter of:

- mapping each in-memory column to an on-disk column file,
- flushing the vector contents to disk in one or a few large writes.

There is no per-row conversion or per-field serialization; the in-memory representation is already very close to what the HDB uses.

Serving Historical Queries

The HDB responds to longer-horizon queries:

- backtests over months or years,
- regulatory or client reporting,
- research into intraday patterns across many days.

Many deployment patterns separate HDB processes from the RDB for isolation:

- HDBs may run on separate hosts with more storage and less strict latency targets,
- RDBs can be tuned more aggressively for low-latency, in-memory workloads.

Nevertheless, because q's query language is the same, analysts often write functions that:

- run over today's RDB for live monitoring,
- and over the HDB for historical analysis,

with nothing more than a change in which process they connect to.

Client Interaction: Subscriptions and Queries

Clients interact with the kdb+tick pipeline in two main ways:

- subscribing to live updates from the tickerplant,
- sending ad-hoc or scheduled queries to the RDB and HDB.

Real-Time Subscriptions

Some clients need immediate notification when specific events occur:

- a risk engine might want every trade in a given portfolio,
- a monitoring system might want all quotes for a benchmark symbol across venues.

These clients subscribe to the tickerplant much like the RDB does, often with filters by table and symbol. The TP then:

- sends each matching update as a small q table or batch of rows,
- does so asynchronously so that it does not block feed handling or logging.

Because IPC messages carry typed vectors, clients can receive data in a form that their local q (or PyKX, C++, etc.) code can consume with little overhead.

Querying RDB and HDB

Other clients, such as dashboards and research tools, send q expressions to RDB or HDB processes over IPC. As discussed earlier, the most efficient pattern is:

- send a small function or query description to the database,
- let the database perform computation close to the data,
- return only the aggregated or filtered result.

In practice, this might mean:

- requesting an intraday VWAP curve from the RDB,
- requesting a multi-year daily volatility series from the HDB,
- combining results in a client or gateway for visualization.

This minimizes network traffic and keeps client applications stateless and simple.

Log and Replay: Recovering and Reconstructing State

One of the most powerful aspects of the kdb+tick design is the tickerplant's ability to *replay* its log. Replay supports both operational resilience and research.

Operational Recovery

If an RDB or subscriber process crashes during the day, the typical recovery sequence is:

1. restart the process,
2. connect to the tickerplant and request a replay from a certain log position (for example, from the start of the day or from the last acknowledged point),
3. as the TP replays entries, rebuild internal tables to the desired state,
4. once caught up, switch to live updates.

Because the log captures every published update in order, replay allows the RDB to rebuild an intraday state consistent with what it would have had without the failure.

Backtesting and Intraday Reconstruction

Researchers can also use log replay to reconstruct the state of the system at any point in the past day, which is particularly valuable for intraday backtesting:

- you can spin up a separate kdb+ environment, feed it historical logs as if they were live,
- run your strategy or analytics in "simulated real time",
- use the same code paths as in production, since data arrives in the same format.

This ability to "time travel" operationally, using the exact tick stream as it originally arrived, is a major advantage over systems that only preserve end-of-day snapshots.

Latency, Backpressure, and Failure Modes

The TP/RDB/HDB trio is simple on paper, but real-world behavior under load depends on how you handle pressure and failures.

Latency and Minimal Copying

By design, the pipeline avoids unnecessary copying:

- feed handlers convert wire messages into q records once,
- the tickerplant appends and forwards mostly as-is,
- RDB and clients receive vectors that map closely to their in-memory tables.

Combined with sequential logging and partitioned, columnar storage, this yields:

- low per-tick overhead,
- predictable latency per batch,
- graceful scaling as you add symbols or venues, as long as you provision enough CPU and network bandwidth.

Backpressure

Backpressure occurs when downstream components cannot keep up with incoming ticks. In a kdb+tick deployment, this can show up as:

- the tickerplant's send buffers filling because subscribers are slow to read,

- RDB tables growing faster than the process can handle queries,
- disk contention if the TP log falls behind due to slow I/O.

Common mitigation strategies include:

- filtering subscriptions so clients receive only what they need,
- aggregating or sampling data in the tickerplant or feed handlers (for example, sending only top-of-book, or coalescing updates),
- moving heavy analytics off the main RDB onto separate processes fed via the same TP or secondary feeds.

Because q IPC is synchronous by default for request/response and asynchronous for TP updates, you must design carefully to avoid blocking the critical path.

Failure Modes

Key failure scenarios and how the TP/RDB/HDB design responds:

- **RDB crash:** restart, replay from TP log, resume; historical data remains intact in HDB.
- **TP crash:** more serious, as live distribution and logging stop. High-availability deployments often run a standby TP that can be switched in, sometimes with feed handlers publishing to both active and standby.
- **HDB host failure:** affects historical queries and end-of-day saves; redundancy and replicated HDBs mitigate this.

We will revisit high-availability topologies in the scaling and deployment section. For now, the important lesson is that the simple log-and-replay mechanism gives robust recovery options for most intraday failures.

The kdb+tick real-time pipeline brings together many of the ideas developed earlier in this chapter:

- q's typed vectors and IPC allow feed handlers, tickerplant, RDB, and HDB to exchange large volumes of ticks with minimal encoding overhead.
- The tickerplant acts as a specialized message broker and write-ahead logger, ensuring that every update is both distributed and durably recorded.
- The RDB maintains today's data in memory, using the same schemas and attributes as the HDB, so that as-of joins and temporal windows can run with low latency.
- The HDB provides long-term, partitioned, columnar storage, loaded efficiently from the RDB at end-of-day.
- Clients interact through subscriptions and queries, often pushing computation to the data rather than pulling raw ticks across the network.

By dissecting the TP/RDB/HDB trio, you can now see the end-to-end path of a tick: from wire, through normalization, into a typed q table, across IPC, into in-memory analytics, and finally into historical storage. In the next section, we will build on this foundation to discuss how to scale this architecture across processes and hosts, and how gateways can help manage growing query loads without sacrificing the latency characteristics that make kdb+ attractive for market data.

4.5 Scaling, Deployment, and Gateways

So far we have treated kdb+ as if it lived on a single powerful server: one tickerplant, one RDB, one HDB. For a surprising number of trading desks, that single-node pattern works well. Modern hardware is fast, and well-written q can process an impressive amount of tick data on one box.

However, as your universe of instruments grows, as you add more venues and more users, a single server eventually becomes a constraint. CPU cores saturate on hot symbols, memory fills with intraday history, and network fan-out to many clients starts to hurt latency.

This section explains how to move from that simple starting point to a horizontally scaled, fault-tolerant deployment. We will focus on three themes:

- **Process sharding**: splitting work across multiple TPs, RDBs, and HDBs.
- **NUMA-aware placement**: using the physical layout of CPUs and memory to preserve the low-latency properties of kdb+.
- **Gateways**: introducing query routers and caches that provide a unified logical view while protecting the core data stores.

Our goal is to make each scaling step feel like an understandable extension of the single-node tick architecture you already know.

Revisiting the Single-Node Architecture

Let us briefly restate the baseline:

- One physical or virtual server.
- One tickerplant receiving normalized feeds and logging them.
- One RDB subscribing to that TP and holding intraday tables in memory.
- One HDB on local or attached storage, serving historical queries and taking end-of-day saves from the RDB.
- Clients directly connecting to the TP (for subscriptions) and to RDB/HDB (for queries).

This setup has many virtues:

- Simplicity: easy to reason about and to operate.
- Low latency: no network hops between TP, RDB, and HDB if they share a host.

- Minimal coordination: all intraday state is centralized.

Its weaknesses show up as you scale:

- **CPU bottlenecks**: one TP and one RDB must ingest and process all ticks. Hot symbols and bursty periods can saturate cores.
- **Memory pressure**: storing deep intraday histories for many instruments can exhaust RAM on a single host.
- **Fan-out**: many client connections to the TP and RDB mean more IPC work, more context switches, and more backpressure risk.
- **Single point of failure**: a hardware or OS issue can bring down the entire pipeline.

Scaling is about addressing these bottlenecks while preserving the core promise: fast, predictable operations on arrays of time.

Sharding: Dividing the Work Horizontally

The most natural way to scale kdb+ is to divide the universe of data and queries across multiple processes and hosts. This is known as sharding. Conceptually, you *partition the problem space*, not just the storage:

- by symbol or symbol ranges,
- by venue,
- by asset class,
- or by a combination of these.

Each shard has its own TP/RDB/HDB set, or at least its own RDB and HDB, possibly fed from a small number of TPs.

Sharding by Symbol

Sharding by symbol is often the simplest and most effective. For example:

- Shard A handles symbols starting with A–M.
- Shard B handles symbols starting with N–Z.

Or, more realistically, you create symbol groups that reflect liquidity and importance, aiming to balance tick volumes across shards.

In this design:

- Feed handlers demultiplex ticks by symbol and send them to the appropriate shard's tickerplant.
- Each shard's TP, RDB, and HDB see only their subset of the universe.
- Clients that care about a specific symbol or basket connect to the relevant shard(s).

The benefits are clear:

- CPU load per shard is reduced.
- Memory footprint per RDB is smaller, because each holds fewer instruments.
- End-of-day saves and HDB storage are spread across multiple hosts or disks.

The main cost is increased coordination complexity:

- A client needing a cross-universe view (for example, an index over all symbols) must query multiple shards.
- Operational tooling must manage multiple TPs, RDBs, and HDBs.

We will see later how gateways help hide some of that complexity from end users.

Sharding by Venue

Alternatively, or in addition, you can shard by venue. This is especially useful when:

- you trade the same set of symbols across many exchanges,
- each exchange has its own distinct feed with its own idiosyncrasies,
- you want to measure and control latency per venue.

In a venue-sharded design:

- Each shard deals with one or a small group of exchanges.
- Intraday tables and HDB layouts carry a venue column but within a narrower venue set.

This can simplify feed handler logic and help isolate problems: an outage in one shard's venue feed affects only that shard.

Write-Heavy and Read-Heavy Separation

Another useful dimension is separating write and read workloads:

- A subset of processes (and hosts) focus on ingesting and persisting data (TP + RDB + HDB for each shard).
- Other processes specialize in serving read-heavy analytics, perhaps subscribing to TPs and querying HDBs, but not involved in ingestion.

This separation allows you to:

- shield ingestion from heavy ad-hoc queries,
- tune some nodes aggressively for CPU and memory (the writers),

- and others for concurrency and network bandwidth (the readers).

In practice, write/read separation is often combined with symbol or venue sharding for even finer control.

NUMA-Aware Deployment on Modern Servers

Even before you move to multiple hosts, modern multi-socket servers are themselves small distributed systems. They have a Non-Uniform Memory Access (NUMA) architecture:

- Each CPU socket has local memory banks.
- Accessing local memory is faster than accessing memory attached to another socket.
- Caches and memory controllers are also per-socket.

If you ignore NUMA considerations, you may get unpredictable latency because:

- a process runs on cores attached to one socket,
- but much of its memory (for example, large columns) resides on another socket.

Pinning Processes and Memory

To mitigate this, you can:

- pin each key kdb+ process (TP, RDB, HDB) to a specific NUMA node or subset of cores,
- allocate memory with awareness of that node, for example by starting the process with the right OS affinity and memory policies.

The aim is:

- for the RDB to keep its hottest columns and working sets in memory local to its cores,
- for the TP to avoid bouncing its log buffers across sockets,
- for HDB processes to access memory close to the cores doing the disk I/O.

q itself does not manage NUMA for you; this is done via OS-level configuration and deployment discipline. However, because kdb+ uses large contiguous vectors and memory-mapped files, the gains from good locality are significant:

- fewer cross-socket memory accesses,
- more predictable cache behavior,
- lower noise in latency-sensitive operations such as as-of joins on hot symbols.

Co-locating Hot Partitions

You can also exploit knowledge of which date partitions and symbol ranges are "hot" intraday:

- the current day's partitions are accessed more than historical ones,
- a small subset of symbols may dominate trading volume and query loads.

On a large host, you might:

- place the current day's RDB and its hottest HDB partitions on the same NUMA node as the RDB cores,
- leave colder historical partitions to other nodes or hosts.

This arrangement reduces contention and improves cache hit rates when intraday analytics reach back into recent history.

Gateways: A Logical View over a Physical Mesh

As you shard processes and pay attention to NUMA placement, the physical topology grows more complex. From a user's perspective, however, you ideally present something simple:

- a single logical database,
- accessible with familiar q queries,
- that "just happens" to be fast and reliable.

Gateway processes are the main tool kdb+ practitioners use to bridge this gap.

What is a Gateway?

A gateway is a kdb+ process that:

- accepts client connections and q queries,
- routes each query to the appropriate RDBs and HDBs based on the data it needs,
- optionally aggregates, caches, or post-processes results,
- returns a unified result to the client.

From a client's point of view, the gateway looks like a single database server. Internally, it knows:

- which shards own which symbols, venues, or date ranges,
- which processes hold intraday versus historical data,
- how to combine partial results from multiple sources into a single table or vector.

Routing by Symbol, Venue, and Time

The gateway's routing logic often mirrors your sharding scheme:

- queries filtered by symbol are directed to the shard that owns that symbol,
- cross-symbol queries are split into sub-queries, one per shard, then merged,
- intraday portions of a query are handled by RDBs, while older data is taken from HDBs.

For example, a client asking for a month of trades for a symbol might trigger:

1. a sub-query to the relevant shard's RDB for today's part,
2. sub-queries to the shard's HDB processes for the previous days,
3. merging and time-ordering the results in the gateway before sending them back.

This hides the physical division between RDB and HDB and between shards.

Protecting the Core from Heavy Workloads

Gateways serve another critical role: shielding core TPs, RDBs, and HDBs from abusive or overly heavy queries. Because gateways are intermediaries, you can:

- enforce limits on data volumes, time ranges, or CPU time per query,
- implement admission control or prioritization for certain clients,
- offload some computations from the core to the gateway itself when appropriate.

In effect, the gateway becomes a guardrail:

- risky experiments by analysts are run through gateways,
- if a query turns out to be too heavy, it harms the gateway first, not the production RDB ingesting live ticks.

Since gateways are stateless or lightly stateful (they do not hold primary copies of data), you can scale them horizontally and restart them without risking data loss.

Caching and Precomputation at the Gateway Layer

Many queries are repetitive: the same dashboards are refreshed every few seconds, and the same summary metrics are requested by multiple users. Gateways are natural places to cache or precompute such results.

Result Caching

A simple yet effective pattern is:

- when a query arrives, the gateway checks if its result (for the specified time range and parameters) is already in cache,
- if so, return the cached result immediately,
- if not, forward the query to the underlying kdb+ processes, cache the result, then return it.

This can dramatically reduce load on RDBs and HDBs when:

- many users share dashboards and reports,
- the underlying data changes slowly relative to refresh frequency,
- queries are expensive relative to the cost of caching.

Precomputing Aggregates

Gateways can also host scheduled jobs that precompute commonly requested aggregates, such as:

- daily volume curves per symbol,
- intraday liquidity and volatility metrics,
- rolling factor exposures for baskets.

These precomputations can:

- run during quieter periods or staggered across time,
- save only aggregated results into small tables in the gateway or a cached store,
- serve user queries from these precomputed tables instead of rederiving metrics from raw ticks.

Because q expressions are compact and composable, the same logic you use for on-the-fly analytics can often be reused in batch jobs, simply wrapped in scheduling logic.

High Availability: Active/Standby and Replication Patterns

Scaling is not only about performance; it is also about resilience. As you distribute work across more hosts and processes, you should plan for how to survive failures.

Active/Standby Tickerplants

The tickerplant is a critical component: if it fails, live distribution of ticks and logging stops. A common pattern is:

- run an active TP that handles live feeds,

- run a standby TP that either:
  - receives a copy of the feeds and logs them, or
  - tails the active TP's log and keeps a synchronized state.
- use orchestration or manual procedures to promote the standby to active if the primary fails.

This reduces downtime and preserves continuity of the log, at the cost of extra complexity and hardware.

Replicated HDBs

For historical data, you can replicate HDB partitions across hosts:

- maintain two or more HDB instances with identical content,
- direct queries to either or both, using gateways to load-balance,
- use OS or storage-level replication, or application-level copy, to keep them in sync.

Replication protects you from hardware failures and allows you to:

- schedule heavy batch jobs on secondary HDBs,
- keep primary HDBs more responsive for ad-hoc queries.

From Proof-of-Concept to Production Mesh

When you evolve from a proof-of-concept single node to a production mesh, it helps to take small, deliberate steps rather than leaping into a complex architecture immediately. A typical progression might be:

1. **Single host**: one TP, one RDB, one HDB. Validate schemas, latency, and correctness.
2. **Add gateways**: insert a simple gateway between clients and the core, mainly as a safety and routing layer.

3. **Shard by symbol**: split into two or more shards, starting with the hottest symbols on their own shard. Update gateways to route queries accordingly.
4. **Introduce NUMA pinning**: on each host, pin processes and tune memory and OS settings as loads grow.
5. **Add standby TPs and replicated HDBs**: once the mesh is stable under load, add high-availability features.
6. **Refine caching and precomputation**: as usage patterns stabilize, move common analytics into precomputed paths behind gateways.

At each stage, you maintain the same logical model:

- ticks are arrays of time flowing from feed handlers through TPs into RDBs and HDBs,
- queries are vector operations in q operating on columnar tables,
- gateways are q processes orchestrating and combining those operations across the mesh.

Scaling kdb+ is less about inventing new mechanisms and more about applying the same principles—arrays, time, locality—at larger scope:

- **Process sharding** lets you divide ingest and query workloads across multiple TP/RDB/HDB sets, typically by symbol or venue, reducing per-node CPU and memory pressure.
- **NUMA-aware placement** keeps hot data close to the cores that process it, preserving latency characteristics even on large multi-socket servers.
- **Gateways** provide a unified logical view over a physically distributed mesh, route queries intelligently, cache results, and protect core data stores from heavy or misbehaving workloads.
- **High-availability patterns** such as active/standby TPs and replicated HDBs turn this mesh into a resilient platform rather than a fragile cluster.

With these deployment patterns in mind, you can design kdb+ environments that grow with your trading business: from a single server supporting a small strategy, to a horizontally scaled, fault-tolerant mesh underpinning a whole firm's market data and analytics stack.

4.6 Integration and Feed Handlers

By now we have treated kdb+ mostly from the inside: the q language, table design and HDB layout, temporal joins and windows, and the kdb+tick TP/RDB/HDB pipeline, including how to scale it and introduce gateways. In production, however, kdb+ is rarely an island. It sits between external market feeds on one side and a wide variety of applications on the other.

This section explains how kdb+ connects to that outside world. We will look at three integration edges:

- ingesting market data from exchanges and vendors via dedicated feed handlers,
- interposing streaming buses such as Kafka or Redpanda between feeds and kdb+,
- serving application clients through APIs and gateways while preserving the performance and consistency of the core store.

Throughout, two architectural themes recur:

- **Backpressure awareness**: making sure downstream components can signal when they are overloaded, and that upstream components react gracefully instead of dropping data or stalling unpredictably.
- **Replayability**: ensuring that the same ticks can be replayed deterministically into new or restarted consumers, for recovery or research.

Feed Handlers: From Raw Feeds to Normalized q Records

On the left edge of the architecture sit *feed handlers*. These are processes, often written in C, C++, or Java, that speak native exchange or vendor protocols. Their responsibilities are to:

- receive raw packets or messages from networks (multicast, TCP, proprietary APIs),
- decode binary formats into structured messages,
- normalize those messages into a schema that maps directly to your kdb+ tables.

Decoding Market Protocols

Each exchange and vendor has its own wire protocol:

- some are binary multicast feeds with compact field encodings and sequence numbers,
- others are TCP-based with framing and keep-alives,
- vendors may provide their own libraries and data models.

Feed handlers must:

- parse these messages in real time,
- track sequence numbers and retransmissions,
- handle gaps, out-of-order packets, and connection resets.

Although this code sits outside kdb+, its design directly affects the downstream tick pipeline. If decoding is slow or prone to backlogs, the tickerplant and RDB will see bursts rather than smooth flow.

Normalization into q-Compatible Structures

The output of a feed handler should be as close as possible to the logical q schema you designed earlier. This means:

- converting timestamps into the q temporal types you use system-wide,
- mapping exchange or vendor symbol identifiers into your canonical symbol representation,
- aligning field names and types with your trade and quote tables (for example, *time*, *sym*, *price*, *size*, *bid*, *ask*).

Crucially, this normalization step should not create per-message heavyweight objects. Instead, feed handlers should accumulate small batches of decoded messages into vector-like structures that can be serialized into q tables with minimal copying.

Once normalized, feed handlers send these batches over q IPC to the tickerplant or, in some designs, to an intermediate bus such as Kafka.

Feed Handler Backpressure

Even at this first stage, you must consider backpressure:

- Network feeds can deliver ticks faster than you can process them in rare, bursty periods.
- Downstream components (TP, Kafka, etc.) may slow down or become temporarily unavailable.

A robust feed handler design:

- uses bounded internal queues rather than unbounded buffering,
- monitors downstream send latencies and queue depths,
- has defined policies for overload: dropping non-critical messages, sampling updates, or temporarily disconnecting and resynchronizing by gap-fill mechanisms.

The key is to avoid a situation where the process keeps buffer-growing in memory until it fails in an uncontrolled manner. Instead, you strive for *controlled degradation*: under extreme load you may reduce fidelity, but you know exactly how and where that happens.

Kafka and Redpanda: Streaming Buses as Intermediaries

Between feed handlers and the tickerplant, many modern architectures insert a streaming bus, typically Kafka or Redpanda. This adds components, but gives two major benefits:

- **Decoupling**: producers and consumers can be scaled and managed independently.
- **Durable, ordered logs**: topics act as partitioned, append-only logs, useful for replay and integrating additional consumers.

Designing Topics and Partitions

Choosing topic and partition keys is analogous to designing table partitioning in the HDB. For market data, common patterns are:

- one topic per asset class (for example, *equities.trades*, *futures.quotes*),
- partitions keyed by symbol, symbol range, or venue.

Partitioning by symbol or venue allows:

- multiple kdb+ consumers to read from different partitions in parallel,
- data locality when mapping topic partitions to specific tick shards,
- better balancing of load across cluster nodes.

Messages placed on these topics should already be normalized as much as possible, so that kdb+ consumers can stream them into trade and quote tables without extra parsing work.

Batching and Latency Trade-Offs

Producers to Kafka or Redpanda control batching parameters:

- how many messages or bytes to accumulate before sending a batch,
- how long to wait before flushing a partially filled batch.

Larger batches improve throughput and compression efficiency but add latency. For trading systems, you typically:

- configure small but non-zero batching to amortize protocol overhead,
- set conservative flush timeouts to limit latency,
- monitor end-to-end delay (from feed wire timestamp to kdb+ ingestion) to ensure it remains within budget.

The right parameters depend on your use case: ultra-low-latency strategies might bypass Kafka altogether, while research or less sensitive workflows can tolerate extra milliseconds.

Idempotent Consumption and Exactly-Once Semantics

When kdb+ consumes from Kafka or Redpanda, it should do so in a way that supports replay without duplication of effects. Two simple disciplines help:

- Each message contains a natural sequence key (for example, exchange sequence number, or a monotonically increasing feed ID plus offset).

- Consumers keep track of their last processed offset per partition, committing progress only after applying updates to kdb+ tables.

If a consumer is restarted and replays from an earlier offset, it can:

- detect older messages by their sequence or timestamp,
- avoid applying them twice, for example by ignoring duplicates or by rebuilding from a clean snapshot.

While strict "exactly-once" semantics end-to-end are hard to guarantee in any distributed system, careful design here makes replay and recovery much more reliable.

kdb+ as a Consumer: Streaming into the Tickerplant

When kdb+ acts as a consumer from Kafka or Redpanda, the flow is:

1. A small adapter process or q script reads batches from topic partitions.
2. It converts those batches into q tables matching your tick schema.
3. It sends these tables over IPC to one or more tickerplants, just as a direct feed handler would.

The adapter should be aware of:

- backpressure from the TP (for example, slow sends or explicit signals),
- lag relative to the head of the Kafka topic, which indicates whether it is keeping up.

An important design choice is where you treat the "system of record" for ticks:

- Some firms treat Kafka topics as the primary log; kdb+ is one of many consumers.
- Others treat the tickerplant's log as primary and use Kafka as a side-channel or for derived streams.

Either approach can work, but you should be clear on which log you trust as authoritative, and how long you retain it.

kdb+ as a Producer: Pushing Out Derived Streams

kdb+ does not only consume data; it often produces derived streams:

- cleaned and normalized ticks,
- enriched events (for example, trades with attached quotes and microstructure features),
- risk and P&L updates,
- alert and monitoring events.

These streams may be published back to Kafka or pushed directly to downstream applications. The production side must also be designed with backpressure and replay in mind:

- use bounded queues between analytics and Kafka producers,
- include sufficient identifiers and timestamps in messages to support downstream replay and deduplication.

A natural pattern is to:

- compute derived metrics in RDB or analytics processes,
- write their outputs into q tables,
- have a publishing process tail those tables and push new rows into Kafka topics.

This keeps computation and integration concerns separate, and lets you re-run the publishing step if necessary, using saved intermediate results.

Client Integration: APIs and Access Patterns

On the right edge of the architecture, kdb+ serves a wide range of clients:

- quant researchers using Python or R,
- production trading systems in C++, Java, or .NET,
- reporting tools and dashboards.

These clients connect either directly to kdb+ processes or, more commonly in larger deployments, through gateways.

Language Bindings and Interfaces

Several common integration points are:

- Native q IPC from another q process.
- Python interfaces (for example, via PyKX), exposing q data as Python objects or array types.
- JDBC/ODBC drivers for BI tools.
- REST-style HTTP gateways that translate HTTP requests into q queries and serialize results as JSON.

Regardless of the surface protocol, the same performance principle applies: *push computation to kdb+ rather than pulling raw data out.* That means:

- send concise q expressions that describe aggregations or filters,
- let RDB or HDB execute them near the data,
- return only the final or intermediate results needed by the client.

Row-by-row pulls—for example, looping in Python and requesting one tick at a time—destroy the benefits of kdb+'s columnar model and IPC design.

Consistent Views Across Real-Time and Historical Data

Applications often need a view that spans both:

- intraday data in the RDB,
- and historical data in the HDB.

Gateways or client-side libraries can hide this split by:

- sending one part of the query to the RDB (for today's slice),
- sending the remainder to HDB processes (for prior days),
- merging and sorting the results before returning them to the client.

To maintain consistency:

- schemas and type representations must align between RDB and HDB,
- attributes such as sorted time and parted date should be preserved across both,
- any aggregations or window functions should behave identically on both sides.

This is one of the strengths of kdb+: the same q code can generally be used on both real-time and historical stores.

Backpressure from Clients

Clients rarely admit to being slow, but they sometimes behave that way:

- a dashboard may refresh many heavy charts simultaneously,
- a researcher may fire off expensive ad-hoc queries,

- downstream systems may struggle to parse or store large result sets.

This client-induced load can ripple back into kdb+ processes. Well-designed integration layers mitigate this:

- Gateways can limit query concurrency, result sizes, or execution time per user.
- Real-time subscriptions can be filtered so each client sees only the tables and symbols it needs.
- Push-based feeds to clients can be throttled or sampled under load.

On the kdb+ side, you can instrument:

- CPU time per query,
- volume of data returned,
- per-client or per-application usage patterns.

This feedback informs both technical tuning and governance (for example, rate-limiting heavy users).

Replayability Across the Whole Stack

We have already discussed replay within kdb+ via the tickerplant log. When you widen the lens to include exterior components (feed handlers, Kafka, clients), replay becomes a cross-system concern.

Ideally, you want the ability to:

- rebuild an RDB or HDB from an authoritative log (tickerplant log or Kafka topics),
- reconstruct exactly what a given strategy or risk system saw at a particular historical time,

- simulate intraday behavior by replaying ticks at original or controlled speeds.

To support this end-to-end:

- Preserve original timestamps and sequence identifiers from the exchange in all downstream messages and tables.
- Ensure that logs (TP and/or Kafka) are retained for a sufficient period, with clear retention guarantees.
- Make feed handlers and kdb+ consumers capable of running in both "live" and "replay" modes, ideally reusing the same code paths.
- Record versions of critical configuration and code so that you can rerun past days with matching logic.

When this is done well, you gain a powerful research capability: intraday backtests and forensics that use the exact tick stream and system behavior as in production.

Putting It Together: A Robust Integration Edge

Let us summarize how the pieces connect and how they preserve backpressure awareness and replayability:

- **Feed handlers** decode raw market protocols and normalize messages into q-compatible records. They implement bounded queues and overload policies to avoid uncontrolled memory growth.
- **Streaming buses** like Kafka or Redpanda optionally sit between feeds and kdb+, providing durable, partitioned logs that multiple consumers can read from. Topic and partition design mirrors your sharding scheme.
- **kdb+ consumers** read batches from topics or from direct feeds, convert them to q tables, and push them into tickerplants. They track offsets or log positions to enable replay and avoid duplicate effects.

- **Tickerplants, RDBs, and HDBs** form the core store, as described in earlier sections, with write-ahead logging and end-of-day saves.
- **Gateways and APIs** expose this core to clients, routing queries, caching results, and enforcing limits. They encourage a pattern of pushing computation to kdb+ rather than exporting raw ticks.

Across this entire path, backpressure is handled by:

- carefully bounded queues and timeouts,
- monitoring lag and resource utilization at each hop,
- choosing when to shed load, sample, or slow down producers.

Replayability is ensured by:

- treating certain logs (Kafka topics, TP logs) as authoritative append-only histories,
- preserving identifiers and timestamps across transformations,
- making components able to consume from these logs in a deterministic replay mode.

With this integration edge in place, kdb+ is not just a fast time-series database but a well-behaved citizen of a larger trading and research stack—one that can keep up with live markets, recover from failures, and reproduce past behavior when you need to understand or improve your strategies.

Chapter 5

ClickHouse for Time-Series Markets

ClickHouse looks like "just another column store" from a distance, but in time-series markets it behaves more like a streaming engine fused to an analytics database. This chapter turns that raw speed into something you can actually trust for ticks, orders, and risk: we'll shape schemas around temporal precision, bend MergeTree to continuous ingest, and wire up replication, sharding, and materialized views so that petabytes of history still feel interactive at the desk.

5.1 SQL Dialect and Temporal Data Types

ClickHouse is often introduced as a "columnar OLAP database," but if you approach it with only a generic warehouse mindset, you will quickly run into trouble with market data. Trading systems care deeply about time: not just the date, not just the second, but sometimes the exact nanosecond in which a trade was matched. They also care about sparse fields, evolving schemas, and compact storage of arrays of prices or sizes.

This section gives you a practical mental model of ClickHouse's SQL dialect as it applies to time-series markets. We focus on three core ideas:

- How ClickHouse's SQL is similar to, and different from, standard relational SQL.
- How to model time correctly with DateTime64 and related temporal types.
- How arrays and nullable columns help you represent real-world tick and bar data without sacrificing precision or scan performance.

The goal is not to cover every corner of the language, but to give you a toolbox that lets you express trades, quotes, and candles accurately and compactly, ready for the storage engines and table designs discussed in later sections.

ClickHouse SQL in a Market Data Mindset

If you know basic ANSI-style SQL, ClickHouse will feel familiar: you still write SELECT, FROM, WHERE, GROUP BY, and ORDER BY. Joins, aggregations, and subqueries work broadly as you expect. For someone coming from kdb+, the syntax will feel more verbose, but the semantics line up with a relational engine: tables, rows, and columns.

There are, however, differences that matter specifically for time-series work:

- ClickHouse is strongly typed. Every column has a fixed, explicit type. There is no automatic promotion from integer to floating point or from string to timestamp without an explicit cast. This is healthy for trading systems, because it makes accidental loss of precision less likely.
- Many functions are vectorized and time-aware. There are built-in functions to manipulate timestamps, truncate to time buckets, and work with arrays, which we will use heavily when forming bars and order-book snapshots.

- The storage engine (a MergeTree variant, discussed in the next section) is exposed more directly in the DDL. You declare primary keys, partition keys, and table engines explicitly. This means your understanding of the SQL layer must already take into account how data will later be sorted on disk.

From a markets perspective, the key mental shift is this:

> In ClickHouse, the types and schema you choose at table-creation time are not a cosmetic concern. They control temporal correctness, compression behavior, and query performance.

The rest of this section develops that idea for the central building block of all market data: time.

Event Time, Ingest Time, and Time Zones

Before choosing concrete types, it is important to clarify which "time" you are recording and why. In market data, at least two notions of time are usually relevant:

- **Event time** When the event actually occurred at the venue or matching engine. For a trade, this might be the exchange's matching timestamp. For a quote, it might be when the quote became effective on the central limit order book.
- **Ingest time** When your system observed and stored that event. This could be when a message was received from a multicast feed, or when it was written to a Kafka topic and later consumed by ClickHouse.

These two clocks can diverge for many reasons: network delays, batching, or clock skew. For compliance, backtesting, and replay, event time is usually the primary axis: if you replay a day's trading, you want the trades and quotes in the same sequence as the market saw them, not as your capture stack happened to receive them.

However, ingest time is still valuable. You may want to analyze latency, detect outages where the ingest pipeline stalled, or reconstruct what was "known" to a strategy at a particular time in your own infrastructure.

A simple rule of thumb is:

- Always model both event time and ingest time as separate columns.
- Make event time the first-class "time axis" for most queries and for physical sorting on disk.
- Use ingest time mainly for pipeline diagnostics and audit trails.

On top of this, you must consider time zones. Exchanges publish timestamps in specific time zones: for example, New York equities in America/New_York, many crypto venues in UTC, and so on. ClickHouse can interpret timestamps either as plain UTC or as a local time zone with daylight savings rules.

For trading systems, a robust pattern is:

- Store all event timestamps in UTC inside ClickHouse.
- If you need to present data in local exchange time, convert for display or reporting, not for storage.

This avoids ambiguities around daylight savings transitions and makes cross-venue joins less error-prone. It also aligns with most upstream capture systems, which often normalize to UTC as early as possible.

With these concepts in place, we can choose the concrete temporal types.

Why DateTime64 Matters for Market Data

Most relational systems offer two broad timestamp types:

- A date or datetime type with second-level precision.

- A higher-precision type (often called timestamp) with fractional seconds.

In high-frequency markets, seconds are far too coarse. You may see thousands of trades per second in a single symbol, and multi-leg strategies that care about microsecond or nanosecond differences.

ClickHouse's DateTime64 type is designed for this world. It stores timestamps as a fixed-point number of fractional seconds since the epoch, with a configurable scale. The scale defines how many decimal places of fractional seconds you retain:

- A scale of 3 gives millisecond precision.
- A scale of 6 gives microsecond precision.
- A scale of 9 gives nanosecond precision.

At table-creation time, you choose the scale once, and every row in that column uses the same precision. For example, a trade table might use:

- DateTime64(6) for event time, capturing microsecond-level detail.
- DateTime64(3) for ingest time, if your capture system only timestamps to the millisecond.

Choosing the scale is a trade-off between:

- **Precision** How finely you can distinguish events that occur close together.
- **Storage size** Higher precision needs more bits. In practice, the difference is small compared to the overall width of a market data row.
- **Interoperability** Some upstream systems only produce millisecond timestamps; storing nanoseconds might be unnecessary and misleading.

For most trading applications:

- Millisecond precision is sufficient for slower markets or for daily bars.
- Microsecond precision suits many equities and futures feeds.
- Nanosecond precision is appropriate when your upstream source already delivers nanoseconds and you do not want to lose information.

The important part is consistency: use the same precision for all event-time columns you later want to compare or join, and avoid "upgrading" or "downgrading" precision in the middle of the pipeline. Conversions can introduce rounding and off-by-one errors that are painful to debug in a trading context.

Encoding Trades and Quotes with Temporal Types

Let us ground this in concrete schemas for the two most basic datasets: trades and quotes.

Trades.

A canonical trade row for liquid instruments often includes:

- Instrument identifier: symbol or a richer instrument key.
- Event time: when the trade occurred at the venue, as DateTime64.
- Ingest time: when the trade entered your pipeline.
- Price and size: usually numeric types with enough precision to represent ticks.
- Side: buyer- or seller-initiated, if known.
- Venue or feed identifier.
- Trade identifier: exchange trade ID or a composite key.

Here, event time should be the leading temporal field and typically participates in the primary sort of the table. Ingest time may be left as a regular column. Both should use DateTime64 rather than a lower-precision type to avoid ambiguity when multiple trades occur within the same second.

Quotes.

Quote data is more complex because each event usually contains multiple fields: bid price, bid size, ask price, ask size, and possibly multiple levels of the book. A basic top-of-book quote row might include:

- Instrument identifier.
- Event time.
- Ingest time.
- Best bid price and size.
- Best ask price and size.
- Quote condition flags.

Here again, DateTime64 models both event and ingest times. The important design decision is to keep the same type and precision across trades and quotes; this will later make temporal joins (such as matching each trade to the most recent quote) straightforward and correct.

Representing Bars and Buckets: Dates Versus DateTime64

Candles or bars aggregate raw ticks into regular time buckets: one-minute bars, five-minute bars, daily bars, and so on. Each bar needs a way to represent its time position. Common choices include:

- A Date for daily bars: one row per symbol per day.
- A DateTime64 for intraday bars: one row per symbol per bar interval.

For daily bars, a pure Date column is often sufficient, because there is no intra-day time component. For intraday bars, it is more flexible to use DateTime64, typically pointing to the start or end of the bar interval. Using the same type as your underlying ticks simplifies roll-ups and checks:

- A one-minute bar at 10:01 can be computed by grouping ticks whose event times fall into the interval [10:01, 10:02).
- The bar's timestamp can be set to 10:01:00.000000 with the same DateTime64(6) type as the ticks.

You can still extract the calendar date component when partitioning or aggregating, but you avoid juggling different temporal types.

Nullable Columns for Sparse Market Fields

Real-world market data is messy. Not every feed supplies every field for every event:

- Some venues may omit a trade condition or a specific flag.
- Certain instruments may not have meaningful sizes or implied quotes.
- Regulatory fields may only appear for certain regions or asset classes.

In a traditional relational system, you have a few options:

- Allow NULLs in the column.
- Use special sentinel values (for example, -1 to mean "unknown").
- Split into separate tables for different instrument types.

ClickHouse supports nullable columns explicitly via the Nullable wrapper type. Conceptually, a Nullable column is a pair of arrays: one for the actual values and one for a bitmap indicating which rows are null.

For example:

- A column Nullable(Float64) can represent either a floating-point value or no value.
- A column Nullable(DateTime64(6)) can represent a timestamp or an absent timestamp.

Using nullable columns in market schemas is generally preferable to sentinel values for several reasons:

- It makes SQL expressions clearer. You can use standard IS NULL and COALESCE-style functions instead of remembering magic constants.
- It preserves type correctness. You do not have to choose a sentinel inside the valid numeric range.
- It compresses well. The bitmap and columnar layout allow ClickHouse to handle sparse fields efficiently.

A common pattern is:

- Use non-nullable types for fields you expect to be always present in your dataset (for example, symbol, event time, price).
- Use nullable types for optional or feed-specific fields (for example, trade condition flags, regulatory indicators).

This keeps the core of your schema clean while still allowing you to extend it as you onboard new feeds or regions with additional fields.

Arrays, Maps, and Tuples for Order-Book and Enriched Data

Quotes and trades are often just the visible tip of the iceberg. Many trading systems work directly with order-book depth, volatility surfaces, or enriched attributes that do not fit neatly into a flat, scalar schema. ClickHouse's complex types—arrays, maps, and tuples—allow you to keep these structures in a single row while retaining columnar efficiency.

Arrays.

An array column stores a variable-length list of values of the same type. For example:

- An array of prices: multiple price levels in an order book snapshot.
- An array of sizes: corresponding quantities at each level.

Arrays are particularly natural for order-book data. Instead of normalizing each price level into a separate row (which would explode row counts and hurt cache locality), you can store an array of the top N levels per side in each snapshot row:

- bid_prices: array of best bid prices, sorted from highest to lowest.
- bid_sizes: array of corresponding sizes.
- ask_prices and ask_sizes: similarly for offers.

This layout keeps all levels for a symbol at a given time point packed together on disk, which is ideal for snapshot-based analyses and for reconstructing book states over time.

Maps and tuples.

Maps are associative arrays: key-value pairs where keys and values have defined types. They can be useful for sparse, dynamic attributes, such as per-venue flags or miscellaneous metrics that vary widely between instruments. Tuples are fixed-size, ordered collections of fields, often used to group a small number of related values.

In a trading context, arrays tend to be the workhorse complex type. Maps and tuples appear more in metadata-heavy datasets or in intermediate computations where you want to package a small structure without creating a separate table.

Avoiding Common Temporal Pitfalls

When modeling time-series data in ClickHouse for markets, there are a few recurring mistakes that are easy to avoid with a bit of discipline.

Ambiguous time zones.

Mixing local exchange timestamps and UTC without a clear convention is a recipe for subtle bugs. Always normalize to UTC upon ingestion into ClickHouse and record any original time zone as a separate metadata field if you need it later.

Lossy casting between timestamp types.

Casting a DateTime64(6) to a DateTime (second-level precision) discards information. Doing that in a join condition or a grouping key may collapse multiple events into the same bucket unexpectedly. When you must change precision, do it consciously and document the choice, preferably at the edges of the system rather than in core tables.

Mixing event and ingest time.

It is tempting to group by "time" without being explicit about which clock you mean. In schemas and queries, use clear, distinct names such as event_time and ingest_time. Decide early which one governs sorting, partitioning, and most analytics, and stick to it.

Overuse of nullable types.

Nullable columns are powerful, but if everything is nullable, you lose the benefit of having clear, guaranteed fields. Reserve nullable types for genuinely optional data. For core attributes that must be present for all instruments and feeds, prefer non-nullable columns and handle missing data upstream.

Schema Sketch: Generic SQL Versus ClickHouse-Oriented Design

To see how ClickHouse's temporal types, arrays, and nullability change a schema, it is useful to contrast a "generic SQL" tick schema with a ClickHouse-aware version. Imagine a simple trades table:

- In a generic relational database, you might use a basic TIMESTAMP type with second or microsecond precision, char-based symbols, and a few optional fields held as loose strings or numbers.
- In ClickHouse, you instead choose a precise DateTime64 for

event and ingest times, make core columns non-nullable, and wrap optional ones in Nullable. You add array columns if you want to keep related structures (for example, multiple fills) inside a single row.

Right after introducing these ideas conceptually, it is helpful to visualize the contrast.

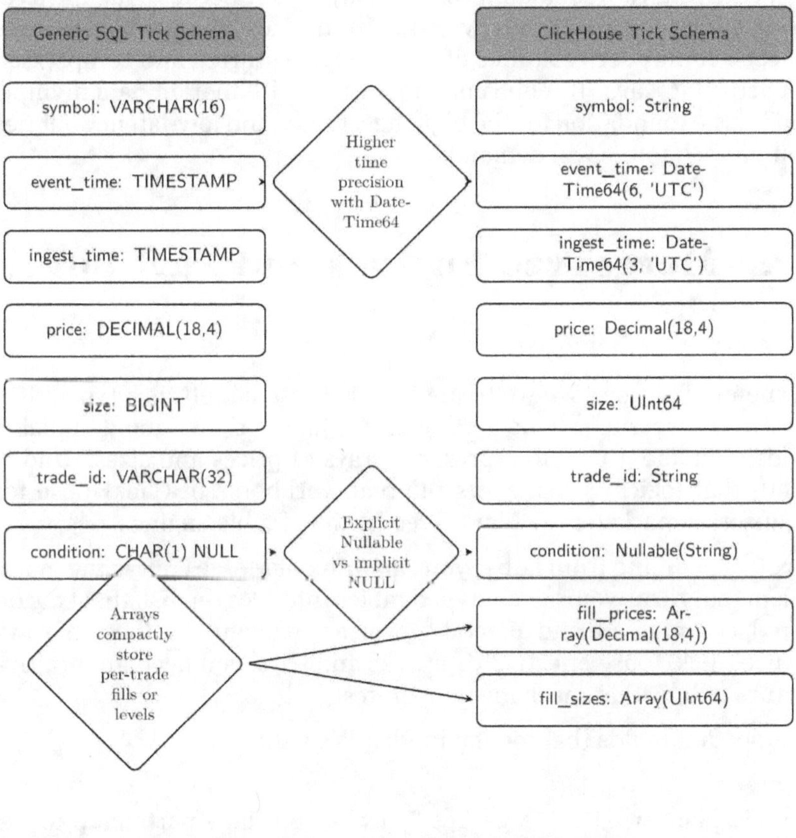

The actual DDL syntax is not important here. What matters is the mindset: you are explicit about temporal precision, about which fields can be absent, and about structured arrays that match market concepts like fills and depth levels.

From Types to Engines

The temporal and structural types discussed in this section—DateTime64, nullable columns, arrays, and related constructs—are the raw material out of which we will build efficient MergeTree tables. In the next section, we will see how these typed columns are stored on disk in parts, sorted by primary and partition keys, and merged over time.

It is essential to understand the SQL layer first because the physical storage model does not know about "trades" or "quotes" as business objects. It only sees columns of specific types, sorted and compressed in particular ways. By choosing those types with market data in mind, you lay the foundation for the high ingest rates and low-latency queries that later chapters will demand.

5.2 MergeTree Engines and Part Lifecycle

In the previous section we treated ClickHouse largely as a typed SQL layer: we worried about getting DateTime64 right, about nullable fields, and about how to represent arrays of prices and sizes. Underneath that logical schema sits the real workhorse of ClickHouse for time-series markets: the MergeTree family of table engines.

If you are coming from kdb+, you can think of MergeTree as the mechanism that turns your nicely-typed tables into files on disk that stay ordered, compressed, and queryable even as you pour in billions of rows. To use ClickHouse effectively for ticks and bars, you need an intuitive picture of how that mechanism operates.

This section builds that mental model. We will:

- Explain what a MergeTree "part" is and how parts map to the filesystem.
- Follow the lifecycle of your data: from insert, to part creation, to background merges, and eventually to eviction by retention rules.

- Highlight the key settings that keep ingest stable while maintaining fast scans, and explain how to reason about them without trial-and-error tuning.

The emphasis is on understanding, not remembering every knob. Once you can picture the lifecycle of a part, most MergeTree issues become much less mysterious.

What a MergeTree Table Actually Stores

At the SQL level, a MergeTree table is just another table: it has columns, types, and constraints. Physically, the table is stored as a collection of *parts* on disk. Each part is:

- A self-contained, read-only mini-table.
- Sorted on disk by the table's ORDER BY (which is closely related to its primary key).
- Placed inside a single partition (for example, a trading day).

You can think of a part as a segment of your time-series: "all trades for 2024-03-18, symbols A–K," or "100 million latest ticks for ES futures between 10:00 and 10:05." MergeTree never updates rows in place. Instead, it creates new parts and merges them in the background.
Each part, in turn, is made of:

- **Data files per column**: Because ClickHouse is columnar, each column lives in its own file or set of files inside the part. Your event_time, price, size, symbol, and other columns are all written separately.
- **Marks (index granules)**: These are small index structures that record, at regular row intervals, where in each column file a particular range of primary key values resides. They enable ClickHouse to "jump" to the relevant portions of a part when scanning, instead of reading every byte.

- **Metadata files**: Checksums, compression information, and minimal/maximal values for certain columns. These are the basis for data skipping and query pruning.

Why does this matter for markets? Because the way you choose ORDER BY (and PARTITION BY in the next section) determines:

- How well the marks can prune away data during queries.
- How compactly values like prices and sizes compress.
- How MergeTree chooses which parts to merge and when.

But before we optimize, we must understand the lifecycle of a part.

From Insert to Part: The Birth of Your Market Data

When you insert new trades or quotes into a MergeTree table, ClickHouse does not stream each row individually to disk. Instead, it works in batches:

1. Your client or materialized view sends a batch of rows. For market data this might be thousands to millions of ticks at a time.
2. On the receiving server, ClickHouse groups rows by partition key (for example, by trading day) and sorts batches according to the ORDER BY expression, often something like (symbol, event_time).
3. It then writes each group of rows as a new part on disk. Each part is immutable once written.

If your table partitions by trading day, a single insert batch that spans multiple days will usually result in multiple parts, one per day. The setting max_partitions_per_insert places an upper bound on how many partitions a single insert may fan out into, which is especially relevant if you do large backfills covering weeks of data. For live feeds, batches typically fall into a small number of adjacent partitions.

From a performance perspective, the critical detail is that writing a part is a sequential disk operation and is therefore relatively efficient. However, you pay a cost for every additional part:

- More parts means more metadata files and marks to maintain.
- Queries must inspect more parts to answer a given time range or symbol.
- There is more work for the background merge process to do later.

MergeTree's solution is to create parts eagerly (to keep ingest simple and low-latency), then merge them gradually in the background.

Background Merges: Keeping Parts Manageable

Over time, as inserts keep producing new parts, you would drown in metadata if nothing combined them. Background *merges* are how ClickHouse maintains a healthy number and size of parts.

Conceptually, a merge does the following:

1. Selects a group of parts within the same partition. These parts often contain adjacent ranges of the primary key.
2. Reads their column files in primary-key order and merges them into a single sorted stream of rows.
3. Writes this stream into a new, larger part on disk, with new marks and metadata.
4. Once the new part is fully written and checksummed, atomically swaps it in and deletes the old, smaller parts.

The result is a hierarchy of parts: many small parts from raw inserts are gradually consolidated into fewer, larger parts. The merging is done asynchronously by background threads, trying to avoid interfering with foreground queries and inserts.

Merges serve three critical functions for time-series markets:

- They improve compression. Larger parts with long runs of similar values let codecs work more efficiently. For example, prices for a single symbol over a day often change smoothly and are highly compressible when stored contiguously.

- They improve query speed. Fewer, larger parts mean fewer metadata checks and fewer seeks when scanning long date ranges.

- They stabilize write amplification. Without merges, repeatedly inserting into the same days and symbols would create a proliferation of tiny parts, each of which must be consulted for every query.

The challenge is balancing merge aggressiveness against ingest load. Merging requires reading and writing large amounts of data, which consumes CPU and disk bandwidth. If merges fall too far behind, you see a "merge backlog": many small parts accumulate and queries begin to slow down. If merges are too aggressive, they compete with ingest and cause latency spikes.

Before we discuss tuning, it is helpful to visualize the full part lifecycle.

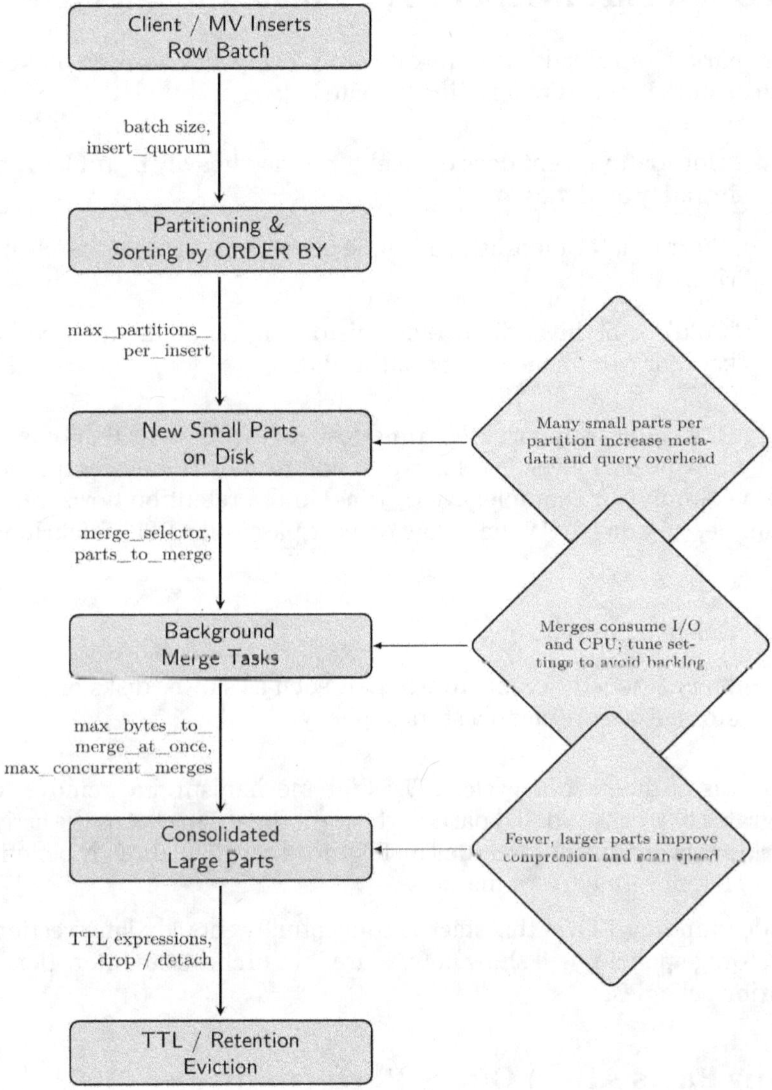
Client / MV Inserts
Row Batch
batch size,
insert_quorum
Partitioning &
Sorting by ORDER BY
max_partitions_
per_insert
New Small Parts
on Disk
Many small parts per
partition increase meta-
data and query overhead
merge_selector,
parts_to_merge
Background
Merge Tasks
Merges consume I/O
and CPU; tune set-
tings to avoid backlog
max_bytes_to_
merge_at_once,
max_concurrent_merges
Consolidated
Large Parts
Fewer, larger parts improve
compression and scan speed
TTL expressions,
drop / detach
TTL / Retention
Eviction

TTL and Part Eviction: The End of the Lifecycle

For market workloads, it is rare to keep every tick forever on your fastest storage. Most teams differentiate between:

- "Hot" data: recent days or weeks, queried heavily by traders and intraday analytics.
- "Warm" data: months to a couple of years, used for research and risk.
- "Cold" or archival data: older history, infrequently queried but kept for compliance or special studies.

MergeTree tables support *TTL* (time-to-live) expressions that operate at the row or part level. A TTL expression usually references a timestamp column (for example, event_time) and a retention horizon (for example, 365 days). When a row or part passes its TTL, ClickHouse can:

- Delete it entirely.
- Move it to a different storage tier, such as slower disks or object storage, according to a storage policy.

In terms of the part lifecycle, TTL is the mechanism that removes or migrates old, consolidated parts at the right time. This keeps the active working set small and contained on fast storage, which directly benefits query latency for current markets.

Understanding TTL at this stage is conceptually enough; later sections on storage policies will show how to use it to orchestrate multi-tier retention schemes.

How Parts Affect Query Performance

Armed with this lifecycle view, we can explain some common observations when working with large tick datasets.

Why does a table with many small parts feel slower?

Even if the total number of rows is unchanged, a table fragmented into thousands of tiny parts per partition imposes overhead on each query:

- Every part has to be considered during query planning and may require opening separate file handles.
- The marks and metadata for each part must be read and checked to see whether the part can be skipped.
- Skipping decisions become less effective because each small part tends to cover a narrow range of primary key values, leading to more files touched overall.

In practice, a few dozen parts per partition is comfortable; hundreds may be acceptable; thousands begin to hurt. Background merges, properly configured, are the antidote.

Why do merges improve compression?

Columnar compression benefits from long runs of similar values. For a single symbol over a day, prices and sizes are usually correlated from one row to the next. If these rows end up scattered across many parts—for example, because small batches were written unsorted or across multiple nodes—the compression algorithm sees shorter runs and cannot compress as effectively.

Merging parts reorders data into a smooth, primary-key-sorted sequence. For schemas where ORDER BY starts with symbol and event_time, this means:

- All events for a symbol on a day are tightly clustered.
- Price and size differences between consecutive rows are small, ideal for delta or time-series codecs.

The practical effect is a lower storage footprint and often faster scans because fewer disk pages must be touched.

Key Settings for Stable Ingest and Fast Scans

The MergeTree engine exposes many settings, but a relatively small subset governs the health of ingest and merges for typical market workloads. Here we highlight a few with intuitive explanations; the exact names may vary slightly between ClickHouse versions, but the concepts remain stable.

Insert and part-creation related settings.

- **Batch size in your client**: Although not a MergeTree setting per se, the number of rows you insert per batch has a direct impact on part sizes. Larger batches usually produce larger initial parts, reducing merge pressure. For market feeds, a good practice is to aim for inserts on the order of tens to hundreds of thousands of rows per batch, depending on hardware.
- max_partitions_per_insert: Limits how many partitions a single insert can touch. This prevents pathological inserts (for example, backfills spanning years) from exploding into thousands of tiny parts at once. For live data, setting this to a small number enforces discipline in how you group rows before insertion.

Merge scheduling and resource limits.

- max_bytes_to_merge_at_once: Caps the total size of parts that a single merge task can combine. A larger value allows building bigger consolidated parts in one go, but also requires more I/O and memory bandwidth. On a modest server, you might prefer more, smaller merges; on a powerful box, larger merges reduce the number of parts faster.
- max_concurrent_merges: Limits how many merges can run at the same time. Too many concurrent merges can saturate disks and CPUs, interfering with queries and inserts. Too few can lead to a merge backlog where small parts accumulate faster than they can be merged.
- Merge selector and priorities: ClickHouse uses internal heuristics to decide which parts to merge next, often preferring smaller parts first. For market data, this generally aligns well with the goal of quickly collapsing tiny parts created by live ingest into healthier sizes.

Background I/O and throttling.

- background_pool_size and related settings: Control the number of background threads shared between merges and other maintenance tasks. These should be sized relative to the number of CPU cores and the I/O capabilities of your storage system.
- I/O priority mechanisms: In some environments, you may configure the operating system or storage layer so that background merges run at a lower priority than foreground queries. The exact mechanics depend on your deployment, but the principle is the same: merges should be steady but not disruptive.

The guiding principle when tuning is to avoid extremes. Stable systems typically show:

- A moderate and slowly changing number of parts per partition.
- A merge queue that is non-empty (indicating useful work is being done) but not growing unbounded.
- Query latencies that are largely insensitive to momentary spikes in ingest volume.

Diagnosing MergeTree Health

Once your trading data is flowing, how do you know whether your MergeTree tables are healthy? While this book does not aim to be an operational manual, it is worth outlining a simple mental checklist.

Number and size of parts per partition.

For each MergeTree table, you can observe how many parts exist in active partitions and what their size distribution looks like. Healthy tables tend to exhibit a "pyramid" shape:

- A small number of large, consolidated parts covering older data.
- Some medium-sized parts for more recent days where merges are still catching up.
- Many small parts only in the very latest partitions, corresponding to recent inserts not yet merged.

If you see many small parts across all partitions, merges are not keeping up. If you see only a handful of very large parts and frequent spikes in I/O, merges might be too aggressive.

Merge queue and background task metrics.

ClickHouse exposes system tables that report pending merges and background task throughput. Watch for:

- A merge queue that grows steadily over hours or days.
- Large parts waiting indefinitely to be merged.
- Frequent failures or retries of merge tasks.

These are signs that your merge-related settings or hardware are mismatched to your ingest rate.

Query latency patterns.

Finally, your traders and analytics provide the ultimate metric: latency when querying typical lookbacks. If simple time-range filters over recent days or weeks suddenly slow down without a corresponding increase in data volume, suspect fragmentation and merge backlog.

Because MergeTree stores every column separately, remember that adding more nullable or array columns (as we advocated earlier) also adds more files per part. This is usually acceptable if merges are healthy; if merges are struggling, the overhead becomes more visible.

Summary: Mental Model and Practical Implications

You can now think of a MergeTree table not as a monolithic lump of bytes but as a living ecosystem of parts:

- Inserts continuously create new, immutable parts, grouped by partition and sorted by your ORDER BY key.
- Background merges steadily combine these parts into larger segments, improving compression and query performance.

- TTL and retention rules eventually remove or migrate old parts, keeping the active working set manageable.

For time-series market data, this model has concrete design consequences:

- Your choices of partitioning and primary key (covered next) directly shape part boundaries and merge behavior.
- Your ingest patterns—batch sizes, how you split by day and symbol—determine how many small parts appear.
- Your merge-related settings must be matched to your data rates and hardware to avoid either merge starvation or merge overload.

In the next section we will build on this understanding to tackle one of the most important design problems in ClickHouse for markets: how to choose PARTITION BY and ORDER BY expressions that both reflect your query patterns and keep the MergeTree part lifecycle healthy over the lifetime of your trading system.

5.3 Partition and ORDER BY Design

In the previous sections we focused first on getting the logical schema right (types, time semantics), and then on how MergeTree actually stores that schema as parts, merges them, and eventually evicts them. We are now ready for the central physical-design decision in ClickHouse for markets: how to choose *partitions* and *ORDER BY* keys.

These two choices determine:

- How efficiently queries can prune away irrelevant data.
- How much work the merge process must do to keep parts healthy.
- How well compression works and how often your system touches disk.

For time-series markets, good partition and ORDER BY design is the difference between sub-second scans over years of history and a cluster that constantly feels overloaded.

Partitions and ORDER BY: Two Different Levers

It is tempting to think of partitions and ORDER BY as variants of the same idea: "how data is split and sorted." In MergeTree they serve distinct roles.

Partition key: units of retention and maintenance.

The *partition key* groups rows into large buckets, each of which becomes a family of parts on disk. Typical partition keys are:

- Trading day for intraday data.
- Calendar month or year for coarser-grained data.
- Occasionally, a combination of date with a coarse symbol bucket or venue.

Partitions exist to give you manageable units of:

- **Retention** You can drop or archive data partition by partition. If each partition is one trading day, deleting a day's data is a constant-time operation.
- **Maintenance** Merges operate within partitions. Index rebuilds, TTL actions, and other maintenance tasks are also scoped by partition.

You can think of partitions as the *largest* blocks in the layout: they define the outer boundaries of where a row can live.

ORDER BY: the true physical sort for skipping and compression.

Within each partition, rows are physically sorted by the *ORDER BY* expression. This sort order is used for:

- Data skipping: marks and min/max metadata allow ClickHouse to quickly determine if a block of rows might satisfy a filter on the ORDER BY keys.

- Compression: consecutive rows with similar values compress more effectively.

- Efficient range scans: scanning all trades for a given symbol and time interval is fast if those rows are clustered together.

The ORDER BY is therefore your main tool to encode the *shape* of your typical queries into the storage layout.

A useful mental model:

> Partitions decide which large files live together and are maintained as a group. ORDER BY decides how rows are arranged *inside* those files.

For time-series markets, we almost always set the partition key to capture time at a coarse granularity, and the ORDER BY to start with a symbol and a precise timestamp.

Core Trade-Offs for Market Data

Designing partition and ORDER BY keys is about balancing three forces:

1. Query pruning: How quickly can ClickHouse ignore data that a query will never need?

2. Ingest and merge load: How much work do merges have to do to combine parts and keep fragmentation under control?

3. Operational convenience: How easy is it to drop, archive, or relocate data as it ages?

These forces often pull in different directions. For example:

- Very fine-grained partitions (for example, hourly) let you drop or scan exactly the time range you want, but they multiply the number of partitions and can increase metadata overhead.
- Very coarse partitions (for example, yearly) minimize partition count and merge complexity, but every intraday query will at least touch the whole year's partition, even if it only needs a single day.
- An ORDER BY that starts with time makes time-range scans very fast, but symbol-specific queries might jump around within the partition.
- An ORDER BY that starts with symbol makes symbol-centric queries extremely cache-friendly, but aggregations across many instruments or the entire market must hop over many symbol ranges.

Because market workloads are dominated by queries of the form:

> "Give me all trades or quotes for symbol(s) S over time interval $[T_{\text{min}}, T_{\text{max}}]$."

we will use them as the primary target and then consider how to adjust for specific scenarios.

Choosing Partition Keys: Time as the Outer Axis

Let us start with partitions, the outermost grouping. For intraday tick data, three patterns appear repeatedly in practice:

Daily partitions by trading day.

This is the most common and often the best starting point. Each partition corresponds to one trading day in the venue's calendar:

- Pros:
- Natural unit for retention and compliance (drop or archive by trading day).

- Merges and TTL actions stay well scoped; you can see merge backlogs on a per-day basis.
- For queries with lookbacks measured in days (for example, "last 30 trading days"), ClickHouse only has to open a bounded number of partitions.

- Cons:

- Very long lookbacks (for example, ten years) involve many partitions.
- If your ingest batches cross day boundaries frequently, you may create more small parts per insert; this is mitigated by batching and by the max_partitions_per_insert setting.

Daily partitions work particularly well for equities and futures where the trading session boundaries are clear.

Monthly partitions for heavier history or slow-changing data.

For bar data or for long-term backtesting datasets, monthly partitions sometimes strike a better balance:

- Pros:

- Fewer partitions overall; metadata and merge overhead is reduced.
- Dropping or archiving months at a time is still operationally intuitive.

- Cons:

- Queries that focus on a single day must at least touch the whole month's partition. If your lookbacks are almost always intraday, this can waste I/O.

Monthly partitions are attractive for daily bars or for datasets where the natural unit of work is a month (for example, regulatory or end-of-month risk reports).

Hourly partitions for extreme volumes.

In ultra-high-frequency environments or multi-venue crypto where throughput is enormous, some teams experiment with hourly partitions:

- Pros:

- Each partition is small enough that merges remain easy even at very high tick rates.
- Intraday queries that target specific hours can prune aggressively at the partition level.

- Cons:

- The total partition count grows very quickly, complicating retention and metadata.
- Dropping an entire hour is less intuitive than dropping a day; compliance requirements often talk about dates, not hours.

Hourly partitions are rarely needed as a first design; they are more of a specialized tool for edge cases.

Designing ORDER BY for Time-Series Markets

Once partitions define the outer time boundaries, ORDER BY defines the inner layout. For market data, the most effective ORDER BY expressions nearly always start with a symbol (or instrument identifier), followed by event time, and optionally additional disambiguating fields.

A canonical pattern for trades and quotes is:

```
ORDER BY (symbol, event_time)
```

This layout has several strong properties:

- All rows for a given symbol within a partition are contiguously stored.
- Within a symbol, rows are sorted by event time, which matches how most analytics and replay operations proceed.
- Data-skipping indices and marks can easily eliminate entire symbol ranges when a query filters by symbol.

You can visualize each partition as containing a sequence of symbol blocks:

> [AAPL on day D] followed by [AMZN on day D] followed by [ES futures on day D], and so on, each internally ordered by time.

This makes queries such as:

- All trades in AAPL on a specific day.
- All quotes in ES futures between 09:30 and 16:00.

extremely efficient: ClickHouse quickly narrows down to the relevant partitions by date and then jumps into the contiguous symbol range within each partition.

Composite ORDER BY with date.

Some designers include the partitioning date inside ORDER BY:

> ORDER BY (trade_date, symbol, event_time)

When partitions are already based on trade_date, repeating it in ORDER BY usually does not harm but also does not help much for data skipping within a partition. Its main value appears when:

- You plan to change the partitioning scheme later and want the on-disk sort order to remain compatible.

- You occasionally query across partitions using the same table, and the engine may leverage the sort order when reading multiple partitions.

For many simple setups, sticking to ORDER BY (symbol, event_time) within daily partitions is sufficient and easier to reason about.

Visualizing Partitions and ORDER BY

Before diving into specific recipes, it is useful to have a mental image of how partitions and ORDER BY combine to structure a MergeTree table for markets.

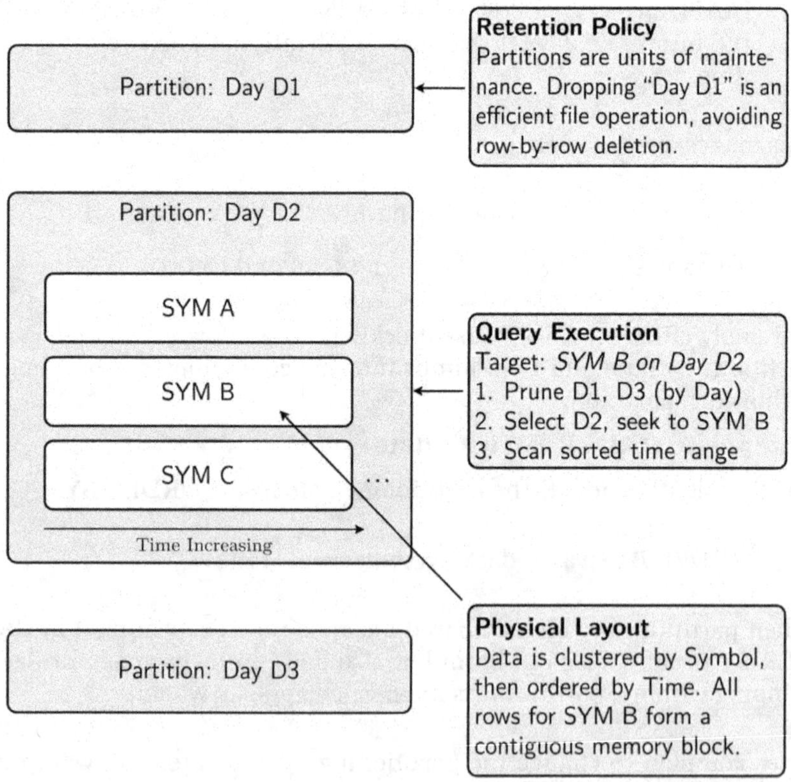

In this diagram, each large horizontal block is a partition (for example, a trading day). Within a partition we show symbol stripes; one of them (SYM B) is highlighted as the range a typical symbol-and-time query will touch.

Design Recipes for Common Market Datasets

With the conceptual groundwork and visualization in place, we can now outline practical recipes for three core datasets: trades, quotes, and bars. The aim is not to prescribe a single design, but to give you starting points that align with MergeTree's behavior.

Tick Trades

Workload characteristics.

- Frequent queries: all trades for one or a few symbols over a recent time interval (intraday to a few months).
- Less frequent: cross-sectional scans across many symbols at a single timestamp (for example, closing prints).
- Write pattern: continuous stream of trades, heavily skewed to a subset of very active instruments.

Recommended design.

- Partition by trading day (or calendar day in UTC if you have normalized timestamps).
- ORDER BY (symbol, event_time, possibly a tiebreaker such as an exchange trade ID).

This design:

- Keeps per-symbol trades for a day dense and contiguous, which is ideal for replay, ASOF joins to quotes, and most analytics.
- Localizes heavy symbols' data into compact ranges, which compress well and are easy for the cache hierarchy to handle.

- Allows the merge process to work partition by partition, combining small parts for each day independently.

If you have a handful of symbols that dwarf all others (for example, a few front-month futures), monitor whether any single symbol's range becomes so large that merges struggle. In extreme cases, you may consider bucketing symbols or splitting the hottest instruments into dedicated tables, but this is more of an advanced optimization than a first-principles design.

Quotes and Order-Book Snapshots

Workload characteristics.

- Quotes typically arrive more frequently than trades; order-book snapshots can be very dense.
- Common queries: best quotes over time, spread analysis, slippage and impact estimation, or reconstructing the book at trade times.
- Data size per row can be larger due to arrays for multiple levels of the book.

Recommended design.

- Partition by trading day, aligning with trades for easier temporal joins.
- ORDER BY (symbol, event_time).

Using the same partitioning and ORDER BY pattern as for trades delivers several advantages:

- Matching trades to quotes by event time (for example, via ASOF JOIN) is very efficient when both tables have the same symbol-and-time sort.
- Compression benefits are amplified because not only timestamps and prices, but also arrays of depth levels for each symbol, change gradually through the day.

- Maintenance and TTL are symmetric between trades and quotes; you can drop or archive both in lockstep by partition.

When building snapshot tables that are especially large, consider whether you need full-depth snapshots for every symbol and every millisecond. For many analyses, storing only top-of-book or sparse snapshots can reduce the part size and merge load significantly.

Bars and Aggregated Data

Workload characteristics.

- Typical queries: OHLCV bars for one or multiple symbols over weeks to years.
- Bars are often at coarser granularity: one minute, five minutes, hourly, or daily.
- Data volume per time unit is much smaller than for ticks.

Recommended design.

The right design depends on bar granularity:

- **Intraday bars (sub-daily).**

- Partition by trading day or calendar month, depending on retention and query horizons.
- ORDER BY (symbol, bar_start_time).

Daily partitions make sense if most queries focus on recent weeks; monthly partitions are attractive if you often scan many months or years at once.

- **Daily bars.**

- Partition by calendar year.
- ORDER BY (symbol, bar_date).

Here, each partition contains one year of daily bars across all symbols. Dropping or archiving old years is straightforward, and a query for a single symbol over ten years will involve about ten partitions, each scanning a single compact symbol range.

Bars are compact enough that you may tolerate slightly coarser partitions than for ticks; this eases operational overhead without significantly hurting query performance.

Special Cases: Sparse Symbols and Multi-Venue Data

The patterns above assume a relatively uniform symbol universe and a single venue or a consistent consolidation strategy. In practice, you often encounter:

Sparse symbols.

Some instruments trade only a few times a week, or only during particular regimes. In the recommended ORDER BY layout, they occupy tiny ranges within each partition. This is generally fine:

- Their rows piggyback on the compression and sorting benefits of the busier symbols.
- They impose almost no incremental cost on merges.

If your workload contains queries that focus exclusively on sparse instruments and never on busy ones, and performance is critical for those sparse instruments, it may be worth putting them in a separate table with a layout tuned to their patterns. But this is an optimization of the second order.

Multi-venue and multi-asset data.

When storing data from multiple venues or asset classes in a single table, you have a few options:

- Include a venue or asset_class column in ORDER BY: for example, ORDER BY (venue, symbol, event_time).

- Keep distinct tables per venue or asset class, each with its own partition and ORDER BY tuned to its characteristics.

Including venue in ORDER BY groups each venue's symbols together, which is beneficial if queries are usually venue-specific. It does, however, widen the sort key and can slightly reduce compression across venues. Separate tables per venue keep each MergeTree instance simpler at the cost of more tables to manage.

The right choice depends on your organizational boundaries and query habits: prop trading desks often favor per-venue tables; centralized research teams sometimes prefer unified schemas.

Balancing Ingest, Merges, and Queries

Finally, how do partition and ORDER BY choices interact with the MergeTree lifecycle you saw earlier?

- Smaller partitions (daily vs monthly) mean merges operate on smaller, more localized data sets. This tends to keep merge tasks lighter and makes backlogs less catastrophic, at the cost of more partitions overall.
- An ORDER BY that matches your insert ordering reduces the amount of sorting work ClickHouse must do on ingest. If upstream pipelines can roughly batch rows by partition and symbol, new parts arrive almost pre-sorted.
- Orderings that heavily interleave unrelated symbols or wildly different time ranges within a partition make merges and compression less effective. Avoid clever composite keys that do not reflect actual query patterns.

As a rule of thumb:

> Start with daily partitions and ORDER BY (symbol, event_time) for tick-level trades and quotes. Observe how parts grow, how merges behave, and how queries perform. Only then consider deviations, and always with a clear workload-driven reason.

This conservative design aligns MergeTree's strengths with the core shape of market data. It gives you a stable baseline on which to layer more advanced features in later sections: replication, sharding, streaming ingest, and temporal analytics.

5.4 Replication and Keeper Coordination

In the earlier sections we treated each MergeTree table as if it lived on a single server. The part lifecycle, partitions, and ORDER BY design were all explained from the perspective of one node writing and merging its own parts. Real trading systems, however, do not trust a single machine with years of tick history or a live feed that must never be dropped.

To cope with machine failures, maintenance, and rolling upgrades, ClickHouse offers *ReplicatedMergeTree* engines. These engines extend MergeTree with replication: several ClickHouse servers hold logically identical copies of the same table. A separate coordination service, called *Keeper* (or ZooKeeper in older deployments), keeps these replicas in sync.

This section builds a practical understanding of:

- How ReplicatedMergeTree uses Keeper to coordinate inserts, merges, and deletions.
- What replication guarantees you actually get in a market-data setting.
- How to configure replication and Keeper so that your cluster tolerates failures without losing ticks or corrupting history.

The aim is not to cover every configuration flag but to give you a mental model that lets you reason about failure scenarios and choose sane defaults.

From MergeTree to ReplicatedMergeTree

A ReplicatedMergeTree table behaves like a MergeTree from the SQL point of view: it has the same columns, partitioning, and ORDER BY, and it stores data in parts. The difference is that:

- There are multiple *replicas* of the same table, usually on different servers or racks.
- These replicas share a logical *replication log* stored in Keeper.
- Each replica has its own local parts on disk but coordinates part creation and deletion via Keeper.

You can think of a ReplicatedMergeTree table as a group of MergeTree instances that agree on what parts exist, which of them are active, and in what order they were created.

Keeper's role is to provide a small, consistent filesystem-like tree where replicas can:

- Append log entries describing new parts, merges, and deletions.
- Discover which parts exist and which they are missing.
- Coordinate operations so that each logical part is created once and replayed in the same order on all replicas.

The actual data files (the columnar parts) still live on the ClickHouse servers' local disks. Keeper stores only metadata: names of parts, logs, checksums, and coordination state.

Roles: Replicas, Parts, and the Replication Log

To understand how replication works, it helps to identify the main actors:

- **Replica**: A ClickHouse server that hosts a copy of a ReplicatedMergeTree table. Each replica has its own local directory of parts on disk and a link to a shared path in Keeper.

- **Replication log**: A sequence of logical operations stored under a path in Keeper. Every action that changes the set of parts (for example, "inserted part P1," "merged parts P1 and P2 into P3," "dropped part P1") is appended as a log entry.
- **Part queue**: On each replica, a local queue of tasks derived from the replication log. If a replica sees a log entry saying "part P3 was created," but does not yet have P3, it enqueues a task to fetch or create that part.

In steady state, all replicas read the same replication log and apply the same sequence of operations. They may be at different positions (one replica can be slightly behind if it is busy or just came back from a restart), but they converge toward the same set of parts as they catch up.

The Life of an Insert in a Replicated Table

Let us follow a batch of trades inserted into a ReplicatedMergeTree table:

1. A client sends an insert to one of the replicas. This is the "coordinating" replica for this insert.
2. The replica partitions and sorts the rows according to the table's partition and ORDER BY, just as a normal MergeTree would, and writes a new part or parts on its local disk.
3. After successfully creating a part, the replica writes a new entry into the shared replication log in Keeper. This log entry contains the part's name, checksums, and other metadata.
4. Other replicas continuously watch the replication log. When they see the new entry, they add a task to their local part queue: "I must obtain part P from some replica."
5. Each replica then downloads or copies the part from a peer (or, in some configurations, regenerates it by merging its own smaller parts) and verifies the checksums. Once done, it marks the task as complete.

The critical point is that:

> The act of inserting data is recorded in the replication log and then replayed by each replica, rather than each replica independently doing its own inserts.

This pattern applies not only to raw inserts but also to merges. When a replica decides to merge parts P1 and P2 into P3, it:

- Performs the merge locally to produce P3.
- Writes a merge entry into the replication log.
- Other replicas, upon reading the entry, either perform the same merge locally or download the resulting P3, and then drop P1 and P2 in a coordinated way.

This is how all replicas stay in agreement about which parts exist and which ones have been superseded by merges.

Keeper as the Coordination Backbone

Keeper is a lightweight, fault-tolerant coordination service. You can picture it as:

- A small replicated key-value tree shared by all ClickHouse servers.
- A place where ClickHouse stores replication logs, replica state, and some configuration.
- A service with its own cluster (an ensemble of nodes) and consensus algorithm, independent of your ClickHouse data nodes.

For ReplicatedMergeTree, Keeper provides three key capabilities:

- **Ordering**: Log entries are written in a total order per replicated table. This means all replicas see inserts and merges in the same sequence.

- **Notification**: Replicas can watch parts of the tree and get notified when new log entries or state changes appear, so they do not have to poll constantly.

- **Consistency**: Writes to Keeper are replicated across its own ensemble, so the replication metadata is durable even if a Keeper node fails.

Importantly, Keeper does not store the actual tick data. It would be both too slow and too expensive to use it as a data store. Its job is to coordinate and describe, not to hold, your market history.

Topology: Replicas and Keeper Ensemble

Right after introducing these roles conceptually, it is helpful to visualize the topology of a typical replicated ClickHouse deployment for market data.

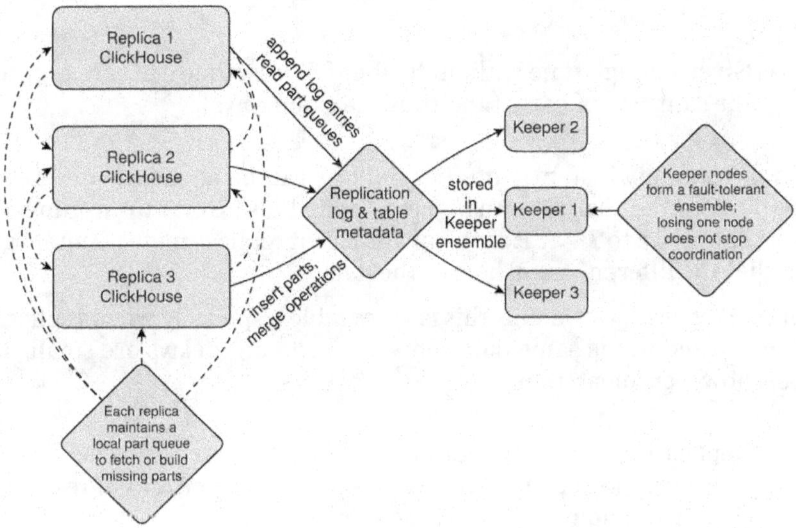

This diagram separates the ClickHouse replicas (on the left) from the Keeper ensemble (on the right). The replication log in Keeper is the bridge: replicas append to it and consume from it to fill their local part queues, while Keeper ensures the log is consistent and replicated.

What Replication Guarantees Do You Actually Get?

With this architecture in mind, we can answer a critical question for trading systems: what does ReplicatedMergeTree guarantee, and what does it not?

Eventual consistency across replicas.

ReplicatedMergeTree provides *eventual consistency* for table contents:

- All replicas see the same sequence of operations in the replication log.
- Given enough time without further failures, they will converge to the same set of parts (and thus the same rows).

However, at any instant, different replicas can be at slightly different positions in the log. One may have applied all inserts up to time T, another only up to $T-\delta$. Reads from different replicas might, therefore, see slightly different snapshots of the data.

For most market workloads this is acceptable, especially when replicas are colocated in the same data center and commit delays are small. It does, however, mean that:

> Replication is not a substitute for transactional consistency. It is a way to keep multiple copies nearly in sync and to recover from node failures without losing data.

Durability against node failures.

Assuming:

- You have at least two replicas for each critical table.
- The Keeper ensemble itself is healthy and can store the replication log.

then:

- If one ClickHouse node fails, its data can be rebuilt by pulling parts from surviving replicas after it comes back.
- If one Keeper node fails (in an ensemble of three or more), coordination can continue, and no data is lost from Keeper.

In other words, ReplicatedMergeTree plus a properly sized Keeper ensemble protects against individual node failures but not against entire data-center outages unless your cluster spans regions.

Insert quorums and write visibility.

By default, when a client inserts data into a ReplicatedMergeTree table, the insert is considered successful once the coordinating replica has written the part locally and added the corresponding entry to the replication log. Other replicas will catch up later.

For some workloads, especially when feeding real-time trading strategies, you may want stronger guarantees. Insert quorum settings allow you to require that:

- An insert is only acknowledged as successful once a specified number of replicas have actually written the part.
- There is a timeout after which the client will see an error if the quorum cannot be reached.

This improves the chance that a freshly inserted tick is available on multiple replicas before the client proceeds, at the cost of increased latency and potential insert failures during partial outages.

Configuring Replication for Market Workloads

With the guarantees understood, we can focus on practical configuration decisions.

Replica count.

For critical market data (trades and quotes), a common pattern is:

- Two replicas per shard for high availability and rolling maintenance.
- Optionally, a third replica in a different failure domain (different rack, or even different data center) for disaster recovery.

More replicas increase resilience but also increase write amplification: each insert eventually results in multiple part copies across disks. For read-heavy workloads such as backtesting, additional replicas can be used to scale out query capacity.

Keeper ensemble sizing.

Keeper itself should be deployed as a small, odd-sized ensemble, often three or five nodes. Consider:

- Keep Keeper nodes isolated from noisy neighbors. They handle only metadata but are sensitive to latency and pauses.
- Place Keeper nodes on reliable hardware and, ideally, on different machines than your busiest ClickHouse data nodes.

Because Keeper's state is relatively small, its resource needs are modest: CPU and disk throughput are not the bottleneck. Stability and low latency are more important.

Read preferences.

Replicated tables support settings that influence which replica a query reads from. For low-latency, in-rack trading applications, it is often best to:

- Prefer the local replica on the same host or rack to minimize network hops.
- Fallback to remote replicas only when the local one is unavailable or lagging.

This pattern keeps the typical read path short and uses replication primarily for resilience and capacity, not for random load balancing across the cluster.

Insert quorums.

For feeds where every tick must be recorded in at least two places before a strategy acts on it, configure:

- A quorum size equal to the number of replicas you consider safety-critical (often two).
- A quorum timeout that is generous enough to handle brief slowdowns but short enough that persistent issues surface quickly.

Remember that quorum failures on inserts will surface as errors for upstream producers (for example, Kafka consumers writing into ClickHouse). Your ingest pipeline must be prepared to handle and retry or reroute such errors gracefully.

Failure Modes and How to Reason About Them

To build confidence in your design, walk through a few concrete failure scenarios.

Single data-node failure.

One ClickHouse replica for a table goes down unexpectedly:

- Inserts continue to be accepted by the remaining replicas.
- The downed replica stops reading the replication log and falls behind.
- When it comes back, it reconnects to Keeper, sees its part queue filled with missing parts, and begins downloading or merging until it catches up.

From the client perspective:

- Queries should route around the failed replica (assuming you have configured read preferences and health checks).
- If insert quorums require more replicas than are available during the outage, inserts may fail or block until quorum can be reached.

Keeper node failure.

One Keeper node in a three-node ensemble fails:

- The ensemble retains a majority of nodes and continues to serve reads and writes.
- ClickHouse replicas can still append to and read from the replication log.

If enough Keeper nodes fail to lose majority, the ensemble becomes unavailable:

- Replication coordination halts: replicas cannot write new log entries or update their state.
- ClickHouse may still serve reads from existing parts, but inserts and merges depending on Keeper may fail.

This is why Keeper's health is critical: you must monitor and maintain its ensemble with the same seriousness as you do your main data nodes.

Network partition between replicas and Keeper.

If a network issue isolates a subset of replicas from Keeper:

- Isolated replicas may not see new log entries or be able to append their own.
- Depending on configuration, they may stop accepting writes that require replication coordination.

To avoid silent divergence (different replicas accepting different, uncoordinated writes), ReplicatedMergeTree relies on Keeper as the single source of truth. If a replica cannot reach Keeper, it should treat itself as unable to participate fully in replication. Configurations and operational practices should reinforce this, preferring temporary unavailability over split-brain behavior.

Operational Practices for Reliable Replication

Beyond static configuration, certain operational habits greatly increase the robustness of replicated ClickHouse clusters in trading environments:

- **Isolate Keeper** from heavy resource contention. Give it dedicated virtual or physical machines, avoid colocating it with CPU- or I/O-bound services.

- **Monitor lag** between replicas: how far behind each replica is in terms of replication log position. Alert when lag exceeds your tolerance for read staleness.
- **Monitor part queues** on each replica: long queues or stuck tasks can indicate networking issues, disk problems, or misconfigurations.
- **Test failover regularly**: simulate taking a replica or a Keeper node down and observe whether inserts, merges, and queries behave as you expect.

In market data systems, it is not enough that replication "usually works." You need confidence that, under stress, it fails in predictable, recoverable ways.

Summary: Replication as Structured Redundancy

ReplicatedMergeTree and Keeper together transform the single-node MergeTree model into a distributed, fault-tolerant storage layer suitable for serious trading workloads:

- Multiple replicas hold the same logical table, each with its own local parts.
- A shared replication log, stored in Keeper, orders inserts and merges and drives per-replica part queues.
- Eventual consistency across replicas and insert quorums give you control over the trade-off between latency and durability.
- A small, carefully managed Keeper ensemble underpins the whole system; its health is as critical as any data node.

With this mental model you can now evaluate replication strategies for your own market data cluster: how many replicas you need, where to place them, and how strictly to enforce write quorums. In the next section we will extend this view from replication to *sharding*: splitting data horizontally across multiple groups of replicas so that you can scale from a single box to a multi-petabyte ClickHouse deployment while keeping latency predictable for traders and researchers.

5.5 Sharding and Distributed Queries

The previous sections treated replication as a way to keep multiple copies of the *same* data synchronized for resilience and read scale-out. Replicas are like mirrors: every replica of a ReplicatedMergeTree table aims to hold the same parts.

At some point, however, a single logical table becomes too large or too busy for one group of replicas. Tick-by-tick data for thousands of instruments over a decade, plus real-time ingest, can exceed the CPU, memory, and storage budget of any single box, even with fast disks and careful tuning.

To go further, you need *sharding*: splitting a logical dataset horizontally into multiple independent subsets, each stored on a different group of servers. Once the data is sharded, you must also be able to query it as if it were still one table. That is the role of ClickHouse's *Distributed* tables.

This section explains:

- How sharding differs from replication, and how they work together.
- How to define shard layouts for market data: what a shard "owns" and why.
- How Distributed tables route queries across shards and combine results.
- How to think about rebalancing as your markets and data volumes grow.

The aim is to give you a clear mental model you can apply whether you run a modest two-shard cluster or a fleet of servers holding petabytes of ticks.

Replication Versus Sharding

It is easy to conflate replication and sharding because both involve multiple servers. The distinction is simple but fundamental:

- **Replication**: Multiple replicas hold the *same* data. They all have the same logical rows, coordinated by Keeper. You add replicas for high availability and read capacity.
- **Sharding**: Different shards hold *different* subsets of the data. Each shard is responsible for only part of the symbol or time universe. You add shards to increase total storage and ingest capacity.

In practice, you usually combine both:

- Each shard is itself a small replicated cluster (for example, two or three replicas).
- A higher-level configuration describes a set of shards that together make up the full logical table.

You can think of the layout as a grid:

- Horizontally: shards, each with its own slice of the dataset.
- Vertically: replicas within each shard, which mirror that shard's slice.

The rest of this section focuses on the horizontal dimension: which rows go to which shard, and how you query across them efficiently.

What a Shard Owns in a Market Data Cluster

A shard is a group of servers that collectively store and query a subset of a logical table. For a trades or quotes table, a shard might own:

- All data for a subset of symbols across all dates.
- All data for all symbols within a certain date range.
- A hybrid combination, such as some subset of symbols in some subset of dates.

To keep systems manageable, you want a simple, deterministic mapping from a row to a shard. That mapping is often based on:

- A hash of the symbol or instrument identifier.
- A bucketing of dates (for example, year, quarter).
- A composite of both, if needed.

The guiding principles are:

- **Balance**: Each shard should hold a comparable volume of data and ingest roughly the same number of rows per unit time. Otherwise, one "hot" shard becomes a bottleneck.
- **Locality**: Queries that focus on a small part of the universe (for example, one symbol) should hit as few shards as possible.
- **Predictability**: It should be easy to reason about where data lives and how moving a symbol or date range to a new shard will affect the layout.

With these in mind, we can examine common shard key strategies for market data.

Shard Key Strategies for Market Data

A *shard key* is the rule that maps logical rows to shards. Common strategies include:

Hashing by Symbol

The simplest and often most effective strategy for large symbol universes is to hash on the symbol (or a stable instrument identifier):

- All rows for a given symbol, across all dates, go to the same shard.
- Symbols are spread pseudo-randomly across shards according to the hash.

This design has several advantages:

- **Locality for symbol-centric queries.** Most queries in trading research and execution focus on one or a small set of symbols. With hash-by-symbol, those queries only hit the shard(s) that own the relevant symbols.
- **Good load balance.** Assuming you have many symbols and you hash evenly, each shard receives a mix of busy and quiet instruments. No single shard ends up with all the hot symbols unless the hash key is poorly chosen.
- **Simple mental model.** "Symbol S lives on shard H(S)" is easy to reason about and debug.

The main trade-off is for queries that span a large cross-section of symbols (for example, all constituents of an index). Those queries will need to fan out to multiple shards and aggregate results. For many clusters, this is acceptable: the point of sharding is that total CPU and I/O increase with the number of shards, making full-universe scans feasible.

Bucketing by Time

Another strategy is to shard by coarse time bucket, such as year or month:

- Shard 1 owns all data up to and including year 2019.
- Shard 2 owns all data for years 2020 and 2021.
- Shard 3 owns all data from 2022 onwards.

This can be attractive when:

- You are primarily concerned with archival history and want to move older years onto cheaper hardware.
- Your queries frequently scan across the entire symbol universe but focus on limited date ranges.

However, pure time-based sharding has drawbacks for live trading data:

- All current writes go to the "latest" shard, creating a write hotspot.
- Symbol-centric queries that span multiple years must hit many shards.

For these reasons, pure time sharding is better suited to deep-history archives or read-mostly research clusters, not to the primary, live tick store.

Hybrid Sharding: Symbol and Time

In very large deployments, a hybrid approach is sometimes used: the key space is divided by both symbol and time. For example:

- Hash the symbol into N buckets.
- Combine that with a coarse time bucket (for example, year) to form a two-dimensional grid of shard assignments.

Such designs allow you to:

- Distribute write load for the current year's busiest symbols across multiple shards.
- Move older years for selected symbols as units, if needed.

The downside is complexity: it becomes harder to reason about which shard holds which rows, and moving data between shards can be more delicate. For most trading teams, hash-by-symbol alone, possibly combined with coarser partitioning by date *within each shard*, is enough.

Distributed Tables: A Single Logical View

Once data is sharded, you need a way for clients to query it without knowing the shard layout. ClickHouse provides this through the *Distributed* table engine.

Conceptually, a Distributed table is:

- A small metadata object that describes:
  - The cluster: which servers and shards exist.
  - The local table name on each shard (for example, the `trades` MergeTree on each shard).
  - The shard key, if any, used for routing inserts.
- A query router: when you run a query against the Distributed table, ClickHouse fans the query out to the relevant shards and then merges results.

From the analyst's perspective:

- You select from the Distributed table as if it were a single massive table.
- You can filter by symbol, time, venue, and other columns as usual.
- The engine decides which shards to contact and how to combine partial aggregates.

Distributed tables are not themselves storage engines. The actual data still lives in local MergeTree or ReplicatedMergeTree tables on each shard. Distributed tables simply orchestrate the multi-shard query.

How Queries Flow Through a Distributed Table

It is helpful to trace the lifecycle of a typical query through a Distributed table:

1. A client connects to one ClickHouse node, which we call the *coordinator* for this query. (In many clusters, every node can act as a coordinator.)

2. The client issues a query against a Distributed table (for example, distributed_trades).

3. The coordinator examines the query:

   - If the query contains conditions on the shard key (for example, symbol IN ('AAPL', 'MSFT')), it can route subqueries only to the shards that own those symbols.
   - If not, it fans the query out to all shards.

4. Each shard receives a subquery against its local MergeTree table, applies local filters and aggregations, and returns partial results.

5. The coordinator combines partial results:

   - For simple SELECTs, it concatenates rows.
   - For aggregations (for example, SUM, AVG), it merges partial aggregates.

6. The combined result is sent back to the client.

The elegance of this model is that:

- Much of the heavy lifting (filtering, grouping, joining) is done on shards where the data lives, reducing network traffic.

- The coordinator's job is mostly to plan the query, dispatch subqueries, and merge intermediate results.

The better your shard key aligns with typical filters, the fewer shards each query must touch, and the more efficient this distributed execution becomes.

Routing Inserts in a Sharded Cluster

Distributed tables can also be used for inserts. When you insert into a Distributed table:

- The coordinator examines the values of the shard-key columns in each row.
- It routes rows to the appropriate shards' local (Replicated)MergeTree tables.

There are two common patterns:

- **Smart inserts via Distributed table**: Your ingest pipeline writes directly into the Distributed table, and ClickHouse automatically routes rows based on the shard key.
- **Direct inserts to local tables**: Your upstream system computes the shard assignment itself (for example, in your Kafka consumers) and writes directly to the appropriate shard's local table. This gives you more control and may reduce a network hop, at the cost of extra complexity in your application layer.

For many teams, letting the Distributed table handle routing is simpler and sufficiently performant, especially when ingesting through materialized views and the Kafka engine, which can be configured per shard.

Avoiding Skew and Hotspots

Sharding can fail if one shard becomes significantly busier or larger than others. In a market context, skew can arise from:

- A few ultra-active symbols that dominate volume.
- A sudden regime where interest concentrates on a limited set of instruments (for example, meme stocks or a particular futures contract).
- Shard keys that correlate poorly with actual load.

A well-designed hash-by-symbol scheme mitigates much of this: hot symbols are spread across shards pseudo-randomly. However, issues can still appear:

- If the symbol universe is small and a few symbols account for most of the traffic, random hashing has less smoothing effect.
- If you pin certain symbol ranges to specific shards (for example, all FX to shard 1, all futures to shard 2), those asset classes can become hotspots.

To detect and address skew:

- Monitor ingest and query rates per shard. Significant differences in CPU, I/O, or latency are red flags.
- If a shard persistently runs hotter, consider:
- Splitting its key space and moving some symbols to a new shard.
- Adjusting the hash or mapping function so that heavy symbols are redistributed.

Planning for such rebalancing upfront (for example, by using an indirection layer in your shard mapping rather than hard-coding shard IDs) makes future changes less disruptive.

Rebalancing: Growing the Cluster Safely

As your data grows, you will eventually need to add shards and migrate some data. Rebalancing is a delicate but manageable process if you approach it in stages.

1. Add new shard hardware.

Provision one or more new shard groups (each with its own replicas) and configure them in the cluster description, initially with no data.

2. Decide what to move.

Choose units of data to move that are:

- Large enough to matter (for example, all symbols whose hash falls into a certain range).
- Operationally consistent (for example, full partitions or symbolic groupings, not random fragments).

3. Copy data.

You can:

- Use ClickHouse's internal copy and attach mechanisms to move partitions between tables.
- Or, in some cases, re-ingest from a durable upstream source (for example, from Kafka or object storage) into the new shard.

During this phase, old and new shards may both hold copies of the same data.

4. Update routing.

Change the shard mapping or the Distributed table configuration so that new inserts and queries for the moved symbols or time ranges go to the new shard. Ensure this change is done atomically from the client's point of view.

5. Remove old copies.

Once you are confident that the new shards hold complete data and that all clients are routing correctly, you can drop the old partitions from the previous shard. For safety, teams often keep old copies for a short overlap period as a fallback.

Throughout this process, Distributed tables help by abstracting away the exact physical location of data from most clients. Only the cluster configuration and shard mapping need to be updated; client queries continue to target the same logical table.

Latency Considerations in Distributed Queries

Distributed queries inevitably involve more network hops and coordination than single-node queries. To keep latency acceptable for trading workloads:

- **Favor locality.** Where possible, route queries from an application to a coordinator in the same rack or data center, and prefer reading from local replicas to reduce network overhead.
- **Push computation down.** Design queries so that filters and aggregations can be applied on shards before returning data. Avoid patterns that require sending large raw datasets back to the coordinator.
- **Align shard keys with filters.** When queries filter on symbol, venue, or asset class, use those in the shard key so that only relevant shards are touched.

For interactive human queries (for example, ad-hoc research), latencies of a few hundred milliseconds to a couple of seconds are often acceptable. For automated trading, you may:

- Maintain a separate, smaller cluster or subset of tables holding only the most recent data for latency-critical strategies.
- Use pre-aggregated tables (for example, materialized views of recent bars) to avoid heavy distributed scans in the hot path.

Distributed tables, replication, and pre-aggregation are complementary tools; you will often combine them in one architecture.

Summary: From Single Box to Market-Scale Cluster

Sharding and Distributed tables complete the picture begun with types, MergeTree parts, and replication:

- MergeTree gives you efficient on-disk parts, sorted and merged according to your partition and ORDER BY design.
- ReplicatedMergeTree plus Keeper give you resilience and read scale within each shard.

- Sharding spreads the logical dataset across multiple shards, each a small replicated cluster, to support higher ingest and larger histories.
- Distributed tables tie the shards together, presenting a single logical table to clients and routing queries and inserts according to a shard key.

For time-series market data, a well-thought-out shard layout-usually starting with hash-by-symbol on top of daily-partitioned, symbol-and-time-sorted MergeTree tables-lets you grow from one server to many while preserving the mental simplicity of a single trades or quotes table.

In the following sections, we will connect this cluster-level view to the rest of the pipeline: how Kafka and materialized views feed data into sharded, replicated MergeTree tables, and how window functions and ASOF joins operate efficiently even when your data lives across many machines.

5.6 Materialized Views and Streaming Ingest

Up to this point we have treated ClickHouse tables as if data simply appeared in them: trades, quotes, and bars were inserted, parts were merged, and partitions were pruned. In production trading systems, of course, data arrives as a continuous stream from external feeds and message buses.

In many architectures today, Apache Kafka (or a similar log-based system) is the backbone for this streaming layer. Trading venues, consolidators, and internal capture services publish trade and quote messages into Kafka topics; downstream consumers transform and store them.

ClickHouse integrates directly into this ecosystem through two key features:

- The *Kafka engine*, which lets a ClickHouse table act as a consumer of one or more Kafka topics.

- *Materialized views*, which automatically transform rows arriving in one table into inserts into another.

Combined, these form an end-to-end path:

> Kafka topics → Kafka-engine tables → Materialized views → MergeTree targets (raw ticks and rollups).

This section explains how to design that pipeline for market data, with special attention to:

- Deduplication and "exactly-once-ish" semantics in the presence of retries.
- Aligning batch sizes and schedules with MergeTree part creation and merges.
- Pre-aggregation and rollups (for example, OHLCV bars) alongside raw tick storage.

The Kafka Engine: ClickHouse as a Consumer

The Kafka engine turns a ClickHouse table into a read-only window onto one or more Kafka topics. It is essential to understand what it is *not*:

- It is not a storage engine. Data in a Kafka-engine table lives in Kafka, not in ClickHouse parts.
- It is not a generic Kafka client library. It is a specialized adapter for pulling messages into ClickHouse's execution engine.

A Kafka-engine table defines:

- Which Kafka topic(s) to subscribe to.
- How to deserialize messages into rows (for example, JSON, CSV, Avro).

- Consumer group and partition settings.

Think of it as a streaming source operator inside ClickHouse: messages enter from Kafka partitions and appear as rows when ClickHouse queries or materialized views read from the Kafka-engine table.

For market data, you commonly have separate topics per feed and message type, for example:

- trades.nyse, trades.nasdaq, trades.crypto.binance
- quotes.nyse, quotes.crypto.binance

Each of these topics might be wired into its own Kafka-engine table, which in turn powers one or more materialized views.

Materialized Views: Declarative Streaming Transforms

A ClickHouse materialized view is a standing query whose output is written into a target table whenever new rows appear in its source. It is defined once and then runs automatically; you do not trigger it manually.

In the streaming ingest context, the usual pattern is:

- Source: a Kafka-engine table.
- Target: a MergeTree or ReplicatedMergeTree table.

Whenever ClickHouse pulls a batch of messages from Kafka into the Kafka-engine table, the materialized view consumes that batch and inserts the transformed rows into the MergeTree table. This achieves:

- Continuous, near-real-time ingest from Kafka into your persistent ClickHouse store.
- Declarative transformation logic: parsing, filtering, enrichment, and aggregation in SQL.

You can chain multiple materialized views off the same Kafka source table to produce different targets, for example:

- A raw tick table holding every trade as-is.
- A rollup table holding one-minute OHLCV bars per symbol.

Both are populated from the same feed without double-consuming Kafka.

End-to-End Pipeline: From Topics to MergeTree Targets

Before discussing deduplication and rollups in detail, it is helpful to visualize the full data path.

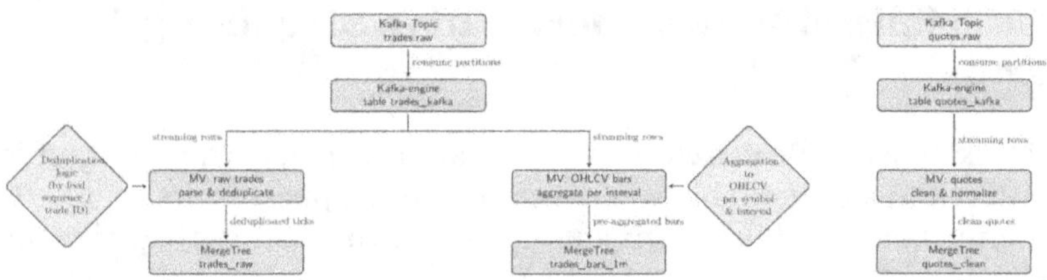

On the left, Kafka topics belong to the external streaming system. In the middle, Kafka-engine tables and materialized views live inside ClickHouse. On the right, MergeTree tables hold the persistent raw and aggregated market data that other sections of this chapter work with.

Raw Tick Ingest: Schema and Transform

For raw trades and quotes, the main goal of the Kafka-to-MergeTree pipeline is to:

- Parse incoming messages into the strongly typed schema we defined earlier (for example, symbol, event_time as DateTime64, price, size, etc.).

- Normalize time zones (often to UTC) and feed-specific quirks.
- Deduplicate messages that may be delivered more than once due to retries or producer behavior.

A typical pattern is:

1. Define the Kafka-engine table with columns that correspond closely to the message format. These might be strings or lightly typed fields, reflecting what is on the wire.
2. Define a materialized view that:
   - Projects only the fields you need for storage.
   - Converts timestamps and numeric types into your canonical schema.
   - Attaches a feed-specific identifier (for example, feed_name) to each row.
3. Insert the transformed rows into a MergeTree or ReplicatedMergeTree table with the production schema, partitions, and ORDER BY keys from earlier sections.

Separating the Kafka-engine schema from the MergeTree schema has practical benefits:

- You can adjust message parsing and normalization without rewriting stored history.
- You can handle multiple message versions by branching logic in the materialized view.
- You keep the MergeTree table clean and focused on the analytics schema, not transport details.

Deduplication and "Exactly-Once-ish" Semantics

Kafka itself provides at-least-once delivery to consumers: a message may be redelivered if the consumer crashes or if commits are retried.

Producers, too, can generate duplicates accidentally. Without care, this would result in duplicate trades or quotes in your MergeTree tables.

ClickHouse's materialized views and MergeTree semantics help you approach an "exactly-once-ish" behavior, where duplicates are highly unlikely or are eliminated downstream.

Common deduplication strategies include:

1. Idempotent upserts by unique key.

If each trade or quote has a unique identifier (for example, an exchange trade ID combined with venue and symbol), you can design the target MergeTree table so that:

- Incoming rows with the same unique key overwrite previous ones.
- Duplicates therefore do not accumulate; later copies simply replace the earlier row.

This can be achieved using special engines or mutation patterns, but it increases write amplification and complexity. It is most appropriate when duplicate rates are modest and unique IDs are reliable.

2. Deduplication in the materialized view.

More commonly, deduplication is done *before* inserting into the MergeTree table:

- The materialized view keeps only the first occurrence of a message with a given key within each batch, or across a sliding window.
- It may, for example, group by trade ID and keep the latest version per ID when building rollups.

This is easier when Kafka partitions are keyed such that duplicates for a given trade always land on the same partition, allowing local dedup per consumer.

3. Sequence-based filtering.

Some feeds include monotonically increasing sequence numbers per channel. You can store, per feed and partition, the highest sequence number you have processed and discard any messages with older sequence numbers.

This logic can live:

- In a materialized view, using stateful functions or auxiliary tables.
- In the upstream consumer layer that populates Kafka, which removes duplicates before they ever reach ClickHouse.

In all approaches, the goal is not mathematical perfection but practical robustness:

> Design the ingest path so that occasional duplicates are either impossible or harmless for downstream analytics and compliance.

For example, some surveillance queries can be written to tolerate idempotent duplicates by using DISTINCT or by focusing on conditions that are unaffected by occasional repetition.

Batching, Offsets, and Backpressure

The Kafka engine pulls messages from Kafka in batches. Each batch:

- Is exposed to materialized views as a group of rows.
- Typically becomes one or more MergeTree parts after transformation and insert.

The size and frequency of these batches are important:

- Too small, and you create many tiny parts, increasing merge pressure and metadata overhead (as discussed in the MergeTree section).

- Too large, and each batch can cause latency spikes or risk exhausting memory.

In practice:

- Aim for batch sizes that produce MergeTree parts in the tens to hundreds of megabytes range.
- Adjust Kafka-engine polling intervals and max message counts so that under normal load you achieve this balance.

Offset management.

The Kafka engine tracks offsets per topic partition. When materialized views successfully process a batch and inserts into MergeTree complete, offsets can be committed. This ensures:

- If ClickHouse restarts, it resumes from the last committed offsets, avoiding data loss.
- If a batch fails to process, offsets are not advanced, and the batch can be re-read (which is why deduplication logic must tolerate replays).

Think of offsets as the integration point between Kafka's delivery guarantees and ClickHouse's ingestion semantics.

Backpressure and lag.

Under heavy markets (for example, during a volatility spike), Kafka topics may accumulate messages faster than ClickHouse can consume them. You observe this as:

- Growing consumer lag: the difference between the high-water mark in Kafka and the committed offsets.
- Increased MergeTree merge backlog and part counts.

To handle backpressure gracefully:

- Scale out consumers where possible: more Kafka-engine tables and materialized views across shards, possibly with partition-specific consumers.
- Prioritize critical topics (for example, trades) over less critical ones (for example, some derived metrics).
- Monitor lag and have operational runbooks for temporary rate limiting or resource scaling.

Because MergeTree writes and merges have finite capacity, the entire pipeline must be designed with worst-case bursts in mind, not just average volumes.

Streaming Rollups: On-the-Fly OHLCV Bars

One of the chief advantages of combining Kafka, materialized views, and MergeTree is the ability to compute rollups continuously as data arrives. Instead of re-aggregating raw ticks for every query, you can maintain pre-aggregated bar tables.

Example: One-minute OHLCV bars.

From a trades feed, a materialized view can:

- Bucket each trade by symbol and one-minute interval based on its event time.
- Compute, per bucket:
  - Open price: first trade price in the interval.
  - High price: maximum price in the interval.
  - Low price: minimum price in the interval.
  - Close price: last trade price in the interval.
  - Volume: sum of trade sizes.
  - VWAP: volume-weighted average price (often stored as a separate measure).
- Insert these aggregates into a bar table with its own schema, partitions, and ORDER BY (for example, by date and symbol).

This bar table becomes the natural target for most charting, backtesting, and factor-construction queries, dramatically reducing read amplification compared to scanning raw ticks.

Consistency with raw ticks.

Because both raw and bar tables are driven from the same Kafka feed and associated materialized views:

- They remain consistent by construction: a bar at 10:01 is computed from the same set of trades that appear in the raw tick table for that interval.
- Late-arriving trades (for example, corrections) can be handled by re-aggregation or by mutation, depending on your policy.

In practice, you may maintain:

- A "live" bar table for recent history, updated in real time and occasionally corrected.
- A "frozen" bar table for older history where all late corrections have been applied and data is stable.

Materialized views can be directed to one or both, depending on the age of the data.

Multiple Targets: Raw, Clean, and Enriched Layers

In mature trading data stacks, you often see a layered approach:

- **Raw layer** A near-verbatim capture of the feed: minimally processed, preserving all fields that may be needed for future forensic analysis or compliance.
- **Clean layer** A schema-aligned table with standardized types, time zones, and naming, suitable for most analytics and joins across feeds.

- **Enriched or derived layer** Tables that include additional features: classification labels, reference data joins, regime indicators, or strategy-specific signals.

Kafka-engine tables and materialized views are a powerful way to implement this layering:

- Kafka-engine → MV_1 → *raw MergeTree.*
- Kafka-engine or *raw MergeTree* → MV_2 → *clean MergeTree.*
- Clean MergeTree → MV_3 → *enriched MergeTree.*

Each materialized view expresses a clear, incremental transformation:

- Parse and store raw.
- Normalize and standardize.
- Enrich and aggregate.

Because the end targets are MergeTree tables, they benefit from all the partitioning, ORDER BY, replication, and sharding strategies developed earlier in the chapter.

Streaming Ingest in a Sharded, Replicated Cluster

All of the above examples can be scaled out across shards and replicas:

- Each shard can host its own Kafka-engine tables and materialized views, consuming a subset of Kafka partitions keyed by symbol or another shard key.
- Materialized views on each shard write into the local ReplicatedMergeTree tables that belong to that shard.
- Distributed tables then unify these per-shard targets into a global logical view.

Designing the mapping between Kafka partitions and shards is crucial:

- Ideally, messages for a given symbol are always sent to the same Kafka partition and consumed by the same shard. This simplifies deduplication and rollups.
- Kafka's own partitioning can mirror your ClickHouse shard key (for example, both hash by symbol), reducing cross-shard coordination.

By aligning partitioning and sharding across Kafka and ClickHouse, you reduce unnecessary data movement and make the entire pipeline more predictable and scalable.

Summary: A Streaming Spine for Market Data

Materialized views and the Kafka engine provide the streaming spine that connects external markets to your ClickHouse-based analytics and storage:

- Kafka-engine tables act as high-throughput adapters, pulling messages from topics into ClickHouse.
- Materialized views define declarative, continuous transformations that turn those messages into well-typed rows in MergeTree tables, with opportunities for deduplication, normalization, and enrichment.
- Additional materialized views compute pre-aggregated rollups such as OHLCV bars, making most queries cheaper and more predictable.
- Batch sizes, offsets, and backpressure handling ensure the pipeline remains stable through both calm and volatile market conditions.
- In sharded, replicated clusters, these patterns scale horizontally, with Kafka partitions and ClickHouse shards aligned to keep ingest and queries local and balanced.

With this streaming ingest framework in place, the remaining sections of the chapter can focus on how to *use* the data once it is inside

ClickHouse: expressing temporal analytics with window functions and ASOF joins, and tuning indices, codecs, and storage policies to keep both latency and cost in check.

5.7 Window Functions and ASOF JOIN

By now we have focused mainly on how to *store* market data well in ClickHouse: choosing precise temporal types, designing partitions and sort orders, and wiring up streaming ingest into MergeTree tables. The natural next question is: how do we *use* that data to answer the kinds of temporal questions that drive trading research and surveillance?

In kdb+, such questions are often expressed with concise q syntax: rolling windows, "prev" operations, and joins on "last known" values. In ClickHouse, these ideas show up as:

- *Window functions*, which compute rolling or running metrics over ordered partitions of your data.
- *ASOF JOIN*, which matches events in one table to the most recent prior event in another, based on time.

In this section we develop an intuitive understanding of both. We assume the schemas and layouts from earlier in the chapter: trades and quotes stored in MergeTree or ReplicatedMergeTree tables, partitioned by day and ordered by (symbol, event_time).

Temporal Analytics as Sequences, Not Just Sets

Traditional SQL views a table as an unordered set of rows. For time-series markets, this is incomplete: the *order* of events matters. Many core metrics rely on the idea of a sequence in time:

- Rolling volume over the last N trades.
- Cumulative inventory over the day, updated trade by trade.
- Realized volatility over the last 5 minutes or 100 ticks.

- The best quote "known" just before each trade.

Window functions and ASOF JOIN both extend SQL to reason about such sequences. They let you say, in effect:

> "For each row, look at nearby rows in time for the same symbol and compute something over that neighborhood."

Window functions handle the "look at nearby rows *within this table*" case; ASOF JOIN handles "look at nearby rows *in another table*."

ClickHouse Window Functions: A Conceptual Overview

A window function in ClickHouse operates over a *window* of rows defined relative to each current row, instead of over the entire result set. You specify that window by:

- **PARTITION BY**: which rows belong to the same logical group (for example, all trades for one symbol).
- **ORDER BY**: how rows are ordered within the group (for example, by event time).
- **Frame**: which subset of ordered rows around the current row are included in the calculation (for example, the last 10 trades, or all trades within the last 5 minutes).

Conceptually, for each symbol:

1. Sort trades by event time.
2. Slide a window along that timeline.
3. At each step, compute metrics (sum, average, standard deviation, etc.) over just the rows inside the current window.

Because our tables are physically ordered by (symbol, event_time), ClickHouse can often evaluate these windows with relatively few random reads, especially when queries are scoped to reasonably small date ranges. This is one of the reasons we insisted earlier on aligning ORDER BY with temporal query patterns.

Rolling Volume, VWAP, and Volatility

Let us look at a few canonical rolling metrics.

Rolling volume over last N trades.

Suppose you want, for each trade, the total volume of the last 50 trades for the same symbol. This is a count-based window:

- Partition by symbol.
- Order by event time.
- Frame: the 49 preceding rows plus the current row.

Intuitively, you can picture a sliding window containing 50 consecutive trades for that symbol. As you move forward one trade at a time, you drop the oldest trade from the window and add the newest. The rolling volume is simply the sum of trade sizes inside that moving window.

Such a metric is useful for:

- Detecting bursts of activity.
- Normalizing trade sizes against recent flow.
- Feeding features into short-horizon models.

Running inventory.

For a trading desk's own fills (as opposed to public trades), you often care about inventory: net position over time. This is a cumulative sum:

- Partition by account or strategy and symbol.
- Order by fill time.

- Frame: from the beginning of the day (or horizon) up to the current row.

As you step through fills in time order, each buy increases inventory, each sell decreases it. Window functions computing a running sum of signed quantities express this directly. The result is a time-series of inventory that can be joined to prices to compute mark-to-market P&L, risk limits, and drawdowns.

Rolling volatility.

Realized volatility measures how much prices fluctuate over time. A simple estimator uses returns over small intervals and computes their standard deviation over a rolling window.

Here, the window might be:

- A fixed number of recent trades (for example, last 100 trades).
- A time-based frame (for example, all trades in the last 5 minutes).

In either case:

- Partition by symbol.
- Order by event time.
- Frame: rows whose timestamps fall in a specified backward-looking interval, or a fixed number of preceding rows.

ClickHouse's support for both row-based and range-based frames allows this: row-based for "last N trades," range-based for "last T seconds or minutes." Because event times are stored as precise DateTime64, range definitions can align exactly with market microstructure needs.

Performance Considerations for Window Functions

Window functions can be CPU-intensive, especially when:

- The frame is large (for example, whole-day running aggregates).
- You compute many different windowed metrics at once.
- Queries span long date ranges and many symbols.

Your earlier physical design choices help here:

- **ORDER BY (symbol, event_time)** keeps each symbol's events contiguous, making symbol-partitioned windows cache-friendly.
- **Daily partitions** limit each query's work to one or a few days when possible.
- **Pre-aggregated bar tables** can be used for rougher-granularity windows (for example, rolling 1-hour volatility computed from 1-minute bars instead of ticks).

A good pattern is to:

- Use tick-level window functions for high-precision, targeted analyses over modest lookbacks and date ranges.
- Use bar-level window functions for long horizons or heavy exploratory work.

The Problem of "Last Known" Values

Many important questions in markets cannot be answered by looking at a single event stream in isolation. You often need to align two streams:

- Trades with quotes (to compute spreads, slippage, and impact).
- Trades with reference curves or benchmark prices.
- Orders with risk limits or portfolio weights.

However, these streams are not synchronized. For example:

- Quotes update whenever the book changes; trades occur when matches happen. A trade may not coincide with a quote update.
- A benchmark price series might be published every second, while trades arrive at sub-millisecond intervals.

To analyze, say, "the spread at the time of each trade," you need to find, for each trade event:

> The most recent quote event for the same symbol whose event time is less than or equal to the trade's event time.

This is the "last known value" problem. Naively, you could:

- For each trade, scan backwards in the quotes table until you find a matching symbol and earlier timestamp.
- Or join on equality of timestamps and then fill gaps with window functions.

Both approaches are painful and inefficient. ASOF JOIN exists to solve exactly this problem.

ASOF JOIN: Last Known Match in Time

An ASOF ("as of") join in ClickHouse is a temporal join that, in simplified terms, says:

> For each row in the left table (for example, trades), find the row in the right table (for example, quotes) that has matching keys (for example, symbol) and the largest timestamp less than or equal to the left row's timestamp.

If no such row exists (for example, before the first quote of the day), the join yields no match or a null, depending on join type and configuration.

Conceptually:

1. For each symbol, imagine interleaving trades and quotes in event-time order along a timeline.
2. At each trade, look backwards along the timeline until you hit the nearest quote event.
3. Attach that quote's fields (bid, ask, sizes, etc.) to the trade.

ASOF JOIN automates this pattern. It uses the fact that both tables are sorted by symbol and time (or at least can be scanned in that order) to avoid quadratic searches.

Aligning Trades and Quotes

This is the most common application of ASOF JOIN in trading research.

Preconditions for efficient ASOF JOIN.

To make ASOF JOIN both correct and fast, you should:

- Store trades and quotes with the *same* timestamp type and precision (for example, DateTime64(6) in UTC).
- Use compatible ORDER BY keys: ideally (symbol, event_time) in both tables.
- Partition in a way that allows queries to touch the same dates in both tables (for example, daily partitions).

These choices ensure that:

- For each symbol, rows in both tables are ordered by time, so the join can advance through both streams in a coordinated way.
- ClickHouse can prune partitions and parts efficiently when you restrict to specific days and symbols.

Interpretation and use cases.

Once such a join is in place, you can compute, per trade:

- **Spread at trade time**: difference between best ask and best bid pulled from the matched quote.
- **Midprice at trade time**: average of bid and ask from the matched quote.
- **Slippage or impact**: difference between trade price and midprice at trade time, or between trade price and subsequent quotes.

This joined dataset becomes the substrate for:

- Transaction cost analysis (TCA).
- Market making performance evaluation.
- Microstructure studies of price impact and information flow.

Other Uses of ASOF JOIN

Beyond trade-quote alignment, ASOF JOIN is useful whenever you want to attach slow-moving or sampled information to a faster event stream.

Examples include:

Reference curves and benchmarks.

Suppose you have:

- A reference price curve (for example, an index level or mid of a synthetic basket) sampled every second.
- Tick-by-tick trades in constituent symbols.

You may want to, for each trade:

- Attach the last known index level.
- Compute deviations or residuals relative to that benchmark.

An ASOF JOIN between trades and the reference curve table, keyed by symbol or by some instrument grouping and time, expresses this cleanly.

Risk limits and configuration.

You might keep a table of risk limits or configuration values that change infrequently (for example, maximum position per symbol, per strategy, as of a given time). When replaying historical trades to check for limit breaches as they would have been perceived in real time, you need to know:

> What was the applicable limit on that symbol at the moment of each trade?

Again, an ASOF JOIN between the trades and the limit-change events, keyed appropriately, gives you this answer.

Comparing ASOF JOIN to Alternative Patterns

You could, in principle, emulate ASOF behavior using more traditional SQL constructs:

- Join trades and quotes on symbol, then filter to quotes with event time less than or equal to trade time, then keep only the "closest" one using a window function or a grouping and max-time trick.

However, this has several drawbacks:

- It is harder to read and easier to get subtly wrong (off-by-one boundaries, incorrect handling of ties, etc.).
- It often performs worse because it creates large intermediate join results before filtering them down.

ASOF JOIN, by contrast:

- Encodes the "last known as of time" semantics directly in the join operator.

- Can exploit the sort order of both tables to stream through them efficiently.

For users familiar with kdb+, this maps closely to the mental model of as-of joins in q, but expressed in ClickHouse's SQL dialect.

Handling Late and Out-of-Order Data

Real feeds are messy. Even if most events arrive in order, you will encounter:

- Trades that arrive late relative to quotes.
- Corrections and cancellations.
- Replayed data with different latencies.

These complications interact with both window functions and ASOF JOIN.

Ordering and event time.

ASOF JOIN semantics are based on the timestamp stored in the tables. If event times reflect true market times (even if messages arrived out of order), then:

- A late-arriving trade with an earlier event time will be matched to the appropriate earlier quote when you query after the fact.
- The join is a function of the underlying event history, not of your system's observation order.

This is why we stressed earlier the importance of distinguishing *event time* from *ingest time* and using event time as the primary axis for analytics.

Corrections and replays.

When corrections appear (for example, a trade is canceled or amended), you have to decide:

- Whether to maintain a strictly historical view that reflects what was *first seen*, useful for reproducing strategy decisions in real time.
- Or to maintain a *corrected view* that reflects the final, authoritative state of the feed.

In the corrected-view case, you may:

- Mutate or overwrite rows in the trades table according to correction messages.
- Recompute impacted rollups and ASOF JOIN-derived metrics (for example, by re-running joins for affected date ranges).

This can be resource-intensive; many teams limit full recomputations to end-of-day or end-of-week cycles and accept that intraday analytics operate on slightly stale or uncorrected data.

Testing Temporal Logic with Small Datasets

Because temporal logic is subtle, it is good practice to validate any window-function or ASOF JOIN query on a tiny, hand-constructed dataset before applying it to billions of rows.

A sensible workflow is:

1. Extract a few minutes of trades and quotes for a single symbol into a scratch table.
2. Manually inspect and annotate them (for example, in a spreadsheet) to determine the correct rolling metrics and last-known matches.
3. Run your ClickHouse queries using window functions and ASOF JOIN on this scratch dataset.
4. Compare the results row-by-row against your manual expectations.

Only once the behavior is verified on a small sample should you scale up to production-sized queries. This process greatly reduces the risk of off-by-one errors, mishandled edge cases (start-of-day, gaps in data), or misinterpreted join semantics.

Putting It All Together

Window functions and ASOF JOIN sit at the top of the ClickHouse stack we have built in this chapter:

- **SQL dialect and temporal types** give you precise timestamps and well-typed schemas for trades, quotes, and bars.
- **MergeTree and ReplicatedMergeTree** store these schemas efficiently in parts, merged and replicated for resilience.
- **Partitions and ORDER BY** arrange data on disk so that symbol- and time-based scans are fast and cache-friendly.
- **Sharding and Distributed tables** let you scale these designs across many nodes.
- **Kafka and materialized views** bring the live streams of market data into ClickHouse continuously, with options for deduplication and pre-aggregation.

On this foundation, window functions and ASOF JOIN provide the expressive power needed for real temporal analytics:

- Rolling metrics for volume, volatility, and inventory.
- Last-known-value joins for aligning trades with quotes, benchmarks, and risk limits.
- Complex temporal logic expressed declaratively, without resorting to procedural code or external processing systems.

For practitioners familiar with kdb+ and q, these features make ClickHouse feel much less like a generic warehouse and much more like a viable engine for serious market microstructure research and surveillance—one that integrates smoothly with the broader data ecosystem of Kafka, object storage, and distributed compute.

In the final section of this chapter, we will turn to the lower-level tuning knobs—indices, codecs, and storage policies—that help you meet strict latency and cost budgets once your temporal analytics are in place.

5.8 Indices, Codecs, and Storage Policies

So far in this chapter we have focused on getting the logical and physical layout of market data right: types, partitions, ORDER BY, replication, sharding, and streaming ingest. With these foundations in place, ClickHouse already delivers excellent performance on many workloads.

However, as datasets grow into trillions of rows and clusters into dozens of nodes, you inevitably face two pressures:

- **Latency**: queries that used to run in milliseconds start creeping into seconds.

- **Cost**: storage footprints become large enough that hardware and cloud bills start to matter.

ClickHouse offers three additional levers to manage these pressures:

- **Data-skipping indices** Extra on-disk structures that help the engine skip over irrelevant data more aggressively than ORDER BY alone.

- **Column compression codecs** Pluggable compression schemes per column that change how values are encoded on disk.

- **Storage policies** Rules that determine which physical volumes hold which data, and how data migrates between "hot" and "cold" tiers over time.

This section explains how to use these features *together* in the context of time-series markets, not as isolated tricks. We will focus on simple, reusable patterns and the reasoning behind them, rather than cataloging every option.

Data-Skipping Indices: Skipping More Than ORDER BY

In earlier sections, we saw that MergeTree already has a built-in notion of data skipping: marks and per-part metadata allow it to avoid reading portions of a part where the ORDER BY keys cannot possibly satisfy a query's filters. For many workloads, a well-designed ORDER BY is enough.

Data-skipping indices extend this idea to other columns. They add auxiliary summaries, stored alongside column data, that allow ClickHouse to decide quickly whether a block of rows can be skipped for a given predicate.

Conceptually, a data-skipping index is:

- Defined on one or more columns.
- Evaluated per "granule"—a contiguous group of rows, often aligned with marks.
- Populated with summary information, such as minimum and maximum values, Bloom filters, or token sets.

At query time, if a predicate such as symbol = 'ESZ4' or regime_flag = 'stress' is incompatible with a granule's summary, ClickHouse can skip that granule entirely without looking at the raw rows.

When Indices Help Market Queries

Indices are not free: they consume storage and CPU during inserts and merges. They make sense when:

- Queries often filter on columns *not* leading in ORDER BY.
- Those filters are selective: they match a small fraction of rows.

- Values show some clustering or structure that makes summaries informative.

In market contexts, good candidates include:

Symbol buckets.

If your ORDER BY is already (symbol, event_time), you may not need an index on symbol itself. But you may benefit from an index on a coarser bucket, such as:

- Sector or industry classification.
- An internal "symbol group" used by a particular strategy.

If many queries filter by a small subset of such groups, a data-skipping index can help ClickHouse avoid scanning irrelevant symbol ranges, especially when the query is not fully constrained by symbol and time at the same time.

Regime or event flags.

Surveillance and research queries often target special regimes:

- Trading halts.
- Auctions and opening/closing crosses.
- Stress periods (for example, days marked as crisis events).

If these regimes are encoded as low-cardinality flags or enumerations, a data-skipping index can quickly exclude granules that contain no flagged rows. This is particularly powerful when such regimes are sparse relative to total tick volume.

Surveillance alert IDs.

Some systems generate alert or anomaly IDs and attach them to specific trades or quotes. These IDs may be sparse and highly selective. A Bloom-filter-based index on the alert ID column can accelerate investigations that repeatedly query by specific alert IDs or small sets of them.

When Not to Use Indices

Indices are not a substitute for good primary design. Avoid them when:

- You are trying to compensate for a poor ORDER BY choice (for example, random ordering in a tick table).
- The column values are high-cardinality and nearly random (for example, unique trade IDs) and queries rarely filter on them.
- Queries are mostly full scans over dates and symbols, where indices cannot skip much.

As a rule:

> First get partitioning and ORDER BY right for your dominant query patterns. Then add indices only where you can point to a specific, recurring query shape that needs extra help.

Column Compression Codecs: Shaping How Data is Stored

ClickHouse stores each column in compressed form. By default, it uses general-purpose codecs that balance compression ratio and CPU cost (for example, LZ4 or similar). For time-series market data, you can often do better by customizing codecs per column.

A *codec* defines how a column's values are transformed before generic compression is applied. Common patterns include:

- **Delta encoding**: store differences between consecutive values rather than absolute values.
- **Gorilla-style codecs**: specialized for time-series with slowly changing values and occasional jumps.
- **Low-cardinality encodings**: map frequent strings or small integer sets to compact codes.

Because MergeTree stores rows ordered by (symbol, event_time), many columns in market data exhibit strong local structure:

- Prices of a given symbol do not jump randomly tick to tick; differences are small.
- Sizes for a symbol may repeat common values (round lots).
- Symbols, venues, and condition codes are drawn from small enumerations.

Good codecs exploit this structure.

Choosing Codecs for Common Market Columns

Timestamps.

Event times and ingest times are often stored in DateTime64. Within a symbol-day partition, successive timestamps are close together and monotonic. Delta-based codecs or time-series-specific codecs can represent these efficiently.

Benefits:

- Smaller storage footprint for time columns.
- Faster decompression when scanning long segments of time.

Prices.

Prices for a given instrument:

- Tend to move gradually.
- Obey tick sizes.

Encoding them as decimals or scaled integers, coupled with delta compression, often yields high compression ratios. Gorilla-style codecs can also perform well, particularly if you store midprices or log-prices where relative changes are small.

Sizes and volumes.

Trade sizes and quote sizes:

- Often repeat common values (for example, 100 shares, 1 contract).
- Are non-negative integers.

These are good candidates for delta plus integer-friendly codecs. In some cases, if the set of possible sizes is small, low-cardinality encodings compress them into tiny codewords.

Symbols, venues, and flags.

String-like identifiers and enums:

- Symbol and venue codes.
- Trade conditions and quote flags.

These are prime candidates for dictionary-based or low-cardinality codecs:

- The distinct set of values is modest compared to row count.
- Compressing them into small integer codes yields excellent ratios.

Because these columns are used in filters and joins, there is a balance: heavier compression can increase CPU cost during decompression; lighter codecs may reduce CPU but increase I/O. In practice, low-cardinality codecs strike a good compromise.

Balancing Compression and CPU

Compression brings two main benefits:

- Less data on disk and in I/O caches.
- Fewer bytes moved from disk to CPU, which often dominates query time.

But it also has costs:

- Extra CPU to compress during inserts and merges.

- Extra CPU to decompress during queries, especially when queries select many columns.

For market data, patterns to keep in mind:

- For **cold history** that is rarely read but expensive to store in bulk, prioritize heavier compression.
- For **hot data** regularly queried by traders and intraday analytics, prefer lighter codecs that trade a bit of storage for lower query CPU.
- For **narrow queries** (for example, scanning only price and size), ensure those columns use codecs that decompress quickly.

The ideal codec mix cannot be guessed; it should be measured. Start with sensible defaults informed by time-series structure, then iterate using ClickHouse's system tables to compare compression ratios and query profiles before and after codec changes.

Storage Policies: Hot, Warm, and Cold Tiers

Even with good codecs, full-depth tick data accumulates rapidly. It is rarely economical to keep a decade of nanosecond-level history on your fastest SSDs. Instead, production systems stratify storage into tiers:

- **Hot** Fast, low-latency storage (NVMe or high-end SSD) for recent, frequently accessed data.
- **Warm** Cheaper disks (SATA SSD or HDD) for moderately recent but less frequently accessed data.
- **Cold** Very cheap storage (network-attached, object storage) for archival history.

ClickHouse's *storage policies* and *volumes* let you capture this structure. You define:

- One or more volumes, each backed by specific disks or storage locations.

- A policy that assigns tables or partitions to volumes, possibly with age-based rules.

TTLs, introduced earlier in the context of MergeTree part eviction, tie into this:

- Instead of only deleting old data, TTL expressions can also move parts from one volume to another once they age past a threshold.

A Typical Market Retention Layout

For a large trade and quote store, a common pattern is:

Hot tier.

- Holds recent days or weeks of ticks.
- Used heavily by intraday analytics, live TCA, and trading support.
- Configured with:
  - Relatively lighter codecs (fast to decompress).
  - High IOPS and low-latency disks.

Warm tier.

- Holds months to a couple of years of data.
- Used for swing trading research, compliance checks, and risk modeling.
- Configured with:
  - Slightly heavier codecs for better compression.
  - Cheaper disks with acceptable but higher latency.

Cold tier.

- Holds deep history beyond operational horizons.
- Accessed infrequently, perhaps via scheduled batch jobs.

- Configured with:
  - Strong compression, even if CPU-heavy.
  - Object storage or low-cost disks.

Queries that scan across these boundaries may experience step changes in latency; for example, scanning the last 10 days might be much faster than scanning the last 400 days. This is not a bug but a consequence of the physical layout; analysts should be aware of these tiers when designing queries.

Combining Indices, Codecs, and Storage Policies

These three tools are most powerful when used together, guided by a clear understanding of your workloads.

Pattern 1: Fast Surveillance on Recent Data

Surveillance teams often need:

- Rapid queries over recent days of ticks and quotes.
- Complex filters on regimes, alerts, and pattern flags.
- Tolerable or looser latencies on older data during rare investigations.

A suitable configuration:

- **Hot tier**: recent days on SSDs, with:
  - Lightweight codecs for prices and sizes.
  - Data-skipping indices on regime and alert flag columns.
- **Warm tier**: older months on slower disks, with:
  - Heavier codecs for better compression.
  - Possibly the same indices, if investigations regularly hit this horizon.

The index ensures that when an investigator queries for a specific alert or rare regime, ClickHouse can skip most granules quickly. The codec choice keeps decompression cheap for the hot window where speed is crucial.

Pattern 2: Research Cluster with Emphasis on Cost

A research or backtesting cluster might:

- Store many years of full-depth data.
- Run long, heavy queries that are not latency-critical.
- Operate under tighter cost constraints.

Configuration might look like:

- One primary tier (no strict hot/cold split), using:
  - Aggressive codecs on most columns (delta, Gorilla, dictionary encodings).
  - Limited use of data-skipping indices, focused on key research dimensions (for example, sector or regime).
- Optional offloading of very old years to object storage, accessed through ClickHouse's support for such backends.

Here, you accept higher CPU per query in exchange for lower storage cost. Since queries are often run overnight or interactively by researchers, this is acceptable.

Pattern 3: Hybrid Tick and Bar Store

Many organizations maintain both:

- Detailed tick tables for compliance and specialized analysis.
- Aggregated bar tables for most modeling and factor construction.

A sensible arrangement is:

- **Bars in a hot tier**: with moderate compression and carefully chosen indices (for example, on sector or custom groups), since they are accessed most frequently.
- **Ticks in warm or cold tiers**: with heavier codecs and minimal indices, since the default ORDER BY and partitioning often suffice and tick-level queries are less frequent.

Researchers first hit bar tables. Only when anomalies or specific hypotheses demand it do they drill down into ticks, accepting the performance cost.

A Metrics-Driven Tuning Process

Because every trading firm's workload is unique, the most important habit is to treat indices, codecs, and storage policies as tunable parameters informed by measurement, not as one-off guesses.

A simple iterative process:

1. **Baseline**: Start with a clean design—good partition and ORDER BY choices, default codecs, no extra indices, a simple two-tier storage policy (hot and warm).
2. **Measure**: Use ClickHouse system tables and query logs to gather:
    - Compression ratios per column and table.
    - Query latency distributions for key workloads.
    - Read amplification: how many bytes read vs. rows returned.
3. **Hypothesize**: Identify friction points:
    - A small set of queries that are too slow.
    - Tables or columns that dominate storage cost.
4. **Adjust**: For each hypothesis, change *one thing*:
    - Add or refine a data-skipping index to target a recurring, selective predicate.

- Change codecs for a small number of columns and rebuild affected parts.
- Adjust storage policies or TTL thresholds for specific partitions.

5. **Re-measure**: Compare metrics before and after. Keep changes that meaningfully improve latency or cost without harming ingest stability.

This loop mirrors good practice in trading strategy development: define the objective, run controlled experiments, and avoid changing many variables at once.

Summary: Fine-Tuning Physical Layout for Markets

By the time you reach this section, you have seen ClickHouse from SQL-level schemas and temporal types down to MergeTree parts, replication, sharding, and streaming ingest. Indices, codecs, and storage policies are the final layer of control:

- **Data-skipping indices** help ClickHouse say "no" quickly to large portions of data that cannot match a query, especially for sparse flags and groupings.
- **Column codecs** shape how market data values are encoded, exploiting temporal and categorical structure to reduce storage and I/O.
- **Storage policies** place different time horizons and data products on appropriate hardware tiers, balancing latency against cost.

Used together, and guided by careful measurement, these tools let you operate a ClickHouse-based market data system that is not only correct and scalable, but also economically efficient and responsive to the evolving demands of traders, quants, and regulators.

Chapter 6

Performance Engineering

Every trading stack eventually hits a wall where more hardware no longer yields faster fills or tighter spreads. This chapter shows how to break through that wall by treating performance as an engineered property-not an accident-using kdb+ and ClickHouse as concrete laboratories. You will learn how to shape data layouts for the CPU you actually run on, make NUMA and the Linux kernel work in your favor, and build a profiling and benchmarking discipline that catches regressions before production does.

6.1 Vectorization and Memory Locality Tuning

In the previous chapters we treated kdb+ and ClickHouse largely as black boxes: we focused on schemas, partitioning, and ingestion patterns that produce good high-level behavior. In this section we open the box a little further and connect those choices to what the CPU actually does cycle by cycle.

The goal is simple to state but subtle to achieve: we want the tight inner loops of our queries to run from L1 cache, using vector (SIMD) instructions on straight-line data, with as few surprises as possible. When we succeed, median and tail latency both improve, and performance becomes more predictable across changing market conditions.

We will first build an intuitive mental model of modern cores, caches, and SIMD. Then we will look at how columnar layouts in kdb+ and ClickHouse map onto that model, and finally we will develop concrete tuning techniques for schemas and queries that keep hot data local and vector-friendly.

A Mental Model of the Core: Pipelines, Caches, and SIMD

You do not need to be a microarchitect to tune market data workloads, but you do need a few stable pictures in your head.

Pipelines and instruction throughput.

Modern x86 CPUs are deeply pipelined. Rather than completing one instruction before starting the next, they break each instruction into stages and overlap many instructions in flight. If dependencies are simple and predictable, the core can retire multiple instructions per cycle.

Conceptually, imagine a small factory line:

- At the front, instructions are fetched and decoded.
- In the middle, arithmetic and logical units execute operations.
- At the back, results are written to registers and memory.

When we write tight loops in kdb+ or ClickHouse that perform simple arithmetic or comparisons on large arrays, the execution engine tries to turn them into these efficient, straight-line sequences that the pipeline loves. Anything that complicates the control flow (many branches) or the data path (random memory access) makes the pipeline stall or idle.

Cache hierarchy and locality.

Main memory (DRAM) is very far away from the core in time, even though it is only a few centimeters away on the motherboard. To hide that distance, CPUs place one or more levels of cache between the core and DRAM:

- L1 cache: very small (tens of kilobytes per core), extremely fast.
- L2 cache: larger (hundreds of kilobytes), a bit slower.
- Last-level cache (L3): shared across cores on a socket, much larger, slower still.

You can think of these caches as tiny, automatic copies of recently used regions of memory. The CPU moves data between caches and DRAM in fixed-size chunks called cache lines, commonly 64 bytes on x86. Every load or store pulls an entire cache line into the cache if it is not already there.

Two kinds of locality drive good cache behavior:

- *Spatial locality*: if you touch element i of an array, you are likely to touch $i + 1$, $i + 2$, and so on.
- *Temporal locality*: if you touch a piece of data once, you are likely to touch it again soon.

Columnar databases are essentially a bet on spatial locality: by storing each column as a dense array of values, they make it likely that a sequential scan will re-use data within the same cache line.

SIMD: doing more work per instruction.

Scalar instructions operate on a single value at a time. SIMD (Single Instruction, Multiple Data) instructions operate on multiple values packed into a wide register.

For example, on a 256-bit SIMD unit:

- You can add eight 32-bit integers in one instruction.
- Or four 64-bit integers in one instruction.
- Or operate on sixteen 16-bit values, and so on.

From our perspective as engine users, the important consequences are:

- Narrower types (32-bit integers instead of 64-bit) allow more elements per SIMD operation and more elements per cache line.
- Clean, contiguous arrays let the query engine feed SIMD units easily.
- Branches inside the inner loop (for example, per-row if conditions) reduce SIMD efficiency, because different lanes want to take different paths.

Both kdb+ and ClickHouse contain hand-tuned vectorized kernels under the hood. Our job is to present data and queries in a shape that lets those kernels run as often as possible, instead of falling back to slower scalar or branch-heavy paths.

How Columnar Layouts Map to the Core

With this mental model, we can now connect engine-level structures to CPU behavior.

kdb+ column vectors.

In kdb+, each column of a table is stored as a contiguous vector in memory. A simple time-price-size table might hold:

- time: an array of timestamps.
- sym: an array of symbols (interned).
- price: an array of doubles.
- size: an array of integers.

When you evaluate an expression like select avg price by sym from t where size>0, the interpreter and underlying C loops walk these arrays sequentially. Filtering and aggregation are implemented in routines that operate over slices of the column vectors, often in batches.

The fact that each column is contiguous is exactly what caches and SIMD want: the engine touches elements in order, and the hardware prefetchers can pull in cache lines ahead of time.

ClickHouse MergeTree parts.

In ClickHouse, a MergeTree table stores each column in its own data file, again as a sequence of values, optionally compressed and often grouped into granules and marks.

A query like SELECT avg(price) FROM trades WHERE size > 0 on a MergeTree table will:

- Read only the price and size columns from disk and decompress them into memory in blocks.
- Pass those blocks through vectorized execution units that apply filters, aggregates, and other operators.

As with kdb+, the key point is that the engine transforms your query into operations over blocks of contiguous column values, designed to drive SIMD-friendly loops. The block size is chosen to balance cache residency against overheads; too small, and there is excessive per-block work; too large, and you exceed L1/L2 and thrash caches.

Why small layout details matter.

Given that both engines are columnar and vectorized, you might expect them to automatically "do the right thing." Often they do, but small decisions we make about types, column ordering, and query shape can dramatically influence:

- How many values fit in a cache line.
- How many values fit in a SIMD register.
- Whether hot loops stay within L1/L2 or constantly reach out to L3 and DRAM.
- How many branches and mispredictions occur in the inner loop.

The remainder of this section focuses on those decisions.

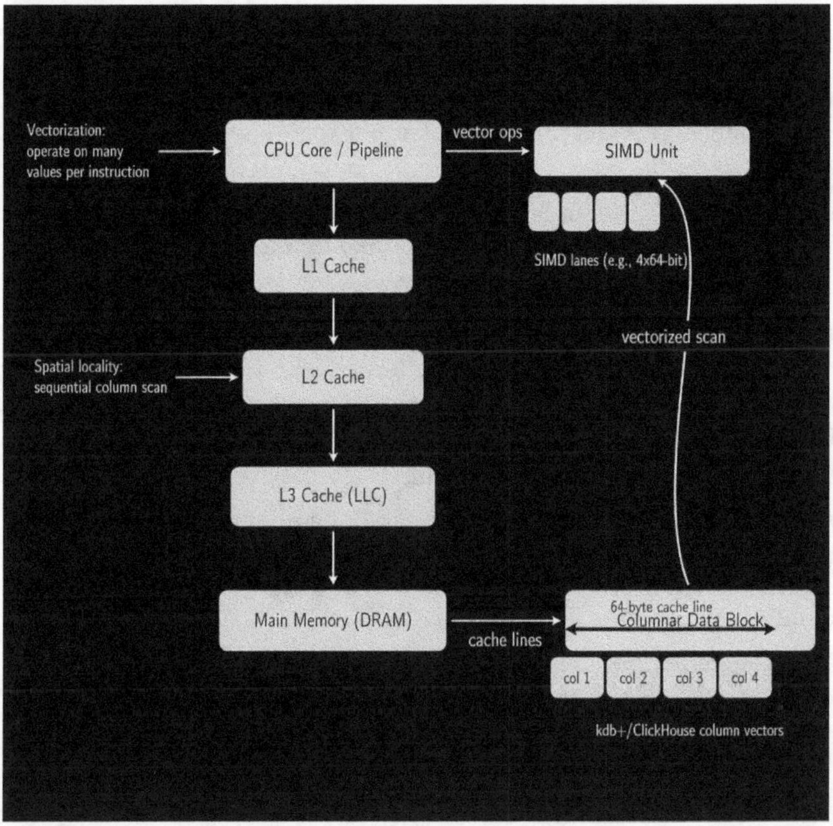

Choosing Types and Layouts for SIMD and Caches

The first and most powerful levers you control are column types and the way columns are laid out and grouped.

Prefer narrow, fixed-width types for hot paths.

SIMD instructions operate on fixed-width lanes. Narrower types give you more lanes per instruction and more elements per cache line. For critical columns that appear in filters, joins, and group-bys, consider:

- Using 32-bit integers instead of 64-bit where the domain allows it (for example, mapping symbols to integer IDs, or compressing exchange codes and venues into small enums).

- Using 32-bit floats instead of 64-bit doubles for some analytics where precision is not critical to the penny. Many P&L and risk applications still prefer doubles, but some signal calculations tolerate floats.
- Avoiding variable-length strings and blobs in hot paths; instead, store fixed-width IDs and keep the human-readable representation in a side table.

In kdb+, this often means using `int` instead of `long`, or symbol columns that map to compact integer keys internally. In ClickHouse, it means choosing `Int32`/`UInt32` or a low-cardinality encoding instead of `Int64` or raw `String` for join keys and group-by dimensions.

Separate hot and cold columns.

A frequent mistake is to add rarely used columns to a core fact table and then always scan them. Columnar storage helps, because unused columns are not touched at all, but within a block, the size and alignment of each column still matter.

Practical guidelines:

- Keep the smallest, most frequently filtered columns close together in memory or in the same family of tables or parts. These should fit comfortably in L1/L2 during a scan.
- Move infrequently used or very wide columns (raw messages, full JSON, debug metadata) into separate tables or projections, joined only when necessary.

For kdb+, this may mean splitting a massive trade table into a compact intraday core with only time, symbol, and prices, and a slower auxiliary table keyed by trade ID with extra fields. For ClickHouse, this can mean using projections or auxiliary tables for heavy columns, so most queries avoid touching them.

Align layout with common filter patterns.

Engines scan data in the physical order it is stored. Partitioning and sorting schemes that group together records likely to be hit by the same query improve locality.

For example:

- If most queries filter by symbol and time range, consider partitioning by day and sorting within a partition by symbol then time.
- If you have many queries by venue, list, or index membership, you might cluster or pre-filter by those dimensions.

The more you can arrange for your primary filters to select contiguous ranges of rows rather than scattered positions, the better your cache behavior and SIMD utilization will be.

Structuring Queries for Vectorized Execution

Even with a good layout, queries themselves can either help or hinder the vectorized inner loops.

Push filters early and keep them simple.

Both kdb+ and ClickHouse try to apply filters as early as possible in the pipeline, ideally in simple, vectorized loops. You can help by:

- Writing filters that are expressible as comparisons and arithmetic on base columns, without user-defined functions or complex control flow.
- Avoiding per-row branching logic in functional constructs where possible; prefer built-in operations that operate on whole arrays.
- In ClickHouse, using built-in functions that are known to be vectorized rather than implementing equivalent logic in less-optimized ways.

On the CPU side, an early filter reduces the volume of data that flows through later stages. This means fewer cache lines touched in group-bys and joins, and more chance that the working set fits in L1/L2.

Order predicates to match selectivity and locality.

When a query has multiple conditions, there is a trade-off between selectivity (filtering out as much as possible early) and locality (staying within a small set of columns).

Often it is best to:

- First apply cheap, highly selective predicates that only touch one or two narrow columns (for example, symbol ID, venue code, or a precomputed bucket).
- Then apply more expensive predicates (time windows, price ranges) on the reduced data set.

Engines already attempt to reorder predicates, but clarity in your query can help the planner and reduce surprises. Importantly, focus early predicates on columns that are already in cache, rather than triggering random lookups into many different columns.

Minimize branches in hot loops.

Branch mispredictions are costly because they flush parts of the pipeline and waste work the CPU speculatively performed on the wrong path. SIMD makes this more delicate: if different lanes want to take different branches, the processor must effectively serialize the work.

At the query level, this means:

- Prefer mask-based operations over explicit branching. For instance, using boolean masks that mark which rows satisfy conditions, then operating on those masks, rather than coding equivalent logic with nested conditional branches.
- Avoid writing queries that depend on per-row decisions in ways that cannot be expressed as pure expressions on columns.

You do not control the exact branching structure the engine emits, but you can favor idioms that map well to masking and vectorization instead of row-by-row branching.

Managing Working-Set Size: Batches, Joins, and Groups

The second half of performance tuning is ensuring that the amount of data touched by a tight loop fits comfortably in the faster caches.

Batch sizes and micro-partitioning.

Both kdb+ and ClickHouse process data in chunks: kdb+ over vector segments, ClickHouse over blocks. If chunks are too large, they do not fit in L1/L2, and cache lines are constantly evicted and reloaded; if chunks are too small, overhead per chunk dominates.

In practice:

- Accept the default block sizes as a good starting point; they were chosen by engine authors with cache sizes in mind.
- Avoid designing your own application-level "micro-batching" that fights the engine's chunking; instead, align your data ingestion and query patterns with the engine's internal blocks.
- For very hot intraday aggregations, consider using smaller, cache-resident summary tables that are periodically folded into larger tables.

Join patterns and locality.

Joins are natural sources of poor locality: they require looking up matching keys in another structure, often producing scattered accesses.

To keep joins cache-friendly:

- Use compact, fixed-width join keys. This keeps hash tables small and improves SIMD usage in key comparisons.
- Keep dimension tables small enough to fit in cache where possible. This is especially valuable for reference data (symbols, instruments, calendars).
- In ClickHouse, exploit join algorithms that favor locality, such as join algorithms based on in-memory hash tables for moderately sized dimensions.
- In kdb+, pre-materialize or pre-join hot reference data for intraday workloads rather than rejoining large dimension tables repeatedly.

The ideal is a join where the right-hand side (dimension table) lives mostly in L2 or L3 during the query, and accesses follow consistent, predictable patterns.

Group-bys and aggregation working sets.

Group-bys and aggregations maintain state per group key. If the number of groups is small and the state per group is tiny, the whole aggregation structure may fit in L1/L2. If there are millions of groups or large per-group state, the aggregation spills into L3 and DRAM, hurting performance.

Design implications:

- Be conscious of group key cardinality. Grouping by raw trade ID is very different from grouping by symbol or by symbol and minute.
- Where possible, perform multi-stage aggregation: first aggregate into coarser buckets or partial summaries that fit in cache, then aggregate those further. This is natural in hierarchical time buckets and symbol lists.
- Avoid adding many rarely used grouping dimensions to core aggregations; they explode the number of groups and blow out working-set size.

In practice, this often leads to a tiered analytics design: small, hot summary tables for most queries, and larger, more detailed tables for occasional deep dives.

From Symptoms to Layout and Query Changes

Even with careful design, you will encounter queries that underperform. The final piece is learning how to reason from observed behavior back to specific layout or query adjustments.

Recognizing cache and SIMD issues in symptoms.

Typical symptoms of poor vectorization or locality include:

- Queries whose median latency is acceptable but whose tail latency (for example, 99th percentile) is wildly unstable, especially during bursts.
- Queries that slow down sharply when an additional column is added to the select-list or group-by, even if that column is rarely used.
- Workloads where adding cores does not increase throughput as expected, because all cores are contending for the same cache and memory bandwidth.

These are signs that your inner loops are spending more time waiting on memory or wrestling with branches than doing useful SIMD work.

Tracing back to cause.

When you see such symptoms, analyze them with the CPU and memory picture in mind:

- Ask which columns are being scanned and in what order; consider whether some could be dropped, moved to another table, or narrowed in type.
- Examine filters, joins, and group-bys to see if they can be reordered or simplified to reduce working-set size early.
- Check whether new columns or dimensions you added recently are changing the shape of blocks or the cardinality of grouping keys.

Often, a small schema change—such as moving a bulky column to a side table or replacing a string join key with an integer ID—will restore vectorized, cache-friendly behavior.

Iterating safely.

Finally, treat these tuning decisions as hypotheses to be tested, not one-off tweaks. Use the profiling and benchmarking techniques from later sections of this chapter to:

- Measure instruction mixes, cache misses, and latency distributions before and after changes.

- Confirm that the improvements hold under realistic, bursty market loads, not just in synthetic microbenchmarks.
- Guard against regressions when schemas or queries evolve.

Vectorization and memory locality are not magic incantations; they are simply ways of aligning your mental model of the workload with the hardware's strengths. When you do this consistently, kdb+ and ClickHouse reward you with predictable, high throughput on even the noisiest market days.

6.2 NUMA Awareness and Memory Mapping

In the previous section we focused on keeping hot loops inside a single core's caches and driving the SIMD units efficiently. We assumed, implicitly, that "memory" was one uniform pool, equally fast from the point of view of any core.

Modern trading servers are not like that. They are almost always multi-socket, and each socket brings its own memory controllers and attached DRAM. Accessing memory local to your socket is much faster and more predictable than reaching across the inter-socket link to touch "remote" memory. This non-uniformity is the essence of NUMA: Non-Uniform Memory Access.

For latency-sensitive engines like kdb+ and ClickHouse, NUMA is the next level of locality after caches. Once you have done a reasonable job with vectorization and cache usage, the biggest remaining source of jitter is often *where* your process's memory lives relative to the cores that execute the queries.

In this section we will:

- Build an intuitive picture of a dual-socket NUMA server and what "local" versus "remote" memory really means.
- Connect that picture to kdb+ and ClickHouse, especially their use of memory-mapped files.

- Develop concrete practices for pinning processes and controlling memory placement so data and threads stay on the same socket.
- Walk through practical recipes using common tools and configuration points.
- End with a short design checklist for new deployments so locality is baked in from day one.

What NUMA Really Means in Practice

Two sockets, two "neighborhoods" of memory.

Consider a typical trading server: two physical CPU packages (sockets) on one motherboard. Each socket has:

- A group of cores.
- One or more memory controllers.
- DRAM channels and DIMMs directly wired to those controllers.

From the point of view of the operating system, each socket plus its directly attached memory is a NUMA node.

When a core on socket 0 reads from memory that physically sits on socket 0's DIMMs, the access travels over the shortest, fastest path. When that same core reads a page that lives on socket 1's DIMMs, the request has to cross an interconnect (QPI, UPI, Infinity Fabric, or similar), wait in the remote memory controller, then come back. This adds latency and consumes shared interconnect bandwidth.

You can think of it like two local neighborhoods in a city:

- Visiting a neighbor on your own block is fast and predictable.
- Visiting someone in another neighborhood across a busy bridge may be much slower, especially at rush hour.

NUMA tuning is, at heart, arranging things so that most of your "visits" stay within the local neighborhood of a socket.

The kernel's default behavior.

By default, Linux tries to be helpful and "fair":

- It can move threads between cores and sockets to balance CPU load.
- It can place memory pages on any NUMA node, often following a "first touch" policy: the node of the core that first writes to a page.
- Under memory pressure or overcommit, it can reclaim or move pages across nodes.

For general-purpose workloads this is reasonable. For low-latency, high-throughput systems, it can be destructive. You can end up with:

- A kdb+ process running mostly on socket 0 but with large parts of its mapped database sitting on socket 1's memory.
- ClickHouse background threads that occasionally run on the "wrong" socket and constantly access remote pages, adding noise to query latency.

Our job is to gently but firmly constrain the kernel so that, for our engines, "local" really means local.

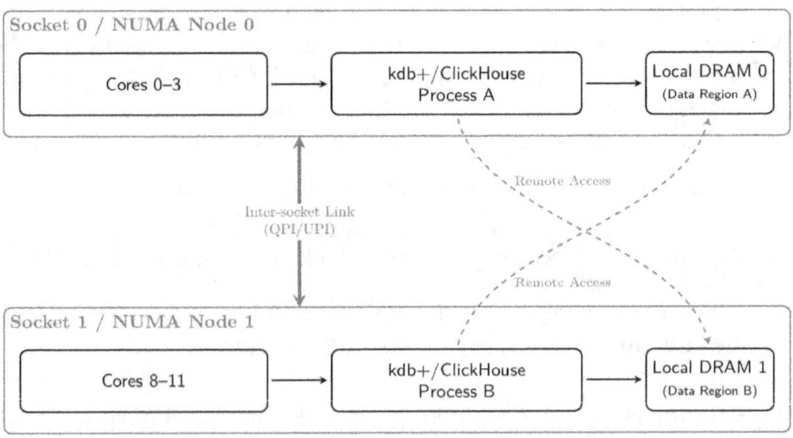

Memory-Mapped Files and NUMA: Why It Matters

kdb+ and memory-mapped databases.

kdb+ famously leans on memory mapping for large historical partitions. When you open a table from disk, the process typically uses mmap under the hood. This tells the kernel:

> "Please make this file appear as a region of my virtual memory. Bring pages into RAM on demand as I touch them. Keep recently used pages cached as long as you can."

The physical pages that back this mapping live in the system's page cache. On a NUMA system, these pages are not magically "everywhere"; they are concrete chunks of DRAM on one node or another.

If kdb+ is running mainly on socket 0, and you warm up a partition by scanning it with threads also on socket 0, the first-touch behavior usually places those pages in socket 0's DRAM. Great: you have a local, warm cache for subsequent queries.

If, however, some other thread on socket 1 (perhaps a background job or an idle shell doing a test query) is the one that first walks the mapping, those pages may land in socket 1's DRAM. Now your critical intraday query on socket 0 is repeatedly pulling pages across the inter-socket link. You will see stable averages, but the tail will be noisy, especially when both sockets are busy.

ClickHouse and mapped parts.

ClickHouse uses file I/O and page cache rather than explicit huge shared mappings for most data paths, but the effect is similar:

- Data parts are read from disk into the page cache.
- Those pages live on specific nodes' DRAM.
- Query threads on one socket may frequently touch pages that were brought in by background merges or other queries on the other socket.

Again, the kernel is simply doing what it always does. It cannot know that a given MergeTree part is "owned" conceptually by one group of cores. If we want that property, we need to impose some structure.

Why remote memory hurts tail latency.

Remote memory access has two main costs:

- Higher average latency per access.
- Extra sensitivity to load on the interconnect and the remote memory controller.

The second point is crucial for trading workloads: at auction open or during a macro news burst, both sockets are busy. If your hot query's data lives mostly on the opposite node, it now competes for inter-socket bandwidth and remote DRAM time just when you need it most. The result is often a "fat tail" in latency distributions that stubbornly resists normal query-level tuning.

Pinning Processes and Threads to NUMA Nodes

The first lever for taming NUMA behavior is deciding where your compute lives.

Affinity: deciding which cores a process may use.

CPU affinity is the mechanism by which you restrict a process (and its threads) to a subset of cores. On a dual-socket machine you might:

- Run your primary kdb+ tickerplant and real-time analytics on socket 0.
- Run less critical jobs (batch backfills, EOD compactions) on socket 1.

With clear affinity, you get:

- More predictable cache usage, because threads are not bounced between sockets.
- A natural hint to the kernel's memory allocator about which node should "own" most of the pages for a process.

You can express this affinity at several levels:

- Using low-level tools (for example, at startup, wrapping your process launch in an affinity-setting command).
- Via systemd unit files, if your engines are managed as services.
- Using engine-specific settings (for example, ClickHouse settings for background pool sizes per NUMA node; wrapper scripts for kdb+ that spawn worker processes per node).

Thread pools and cores.

Both kdb+ and ClickHouse use thread pools for parallel work: scans, merges, compactions, network I/O, and so on. Once you have decided that, say, socket 0 is the home of a given server, you should:

- Size thread pools to match the number of *physical* cores on that socket, leaving headroom for the kernel and network interrupts.
- Ensure threads in those pools are restricted to socket 0's cores, not the entire machine.

In many shops, this pattern emerges:

- Socket 0: Real-time path (tickerplant, intraday kdb+ instance, read-mostly ClickHouse replica).
- Socket 1: Heavy background work (backfill writers, merge jobs, large historical queries, monitoring agents).

This separation both reduces cross-node traffic and isolates latency-sensitive tasks from intensive maintenance jobs.

Controlling Memory Placement and Mappings

Affinity alone is not enough; we also care about *where* the memory pages used by a process actually live.

First-touch and warm-up discipline.

Recall that, with first-touch placement, the NUMA node of a page is determined by which core first writes to it. This leads to a simple but powerful rule:

> Make sure the warms and initial scans of large mappings happen on the same socket where you expect most queries to run.

Applied concretely:

- For kdb+, when you start your intraday process for a given partition, run any warm-up scripts (for example, simple full scans, pre-loading of key tables) with affinity pinned to the target socket.
- For ClickHouse, let the background merges and part creation that "prepare" data for queries be driven predominantly by threads on the same node that will host the hot queries.

This gives the kernel a strong hint: "these pages belong over here."

NUMA policies for processes.

Beyond first-touch, Linux offers more explicit NUMA policies. You can, for example, ask the kernel to:

- Allocate all memory for a process strictly from node 0.
- Interleave pages evenly across nodes (not helpful for most low-latency work).
- Prefer one node but fall back to others if needed.

For engines that you want to "live" on one socket, a policy of "bind to node N" or "prefer node N" is usually appropriate, as long as you have sized memory and caches accordingly.

This becomes especially important when your working set is large compared with a single node's DRAM. In such cases, you may deliberately run separate engine instances per node, each owning a shard of the data, rather than one giant instance spanning both.

Memory-mapped regions and overcommit.

Memory mapping interacts with NUMA in another, less obvious way: the kernel's overcommit and reclaim behavior.

If the system is under memory pressure, the kernel may decide to reclaim pages from the page cache, including pages that back your mapped databases. When those pages are later faulted back in, they may be reallocated on a different node than before, especially if the original node is tight on free memory.

To reduce surprises:

- Reserve enough DRAM per NUMA node so hot mapped regions rarely face reclaim.
- Avoid letting many unrelated processes on another socket chew into your hot node's free memory.
- Consider limiting the maximum page cache usage for background jobs or moving them to the "cold" socket.

The core idea is to keep each socket's DRAM primarily serving the engine processes that are pinned there, rather than treating memory as a global free-for-all.

Detecting When NUMA Is Hurting You

Once you begin thinking in NUMA terms, you want feedback: is cross-node traffic actually a problem in your environment?

Typical symptoms.

NUMA-related issues often show up as:

- Queries that occasionally "spike" in latency even though CPU and I/O utilization look modest.
- Performance that is good when the box is otherwise idle but degrades unpredictably when background jobs or other services are active.

- Strong dependence on which specific cores the OS happens to schedule your queries onto.

These are similar to cache issues but with a spatial twist: the problems worsen when the other socket is busy.

What to look for in metrics.

At the system level, you can watch for:

- Remote memory access counters increasing faster than expected relative to local accesses.
- Inter-socket link utilization rising during periods of query latency spikes.
- High page-fault activity for your engine processes, especially major faults that indicate pages being pulled from another node or disk.

At the engine level:

- Compare latency distributions when traffic is constrained to a single socket versus spread across both.
- Monitor per-thread or per-pool behavior; a specific set of threads might correlate with bad outliers if they wander onto the wrong node.

The aim is to see whether your nicely vectorized, cache-tuned loops are being forced to fetch data from across the board just when they should be humming along locally.

Concrete Deployment Patterns

To bring all the pieces together, let us outline a few concrete patterns you can adapt.

Pattern 1: One engine per socket, sharded data.

This pattern is common in large kdb+ plants:

- Socket 0 runs a kdb+ instance that holds "A-M" symbols.
- Socket 1 runs another instance that holds "N-Z" symbols.
- Each instance is pinned to its node's cores and bound to its local memory.

Client queries are routed based on symbol, either at the application layer or via a lightweight router process. Each query touches only one socket's memory and cores.

The advantages are:

- Strong locality: each instance's working set lives almost entirely on its own node.
- Natural horizontal scalability: you can extend the scheme to more nodes or machines.

The downside is added complexity in routing and aggregation when cross-shard queries are needed, but for many intraday workloads the benefits outweigh the costs.

Pattern 2: ClickHouse replicas segmented by NUMA node.

A similar idea for ClickHouse:

- On a dual-socket box, run two ClickHouse server instances, each bound to a different NUMA node.
- Shard or partition MergeTree tables such that each instance owns a subset of the data, perhaps by time slice or symbol range.
- Configure the query layer (distributed tables or the client logic) to target the correct instance for a given query.

Because ClickHouse already embraces sharding and replication, this pattern often fits naturally into an existing cluster design.

Pattern 3: Hot/cold separation across sockets.

Another approach is to use sockets for different tiers:

- Socket 0 hosts the "hot" datasets: today's and yesterday's partitions, real-time views, and critical summary tables.
- Socket 1 hosts "cold" or background activity: historical partitions, large risk runs, administrative queries, ETL processes.

In kdb+, that might mean your intraday HDB and RDB processes are bound to socket 0, while your historical HDB and analytics engines live on socket 1. In ClickHouse, you might assign recent partitions to MergeTree replicas on socket 0 and older data to instances or disks bound to socket 1.

The key is that latency-sensitive queries spend most of their time in one NUMA neighborhood, while large, noisy jobs are fenced off in another.

Design Checklist: Baking NUMA Locality in from Day One

Finally, to make NUMA awareness a habit rather than an afterthought, incorporate the following points into your design process:

- **Topology awareness**: Before deploying, document the core and memory layout of your servers. Know how many NUMA nodes there are, how many cores per node, and how much DRAM per node.
- **Role assignment per socket**: Decide up front which workloads should live on which nodes: hot vs cold, real-time vs batch, engine A vs engine B.
- **Affinity policies**: Capture CPU and NUMA affinity for each engine in a repeatable configuration (service files, deployment scripts), not as manual commands typed into shells.
- **Warm-up discipline**: Define a standard warm-up routine that is run with correct affinity so that large mapped regions are "owned" by the right node from the start of the trading day.
- **Data shard mapping**: For sharded or partitioned data, map shards or partitions explicitly to sockets in a way that matches query patterns (by symbol range, time, venue, or similar).

- **Background job isolation**: Place heavy maintenance jobs, compactions, and backfills on nodes that are not responsible for the most latency-sensitive queries.
- **NUMA monitoring**: Add basic NUMA metrics to your observability stack so you can see local vs remote memory traffic and inter-socket link utilization alongside query latency.

Once you view your servers as a small NUMA cluster rather than a single monolithic box, many performance mysteries become easier to explain. A predictable, low-latency kdb+ or ClickHouse deployment is not just about fast code; it is about making sure that the code and the data live in the same "neighborhood" most of the time, and that the operating system understands and respects that design.

6.3 Linux and Network Stack Optimization

The previous sections in this chapter operated "inside the box": we focused on getting the most from individual cores, caches, and NUMA nodes once data had already arrived in memory. In practice, however, a kdb+ or ClickHouse system lives at the end of a long chain. Market data must cross network interfaces, kernel code paths, and user-kernel boundaries before any query plan can touch it.

If this path is not engineered carefully, it becomes a major source of jitter. You may have perfectly vectorized queries pinned to the right NUMA node, yet still see ingest stalls, replication lag, or sporadic query spikes during the busiest parts of the trading day. Often the culprit is not the database at all, but the Linux and network stack carrying data to and from it.

In this section, we will:

- Build a simple, intuitive picture of the journey a packet takes from the wire into your kdb+ or ClickHouse process.
- Identify where the Linux networking and I/O subsystems most often introduce latency and loss under bursty loads.

- Describe practical tuning levers: interrupt handling, receive-side scaling (RSS), socket buffers, offloads, and congestion control.
- Connect those tunings to market-data-specific concerns like replication, fan-out, and time synchronization.
- Outline a disciplined approach to validating changes so you rely on measurement rather than folklore.

Throughout, the theme remains consistent with earlier sections: align the environment with the workload so that the entire path, not just the core, behaves predictably under stress.

From Wire to Userspace: A Mental Model

Before touching any tunables, it is helpful to visualize the basic data path.

The packet's journey.

For an incoming market data message, the journey is:

1. **Network interface card (NIC).** The NIC receives Ethernet frames off the wire and performs basic parsing (Ethernet, IP, UDP/TCP). It places packet data into receive queues in host memory using DMA.
2. **Interrupt and polling.** The NIC signals the CPU that work is available, either by raising interrupts or through a polling mechanism (such as NAPI in Linux). Each queue is usually associated with one or more CPU cores.
3. **Kernel network stack.** The kernel processes the packet: routing decisions, firewall hooks, TCP or UDP handling, checksum verification, and queuing into socket receive buffers.
4. **Userspace.** The application (your kdb+ feed handler, ClickHouse replication task, or front-end query service) calls a system call to read from its socket. The kernel copies data from the socket buffer into the process's memory space.

5. **Ingest / replication logic.** The userspace code decodes messages, batches them into tables or blocks, and hands them off to query or storage paths.

Each step has limited capacity and its own buffering. Under bursty conditions—such as exchange opens, closes, or news events—data can accumulate at any of these stages, leading to increased latency or outright drops if buffers overflow.

Why defaults are not enough for markets.

Linux is tuned by default for fairness and generality, not for "lowest possible jitter during a 200 millisecond data storm." Untuned systems often exhibit the following behavior:

- Interrupts for NICs shared with unrelated workloads, causing cache thrash on hot cores.
- Socket buffers too small for the largest bursts, leading to drops in the kernel before your application can see them.
- Receive-side scaling that hashes flows poorly across cores, overloading one core while others sit mostly idle.
- TCP stack parameters tuned for bulk throughput over wide-area networks instead of low latency on a local, high-bandwidth backbone.

The result is that peak loads, rather than average loads, dominate observed behavior. For a trading system, we care deeply about those peaks.

Interrupts, Queues, and Core Affinity

We begin tuning at the boundary between NIC and CPU, since it is the first place where locality and contention can go wrong.

Receive queues and RSS.

Modern NICs expose multiple receive queues. Incoming packets are distributed across these queues based on a hash of the packet's headers (source/destination addresses and ports). This mechanism, called receive-side scaling (RSS), lets parallel cores handle distinct flows.

From a market-data point of view:

- A "flow" might be a unicast TCP connection carrying feed A, or a UDP multicast group, or a replication channel between two ClickHouse nodes.
- Each queue can be tied to one or more CPU cores, so that packets for a flow are preferentially processed on particular cores.

If RSS is poorly configured, you might see:

- Too few queues, causing one core to become the bottleneck while others remain idle.
- All queues mapped to cores on one NUMA node, while your database resides mainly on another node, forcing cross-node traffic.
- Many different, unrelated flows sharing a single busy queue, creating burst amplification and jitter.

Well-configured RSS spreads the work across cores in a way that matches how your software handles different feeds and clients.

Interrupt handling and affinity.

When packets arrive, the NIC either raises interrupts or is polled by the kernel. In both cases, specific cores do the work. You can and should control which cores handle which queues.

The pattern to aim for is:

- For a given feed or replication flow that primarily serves a kdb+ or ClickHouse instance on NUMA node 0, bind its NIC queue interrupts to cores on node 0.
- Reserve specific cores for "network duties," separate from the hottest query-processing cores, to avoid head-of-line blocking when network work spikes.
- Avoid sharing NIC interrupts with unrelated processes that could cause cache pollution or unexpected bursts of work.

This preserves the locality you established in the NUMA-aware design: data lands in memory attached to the same socket where it will be processed, and the cores that handle the packets are near the cores that run the ingest or query code.

Balancing polling and interrupts.

Linux's NAPI model blends interrupt-driven and polling behavior. Under light load, interrupts wake up the kernel to process each batch of packets. Under heavy load, the kernel switches to polling mode, processing larger batches per wake-up to reduce interrupt overhead.

Tuning here is environment-specific, but the guiding principle is:

> Avoid tiny per-packet overhead at the cost of flooding your cores with interrupts, but do not batch so aggressively that bursts sit in queues too long before they are noticed.

In most trading environments, the main levers you adjust indirectly—by setting NIC interrupt moderation and ensuring kernel polling runs on appropriate cores—rather than directly altering NAPI behavior.

Socket Buffers and Burst Tolerance

Once packets are in the kernel, data flows into per-socket receive and send buffers. These buffers are often the narrowest parts of the pipeline during real-world bursts.

Right-sizing receive buffers.

Receive buffers for sockets serve as short-term parking lots between "the speed of the network" and "the speed of your application." If a burst arrives faster than your application can call into the kernel to read it, the buffer starts filling. When it fills completely, the kernel must drop incoming data.

For market data ingest or replication:

- Drops in the receive buffer translate directly into lost messages, gaps in feeds, or retransmission storms, depending on the protocol.

- Even before drops, buffers that are near full increase latency, because data sits queued for longer before being delivered to userspace.

You should:

- Increase the maximum allowed size of socket receive buffers at the system level, to accommodate large but short-lived bursts at the open and during news events.
- Set per-application or per-socket buffer sizes based on observed worst-case burst patterns, leaving enough headroom for safety.
- Monitor buffer utilization and drops to validate that your chosen sizes are effective without being excessive.

Note that buffers that are too large can hide problems and increase variance in latency. You want "as big as necessary, but no bigger."

Send buffers and replication.

On the sending side, buffers smooth out the difference between application write rates and network transmission rates. For ClickHouse replication or kdb+ log shipping:

- Too-small send buffers can throttle throughput and cause backpressure into the application, especially when round-trip times spike temporarily.
- Too-large send buffers can introduce long tails in replication lag, as data piles up in the kernel before being pushed over slower paths.

As with receive buffers, your goal is to size send buffers to absorb normal fluctuations but not to support sustained overproduction.

Offloads and Packet Shape

NICs today implement a variety of offload features: checksum calculation, segmentation offload, and more. These can improve CPU efficiency, but they also change how work is presented to the kernel and, consequently, your application.

Checksum offload.

Checksum offload lets the NIC validate or generate checksums instead of the CPU. In most settings this simply frees CPU cycles; it rarely harms latency and is typically left enabled.

Segmentation and coalescing.

More significant are features that change packet size and timing:

- Large receive offload (LRO) and generic receive offload (GRO) coalesce multiple small incoming packets into larger "super-packets" before handing them to the kernel.
- TCP segmentation offload (TSO) allows the kernel to hand large chunks of data to the NIC, which then chops them into MTU-sized packets for wire transmission.

These can be a mixed blessing for low-latency systems:

- Larger chunks mean fewer function calls and context switches, which improves throughput.
- But coalescing or deferring segmentation can add microseconds or even milliseconds of delay before data becomes visible higher up the stack.

For pure ingest or replication paths where latency is important but not ultra-critical (for example, copying data to a disaster recovery site), some offloads are beneficial. For feeds or query responses where individual message timing matters, excessive coalescing can introduce unwelcome jitter.

The practical approach is:

- Understand which offloads your NIC and driver support.
- Test configurations with and without specific offloads on representative workloads.
- Standardize on a configuration that balances throughput and latency for your particular mix of traffic.

Jumbo frames.

Jumbo frames increase the maximum Ethernet payload size beyond the standard value. This can significantly improve efficiency for large sequential transfers, such as backfills or bulk replication, by reducing per-packet overhead.

However:

- Every device along the path must support the larger MTU; mismatches cause fragmentation or drops.
- For tiny messages, such as typical top-of-book updates, jumbo frames bring little benefit; they may even complicate upstream network design.

In many trading environments, a common compromise is to enable jumbo frames on dedicated backfill or replication networks, while keeping standard MTUs on feed and client-access networks.

Congestion Control and Transport Choices

At transport level, most kdb+ and ClickHouse deployments use TCP for replication, client queries, and higher-value ingest. Some market data feeds use UDP multicast, but even then, you often have a TCP-based distribution layer internally.

TCP congestion control.

Linux offers several congestion control algorithms, each balancing throughput and latency differently. Traditional defaults favor bulk transfers over the public internet. Inside a data center, especially on a private, well-provisioned network, you can choose lighter-weight algorithms that react more quickly without being overly cautious.

While the specific choice depends on your distribution, the general guidelines are:

- For short-lived, latency-sensitive connections (client queries, small replication bursts), favor controllers that ramp up quickly and do not maintain overly large queues.

- For long-lived, high-throughput replication streams across data centers, controllers with stable behavior and good fairness may be preferable even if they add some milliseconds of queueing.

Whatever you choose, keep it consistent across nodes that participate in the same cluster, and validate with measurement.

UDP and loss handling.

When you use UDP for market data, the kernel provides less built-in protection. There is no congestion control or retransmission; packet loss is simply loss. This amplifies the importance of:

- Sufficient NIC and kernel buffering for bursts.
- Careful core and queue affinity to avoid overload on a single core.
- Application-level gap detection and recovery logic (for example, sequence numbers and replay mechanisms).

Because UDP bypasses some TCP machinery, it can be more predictable under certain patterns, but it also gives you more rope to hang yourself with. The Linux and NIC tunings discussed earlier matter even more for UDP feeds.

Time Synchronization as a Performance Concern

Time synchronization seems unrelated to network tuning, but for trading systems it is a first-class performance concern. Timestamps tie together ingest, replication, and query results. If clocks diverge or jump, you will misinterpret latencies—and you may tune in the wrong direction.

Why precise time matters.

Consider a simple example:

- kdb+ tickerplant timestamps a message as it arrives.
- Downstream ClickHouse node timestamps the same event upon insertion.

- You later measure "ingest delay" as the difference between the two timestamps.

If those two hosts disagree by hundreds of microseconds or more, your measurements will be misleading. You cannot tell whether a delay is due to actual network congestion, kernel queuing, application overhead, or just skewed clocks.

Practical guidelines.

For our purposes:

- Use a modern time synchronization protocol suited for low-latency environments, and ensure all trading-related hosts participate in a carefully managed time domain.
- Monitor not only offsets but also jitter and step corrections; sudden time adjustments can appear as false spikes or dips in latency metrics.
- When evaluating network or kernel tuning, always confirm that clocks between sender and receiver are well-aligned before drawing conclusions.

Treat time sync drift as a "performance bug" with the same seriousness as packet drops or buffer overflows.

Validation: From Folklore to Evidence

Perhaps more than any other area of performance engineering, Linux and network tuning is full of rules of thumb and anecdotes: "Everyone disables feature X," "Y is always bad for latency," and so on. Some of this guidance was valid on older kernels or NICs, some is specific to environments very different from yours.

To avoid cargo cult configuration, follow a simple discipline:

Start from a baseline.

Before changing anything, capture:

- End-to-end metrics: ingest throughput, replication lag distributions, and query latency distributions under a repeatable load.
- Relevant system metrics: NIC queue drops, socket buffer utilization, CPU usage per core, inter-socket link utilization.
- Configuration snapshots: current NIC, kernel, and TCP settings.

This gives you a concrete, measurable "before" picture.

Change one thing at a time.

For each tuning experiment:

- Alter a small number of related parameters together (for example, NIC interrupt affinity and RSS queue mapping), not an entire page of settings.
- Re-run the same workload and compare metrics.
- Record the configuration and results, even if there is no improvement.

This mirrors the structured profiling and regression techniques discussed elsewhere in this chapter: hypotheses, experiments, and evidence.

Test with realistic bursts.

Synthetic uniform loads can hide burst-related problems. To test the robustness of your Linux and network stack configuration:

- Use recorded market data from busy days to drive replay-based ingest and query testing.
- Include open and close phases, and known news spikes, in your test windows.
- Observe not only averages but high-percentile latencies and drop rates.

Optimizations that look good under a smooth load but fail during real bursts are not acceptable in production.

Connecting Back to the Engines

Ultimately, Linux and network tuning is not an end in itself; it is a supporting layer for kdb+ and ClickHouse.

When your core and NUMA tuning is sound, but you still see:

- Ingest backlogs that slowly resolve after busy intervals.
- Replication lag that occasionally spikes for seconds without obvious CPU or disk bottlenecks.
- Queries whose latency distribution broadens significantly at the same times across the cluster.

it is often the network and kernel path that needs attention. A well-tuned stack will:

- Deliver packets to the right cores with minimal queuing and no surprises.
- Provide enough buffering to absorb natural bursts without hiding fundamental bottlenecks.
- Support clear, trustworthy measurement of true engine performance under load.

By treating NIC, kernel, and transport configuration as part of the same performance story as vectorization and NUMA locality, you build systems where ingest, replication, and queries remain stable and predictable even on the noisiest trading days.

6.4 Profiling and Bottleneck Analysis

In the earlier sections of this chapter we focused on *what* makes kdb+ and ClickHouse fast when everything is going well: vectorized execution, cache and NUMA locality, and a well-tuned Linux network stack. In practice, however, you will spend much of your time dealing with the opposite situation: something has slowed down, and you need to understand *why*.

Many production teams respond to performance problems with intuition: "it must be the network," "let's add an index," "maybe we should repartition by symbol." Sometimes this guesswork works; more often it wastes days and risks introducing new regressions.

This section aims to replace intuition-driven tuning with a repeatable investigative process. We will:

- Define a simple profiling workflow that starts from observed symptoms and narrows down to specific causes.
- Introduce CPU and I/O profiling tools, with a focus on sampling profilers that produce flame graphs.
- Show how to interpret flame graphs and tracing data in the context of kdb+ and ClickHouse internals.
- Work through an example path from a tail-latency regression to a concrete schema or query-plan adjustment.
- Emphasize documentation and success criteria so performance fixes are auditable and reproducible.

The goal is not to turn you into a kernel hacker, but to give you enough structure and tools to identify the *true* bottleneck before you touch code, schemas, or operating system settings.

From Symptom to Hypothesis: A Structured Workflow

A good profiling process starts not with tools, but with a clear description of the problem.

Step 1: Precisely describe the symptom.

Begin by writing down, in precise and measurable terms, what changed or what is unacceptable. Examples:

- "The 99th percentile latency of select vwap by sym from trades where date=today doubled during the first five minutes after market open."
- "Replication lag between primary and secondary ClickHouse replicas sometimes spikes to 5 seconds during bursts in the futures feed."
- "CPU utilization on the kdb+ RDB stays low, yet clients experience intermittent timeouts."

Notice that good problem statements include:

- **Who** is affected (which query or service).
- **When** it happens (time-of-day, load conditions).
- **How** it manifests (latency, throughput, errors).

Without this, profiling often degenerates into random poking at systems.

Step 2: Reproduce under controlled conditions.

Next, you need a way to reproduce the symptom on demand, or at least capture it reliably:

- For query regressions, construct a load-generator that issues the problematic queries with realistic concurrency and data distributions.
- For ingest and replication issues, build a replay harness that feeds recorded packets from busy days into your system.
- Control as many external variables as possible: run in a known environment, pin processes to the same cores and NUMA nodes used in production, and avoid unrelated background jobs during tests.

The profiling tools we will use (such as sampling profilers and tracers) can add overhead and require privileges. You do not want to experiment for the first time during the live open; a reproducible test harness is essential.

Step 3: Collect coarse-grained metrics first.

Before jumping into micro-level profiling, collect the basics:

- CPU utilization per core and per process.
- Memory usage and page-fault activity.
- Disk and network throughput, I/O wait, and queue depths.
- Latency distributions (p50, p95, p99) for the affected queries or operations.

At this stage, you are answering questions like:

- Is the system CPU-bound, I/O-bound, or waiting on locks?
- Does the problem correlate with spikes in network or disk usage?
- Is the slowdown localized to one node or visible across a cluster?

Only once you have this high-level picture should you narrow your focus with detailed profiling.

Sampling Profilers and Flame Graphs

Sampling profilers measure where a process spends its time by taking snapshots ("samples") of the call stack at regular intervals. Over many samples, functions that appear more often are those in which the process spent more time.

Why sampling instead of tracing everything?

You could, in principle, log every function call or every event. But:

- The overhead would be enormous on busy trading systems.
- The volume of data would be unmanageable.

Sampling gives you a lossy but highly informative picture with much lower overhead. You do not see every event, but you see enough to find the dominant hotspots.

From samples to flame graphs.

A flame graph is a visual summary of sampled stacks:

- Each box represents a function or code path.
- The width of a box corresponds to how much time was spent there (how often it appeared in samples).
- The vertical axis represents the stack: boxes at the bottom are closer to the hardware, boxes on top are higher-level functions called by those below.
- Colors are generally arbitrary, used only to distinguish adjacent boxes.

Conceptually, you can think of a flame graph as a sideways histogram of time, broken down by call stack. The widest plateaus show where your system truly spends most of its time.

Right after introducing this idea is a good place to show a simplified example.

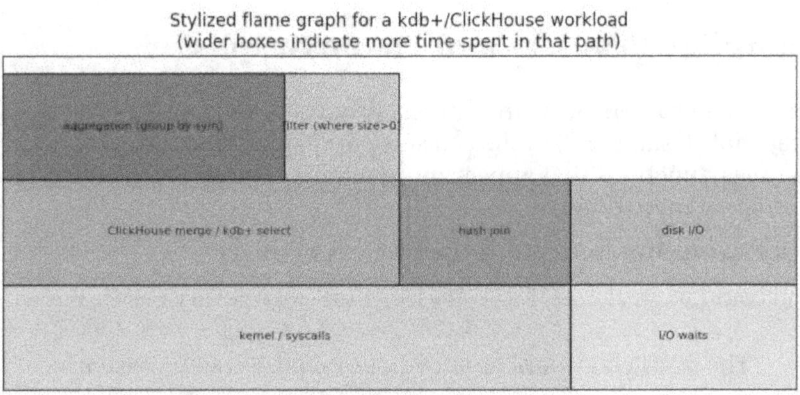

Figure 6.1: Simplified flame graph illustrating a dominant aggregation hot path and secondary time spent in I/O waits.

Interpreting a flame graph.

When you look at a flame graph for a kdb+ or ClickHouse workload, ask:

- **What are the widest stacks?** These represent your primary hotspots. If most of the width is in aggregation functions, for example, you may be CPU-bound in group-by logic.
- **How deep is the stack?** Very deep stacks can indicate excessive abstraction or layers of wrappers; shallow stacks often capture tight, optimized loops.
- **Are there separate plateaus?** One plateau dominated by I/O-related functions and another by CPU-intensive operators may indicate a mixed workload where some queries are CPU-bound and others are I/O-bound.

In short, flame graphs convert tens of thousands of stack samples into a picture you can reason about relatively quickly.

CPU-Bound vs I/O-Bound Behavior

A central question in bottleneck analysis is whether you are limited by CPU cycles or by waiting on something else (disk, network, locks, or external services).

Signs of CPU-bound workloads.

A workload is likely CPU-bound if:

- CPU utilization on the relevant cores is consistently high during the slow period.
- Flame graphs show wide plateaus in compute-heavy functions: aggregation kernels, join operators, compression/decompression routines, parsing code.
- System metrics (disk, network) show headroom; queues and I/O waits are modest.

In this case, optimization efforts should focus on:

- Query shape: can we simplify expressions, reduce group-by cardinality, or pre-aggregate?

- Data layout and types: can we narrow types, split hot and cold columns, or improve partitioning?

- Parallelism settings: are we underutilizing cores due to overly conservative thread pools, or over-subscribing and inducing contention?

Signs of I/O-bound or wait-bound workloads.

A workload is likely I/O-bound or otherwise wait-bound if:

- Overall CPU utilization is moderate, yet latency is high.

- Flame graphs show significant width in functions labeled with "read," "write," "fsync," "poll," or other blocking operations, often near the base of the stack.

- System metrics show increased disk or network queue depths, or high percentages of time in I/O wait.

In that case, attention should shift to:

- Disk layout and hardware: are we saturating IOPS or bandwidth, especially for merges and compactions?

- Network behavior: are replication or ingest channels experiencing bursts, drops, or congestion?

- Concurrency and scheduling: do long-running background tasks monopolize I/O, starving latency-sensitive queries?

In both CPU and I/O cases, the profiler and flame graphs help you avoid misdiagnosis. For example, you may suspect a "slow disk," but the flame graph reveals that most time is spent in string parsing inside a user-defined function; the disk is innocent.

Engine-Specific Hotspots in kdb+ and ClickHouse

While flame graphs are generic, it is helpful to recognize common patterns specific to our two engines.

kdb+ patterns.

In kdb+, profilers often reveal:

- Time spent in evaluation of q expressions for joins, where clauses, and aggregations.
- Overheads from repeatedly materializing intermediate results due to non-fusible query constructs.
- Time in symbol resolution or string handling when queries use text-heavy keys or filters.
- System-level overhead in IPC handling for heavily sharded plants, where many small messages are passed between processes.

These hotspots may indicate opportunities to:

- Rewrite q expressions to use more vectorized primitive operations and fewer nested control structures.
- Precompute derived columns, such as bucketed times or normalized symbol IDs, to simplify query logic.
- Reduce cross-process chatter by consolidating functions or moving certain transforms closer to the data.

ClickHouse patterns.

In ClickHouse, common hotspots include:

- Aggregation code, especially for high-cardinality group-bys or poorly chosen keys.
- MergeTree read paths, including decompression and decoding of columns.

- Background merges and mutations, which can consume CPU and I/O in ways that interfere with foreground queries.
- Network stack and serialization code for distributed queries or replication.

Flame graphs and profiling data may suggest:

- Adjusting aggregation strategies or approximate algorithms for very heavy roll-ups.
- Rebalancing compression levels or codecs for hot columns to trade off CPU against I/O.
- Scheduling merges so they avoid peak query periods or assigning them to less contended nodes.
- Tweaking distributed query plans or replication settings to minimize redundant data movement.

Recognizing these patterns lets you jump more quickly from "this function is hot" to "this query or schema construct is likely responsible."

Tracing and Lock Contention

Sampling profilers are excellent at showing where time is spent on average. They are less effective at revealing short, rare events that cause tail latency spikes, such as occasional lock contention or bursts of garbage collection in application layers built on top of kdb+ and ClickHouse.

For these, you may need tracing techniques:

- Lightweight kernel and user-space tracing tools that can log events like lock acquisitions, context switches, and I/O completes with timestamps.
- Engine-specific diagnostic hooks that record when queries enter and leave key stages (parsing, planning, execution, aggregation, disk access).

By correlating traces across layers, you can spot patterns such as:

- Queries that pause while waiting for a global metadata lock or a shared resource.
- Periodic spikes in flush or commit operations that block dependent operations.
- Garbage collection or memory compaction cycles in application code that runs near your database processes.

While tracing is more complex and potentially intrusive than sampling, it is invaluable when your problem is not "where does time go on average?" but "why do 1% of these operations suddenly get stuck?"

Case Study Outline: Tail-Latency Regression at the Open

To illustrate the full workflow, consider a typical scenario in outline form.

Symptom.

After a schema change that added a new column and altered partitioning, you observe that:

- Median latency for a key intraday aggregation query is unchanged.
- However, the 99th percentile latency during the first five minutes of trading has doubled.

Initial metrics.

Coarse-grained metrics show:

- CPU utilization on relevant cores is high but similar to before.
- Disk and network usage increased modestly, but not dramatically.

- No obvious increase in error rates or drops.

Profiling and flame graphs.

Running a sampling profiler during the open, you compare flame graphs before and after the schema change:

- In the new version, a wide additional plateau appears in aggregation and group-by functions.
- Deeper in the stack, new code paths related to the added column's type handling and grouping logic show up.

This suggests the change increased the work per row in the aggregation step, even though average performance is still acceptable.

Tracing and working-set analysis.

Further tracing indicates:

- During bursts, the number of distinct group keys increases sharply due to the new column being included in the group-by.
- The aggregation state spills out of L2 cache into L3 and sometimes DRAM, leading to more cache misses and occasional contention on shared structures.

Combining this with earlier vectorization and locality concepts, you infer that the new dimension blew up the working-set size in hot loops.

Remedy.

Rather than blindly "tuning the kernel," you propose:

- Removing the new column from the primary group-by for real-time queries and instead aggregating it in a secondary, less frequent batch job.
- Or, pre-encoding the new dimension into a smaller number of buckets or IDs to control cardinality.

You implement the change in a test environment, rerun the open simulation, and observe:

- Flame graphs now resemble the original version, with narrower aggregation plateaus.
- 99th percentile latency returns close to its prior level.

Because you have before-and-after profiles and traces, you can document the fix with confidence rather than anecdote.

Documenting Bottlenecks and Defining Success

Profiling and bottleneck analysis are only as useful as your ability to communicate and preserve their findings. In collaborative trading technology teams, people come and go; code and schemas evolve. Without documentation, lessons are often relearned at great expense.

What to record.

For each significant performance issue and its analysis, keep a short but complete record:

- The precise symptom, including quantitative metrics and time periods.
- The environment: engine versions, schemas, key configuration settings, and workload description.
- The profiling and tracing commands used, along with representative flame graphs or summaries.
- The hypotheses considered and which were ruled out.
- The final identified bottleneck and the rationale linking it to the observed behavior.
- The change implemented (schema modification, query rewrite, configuration adjustment).
- The before-and-after metrics that demonstrate improvement.

This is not bureaucracy; it is how you build institutional knowledge about the interaction between kdb+, ClickHouse, and your trading workloads.

Defining clear success criteria.

Before making any change, define what "success" means. For example:

- "Reduce p99 latency for query X during the open by at least 30% without increasing error rate or ingest lag."
- "Keep replication lag below 500 milliseconds under the baseline replay workload."

These criteria guide your experiments and protect you from "fixes" that simply move the problem elsewhere or trade one form of instability for another.

Integrating Profiling into Routine Practice

Finally, profiling and bottleneck analysis should not be reserved only for emergencies. Integrated into your regular workflow, they can:

- Catch regressions early when introducing new schemas, query paths, or engine versions.
- Provide baseline flame graphs and metrics for "healthy" behavior, against which anomalies are easier to spot.
- Help educate new team members, giving them concrete visualizations of how kdb+ and ClickHouse behave under load.

Combined with the benchmarking and regression-guard techniques discussed in the next section, a disciplined profiling practice turns performance from a reactive scramble into a managed, trackable dimension of system quality.

In short, by learning to observe where time is actually spent—through sampling, flame graphs, and targeted tracing—you put yourself in a position to make small, focused changes that deliver large, reliable gains in how your market data stores perform.

6.5 Benchmarking Methodology and Regression Guards

The previous section focused on how to investigate a performance problem once it appears: profiling workloads, reading flame graphs, and tracing bottlenecks through kdb+, ClickHouse, and the underlying system. In this final section we turn the story around. Instead of reacting to regressions, we want a framework that *prevents* them from reaching production.

A high-performance market data store is not a static artifact. Schemas evolve, new queries are added, engines and Linux kernels are upgraded, hardware changes, and data volumes grow. Any of these can subtly degrade performance, particularly in the tail of the latency distribution where trading P&L is most sensitive.

Our objective here is twofold:

- Define how to build realistic, repeatable benchmarks for kdb+ and ClickHouse market workloads.
- Show how to turn those benchmarks into automated regression guards that enforce performance as a versioned, testable contract.

Clarifying Terminology and Goals

Before designing benchmarks, it is helpful to distinguish three common types of performance tests. They answer different questions and should not be conflated.

Benchmarks.

A benchmark is a controlled test that runs a specific workload under specified conditions and reports metrics. It is usually short to medium duration and is meant to be repeatable. Typical goals:

- Compare engine versions or configuration options.
- Validate the impact of a schema or query change.

- Calibrate capacity planning assumptions.

Think of benchmarks as unit tests for performance: targeted, scoped, and fast enough to run frequently.

Load tests.

A load test explores behavior as intensity grows:

- Increase request rates, parallelism, or data volume up to and beyond expected production levels.
- Observe where throughput saturates and how latency changes approaching and past that point.

Load tests are about *scaling*: how far can you push the system before it breaks down?

Soak tests.

Soak tests run representative workloads for long periods (hours to days) to surface slow-burn issues:

- Memory leaks or fragmentation.
- Gradual growth in replication lag.
- Cumulative effects of merges, compactions, and background tasks.

They complement benchmarks by answering, "What happens over a whole trading day or week?"

In this section we emphasize benchmarks, while recognizing that load and soak tests are also important in a comprehensive performance program.

Defining SLAs and SLOs for Market Data Stores

A benchmark must measure something meaningful. For trading and analytics workloads on kdb+ and ClickHouse, the key metrics are remarkably consistent across firms.

Core metrics.

At minimum, define the following:

- **Ingest throughput:** rows or messages per second that can be reliably ingested, both for real-time feeds and for batch backfills.
- **Query latency:** full latency distribution (p50, p90, p95, p99, and sometimes p99.9) for representative queries under representative concurrency.
- **Replication lag:** delay between data fully committed on a primary and visible on a replica or downstream consumer.
- **Durability and recovery time:** time to recover from a node restart or failover to a replica under load.

For each metric, you should agree on:

- **Service Level Objective (SLO):** for example, "99% of trades-by-sym queries must complete within 150 milliseconds during market hours."
- **Service Level Agreement (SLA):** if relevant, a contractual commitment to an internal or external stakeholder.

These targets give your benchmarks a purpose: they are not just numbers, but tests of whether you are meeting trading needs.

Designing Representative Benchmarks

The quality of a benchmark depends on how well it resembles reality. Overly synthetic tests may be consistent but tell you little about production behavior.

Capture realistic data shapes.

Markets generate data with specific structures:

- Highly skewed symbol distributions (a few very hot names, many cold ones).

- Bursts around opens, closes, auctions, and news events.
- Intraday patterns: heavier in the morning, quieter at midday, with occasional spikes.

Your benchmark data sets should reflect these patterns:

- Use recorded production data, anonymized if necessary, as the basis for replay and query tests.
- Preserve skew and burstiness rather than smoothing them away.
- Include recent schema features, such as new columns for flags, derived features, or risk metrics.

For kdb+, that might mean historical HDB slices replayed into an RDB-like process. For ClickHouse, it could be a snapshot of MergeTree parts from key partitions.

Include concurrent read and write activity.

Real systems do not operate in neat phases of "only ingest" or "only queries." Typical patterns include:

- Continuous ingest while traders and algos submit queries.
- Background merges and compactions running alongside foreground queries.
- Replication and backup processes consuming disk and network capacity.

Benchmarks should therefore:

- Combine ingest streams (tick feeds, order books, reference data updates) with concurrent query streams (dashboards, risk reports, model evaluations).
- Reflect realistic query mixes: some small, point-in-time lookups; some large aggregations; some ad hoc exploratory queries.

- Run engine maintenance tasks at their usual schedules or simulate them.

This ensures that bench results incorporate the contention and interference patterns of real trading days.

Focus on critical query paths.

Not every query deserves equal weight in benchmarks. Identify a small set of *critical paths*:

- The queries that directly support trading decisions (for example, intraday VWAPs, liquidity heat maps, cross-asset correlation snapshots).
- The jobs that must finish within strict windows (for example, pre-open risk, pre-close TCA).
- System processes critical to data integrity (for example, log replay, replication).

For each, define a canonical benchmark version:

- The exact query text or API call.
- The typical parameter ranges (symbols, time windows, filters).
- The expected concurrency (how many clients or threads).

These become your "golden queries," run repeatedly in benchmarks and watched closely in regression guards.

Measuring Tail Latency and Resource Utilization

Once your benchmark workload is defined, the next step is to capture the right metrics with enough resolution.

Why tails matter more than averages.

Average latency is easy to improve by sacrificing consistency. For example:

- Running aggressive background merges might reduce typical query cost, but occasionally block critical queries on I/O.
- Compressing data more heavily might improve typical disk usage, but sometimes cause long decompression stalls.

From a trader's perspective, those occasional stalls matter more than the typical case. Therefore:

- Always record and report percentiles, especially p95 and p99, not just means.
- Track maximum observed latencies as a sanity check; a single outlier may reveal a serious bug.

Benchmark harnesses should compute and store these percentiles as first-class outputs.

Separating engine behavior from environmental noise.

To make benchmarks comparable over time, you must minimize external noise:

- Run benchmarks on dedicated hardware or reserved virtual machines where other activity is controlled.
- Pin processes and threads to predefined cores and NUMA nodes, reusing the affinity strategies from earlier sections.
- Keep network and disk configurations fixed unless they are the subject of the test.

In addition to latency metrics, capture:

- CPU utilization per core, to see whether changes increase contention or imbalance.
- Disk I/O (throughput, IOPS, queue depths), to identify saturation and shifting load.
- Network statistics (throughput, retransmissions, drops), important for replication and distributed queries.

These metrics help interpret whether a regression is due to the engine itself or changes in the system environment.

Designing Regression Guards

Benchmarks are useful, but they only protect you if they run automatically and draw clear red lines. That is the role of regression guards.

What is a regression guard?

A regression guard is an automated test that:

- Runs a benchmark workload under specified conditions.
- Compares key metrics against a baseline or SLO.
- Fails (and alerts) if degradation exceeds agreed thresholds.

Conceptually, it is a performance equivalent of a unit test that asserts functional correctness-but here we assert that "this query still runs within 150 milliseconds in the 99th percentile."

Choosing guard triggers.

Decide when regression guards should run. Common triggers include:

- Schema changes: adding or removing columns, changing types, or altering partitioning and clustering keys.
- Engine upgrades: new versions of kdb+ or ClickHouse, or significant configuration changes (for example, new compression codecs, different merge strategies).
- OS and infrastructure changes: kernel upgrades, NIC driver updates, storage migrations.

For some changes, a full benchmark suite may be too heavy; in those cases, run a targeted subset that covers the most sensitive critical paths.

Defining thresholds and tolerances.

Every guard must specify acceptable ranges. Absolute equality is unrealistic; small fluctuations are normal. Practical examples:

- "p50 latency may increase by at most 10%, p95 by at most 15%, p99 by at most 20% relative to baseline."
- "Ingest throughput must not decrease by more than 5% at the target rate."
- "Replication lag p99 must remain below 500 milliseconds in the standard test window."

It is better to be explicit than to argue informally after the fact. Thresholds can be tightened as your confidence grows.

Comparing against baselines.

A baseline is a snapshot of performance under a known-good configuration. For each benchmark scenario, store:

- Metrics from the last "approved" run.
- The code, schema, configuration, and environment descriptions used in that run.

Regression guards then:

- Re-run the same scenario under the new candidate configuration.
- Compute relative changes and check them against thresholds.
- Flag any metric that crosses its limit.

By tying baselines to specific versions, you preserve a historical record of how performance evolves.

Integrating Guards into CI/CD Pipelines

To be effective, regression guards must fit naturally into your development and deployment lifecycle.

Layers of performance checks.

You can think of performance checks as layered, each with different scope and runtime:

- **Developer-level microbenchmarks:** small, fast tests that run on individual workstations or shared test machines, focused on specific functions or queries.
- **Pre-merge or pre-release benchmarks:** targeted suite running on dedicated hardware, triggered by changes affecting schemas, engines, or critical infrastructure.
- **Periodic baseline refreshes:** larger benchmark or soak runs updating the "golden" baselines for major versions or quarterly releases.

CI/CD systems can orchestrate these layers:

- Developers see immediate feedback on small changes.
- Release managers see concise "go/no-go" performance reports.
- Operations teams see whether long-term trends are improving or degrading.

Automating environment setup.

For reproducibility, automate as much of the test environment as possible:

- Provision benchmark nodes with declarative configuration (for example, infrastructure-as-code), including CPU, memory, NUMA layout, NICs, and disks.
- Apply consistent Linux and network tunings, matching those used in production or in a planned rollout.
- Deploy kdb+ or ClickHouse with standardized scripts or orchestration tools, ensuring consistent startup options and affinity settings.

Automation reduces the risk that a subtle environment change will invalidate comparisons or hide a regression.

Reporting and visibility.

When guards run, their output must be visible and actionable:

- Generate concise summaries showing pass/fail status and key deltas for each benchmark scenario.
- Attach links or references to more detailed logs, profiles, and flame graphs for failed runs.
- Integrate with your existing alerting or ticketing systems so failures are triaged like functional test failures or build breaks.

Over time, these reports also become a performance history that informs capacity planning and architectural decisions.

Examples of Subtle Regressions Caught by Guards

To appreciate the value of regression guards, consider a few realistic examples.

Example 1: Adding a column to a hot table.

A team adds a new, wide JSON column to a core kdb+ trade table to store raw exchange messages. They intend this for occasional debugging and analysis, not routine use.

Without careful design, this change could:

- Increase the table's footprint enough that hot working sets no longer fit comfortably in caches.
- Change disk I/O patterns for persisted data, affecting load times and mapping behavior.

A regression guard that runs a standard "intraday VWAP by symbol" benchmark before and after the change might reveal:

- Little change in median latency.
- A meaningful increase in p99 latency, especially during high-volume periods.

Armed with this data, the team might decide to move the JSON column to a side table, preserving debug capability without harming core performance.

Example 2: Changing partitioning in ClickHouse.

Another team modifies a ClickHouse MergeTree table to partition by day instead of by (day, venue), simplifying maintenance and potential joins.

The change seems harmless, but in practice:

- Certain hotspot venues now share partitions with many others, reducing clustering quality.
- Queries that previously scanned compact ranges must now read larger parts, stressing caches and I/O.

A regression guard running the standard "depth-of-book by venue" queries detects:

- A 40% increase in p95 latency for venues with heavy activity.
- More time spent in disk read and decompression functions in flame graphs.

The team then iterates on partitioning and primary-key design with this concrete feedback, perhaps choosing a composite key or using projections to restore locality.

Example 3: Kernel upgrade and NIC driver changes.

Operations upgrades the Linux kernel and NIC drivers to pick up security fixes and new NIC features. Functional tests pass; the system appears healthy.

However, performance guards that focus on replication and ingest reveal:

- Slightly increased p99 replication lag under the standard bursty replay workload.
- Higher variance in ingest latency, correlating with changes in NIC interrupt behavior.

Instead of rolling out widely and discovering issues in production, the team investigates:

- Adjusting NIC interrupt moderation and RSS settings for the new driver.
- Confirming that NUMA and affinity assumptions still hold.

Regression guards thus turn a potentially disruptive change into a controlled, measurable adaptation.

Making Performance a First-Class Contract

The common thread through this section is a shift in mindset:

> Performance should be treated as a contract, not a side effect.

For kdb+ and ClickHouse in trading environments, that contract includes:

- How quickly and reliably data arrives (ingest and replication).
- How fast and predictably key queries respond (latency distributions).
- How robustly the system recovers from failures (recovery times).

By building:

- Realistic benchmark workloads grounded in actual market data.
- Clear SLOs and thresholds for critical metrics.
- Automated regression guards tied into your CI/CD process.

you create a system where:

- Developers can evolve schemas and queries with confidence, knowing that significant regressions will be caught early.
- Operations teams can manage infrastructure changes without guessing about performance impacts.

- Quant and trading teams can rely on stable, predictable behavior even as underlying components change.

Combined with the tuning and profiling techniques from earlier sections, a disciplined benchmarking and regression-guard strategy closes the loop: you not only understand *how* to make kdb+ and ClickHouse fast and stable today, you also put in place mechanisms to keep them that way as your markets, models, and systems evolve.

Chapter 7

Ingestion, Reliability, and Operations

Trading systems rarely fail when you run a backtest at midnight; they fail when non-farm payrolls hit, a primary broker disconnects, and a backfill is still chewing through last month's options tape. This chapter shows how to make kdb+ and ClickHouse behave like industrial infrastructure under real market stress: how to ingest at exchange speed, replay history safely, bridge stores without double-counting, survive outages, and keep auditors and FinOps happy-while still leaving enough headroom for the next volatility spike.

7.1 Kafka/Redpanda Ingestion at Scale

In the previous chapters we treated kdb+ and ClickHouse mostly in isolation: how they store data, how queries behave, and how to design schemas that work under market workloads. In production, however, neither system sits directly on exchange lines. Between the noisy, bursty world of market feeds and the more structured world of databases, you almost always place a durable messaging layer.

Kafka and Redpanda are the most common choices for that layer today.

They act as the "shock absorbers" of your data platform: they smooth bursts, decouple producers and consumers, and give you a clear place to measure and manage ingestion health. In this section we design a practical blueprint for using Kafka/Redpanda in front of kdb+ and ClickHouse, with a particular emphasis on two properties:

- Sustaining very high peak throughput under bursty conditions without losing ordering guarantees where they matter.
- Keeping consumer lag understandable and controllable, so the trading desk knows how "fresh" its views are.

We will start with the end-to-end architecture, then drill down into topic and partition design, producer tuning, consumer behavior, and finally the operational instrumentation you need to run this in anger on volatile market days.

An End-to-End Ingestion Blueprint

At a high level, the ingestion path from the exchange to your databases has four layers:

- **Producers**: Feed handlers and adapters that normalize raw exchange messages and publish them into Kafka/Redpanda.
- **Brokers**: The Kafka/Redpanda cluster itself, with topics and partitions that sequence and buffer events.
- **Consumers**: kdb+ and ClickHouse ingestion processes that read from topics and write into database tables.
- **Monitoring**: Metrics, logs, and dashboards that track throughput, latency, and lag across the entire pipeline.

Immediately after we set out that blueprint, it is useful to anchor it visually.

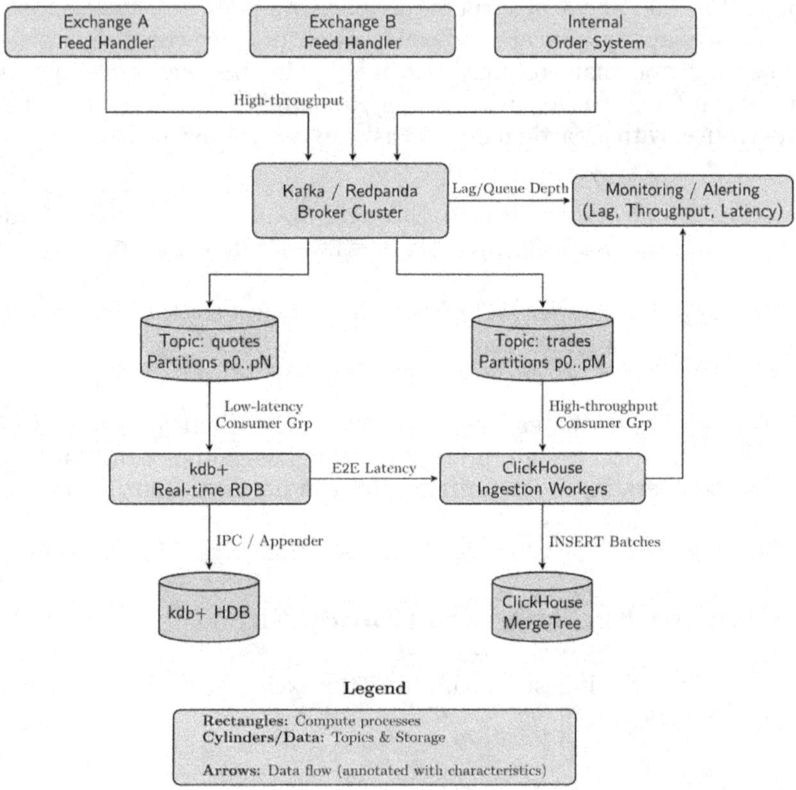

This diagram emphasizes two ideas that will reappear:

- There are *multiple* consumer groups—for example, one optimized for low-latency kdb+ ingestion, another for high-throughput ClickHouse bulk loads—sharing the same topics.
- Monitoring is a first-class component; it receives metrics from both the broker layer and the consumers.

With this mental model in place, we can reason systematically about how to design each part.

Market Data Characteristics and Their Impact

Market data is not a generic event stream. Three properties drive the shape of your Kafka/Redpanda design:

Many small messages. Quotes, trades, order book deltas, and internal risk events are all small records, often a few hundred bytes. At peak, you may see millions of these per second across venues. This leads to overhead per message becoming important: network headers, protocol framing, and Kafka metadata can dominate if you are not careful about batching and compression.

Symbol skew. Activity is not evenly spread across instruments. A small set of symbols (for example, a few large-cap equities or popular futures contracts) can account for the majority of message volume at any given time. If you naively partition by symbol, you risk concentrating hot symbols in a few partitions and overloading them.

Intraday bursts. Volume is highly variable over the day and across days. The open and close auctions, macroeconomic data releases, or company earnings can all cause short, intense spikes. These spikes are exactly when you *most* care about data freshness, so your pipeline must degrade gracefully under stress.

The rest of this section is, in a sense, a response to these three constraints.

Topics and Partitions: Shaping the Data Flow

A topic in Kafka/Redpanda is a logical stream (for example, "equity quotes"), and a partition is an ordered subset of that stream. Partitions are the unit of parallelism: each is consumed by one consumer instance in a group at a time.

Two questions matter:

- How do you split data into topics?
- How do you assign events to partitions within a topic?

Topic Design

Think of topics as representing *contracts* between producers and consumers. They group messages with similar schema, retention, and usage patterns. Common patterns in market data include:

- **By product type**: Separate topics for quotes, trades, order book depth, reference data, risk events. This allows consumers to subscribe only to what they need, and lets you set different retention policies.
- **By venue**: For example, quotes_NYSE, quotes_NASDAQ, trades_CME. This is helpful when venues have different regulatory handling or different internal owners.
- **By criticality**: A separate topic for order and execution history (which may require stricter durability and longer retention) versus less critical analytics events.

In practice you often combine dimensions in the topic name, but be cautious: too many small topics are hard to manage. It is better to use *few* topics with many partitions than a combinatorial explosion of tiny topics.

Partitioning Strategies

Within each topic, you need a partitioning rule. This rule determines ordering and parallelism, so it directly affects your ability to scale while preserving the invariants your applications expect.

Common strategies include:

Symbol-range partitioning. Assign ranges of symbols (for example, by ticker prefix or a hashed identifier) to partitions. This is simple and tends to spread load, but if a few symbols dominate volume they can still overload their partition. You can move from naive ranges to *buckets*: map symbols to a large number of logical buckets (e.g., 1024), then map buckets to partitions. This allows more fine-grained rebalancing as you add brokers.

Venue-based partitioning. For multi-asset setups, you may assign partitions per venue within a topic. This works well when venue-level ordering matters. For example, you might require strict ordering of trades from a given exchange, but are happy to process different venues in parallel.

Product-class partitioning. Group by asset class or product family (equities, futures, options). This can align nicely with downstream table partitioning in ClickHouse and directory structure in kdb+ HDB, simplifying ingestion code.

The key trade-off is between **ordering guarantees** and **parallelism**. Within a partition, Kafka/Redpanda preserves message order. Across partitions, it does not. If your kdb+ RDB expects all updates for a single symbol to be processed in order, those updates must land in the same partition and be handled by only one consumer instance at a time. That constrains parallelism to be "at most one consumer per hot symbol." You then seek parallelism across many symbols and venues, not within a single one.

Dimensioning Partitions for Peak Load

Once you have a partitioning scheme, you must choose *how many* partitions to create for each topic. Too few, and you cannot scale consumers; too many, and the brokers waste resources and controller operations managing idle partitions.

A practical approach is:

- **Start from peak expected throughput.** Work in terms of records per second and megabytes per second per topic at known stress points such as market open.
- **Estimate per-partition capacity.** For a given hardware profile and network, benchmark how many messages per second a single consumer instance can comfortably process from a single partition with your real serialization and write pattern into kdb+ or ClickHouse.
- **Add safety margin.** Because of symbol skew and unpredictable spikes, aim for each partition to run at no more

than half of your benchmarked capacity under expected peaks, leaving room for outliers.

- **Consider consumer concurrency.** The maximum number of concurrent consumers in a group that can read a topic is the number of partitions. If you plan to run, say, eight kdb+ ingestion workers for a topic, you need at least eight partitions.

Do not be afraid to over-partition moderately at the start, especially in cloud environments where brokers are relatively easy to scale. It is easier to leave some partitions underused than to repartition a critical topic in production. The risk of thousands of tiny partitions is mostly about operational complexity and controller load at very large scale; most trading shops will hit ingest bottlenecks long before they hit the theoretical partition limits.

Producer-Side Design and Tuning

Producers are your first line of defense against data loss and unpredictable latency. In a market environment you want producers that are:

- **Idempotent**: A retry should not produce duplicate visible events.
- **Durable enough**: A broker or network hiccup should not drop acknowledged messages.
- **Efficient**: They should use batching and compression to reduce overhead without adding unacceptable latency.

Idempotent Producers and Acknowledgment Settings

Kafka and Redpanda support idempotent producers and different "ack" levels to balance durability and latency.

- **Idempotent producers** assign unique sequence numbers per partition and ensure that retries do not duplicate data. Always enable this for market feeds; it is an easy win for correctness.

- **Acknowledgment levels** control when the broker tells the producer "your message is safely written." At one extreme, waiting for only the leader broker is fastest but more fragile; at the other, waiting for all in-sync replicas adds safety and latency. For critical data such as trades and orders, most shops prefer waiting for multiple replicas even at a slight latency cost.

Conceptually, think of this as deciding how many copies of an event must exist before you are willing to tell the trading platform "we have recorded this." For analytics-only streams (for example, non-critical derived metrics), you may choose weaker guarantees to reduce latency further.

Message Keys and Ordering

The message key determines which partition a record is sent to. To preserve ordering by symbol, use a stable key such as the instrument identifier. For venue-based ordering, use a combination of venue and symbol. This ties back to your partitioning strategy; misaligned keys will undo your careful design.

One subtle point: not all streams require strict ordering. For example, some risk metrics and aggregated bars can tolerate slight reordering as long as they converge to the same result. Reserve strict, key-based ordering for feeds where it truly matters, and use more flexible partitioning where possible to gain parallelism.

Batch Size, Linger, and Compression

Sending every market message individually is wasteful. Kafka and Redpanda are designed around batches: groups of records sent together over the network and written as a unit to disk.

Three knobs matter:

- **Batch size**: Maximum accumulated bytes per partition before a batch is sent. Larger batches improve throughput and compression ratio but increase the time a message may wait in the producer buffer.

- **Linger time**: How long the producer waits (up to a limit) before sending a batch, even if it is not yet full. Setting a small but non-zero linger can significantly increase average batch size without adding much latency.

- **Compression**: Algorithms like LZ4 or ZSTD can drastically reduce network and disk usage for repetitive market data. LZ4 is a good default, offering a balance between compression ratio and CPU cost.

It is useful to distinguish two traffic patterns:

Tick-level streams (quotes, trades). Here, latency budgets are tight. Set batch sizes moderately (to avoid tiny batches) but keep linger very small. Think in terms of a few milliseconds of extra delay at most. Compression should be fast; LZ4 or Snappy are commonly used.

Bar and analytics streams. Bars at one-second or longer intervals, and derived analytics, can tolerate more buffering. Larger batches and slightly higher linger times substantially reduce overhead. You can also use heavier compression, like ZSTD, if CPU is available.

Align these settings with the expectations of your downstream kdb+ and ClickHouse consumers. For example, if your kdb+ RDB ingests in micro-batches of a few milliseconds, your Kafka batches should be tuned to match that cadence.

Consumer Groups, Lag, and Exactly-Once Semantics

On the consumer side, the key concepts are consumer groups, offset management, and how you handle duplicates or failures when writing into kdb+ and ClickHouse.

Consumer Groups and Rebalancing

A consumer group is a logical application reading from a topic. Within a group, partitions are divided among instances. If you add more instances, Kafka/Redpanda *rebalances* the assignment.

For our blueprint, you will typically have at least two groups:

- A **kdb+ ingestion group**, with multiple worker processes each feeding one or more symbols into an RDB or intraday HDB partition.
- A **ClickHouse ingestion group**, perhaps with more instances, optimized for bulk inserts into MergeTree tables.

Rebalancing matters. When an instance dies or you deploy a new version, partitions are reassigned. During this time, no instance is consuming from the affected partitions, and lag grows. To minimize disruption:

- Avoid frequent consumer restarts during peak trading hours.
- Use cooperative rebalancing modes where available, which reduce the number of partitions moved at once.
- Keep consumer processing time per message bounded, so that catching up after a rebalance is quick.

Offset Management and Lag Visibility

Each consumer keeps an *offset*: the position in the partition of the next record to read. Kafka/Redpanda track the latest produced offset as well. The difference between these is *consumer lag*.

Conceptually, lag is your "distance from now" in the stream. For trading desks, this is often translated into:

- **Record lag**: How many messages behind the tip of the topic a given consumer group is.
- **Time lag**: How old the newest record processed by that consumer is, compared to wall-clock time.

Operationally, you should:

- Export lag metrics per topic, partition, and consumer group into your monitoring system.
- Set alert thresholds based on business expectations. For example, kdb+ may be allowed at most a few hundred milliseconds of lag for quotes, while ClickHouse batch ingestion may tolerate seconds or tens of seconds.
- Display lag alongside end-to-end latency metrics computed from event timestamps in the messages and their arrival times in the database.

Offset commits—the act of recording "I have processed up to here"—must be carefully placed. Committing too early risks data loss on failure; committing too late can cause duplicate processing. A common pattern is:

- Consume a batch of messages from Kafka/Redpanda.
- Write them to kdb+ or ClickHouse, ensuring the write completed successfully.
- Commit the offset for that batch.

This yields *at-least-once* delivery: failures may cause reprocessing of some messages, but you will not silently drop data.

Exactly-Once vs Effectively-Once into kdb+ and ClickHouse

Kafka and Redpanda support transactional consumption and production for certain clients, enabling end-to-end exactly-once semantics for some flows. However, integrating this cleanly with kdb+ and ClickHouse is non-trivial, since they have their own transaction and commit models.

In practice, most trading platforms aim for *effectively-once* semantics, which means:

- The system may technically reprocess a message, but

- The resulting state in kdb+ or ClickHouse is as if each message was applied exactly once.

You achieve this by making your writes idempotent:

- Include **business keys** and **sequence numbers** (for example, exchange sequence or order ID) in your tables.
- On ingest, use merge or upsert patterns keyed by these identifiers, so that reprocessing the same message does not create duplicates.
- For kdb+, that may mean writing into staging tables and periodically applying a deduplication pass keyed by (symbol, time, sequence).
- For ClickHouse, it often means using engines and table designs that can collapse duplicates by a primary key or implementing periodic deduplication materialized views.

The design of these deduplication and conflict resolution strategies is covered more deeply in the later section on backfill and late data. For now, the important point is that your Kafka/Redpanda ingestion design must carry the necessary keys and sequence fields through, so that downstream stores can make reliable decisions.

Back-Pressure and Graceful Degradation

Even with careful sizing, there will be times when downstream systems fall behind: a kdb+ node may be under heavy query load, or a ClickHouse cluster may be compacting large partitions. Kafka/Redpanda give you room to absorb such slowdowns, but only up to a point. You need explicit back-pressure strategies.

Short-term buffering. The primary mechanism is the broker itself: as consumers slow down, lag grows and more data sits in topic partitions. This is acceptable over short periods, as long as you monitor lag and have enough disk space.

Prioritization. Not all streams are equally important. If necessary, you can:

- Temporarily slow or pause consumption of non-critical topics, allowing ingestion capacity to focus on critical ones.
- Run separate consumer groups with different resource allocations for high-priority data.

Load shedding. In extreme conditions where even Kafka/Redpanda risk running out of storage, you may need to apply deliberate load shedding on non-critical topics at the producer layer, or temporarily decrease retention. This should be a last resort and should be explicitly codified in your operational runbooks with clear business sign-off.

Consumer throttling. Kafka and Redpanda support quotas and rate limits. These are more commonly used to protect the brokers from abusive clients, but can also help smooth consumption so that downstream kdb+ and ClickHouse nodes are not overwhelmed by sudden catch-up bursts that compete with queries.

The goal is not to avoid all lag—that is impossible—but to avoid *uncontrolled* lag growth and unpredictable behavior under stress.

Operational Dashboards and Runbooks

Lastly, an ingestion pipeline is only as good as your ability to see what it is doing and to act when it misbehaves. For market data, operational visibility is itself a form of risk control.

At minimum, your dashboards should show, per topic and per consumer group:

- **Produced throughput**: messages per second and bytes per second.
- **Consumed throughput**: matching metrics on the consumer side.
- **Consumer lag**: in messages and as an estimated time delay.
- **End-to-end latency**: derived from timestamps in messages and arrival times in kdb+ and ClickHouse.

- **Error rates**: producer retries, consumer failures, deserialization errors, and ingestion failures in kdb+/ClickHouse.

On top of dashboards, you should maintain concise *runbooks* for common scenarios:

- What to check when lag for the kdb+ group exceeds a threshold.
- How to safely restart consumers without causing excessive rebalancing during market hours.
- How to temporarily switch some consumers into a reduced-load mode (for example, dropping less critical derived streams) to protect core ingest.

Over time, this operational layer becomes as important as the technical design. Traders will inevitably ask, during a volatile day, "How far behind are we?" A well-instrumented Kafka/Redpanda ingestion path gives you precise, quantitative answers, and clear levers to bring the system back within its service-level objectives.

By treating Kafka and Redpanda as integral parts of your market data architecture—not just pipes—you can design ingestion that is both fast and predictable. The next sections will build on this foundation to handle historical backfill, late data, and cross-store interoperability, all of which rely on the guarantees and structures we have established here.

7.2 Backfill, Late-Data, and File-Format Strategy

In the previous section we built an ingestion blueprint where Kafka or Redpanda sits in front of kdb+ and ClickHouse, smoothing bursts and giving us predictable lag. That design answers the question: *how do we keep up with the market right now?*

Real trading platforms also have to answer a second, less glamorous question: *how do we repair and extend history when the world is messy?* Exchanges resend corrections. Vendors deliver delayed feeds.

Internal systems discover gaps weeks later. Regulators ask for replay of specific days or instruments years after the fact. None of this fits neatly into the "real-time stream" mental model.

This section focuses on that second question. We will:

- Define backfill, replay, and late data in concrete trading terms.
- Show how to use Parquet and ORC files as the backbone for historical loads, aligned with the partitioning and indexing schemes of kdb+ and ClickHouse.
- Explain strategies for deduplication and conflict resolution when old and new views of the same event collide.
- Discuss how to deal with schema evolution so that history stays usable, not fractured into incompatible slices.

Throughout, the goal is to treat history as a *first-class workload*, with repeatable processes and clear contracts, not a series of one-off emergency jobs.

What We Mean by Backfill, Replay, and Late Data

It helps to distinguish three related but different scenarios. The underlying technical machinery can be shared, but the intent and requirements differ.

Backfill. Backfill is loading data you never had before into your system. For example:

- A trading desk onboards a new asset class and buys five years of historical trades and quotes from a vendor.
- You discover that a particular venue feed was not ingested properly for a week after a system change; the vendor resends that week.

In both cases there was a long period where your databases did not contain these records at all. The key point is that you are *adding* blocks of history, sometimes overlapping existing data, sometimes not.

Replay. Replay means reprocessing data you already have, possibly with new business logic. For example:

- Risk models are upgraded, and you want to recompute risk metrics for the past month while preserving the original market ticks.
- You discover a bug in a derived dataset and need to recompute it from raw trade and quote history.

Replay often reads from your own kdb+ or ClickHouse history and writes back into new tables or partitions. The focus here is less on file formats and more on deterministic processing, but the same partitioning and idempotency ideas still apply.

Late data. Late data is data that *belongs* to a time window you have already processed but *arrives* later, often through the same Kafka or Redpanda streams:

- An exchange sends cancel/correct messages for trades a few days after execution.
- A vendor reconnects after an outage and sends missing ticks for the previous hour.

Late data forces you to make a choice: do you update history and potentially rewrite downstream results, or do you keep the original view and store corrections separately? Whichever you choose, your design must be deliberate and consistent.

With these definitions in place, we can design storage and ingestion paths that handle all three without surprises.

Why File Formats Matter for History

In real-time ingestion we mostly deal with streams and in-memory structures. For history, the unit of work is usually a *file*: a chunk of rows written in a structured format, stored on a filesystem or object store, and later loaded into kdb+ and ClickHouse.

Parquet and ORC are the dominant choices for these files. They share several properties that are particularly useful for market data:

- **Columnar layout.** Data is stored by column rather than by row, which matches how ClickHouse and kdb+ HDBs are organized and enables fast scans and compression.
- **Self-describing schema.** The file contains metadata describing its columns and types. That makes it possible to detect mismatches early and manage schema evolution.
- **Block-level statistics.** Parquet and ORC can store min/max and other statistics per block, which can speed up loading and, when needed, targeted rewrites.

Using Parquet or ORC as the *canonical* representation for backfill and late data gives you a consistent, inspectable foundation. Think of these files as the "shipping containers" of your historical pipeline: standardized units that move between staging areas and final storage.

Aligning File Layout with Database Partitions

Both kdb+ and ClickHouse gain much of their performance from partitioning and indexing strategies:

- kdb+ HDBs are typically partitioned by date (and often further organized by table and symbol).
- ClickHouse tables based on MergeTree engines use partition keys (commonly by date or month) and sort keys (often including symbol and time).

If your Parquet/ORC file layout aligns with these partitions, backfill and late-loading become straightforward. If not, you will constantly fight the storage engines, copying and reshuffling data during every load.

Three practical design decisions help keep things aligned.

Logical Partition Keys in File Naming

Your file paths and names should encode the *logical* partition keys you use in kdb+ and ClickHouse. Common keys include:

- Trade or quote date.
- Symbol or symbol bucket.
- Venue or market segment.

For example, a path could embed these as:

- A date directory (for example, 2025-03-31/), which maps directly to a kdb+ date partition and a ClickHouse partition key.
- A symbol-bucket directory or file suffix, such as grouping symbols into ranges or hashed buckets, which mirrors your internal partitioning of large symbol universes.
- A venue or asset-class tag, useful for routing to different databases or tables.

The exact naming convention is less important than its *stability* and *predictability*. Given a day, a symbol, and a venue, an operator should be able to tell where the corresponding backfill files will live.

Physical Partition Alignment

When you load these files:

- Into kdb+, you typically write directly to the corresponding date partition directory, possibly into a staging area before a final swap.
- Into ClickHouse, you try to map each file or batch of files to a natural partition, so that the engine can write them as a small number of parts aligned with your partition key.

If you mix many logical dates inside a single Parquet or ORC file, you will have to split and scatter the rows at load time, which is slower and more error-prone. Conversely, if you use many tiny files per symbol and minute, you will create excessive metadata and overhead. The art is in choosing a granularity that is:

- Large enough for efficient scanning and insertion.
- Small enough that targeted corrections do not require rewriting huge swaths of history.

Daily or hourly files per symbol bucket and venue are a practical compromise for many equity and futures datasets.

Schema Version Metadata

Your files should carry a clear schema version identifier in their metadata and, ideally, in their path or name. Over time, you will add columns, deprecate others, and sometimes change types. Without schema versioning you will end up guessing which historical files match which table layout.

By recording the version explicitly, you can:

- Detect attempts to load incompatible files into a given table schema.
- Apply targeted transformations to older versions during load (for example, filling new columns with defaults).
- Maintain multiple reader configurations for different historical eras if needed.

The important point is to treat schema as a versioned contract, not an undocumented guess.

Idempotent Historical Loads

Backfill and late-data processes often need to be rerun. A file may fail mid-load. A vendor may resend the same batch. You may need to adjust deduplication logic and reapply it. For this to be safe, historical loads must be *idempotent*: applying the same file twice leaves your database in the same state as applying it once.

To achieve this, design your load processes around three ideas.

Stable File Identifiers

Every Parquet or ORC file should have a stable identifier, such as a combination of:

- The logical partition keys (date, symbol bucket, venue).
- A sequence number or UUID for that particular correction or backfill.

You can then maintain a small control table in kdb+ or ClickHouse that records:

- Which files have been fully loaded.
- Which tables or partitions they affected.
- When the load occurred and under what schema version.

Before loading a file, the process checks this control table. If the file has already been applied with the same content and logic, it can be skipped or treated differently (for example, used only for validation).

Staging and Swap Patterns

Rather than writing directly into final production partitions, it is often safer to:

- Load data into *staging* tables or directories that mirror the structure of the final ones.
- Perform deduplication, validation, and any necessary aggregation there.
- Swap the staging partition into place atomically, or merge it in a controlled way.

In kdb+, this may mean writing new HDB directories and adjusting symlinks or mount points once checks pass. In ClickHouse, it might involve inserting into dedicated staging tables and then using INSERT_-SELECT operations to move cleaned data into the main tables.

This pattern reduces the chance that a half-loaded backfill corrupts live analytics.

Deterministic Deduplication Rules

For idempotency, deduplication logic must be deterministic: given the same set of source rows, it must produce the same result every time. That means:

- Defining clear keys that identify unique events, usually including instrument, business event time, and an exchange or internal sequence number.

- Establishing tie-breaking rules for conflicting records with the same key. For instance, you might always keep the record with the highest sequence number from the exchange, or the most recent vendor delivery time.

- Avoiding reliance on load-time timestamps or other incidental metadata when deciding which record to keep.

With deterministic rules, you can safely rerun backfills, confident that the same files will yield the same final state.

Dealing with Late and Corrected Events

Late and corrected events blur the line between streaming and historical workflows. They often arrive via Kafka/Redpanda, not as bulk files, but they refer to historical time windows that may already be archived.

You can handle them in two complementary ways.

Real-Time Late-Data Path

For small volumes of late data, it is often easiest to let them flow through the same streaming path as on-time events and handle them incrementally. This requires:

- Including enough business keys and sequence information in each message for the consumers to recognize duplicates and corrections.
- Having ingestion code in kdb+ and ClickHouse that can perform point updates or corrections, not just append-only inserts.

For example:

- A late cancel/correct trade message could identify the original trade by a composite key and specify the corrected fields.
- The consumer can then locate and update or replace the original row in the relevant table.

This path is well-suited to exchange-driven corrections, which are typically sparse relative to the full data volume but important for compliance and P&L.

Batch Correction Path

When late data is large (for example, an hour of missing ticks) or when corrections affect entire ranges, a batch path using Parquet or ORC is more practical:

- Collect late or corrected events into partition-aligned files, using the same naming and schema conventions as backfill.
- Run a batch pipeline that:
  - Reads the relevant historical partitions from kdb+ or ClickHouse.

  - Merges them with the late events according to the same deterministic deduplication rules as backfill.
  - Writes out new partitions, either overwriting the old ones or versioning them.

Here, Parquet/ORC serve not only as input but also as intermediate formats during the correction process. They provide a clear audit trail: you can retain both the "before" and "after" files for future review.

Conflict Resolution: Which Version of History Wins?

Once you allow both on-time and late data, often from multiple vendors or feeds, you will encounter conflicts: two different records claim to represent the same event. You need explicit rules for which version of history is authoritative.

Common conflict-resolution strategies include:

Source priority. Some sources are more trusted than others. For example, direct exchange feeds may override vendor-consolidated feeds for critical fields, or a particular vendor might be designated the "golden source" for reference data. In this model, each row carries a source identifier, and your deduplication logic compares both business keys and source priority.

Sequence and event time. Exchanges often provide sequence numbers or event identifiers that make it clear which message supersedes which. You can:

- Treat earlier messages as provisional.
- Replace them with later messages that carry the same key but higher sequence.

This is especially important for order book events and trade corrections.

Delivery time windows. For some analytics, you may decide that corrections arriving after a certain delay are tracked but do not change past published results. For example, an intraday dashboard might use only data that arrived within five minutes of event time, while end-of-day reports incorporate all known corrections as of midnight.

Technically, you can represent this by:

- Storing both the *event time* and the *data-arrival time*.
- Maintaining multiple derived views optimized for different consumers (real-time trading versus audit and compliance).

The important point is to make these policies explicit and to encode them in your pipelines, not as tribal knowledge.

Managing Schema Evolution in Historical Pipelines

Over the life of a trading platform, schemas will change. You may add new fields (for example, new risk measures or identifiers), change cardinalities, or refine data types. If you do not plan for this, history will fragment: older files will be unreadable or misleading to newer tools.

To keep history coherent, apply a few discipline rules.

Additive Changes as the Default

Whenever possible, evolve schemas *additively*:

- Add new columns with sensible defaults or nullability for older data.
- Avoid changing the meaning of existing columns; if semantics change, introduce a new field.

Parquet and ORC make additive changes natural: you can write files that do not contain the new column, and readers can fill in defaults when they see missing fields.

Deprecation, Not Deletion

When you decide to stop using a column:

- Mark it as deprecated in schema metadata and documentation.
- Remove it from new computations and exports.
- Delay physical removal until you are confident no important historical processes depend on it.

This gives you time to adjust backfill and replay code, and avoids hard breaks when loading older files.

Versioned Readers and Writers

Treat your backfill and late-data loaders as versioned components that know which schema versions they support. A mature setup often has:

- A small, central schema registry or catalog describing each table, its history of changes, and associated file schemas.
- Loader configurations that specify which schema versions they accept and how to map them to the current in-database schema.

For example:

- A loader might know that files with schema version 1 lack a `tradeCondition` column and should fill it with a default value.
- Another loader might be restricted to newer versions and explicitly reject older files, signaling the need for an intermediate transformation step.

This approach turns schema evolution into a controlled process rather than a series of ad-hoc fixes.

Protecting Downstream Analytics from Inconsistent Slices

Even with good design, there will be periods where some history has been corrected or backfilled and other parts have not. Risk managers and quants are particularly sensitive to this: they want to know whether a backtest or report is based on a coherent slice of history.

A few practical techniques help here.

Partition-level status flags. For each logical partition (for example, each day and venue), maintain a small metadata record indicating:

- Whether initial load is complete.
- Whether all known corrections up to a certain cut-off time have been applied.
- Which schema version applies.

Downstream processes can then:

- Filter to partitions that meet their consistency requirements.
- Delay or annotate reports that depend on incomplete or partially corrected data.

Versioned historical views. For certain critical analyses, it may be worth creating *versioned snapshots* of history: for example, "history as of month-end" and "history as of regulatory filing date." These can be implemented as separate databases or schemas that you update only during controlled reconciliation windows.

Clear communication of data freshness. Finally, your user-facing tools should surface key facts about history quality: up to which date backfill is complete, whether recent days are still subject to corrections, and similar information. Technically, this information is derived from the same metadata tables your pipelines use.

Bringing It All Together

Backfill and late-data handling are sometimes seen as chores, tackled in a rush when something goes wrong. The perspective in this chapter is different: if you design for history from the start, you gain robustness, auditability, and flexibility.

The key ingredients are:

- Using Parquet or ORC as standardized, schema-rich containers for historical and late data.
- Aligning file layouts with kdb+ and ClickHouse partitioning and indexing, so loads are natural and efficient.
- Making loads idempotent through stable file identifiers, staging-and-swap patterns, and deterministic deduplication.
- Explicitly defining conflict-resolution policies and schema evolution contracts.
- Providing metadata and status indicators so that downstream analytics can select coherent slices of history.

In the next section, we will build on this historical machinery to connect kdb+ and ClickHouse more tightly, creating reliable batch and streaming bridges between them. Those bridges will rely heavily on the partitioning, file-format, and idempotency principles you have just seen.

7.3 kdb+ ↔ ClickHouse Interoperability

So far in this chapter we have treated kdb+ and ClickHouse primarily as *destinations*: Kafka or Redpanda feeds them, and backfill files land neatly in their partitions. Real platforms, however, almost never keep them as isolated silos.

Instead, you use each system where it shines:

- kdb+ as the ultra-low-latency capture and intraday analytics engine.

- ClickHouse as the scalable, cost-efficient store for large historical ranges and heavy ad-hoc queries.

To make this work, you must move data *between* them in predictable ways. That means designing bridges—both batch and streaming—that preserve three properties:

- **Schema compatibility**: columns and types mean the same thing on both sides.
- **Ordering where it matters**: events that must be processed in sequence arrive in that sequence.
- **Idempotency**: if a message or file is processed twice, the final state looks as if it were processed once.

This section develops those bridges step by step. We start with the main use cases, anchor them in a logical topology diagram, and then work through batch exports, streaming flows, and operational reconciliation.

Interoperability Use Cases

There are many ways to connect kdb+ and ClickHouse. In practice, three patterns dominate.

kdb+ as real-time ingest, ClickHouse as analytics lake. Here:

- kdb+ RDB and intraday HDB ingest from exchanges and internal systems through Kafka or Redpanda.
- kdb+ retains a rolling intraday window for fast, flexible queries.
- ClickHouse holds longer history (months or years) plus heavier aggregates and derived views.

Data flows one way for most tables: kdb+ $\rightarrow$ ClickHouse, either intraday in micro-batches or at end-of-day.

ClickHouse as archive for older kdb+ partitions. In many shops, kdb+ HDB is kept relatively small for performance and operational reasons:

- Recent days or weeks live in kdb+, where q scripts and analytics can run with minimal latency.
- Older partitions are periodically offloaded to ClickHouse, where they can still be queried but at slightly higher latency and lower storage cost.

Here the bridge is a scheduled process that transfers entire date partitions from kdb+ to ClickHouse, and possibly prunes them from kdb+ afterward.

Bidirectional replication for derived views. Sometimes you need:

- A derived view computed in ClickHouse (for example, long-window statistics) to be visible in kdb+ for intraday strategies.
- Or, conversely, a complex intraday analytic computed in kdb+ to be captured in ClickHouse for longer-term reporting and machine learning.

In these cases, a subset of data flows in both directions, often using Kafka/Redpanda or file drops as intermediaries.

Right after outlining these use cases, it is helpful to ground them in a single topology.

This diagram highlights that there is no single "magic bridge." Instead, you compose several simple, well-understood flows, each with clear responsibilities.

Batch Bridges: Moving Partitions Safely

Batch movement is conceptually simpler than streaming: you are not trying to keep two systems in perfect real-time sync, just to make sure they agree on certain blocks of history.

We will focus on the most common direction, kdb+ → ClickHouse, but the same ideas apply in reverse.

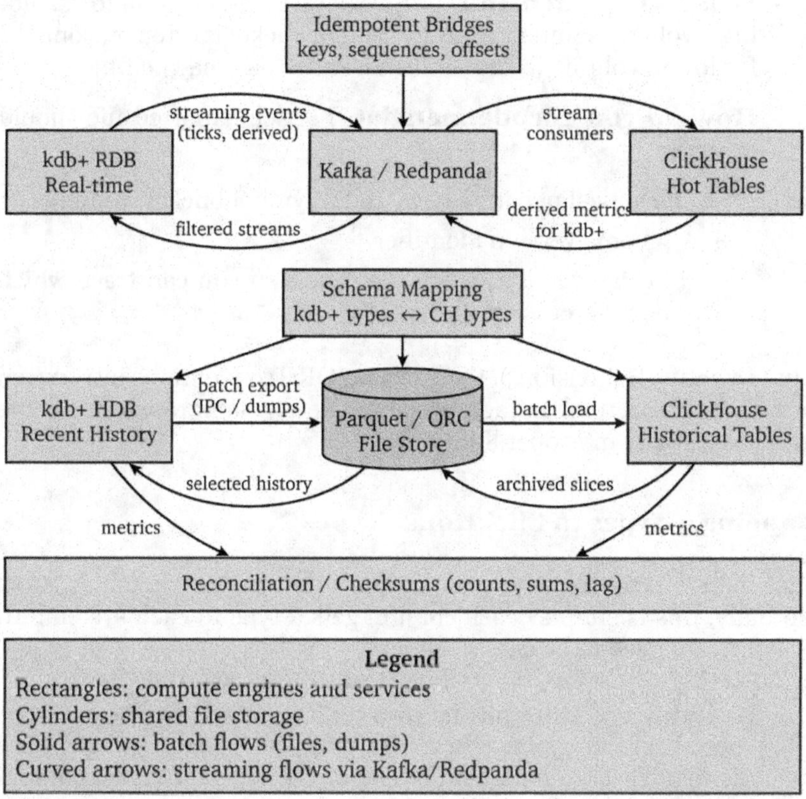

Exporting from kdb+

From kdb+, you typically export at the level of date partitions, symbol buckets, or both, using either:

- IPC-based readers that pull data from q processes and write to Parquet or ORC, or
- Direct file-based dumps from HDB partitions into those formats.

The key design questions are:

- **What is the batch unit?** Whole days, or smaller windows? For high-volume equities, a day by symbol bucket is often reasonable; for lower-volume instruments, an entire day may be fine.
- **How do you encode metadata?** Each exported file should carry:
  - The logical partition keys (date, symbol bucket, venue).
  - A schema version identifier.
  - A bridge version or job identifier, so you can trace which export process created it.

This is a natural extension of the Parquet/ORC conventions introduced in the backfill section. In fact, the same file-format strategy can serve both backfill and interoperability.

Mapping q Types to ClickHouse Types

Once data is exported, you must map it into ClickHouse tables. Conceptually, this is simple: each column gets a type in each system. In practice, you need to be careful about:

- **Nullability.** kdb+ has its own null conventions (for example, special sentinel values for missing ints and floats). ClickHouse distinguishes nullable and non-nullable types. Decide, column by column, whether nulls are allowed and how to represent them.
- **Time and timestamp semantics.** kdb+ uses high-precision times and timestamps with implicit time zones (often UTC). ClickHouse has types for dates, datetimes, and higher-precision timestamps. You must standardize on how you represent:
  - Event time (the time the trade or quote happened).
  - Insertion or processing time, if you carry it.
- **Enumerations and symbols.** In kdb+, symbols are interned strings with performance advantages. In ClickHouse, you may use low-cardinality string types or dictionary-encoded representations. Plan this up front, especially for fields like symbol, venue, and status codes.

The safest pattern is to maintain a small, human-readable mapping document or catalog that states, for each logical column:

- Its meaning.
- Its kdb+ type.
- Its ClickHouse SQL type.

Your batch loading scripts then refer to this mapping, rather than embedding type assumptions ad hoc.

Aligning Partitions and Sorting Keys

For ClickHouse to perform well on queries, you must align its physical layout with your typical access patterns and with the structure of your exports.

Two aspects matter:

- **Partition key.** This is used to group data into larger chunks, often by date or month. For trading data, partitioning by trade or quote date is a common default.
- **Sorting (or primary) key.** Within each partition, rows are stored in sorted order by one or more columns, such as symbol, then event time. This matching of sort key to query patterns is critical for ClickHouse efficiency.

If your kdb+ exports are already organized by date and symbol bucket, you can:

- Create ClickHouse tables partitioned by date (matching kdb+ HDB).
- Use sort keys like (symbol, event time) that align with kdb+ table ordering.
- Load each exported file into the matching partition, which reduces the amount of merging and re-sorting ClickHouse must do.

This alignment increases both performance and predictability. It also simplifies reconciliation, because you can compare record counts partition by partition.

Idempotent Batch Loading

As with backfill, batch interoperability must be idempotent. Files may be re-sent, load jobs may restart, and corrections may involve re-exporting a partition.

To achieve idempotency on the ClickHouse side:

- Embed a stable file identifier (for example, date, symbol bucket, and export job ID) in both the file name and a control table.
- Before loading a file, check whether it has already been applied successfully. If yes, decide whether to skip or treat it as a replacement.
- Load into staging tables or partitions first, then merge or swap into the main tables only after validation.
- Design tables and merge logic to handle duplicate rows gracefully, using primary keys or deduplication queries when needed.

This mirrors the idempotent historical-load patterns from the previous section, but now the "source" is not an external vendor, it is your own kdb+ system.

Streaming Bridges: Keeping Systems in Sync

Batch transfers work well for overnight or infrequent synchronization. When you want ClickHouse to stay close to real time, or when you want kdb+ to see ClickHouse-derived metrics intraday, you need streaming bridges.

Kafka or Redpanda is usually the backbone for these bridges, for the same reasons discussed earlier: durable buffering, parallelism, and clear lag metrics.

We focus on two directions.

kdb+ Publishing to Kafka for ClickHouse Ingestion

In this pattern:

- kdb+ processes acting as producers publish events (ticks, bars, derived metrics) into Kafka/Redpanda topics.
- ClickHouse consumers (for example, ingestion workers or materialized views) read those topics and write into ClickHouse tables.

Designing this flow involves several steps.

Topic and message design. For each logical stream, define:

- A topic name and partitioning strategy consistent with your overall Kafka design (for example, partition by symbol hash).
- A message schema that includes:
  - All business fields you care about (prices, sizes, identifiers).
  - Business keys and sequence numbers to support idempotency and deduplication.
  - Schema version identifiers, so ClickHouse consumers can evolve gracefully.

Ordering and parallelism. If ClickHouse tables require that all events for a given symbol arrive in order, you must:

- Use a key-based partitioning scheme ensuring that all messages for that symbol land in the same partition.
- Run consumer instances in a group such that each partition is processed by only one instance at a time.

If strict symbol-level order is less important (for example, for certain aggregates), you can prioritize throughput and distribute keys more flexibly.

Idempotent ingestion into ClickHouse. ClickHouse writes are usually append-heavy, but you can approximate exactly-once semantics by:

- Including unique identifiers or composite keys for each event in the messages.
- Designing target tables and materialized views to detect duplicates by these keys.
- Committing Kafka consumer offsets only after successful inserts into ClickHouse.

Where data volumes are very high, you might accept a small window where duplicates are possible and periodically run lightweight deduplication queries, relying on primary-key-like logic to collapse duplicates.

ClickHouse Publishing Back into kdb+

The reverse direction is less common but powerful. Examples include:

- Streaming long-window volatility measures computed in ClickHouse back into kdb+ to be joined with intraday signals.
- Publishing aggregated liquidity metrics or cross-asset spreads.

The mechanics are symmetric:

- ClickHouse processes (for example, external jobs, materialized views, or scheduled queries) produce messages into Kafka/Redpanda.
- kdb+ RDB or gateways consume them, writing into in-memory tables or small HDB partitions.

You still need:

- Schema contracts: message fields must map cleanly into kdb+ columns.
- Keys and versions: to detect duplicate metrics or outdated values.

- Lag visibility: to understand how far behind ClickHouse-derived views are relative to raw ticks.

Because these flows typically involve aggregates rather than raw ticks, volumes are lower and you can be more generous with CPU-intensive serialization or encryption if needed.

Schema Compatibility and Evolution Across Stores

Connecting two systems doubles your schema concerns. You must avoid situations where:

- kdb+ adds a column, but ClickHouse does not, leading to silent truncation.
- ClickHouse changes a type (for example, widening an integer) in a way that confuses kdb+ readers.

To manage this:

Treat schemas as shared contracts. For each logical dataset that crosses the bridge (for example, trades, quotes, risk_metrics):

- Maintain a single logical schema definition, independent of any specific technology.
- Derive kdb+ table definitions and ClickHouse table definitions from that shared contract.

Use versioned schemas. As with file formats:

- Attach schema version identifiers to messages and files.
- Ensure consumers can handle a range of versions, at least during transitions.
- Avoid "breaking" changes that would require simultaneous upgrades of all producers and consumers.

In practice, additive changes (adding nullable columns) are easiest to roll out. Removals or type changes should be rare and tightly controlled.

Handle nullable vs non-nullable differences explicitly. Decide for each field whether:

- It is truly optional, in which case ClickHouse should use a nullable type and kdb+ should have a clear null representation.
- It is required, in which case you should enforce non-nullability in both systems and validate at ingestion.

Doing this systematically avoids subtle bugs down the line, such as treating sentinel values as real data.

Idempotency and Exactly-Once Semantics in Practice

Between kdb+, ClickHouse, and Kafka/Redpanda, you have several layers of offset tracking, transaction support, and batching. It is tempting to aim for strict end-to-end exactly-once semantics, but in practice:

- Network partitions, process restarts, and client limitations often make this hard.
- The performance overhead of heavy transactional guarantees can be significant.

Most trading platforms therefore aim for *effectively-once* semantics across these bridges. That means designing for:

- **At-least-once delivery** between components: messages and batches may be redelivered or reprocessed.
- **Idempotent application** in each sink: applying the same input twice does not change the final result.

This requires:

- Carrying stable identifiers and sequence numbers through all layers.
- Using merge/upsert or deduplication logic in ClickHouse where needed.
- Using keyed updates or deduplication in kdb+ when consuming from ClickHouse-derived streams.

It is worth revisiting your earlier design choices (in Kafka topic structures and backfill file layouts) to ensure those identifiers are consistently present.

Operational Reconciliation and Health Checks

Finally, interoperability is not only about designing bridges; it is about being confident that they are doing what you think they are doing. This is where reconciliation enters.

At a minimum, you should regularly compare:

- **Row counts**, per partition, between kdb+ and ClickHouse for tables that are meant to match.
- **Simple aggregates**, such as sums of traded volume or notional, per day and per symbol or bucket.
- **Lag metrics**, indicating how far ClickHouse is behind kdb+ for recent data.

You can implement this as:

- Scheduled jobs that run on both systems, compute metrics, and write them into a small "reconciliation" table (as suggested in the diagram).
- A dashboard that surfaces discrepancies and trends over time.
- Alerts when differences exceed thresholds, especially for regulatory-critical datasets like orders and trades.

For more advanced setups, you may compute checksums or hash-based fingerprints over partitions, but even simple counts and sums catch a large fraction of integration errors.

Bringing the Pieces Together

When you combine:

- Well-defined batch exports from kdb+ to ClickHouse, aligned with partitioning and file-format strategies.
- Streaming bridges using Kafka/Redpanda, with keys, schemas, and lag metrics designed for interoperability.
- Shared, versioned schema contracts across both systems.
- Idempotent application logic and regular reconciliation checks.

you turn kdb+ and ClickHouse from separate tools into a coherent platform.

kdb+ can focus on capturing and analyzing the sharp edges of intraday trading, while ClickHouse can soak up vast amounts of history and heavier workloads. The bridges we have described allow data and insights to flow between them without guesswork, manual fixes, or constant fear of silent divergence.

In the next sections, we will zoom out from data movement to data survival and operations: how to back up these systems, design disaster recovery plans, and run them economically at scale.

7.4 Backup, DR, and Storage Governance

In the earlier sections we built ingestion pipelines, designed historical file strategies, and connected kdb+ and ClickHouse into a coherent platform. All of that work assumes something important: that the data *stays there*.

In reality, disks fail, operators make mistakes, data centers lose power, and cloud regions suffer outages. Traders and regulators, however, care about a simpler pair of questions:

- **How much data can we afford to lose?**
- **How long can we afford to be down?**

This section answers those questions in the language of backup, disaster recovery (DR), and storage governance for kdb+ and ClickHouse. We will:

- Define recovery point objective (RPO) and recovery time objective (RTO) in trading terms.
- Design layered backup and snapshot strategies for kdb+ HDBs and ClickHouse clusters.
- Discuss geo-replication patterns and their latency trade-offs.
- Introduce storage governance: deciding what deserves full protection, for how long, and how to verify that your DR plan actually works.

The emphasis is on practical patterns you can simulate and test, not just theoretical resilience.

RPO and RTO in Trading Language

Two simple metrics anchor any backup and DR strategy:

Recovery point objective (RPO). RPO is how far back in time you are willing to lose data if a failure occurs. In a market-data context:

- An RPO of five minutes means that if your primary cluster fails at 10:00:00, you are willing to restart with data only up to 9:55:00.
- A stricter RPO—for example, a few seconds—means you will invest more in real-time replication.

Different datasets can have different RPOs. Traders may insist that order and execution history never miss more than a second of events, while a derived analytics table might tolerate a few minutes.

Recovery time objective (RTO). RTO is how long you can operate without a given system or dataset. Continuing the example:

- An RTO of 30 minutes for your main ClickHouse analytics cluster means the business can cope with a half-hour outage, perhaps by falling back to kdb+ for recent history only.
- An RTO of five minutes for the intraday kdb+ environment implies much more aggressive DR planning.

RPO and RTO are not purely technical; they are business choices. Once you set them, they act like design constraints on your backup and replication architecture.

kdb+ HDB: Snapshots and Backups

kdb+ HDB (historical database) is usually file-based: a tree of directories and files on local disks or network storage. This simplicity is an advantage for backup and DR, but only if you respect how kdb+ uses the filesystem.

Filesystem Layout and Consistency

Recall that:

- HDBs are typically partitioned by date directories.
- Within each date, tables are stored as column files, often with symbol-level subdirectories.

For a consistent backup, you need a view of this tree where:

- No files are being modified while the snapshot is taken, or
- The underlying storage provides atomic snapshots that freeze the view at a consistent instant.

Two broad approaches are common.

Quiesced backups. Here you:

- Pause writes to the HDB (intraday writes usually go to RDB/mid-tier instead).
- Take a filesystem-level backup or copy.
- Resume normal operations.

This is simple but introduces a brief write freeze. Many shops schedule this during low-activity windows (for example, after cash-market close but before overnight sessions become busy).

Storage snapshots. Many modern filesystems and cloud storage backends support snapshots: point-in-time, copy-on-write views that can be created without stopping the database:

- The snapshot freezes the logical state of the HDB.
- Data files that are not changed after the snapshot share physical blocks, so the snapshot starts small.
- You can later expose the snapshot on another host or region for backup or DR.

This is often the preferred method, because it reduces downtime and enables frequent snapshots with modest overhead.

Backup Frequency and Granularity

With RPO in mind, you decide how often to snapshot or back up the HDB:

- If your RPO for historical ticks is a few hours, a daily snapshot might be enough.
- If you cannot afford to lose more than 15 minutes of intraday history, you may combine:

- A daily full snapshot of the HDB.

- More frequent incremental backups or replication of RDB/mid-tier logs.

It is also useful to think in terms of *change rate*. For many trading datasets:

- Older partitions do not change; only the most recent dates receive new data or corrections.
- This means you can back up older partitions once and treat them as immutable.

A practical pattern is:

- For current and recent dates, take daily snapshots and store them in off-cluster storage.
- For partitions older than a threshold (for example, 30 days), after one verified backup, mark them as "frozen" and exclude them from frequent backup runs.

This reduces backup volume and long-term costs.

Off-Site Copies and Retention

Snapshots on the same storage system protect against accidental deletion or local corruption, but not against data-center or region-level failures. You therefore need at least one *off-site* copy of critical HDB data:

- In another availability zone or region.
- Or in a different storage system (for example, copying snapshot contents to object storage).

Retention policies then determine how long you keep:

- Daily backups (for example, 30 days).
- Weekly or monthly backups (for example, 1–7 years, depending on regulation).

Storage governance, discussed later, will help decide these numbers per dataset.

ClickHouse: Replication, Backups, and Storage Policies

ClickHouse is a distributed, replicated columnar database with its own tools for resilience. Its design suggests a slightly different approach to backup and DR than kdb+.

Replication Within a Cluster

In most production setups:

- Tables use replicated MergeTree engines.
- Data for each shard is stored on multiple replicas (often in different racks or availability zones).

This gives you resilience against single-node failures without involving traditional backups:

- If a node fails, remaining replicas for that shard continue serving queries and taking writes.
- When the failed node returns or is replaced, ClickHouse automatically synchronizes data from peers.

However, replication is *not* a substitute for backups:

- A bad query or bug that deletes data replicates the deletion to all replicas.
- Corruption at the logical level is faithfully mirrored.

Thus you still need backups and, for DR, cross-region replication.

Backups and Snapshots for ClickHouse

You have two main categories of protection:

Logical backups. These are created using ClickHouse's backup mechanisms or by exporting table data:

- They capture table contents and metadata at a logical level.
- They can be restored into different clusters or versions.
- They are often stored in object storage or other external systems.

Logical backups are flexible but can be heavier and slower than low-level snapshots.

Volume or filesystem snapshots. Similar to kdb+, you can snapshot the underlying storage volumes that hold ClickHouse data directories:

- Snapshots are fast and space-efficient initially.
- They allow you to roll back an entire node to a previous point in time.

The trade-off is that volume snapshots are typically tied to a specific storage backend and may be less portable across environments.

In practice, many organizations use a mix:

- Regular logical backups of critical tables to external storage (for long-term retention and cross-cluster restore).
- Frequent volume snapshots for fast, local rollbacks and short-RPO protection.

Storage Policies and Lifecycle Management

ClickHouse includes storage policies that can automatically move data between:

- High-performance local SSDs or NVMe drives (for hot data).
- Slower, cheaper disks or network storage (for warm or cold data).
- External object storage for long-term archival.

You can tie these to:

- Time-to-live (TTL) rules on tables or columns, which automatically mark older data for movement or deletion.
- Partitioning schemes (for example, monthly partitions that can be moved or detached wholesale).

Used carefully, storage policies can:

- Reduce backup volume by pruning unneeded data early.
- Make it easier to maintain different retention periods for different datasets.

Used carelessly, they can surprise you by silently dropping data that certain desks still rely on. This is why storage governance, discussed later, must drive policy settings.

Geo-Replication and Cross-Region DR

Backups and local replication protect you from many failures but not all. To handle the loss of an entire data center or cloud region, you need geo-replication: keeping secondary copies of key datasets in a different location.

Active-Passive vs Active-Active

At a high level, you face a choice:

Active-passive.

- One region is the primary, handling all writes and most reads.
- Another region holds replicas or backups and is used only in an emergency.
- RPO is determined by how often you replicate or back up to the secondary.

This is simpler operationally, and good when regulatory or latency constraints make a single primary region natural.

Active-active.

- Multiple regions accept writes and serve users.
- Data must be synchronized across regions, potentially with conflict resolution.

For low-latency trading data, full active-active is rare, because:

- Cross-region latencies can be tens of milliseconds.
- Coordinating writes in two directions in real time is complex and may degrade latency beyond acceptable limits.

A more typical "active-active" compromise is:

- Each region is primary for its local users and perhaps a subset of data.
- Selected datasets (for example, reference data, aggregated analytics) are replicated asynchronously to other regions.

kdb+ Geo-Replication Patterns

kdb+ does not have built-in cross-region replication; you build it using the tools you already know:

- Streaming feeds replicated via Kafka/Redpanda, where:
- Producers or mirror topics send the same real-time data to consumers in multiple regions.
- Each region has its own kdb+ RDB/HDB ingesting the stream.
- Periodic copying of HDB partitions:
- Using snapshots or rsync-like tools to copy partition directories.
- Often lagged by hours or days, depending on RPO.

This gives you flexibility to choose:

- A near-real-time replica (low RPO) at the cost of more bandwidth and storage.
- A delayed, lower-cost replica for regulatory and audit purposes, with a higher RPO.

ClickHouse Cross-Region Replication

ClickHouse offers features to replicate tables across clusters, and many organizations use asynchronous replication to:

- Maintain a warm standby cluster in a second region.
- Offload heavy read workloads to another location.

The critical point is to align replication lag with your RPO:

- If replication is asynchronous, and the secondary cluster lags by, say, two minutes, then your RPO in a full-region failure is at least two minutes.
- If you require a sub-minute RPO, you must invest in tighter replication or additional mechanisms (for example, streaming logs and applying them on the secondary more frequently).

Cross-region replication also interacts with network design:

- You must provision sufficient bandwidth so that replication does not fall behind during peak activity.
- You should monitor replication lag as a first-class metric.

Designing for Different RPO/RTO Tiers

Not all datasets deserve the same level of protection. Trying to give every table the strictest RPO and RTO is:

- Technically challenging.

- Financially inefficient.

A more realistic approach is to classify datasets into tiers.

Tier-1: Mission-Critical Trading Data

Examples:

- Orders and executions.
- Raw trades and quotes for traded instruments.
- Positions and margin calculations.

Typical targets:

- RPO measured in seconds or a small number of minutes.
- RTO short enough that traders can continue operating (for example, under 15 minutes in most contingency plans).

Protection strategies might include:

- Multiple replicas within a region (for ClickHouse).
- Real-time or near-real-time replication to a secondary region.
- Frequent snapshots and logical backups.

Tier-2: Important but Not Time-Critical Data

Examples:

- Daily risk reports derived from raw ticks.
- Long-horizon analytics and factor models.
- Certain reference data snapshots.

Typical targets:

- RPO of several hours, possibly up to one day.

- RTO of hours, acceptable outside strict trading hours.

Protection may rely more heavily on:

- Daily backups.
- Object storage copies.
- Less aggressive cross-region replication.

Tier-3: Recomputable or Low-Value Data

Examples:

- Intermediate datasets in analytic pipelines.
- Temporary research outputs.

These may have:

- Loose or no explicit RPO/RTO, assuming they can be recomputed from Tier-1 and Tier-2 inputs.

Here you deliberately accept the risk of loss to save on storage and DR complexity.

Testing DR: From Runbooks to Drills

A DR plan that exists only as documentation is not reliable. To build confidence, you must practice.

Runbooks

For each major failure scenario, maintain a concise runbook that covers:

- Symptoms and alerts that indicate the failure (for example, loss of a ClickHouse shard, corrupted kdb+ partition, regional outage).

- Immediate actions to stabilize the situation (for example, fail load-balancers to replicas, pause certain ingest pipelines).
- Step-by-step recovery procedures:

- Where to find backups or snapshots.
- How to restore them.
- How to validate that restored data is consistent.

- Communication steps: who to notify, what to tell traders and risk managers.

Runbooks should be short and specific enough that an on-call engineer can follow them under pressure.

Regular Restore Tests

To ensure backups and DR mechanisms actually work:

- Periodically restore a subset of data into a test environment:

- For kdb+, bring up a test HDB from snapshots.
- For ClickHouse, restore tables from logical backups.

- Measure how long the restore takes (informing real RTO).
- Verify data integrity using reconciliation techniques (counts, sums, checksums).

These drills often uncover:

- Missing permissions or configuration.
- Backups that were incomplete or misconfigured.
- Gaps between documented and actual procedures.

Discovering such issues during a drill is far cheaper than discovering them during a crisis.

Storage Governance: Making Intentional Trade-offs

Storage governance ties everything together. It is the process of deciding:

- What data you keep.
- For how long.
- At what level of protection and cost.

Without governance, clusters accumulate data indefinitely, backups grow without bound, and no one can explain why a given table exists or how critical it is.

Classifying Datasets

For each major table or dataset, record:

- Business owner (desk, risk team, operations).
- Intended usage (trading, risk, compliance, research).
- Required retention (regulatory minimum, business preference).
- RPO/RTO classification (Tier-1, Tier-2, or Tier-3).

This can be a simple catalog or metadata table that both data and infrastructure teams can see.

Aligning Technical Policies

Then, align:

- kdb+ HDB snapshot and replication schedules.
- ClickHouse storage policies and TTLs.
- Backup retention periods.

with those classifications. For example:

- Tier-1 trade history: replicated, backed up frequently, with long-term archival.
- Tier-2 analytics: fewer replicas, daily backups, medium retention.
- Tier-3 scratch data: temporary storage, minimal or no backups, short TTLs.

Cost and Visibility

Finally, connect storage governance to cost:

- Tag storage and compute resources by dataset, environment, and owner.
- Build dashboards that show how much each dataset and tier costs over time.
- Use this visibility to challenge unnecessary retention or excessive protection levels.

When desks see the cost of storing every intermediate dataset forever, they are often more willing to make reasonable trade-offs.

From Theory to Practice

Designing backup, DR, and storage governance for kdb+ and ClickHouse is not about achieving perfect resilience. It is about:

- Making clear, explicit choices about what matters most.
- Using the strengths of each system—kdb+'s simple file layout, ClickHouse's replication and storage policies—to implement those choices.
- Regularly testing and revisiting your assumptions as volumes, regulations, and business needs evolve.

With RPO and RTO targets set, layered backups and snapshots in place, cross-region replication designed where needed, and governance guiding retention and cost, you can approach outages and failures with a plan rather than panic.

In the next sections we will add the remaining pieces: security and compliance controls around these data stores, and operational practices for deployment, automation, and cost management, so that the platform you have designed can be both trusted and sustainable.

7.5 Security, Compliance, and Data Lineage

So far in this chapter we have focused on getting data *in*, keeping it *safe* through backup and DR, and moving it reliably between kdb+ and ClickHouse. The next layer of responsibility is ensuring that only the right people and systems can see or change that data, that regulators can reconstruct what happened, and that you can quickly understand how a wrong input propagates into trading and risk decisions.

This section connects three themes:

- **Security**: protecting data in transit and at rest, and controlling who can do what.
- **Compliance**: recording activity and preserving key datasets in ways that meet regulatory rules.
- **Data lineage**: understanding and documenting how data flows from raw feeds to analytics and reports.

The goal is to apply these controls in a practical way that respects performance constraints, especially for latency-sensitive ingestion paths.

Threat Model for Market Data Stores

Before choosing tools and settings, it is useful to be explicit about what you are defending against. In a trading data platform, typical concerns include:

Unauthorized strategy leakage.

- Raw and derived data encode trading signals, positions, and P&L.
- If exported or exposed to competitors, they reveal valuable intellectual property.

Tampering with analytics and reports.

- An insider might try to manipulate risk figures or historical prices.
- A bug in a pipeline could corrupt a key dataset unnoticed.

Misuse of privileged access.

- Administrators, SREs, or database engineers often have broad powers.
- Without proper controls and audit trails, these powers can be abused or misused accidentally.

Data exfiltration via interfaces.

- Unsecured APIs, poorly configured JDBC/ODBC endpoints, or shared credentials can give wider access than intended.

With this threat model in mind, we can design protections where they matter most: around network boundaries, database access paths, and critical datasets such as orders, executions, and risk reports.

TLS and Secure Transport Without Excess Latency

The first line of defense is encrypting data in transit. Even if your systems live "inside" a corporate network or VPC, you should assume that network boundaries are porous over the lifetime of the system.

The challenge is to enable transport-layer security (TLS) while staying within latency budgets for real-time ingestion.

Where TLS is Required

In most modern environments, you should secure at least:

- **Kafka/Redpanda brokers**: encrypt traffic between producers, brokers, and consumers, especially if they span subnets or data centers.
- **kdb+ gateways and client connections**: secure connections from user-facing tools, applications, and other services into kdb+ RDB/HDB gateways.
- **ClickHouse server connections**: secure native and HTTP interfaces, especially for external clients and cross-region replication.

For intra-node communication (for example, between kdb+ processes on the same host), you may decide that plain connections are acceptable, but this should be a deliberate risk decision, not an accident.

Certificate Management

TLS is only as strong as its certificate practices. Basic disciplines include:

- **Using a private CA or well-managed internal PKI**: avoid self-signed certificates scattered around; use a central authority to issue and revoke server and client certs.
- **Short-lived certificates**: shorter lifetimes reduce the impact of credential leaks; automated renewal tools lessen the operational burden.
- **Certificate-based client authentication where feasible**: for high-value service-to-service paths (for example, Kafka producers carrying orders), use mutual TLS so that both client and server identities are strongly verified.

From an operational perspective, aim for:

- Automated certificate deployment and renewal pipelines.

- Clear ownership of certificates per system (Kafka cluster, kdb+ gateway, ClickHouse cluster).

Performance Considerations

TLS does add CPU overhead and can increase connection setup time. However:

- For long-lived connections (such as Kafka producers/consumers and database clients), the handshake cost is amortized over many messages.
- Modern CPUs and TLS libraries are highly optimized; for most market-data volumes, the overhead is acceptable if you avoid creating and tearing down connections unnecessarily.

Practical guidelines include:

- Use connection pooling and long-lived sessions where possible.
- Terminate TLS close to the workloads but not inside them unnecessarily; for example, front kdb+ and ClickHouse with proxies that handle TLS termination, if this simplifies configuration without undermining security zones.
- Measure end-to-end latency with and without TLS in a controlled test, and adapt batch sizes or parallelism if needed.

In most cases, you can achieve strong encryption in transit without exceeding typical sub-millisecond to low-millisecond budgets for intra-data-center communication.

Access Control: Roles, Least Privilege, and Gateways

Encrypting traffic is necessary but not sufficient; you must also control *who* can read or write data and what operations they can perform.

Role-Based Access Control (RBAC)

Rather than thinking in terms of individual users, it is usually better to define a small set of *roles* aligned with functions:

- **Ingestion roles**: processes that write data (Kafka consumers into kdb+/ClickHouse, backfill jobs).
- **Analytics roles**: users and services that query data but do not change it.
- **Admin roles**: operators who manage schema, storage, and performance, but may not be allowed to read all business data.

For ClickHouse, this translates naturally into:

- User accounts mapped to roles and profiles.
- Privileges granting specific rights (SELECT, INSERT, ALTER, etc.) on particular databases and tables.

For kdb+, RBAC is often implemented using:

- Gateway processes that handle authentication and then route queries to internal processes.
- Access-control logic in the gateway that inspects the user, the query, and sometimes the target tables or columns.
- OS-level controls (process ownership, file permissions) to prevent direct access to HDB directories.

The principle of *least privilege* should guide your designs:

- Ingestion roles can insert into specific tables but not read broad swathes of historical data.
- Analysts can query production data but cannot change schemas or execute dangerous administrative functions.
- Admins can manage clusters but may have restricted access to sensitive business data unless explicitly required.

Segregation of Duties

Regulators often expect that no single person can, on their own, both change and approve critical data. In technical terms:

- Separate operational roles (SRE/DBA) from business-owner roles (desk heads, risk managers).
- Require dual control or approval for high-impact changes (for example, dropping large tables, changing retention of order history).

Some of this is handled by process and governance rather than software, but your access-control setup should at least make it possible:

- Give operational teams only the access they need.
- Implement change workflows (for example, code-reviewed schema changes, configuration in version control) so that changes are visible and auditable.

Gateway Patterns for kdb+

Because kdb+ encourages direct, powerful scripting, it is especially important to place gateways between end-users and core processes:

- **External clients** connect only to the gateway, not directly to HDB or RDB processes.
- The gateway:
  - Authenticates users.
  - Applies query filters based on roles (for example, restricting instruments or desks).
  - Logs queries for audit and performance analysis.
- Internal kdb+ components (such as ingestion scripts) may bypass some of these controls under strict operational accounts, but these exceptions should be rare and well documented.

This pattern both centralizes access control and provides a natural point for implementing lineage tagging and usage metrics, as we will see later.

Compliance: Audit Trails and Immutable Storage

Regulatory regimes for trading data have two recurring themes:

- **You must keep certain data for a defined period.**
- **You must be able to show who did what and when.**

Designing your kdb+ and ClickHouse environments with these in mind avoids painful retrofits later.

Audit Logging

Audit trails should cover at least:

- **Authentication events**: logins, logouts, failed attempts, certificate use.
- **Administrative actions**: schema changes, configuration updates, execution of maintenance scripts.
- **Access to sensitive datasets**: queries against orders, trades, risk metrics, and other critical tables.

For ClickHouse, you can:

- Enable query and access logs.
- Feed them into a centralized log platform.
- Tag entries with user, role, source IP, and timing.

For kdb+, because queries are more free-form, it is often helpful for the gateway layer to:

- Log the full query text (with size and privacy limits as needed).
- Capture metadata such as user ID, desk, and any applied filters.

From a compliance perspective, what matters is not only that logs exist, but that:

- They are retained for an appropriate period.
- They are themselves protected from tampering (for example, stored in append-only systems).

Immutable or WORM Storage for Critical Data

Certain categories of data, such as order and execution history, may need to be stored in a way that prevents modification or deletion for a fixed period (Write Once, Read Many-WORM).

You can approximate or implement this by:

- Using object storage classes with legal hold or WORM features for archived snapshots and backups.
- Designing kdb+ and ClickHouse partitions for those datasets such that:
  - After a short correction window has passed, partitions are marked as immutable.
  - Processes that attempt to modify them are blocked or must go through a controlled exception process.

Conceptually, this mirrors practices you already saw for "frozen" partitions in backup design, but here the driver is regulatory retention rather than performance.

Data Lineage: From Raw Feeds to Reports

Security and compliance controls help you avoid or detect misuse. Data lineage answers a different but related question: *How did this number come to be?*

For a risk report, a backtest, or a regulatory filing, you often need to know:

- Which raw feeds and reference data contributed to it.
- Which transformations and models were applied.

- Which versions of those models and datasets were in use at the time.

This is lineage: the chain of derivations from source to output.

Lineage at Three Levels

To make lineage manageable, think in terms of three levels:

Table-level lineage.

- Which upstream tables feed a given downstream table?
- For example, a daily_risk table might depend on trades, positions, and market_data tables.

Column-level lineage.

- How is a given column computed?
- For example, a var_95 column might be computed from returns derived from adjusted close prices.

Job or pipeline lineage.

- Which scheduled jobs or streaming processes produce or update each table?
- When were they last run, and under which code version?

You do not need a perfect graph from day one. Start with table-level lineage, then refine as needed for sensitive reports and metrics.

Tagging and Metadata

Practically, you capture lineage by attaching metadata to:

- Tables and views in ClickHouse (for example, using comments, a separate metadata database, or external catalogs).
- kdb+ tables and scripts (for example, conventions in table names, config files, or external metadata stores).

For each table, store attributes like:

- Business owner and description.
- Upstream dependencies (as a list of table names).
- Sensitivity classification (public, internal, confidential, restricted).
- Retention and RPO/RTO tier (from the previous section).

Over time, you can build a lineage graph from these relationships. Even a simple graph—"this risk report table depends on these three upstream datasets"—is valuable during incident analysis.

Integrating Lineage with Pipelines

Your ingestion and transformation pipelines are natural places to update lineage:

- When a Kafka-to-ClickHouse job loads data into a table, it can record:
  - The input topics and partitions.
  - The code version or configuration hash.
- When a backfill job recomputes a derived table from raw history, it can log:
  - Which input partitions were used.
  - Which date range was affected.

Storing this in small, dedicated "lineage events" tables makes it easier to reconstruct, for example:

> "Which trades, and which version of the pricing model, contributed to the VaR number on last Friday's risk report?"

You will not answer such questions perfectly in all cases, but a disciplined lineage approach greatly narrows the search.

Balancing Security and Performance

One common fear is that adding security and compliance features will slow the system or make operations cumbersome. To avoid that, apply two guiding principles.

Protect the Highest-Value Paths First

Not all data and all paths are equally sensitive. Focus your strongest controls on:

- Order, execution, and position data.
- Proprietary analytics and models.
- External interfaces (APIs, user-facing query endpoints).

For example:

- Require mutual TLS and strong authentication for ingestion of order data and its storage.
- Apply stricter RBAC and query logging to tables that contain position and P&L data.

Less critical paths—for example, intermediate analytics with no direct business sensitivity—can use simpler controls, as long as the residual risk is acceptable.

Shift Left: Design Security into Pipelines

Security and lineage should not be bolted on after the fact. Instead:

- Design Kafka topics, kdb+ tables, and ClickHouse schemas with security and lineage metadata from the start.
- Include access-control and logging considerations when defining ingestion jobs and backfill processes.

For instance:

- When adding a new table, decide immediately:

  - Who should be able to read and write it.
  - How long data should be retained.
  - How it will be tagged in the lineage graph.
- When deploying a new ClickHouse cluster, bake TLS and RBAC into the initial configuration rather than as later "hardening" work.

This approach keeps the operational burden manageable and reduces the odds of hidden, insecure defaults.

Using Lineage in Incident Response and Change Management

Lineage is not just documentation; it is a powerful tool during incidents and changes.

Responding to Data Quality Incidents

When you discover a problem—say, a corrupt options feed for a few hours—the key questions are:

- Which downstream tables and reports are affected?
- Which desks or strategies consumed those reports?
- How do we repair the data and recompute affected outputs?

With table-level lineage and pipeline metadata, you can:

- Trace from the faulty raw table to all derived tables.
- Identify batches or time windows that need backfill and replay.
- Communicate clearly which reports are being recomputed and which are unaffected.

This reduces both the time to resolution and the "blast radius" of uncertainty.

Assessing the Impact of Changes

Before making a schema or pipeline change, ask:

- Which downstream consumers depend on this table or column?
- Will changing or dropping it break any critical reports?

A lineage catalog can help by:

- Listing known downstream tables and jobs.
- Highlighting which are marked as high criticality.

Armed with this, you can plan:

- Phased rollouts with compatibility layers.
- Coordination with affected teams.

Again, the aim is not perfection but a meaningful reduction in surprise breakages.

Bringing It Together

Security, compliance, and data lineage are sometimes viewed as separate concerns from performance and reliability. In a high-performance trading data platform, they are tightly coupled:

- TLS and access control protect data as it moves through the ingestion and interoperability pipelines.
- Audit trails and immutable storage connect naturally to the backup and DR strategies you already designed.
- Lineage builds on your understanding of partitions, topics, and pipelines to explain how data turns into decisions.

By treating these capabilities as core architectural elements rather than add-ons, you build a platform that is not only fast and scalable, but also trustworthy and auditable.

In the remaining sections of this chapter, we will zoom out one more level to discuss deployment topologies, capacity planning, automation, and cost management, showing how to operate such a secure, compliant, and lineage-aware platform sustainably over time.

7.6 Deployment Topologies and Capacity Planning

The previous sections answered questions about *what* your platform must do: ingest bursts safely, keep history consistent, move data between kdb+ and ClickHouse, survive failures, and remain secure and auditable. This section addresses a more physical question: *where* and *how big* should all of this run?

Architecturally, you now need to:

- Choose deployment topologies that balance latency, resilience, and operational complexity.
- Translate business-facing load descriptions (symbols, messages per second, retention) into concrete capacity for CPU, memory, network, and storage.
- Ensure there is enough headroom to survive peak market stress and growth over time, not just average days.

We begin with deployment patterns, then place a visual comparison, and finally build a simple but robust way to think about capacity planning.

Core Deployment Topologies

For market data platforms centered on kdb+ and ClickHouse, three broad deployment patterns recur:

- Single-region, multi-availability-zone (multi-AZ).
- Active-passive across regions.
- Active-active across regions.

Each pattern must handle:

- kdb+ RDB/HDB tiers for ultra-low-latency intraday and recent history.
- ClickHouse clusters for heavy analytics and longer retention.
- Kafka/Redpanda as the ingestion backbone tying them together.

To frame the discussion, it is helpful to visualize these options side by side.

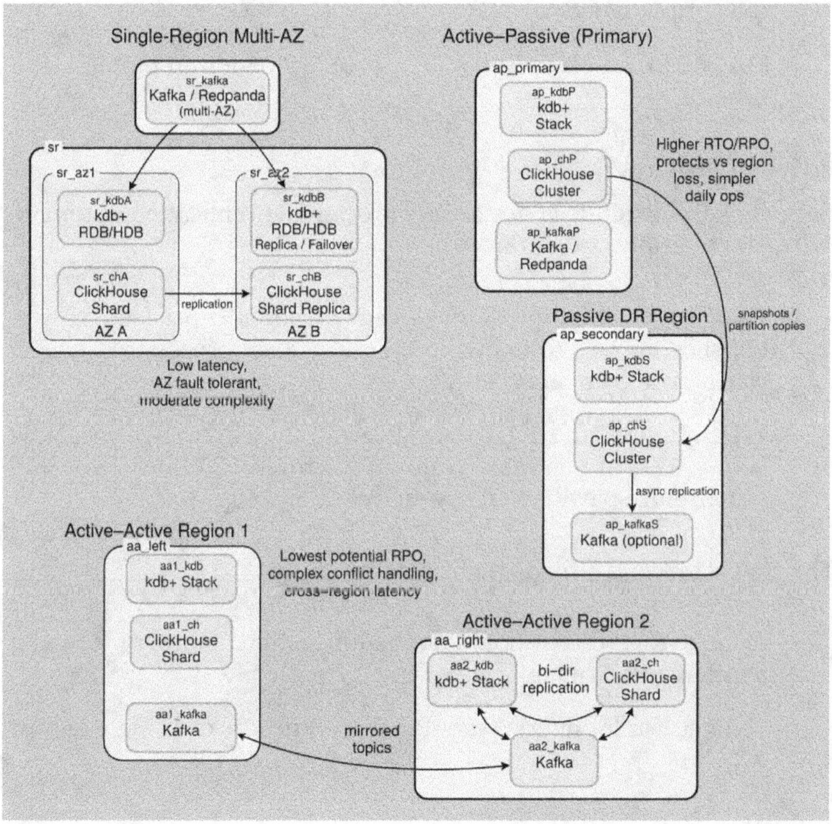

This visual emphasizes that as you move from left to right, you typically gain resilience against large-scale failures but also increase complexity, cross-region latency, and operational burden.

Single-Region Multi-AZ: The Baseline Topology

Most trading platforms start with a single-region, multi-AZ deployment:

- **Low latency**: all components are within a few milliseconds of each other.
- **Reasonable fault tolerance**: one AZ can fail without losing the entire platform.
- **Operational simplicity**: one primary region to monitor and tune.

kdb+ in Multi-AZ

Because kdb+ itself does not handle cross-node replication automatically, you typically structure:

- **RDB layer**: multiple RDB processes, possibly per feed or symbol slice, pinned to nodes across AZs. Each process can have a warm standby in another AZ.
- **HDB layer**: the HDB may live on shared storage available across AZs, or you may maintain mirrored HDB instances and synchronize partitions using snapshot and copy tools.

The goal is to avoid a single point of failure:

- A single RDB crash should not halt ingestion; another process in a different AZ can take over.
- HDB access for queries should survive the loss of a single rack or AZ.

ClickHouse in Multi-AZ

ClickHouse lends itself naturally to this pattern:

- Shards are distributed across AZs.

- Each shard has multiple replicas, ideally in different AZs.
- ZooKeeper or its replacement (depending on deployment) is also deployed across AZs with quorum.

Under normal operations:

- Queries are distributed across shards and replicas.
- A single-node or AZ failure results in temporary load shifting; the cluster continues serving queries and taking writes.

This topology yields high availability for local infrastructure failures while keeping administration focused on one geographic region.

Active-Passive: Regional DR with Simpler Operations

If regulatory constraints, business continuity plans, or risk appetite require surviving the loss of an entire region, an active-passive design is often the next step:

- The primary region handles all normal traffic.
- A secondary region holds a warm or cold copy of critical data and services.
- Failover procedures are tested but invoked only in major incidents.

Data Flow Between Regions

For kdb+:

- HDB partitions are periodically copied or snapped from the primary to the secondary.
- Real-time feeds may be mirrored into both regions via Kafka/Redpanda or separate feed handlers.

For ClickHouse:

- Asynchronous replication streams changes from primary tables to secondary tables, possibly with some lag.

The resulting RPO is roughly:

- The maximum replication lag plus any delay between backups, for datasets not replicated continuously.

Operational Implications

Compared to active-active, active-passive is simpler:

- Only one region is actively serving users at any time.
- You avoid bidirectional conflict resolution.
- Capacity planning is still primarily focused on the primary region, with the secondary sized to take over if needed.

The trade-off is that:

- Failover takes time (affecting RTO).
- Some recent data may be lost, depending on lag (affecting RPO).

These trade-offs must align with the RPO/RTO decisions you made in the backup and DR section.

Active-Active: Low RPO, High Complexity

True active-active deployments, where two regions accept writes for the same datasets, are rare in market data because:

- Cross-region latencies are relatively high.
- Reconciling concurrent writes from multiple regions is complex.

That said, some organizations adopt partial active-active patterns:

- Each region is primary for some desks or asset classes.
- Certain shared datasets (for example, reference data or aggregates) are replicated bidirectionally.

The capacity-planning implication is that:

- Each region must be capable of handling its own local peak plus some fraction of remote load during failover.
- Network bandwidth and replication settings must be dimensioned for steady cross-region flow plus spikes.

Because of the complexity, we will focus capacity-planning techniques on the more typical patterns: single-region multi-AZ and active-passive.

From Business Metrics to Resource Estimates

Regardless of topology, you must answer: *How much capacity do we need?* A disciplined way to approach this is to:

- Express loads in terms the business understands.
- Translate them into technical load drivers.
- Map drivers to CPU, memory, network, and storage.
- Add headroom for peaks and growth.

Step 1: Business-Facing Load Description

Start with simple, concrete questions to the trading and data teams:

- How many instruments do we trade and monitor?
- What are typical and peak messages per second at:

  - normal market conditions,
  - known stress events (open, close, macro announcements)?

- How long must we retain:
  - tick-level data,
  - derived aggregates,
  - orders and executions?

- What query patterns matter most?
  - Tick-by-tick for recent hours?
  - Intraday aggregates per symbol?
  - Multiyear backtests and factor calculations?

From this, derive key parameters such as:

- Peak ingest message rate (per feed, per asset class).
- Average payload size.
- Required daily data volume.
- Query concurrency (how many heavy queries simultaneously).

Step 2: Technical Load Drivers

Next, map these into drivers that kdb+ and ClickHouse experience:

kdb+.

- **Ingestion**: messages per second into RDB/HDB; per-symbol skew; number of parallel streams.
- **Query**: typical window sizes (for example, last hour vs last month), selectivity (per symbol vs wide scans), and concurrency.
- **Storage**: daily footprint of HDB partitions (rows and columns times data type sizes).

ClickHouse.

- **Insert load**: rows per second from Kafka streams and batch loads, partition sizes, merge frequency.
- **Query load**: number and complexity of heavy analytical queries, joins between large tables, groupings across wide ranges.
- **Storage**: on-disk size of partitions after compression, number of parts per partition.

These drivers, combined with small-scale benchmarks or prior experience, help you estimate per-node capacity.

Step 3: Mapping to Resources

Without explicit formulas, we can follow some simple reasoning patterns.

CPU.

CPU is consumed by:

- Parsing and writing data (kdb+ ingestion, ClickHouse INSERTs and merges).
- Query execution (filters, joins, aggregations).
- Background tasks (merges, compactions, replication).

You want enough cores so that:

- Ingestion processes can handle peak message rates without saturating.
- Queries have cores available even during heavy ingest.
- Background tasks do not starve or fall behind.

Practically, this often leads to:

- Dedicated or reserved cores for ingestion and for queries on kdb+ hosts.

- Oversizing ClickHouse shards so that average CPU utilization is well below 100% even during peaks, leaving room for merges.

Memory.

Memory is needed for:

- kdb+ RDBs (in-memory tables).
- Caches in both kdb+ and ClickHouse (hot data, dictionary caches).
- Query working sets and intermediate results.

You estimate memory by:

- Calculating the size of in-memory windows (for example, last N hours of quotes in the RDB).
- Adding overhead for temporary objects and queries.
- Providing safety margin to avoid swapping, which is disastrous for latency.

Network.

Network capacity must cover:

- Ingestion from feeds into Kafka/Redpanda.
- Kafka/Redpanda to kdb+/ClickHouse flows.
- Cross-node replication and query traffic.

To size it:

- Multiply peak messages per second by average message size, adjust for compression.
- Add estimates for replication and query result traffic.

- Ensure underlying links (between AZs, and between regions where applicable) have sufficient headroom even under stress.

Storage and IOPS.

On-disk storage must:

- Hold all retained partitions and replicas.
- Support sufficient throughput and operations per second for ingest and queries.

Tick data compresses well, but you should:

- Estimate raw daily volume, then apply realistic compression ratios.
- Factor in multiple copies (replication, backups, DR).
- Ensure disk I/O and file-system behavior match expected merge and scan patterns in ClickHouse and read patterns in kdb+.

Step 4: Headroom for Peaks and Growth

Finally, avoid sizing purely to average conditions. Markets are volatile; so should your capacity planning be.

Two axes of headroom matter:

Volatility headroom. How much extra load can you handle when volumes spike (for example, during a crisis or unexpected event)? A common practice is to size for:

- A multiple of normal-day peak (for instance, 2–3x) for ingestion and query load.

Growth headroom. How long do you want the current cluster design to last before a major expansion?

- If the business expects volumes to grow steadily, build in enough capacity to avoid constant re-architecture.

Combined, these headroom policies tell you how many instances and what node sizes are appropriate for kdb+, ClickHouse, and Kafka/Redpanda.

Avoiding Hotspots: Sharding and Partitioning in Practice

Even with enough global capacity, you can experience local overloads:

- A single kdb+ process responsible for too many hot symbols.
- A single ClickHouse shard holding a disproportionate share of active data.

To prevent this:

kdb+ Sharding

Sharding in kdb+ is typically done by:

- Splitting instruments into symbol ranges or hashed buckets.
- Assigning each shard to a pair of RDB/HDB hosts (primary and standby) across AZs.

As you grow:

- Monitor per-shard CPU, memory, and latency.
- Rebalance symbol ranges or buckets periodically to spread hot symbols.

This sharding should align with Kafka partitioning, so that ingest traffic for each shard stays roughly balanced.

ClickHouse Sharding and Partitions

ClickHouse shards and partitions must be planned together:

- Use partition keys (for example, by day or month) to group data at a coarse level.

- Use sort keys (for example, symbol and time) to optimize within-partition access.
- Distribute shards so that heavy-query workloads and ingest are spread across hosts.

Avoid:

- Too many tiny partitions and parts, which increase overhead.
- Huge, monolithic partitions that are hard to move and back up.

Balance is again the theme: enough partitions for flexibility, not so many that metadata dominates.

Putting It All Together: A Practical Sizing Workflow

To move from theory to an actionable design, you can adopt a simple workflow:

- **Profile representative workloads.**
  - Replay real or synthetic peak-day traffic into test clusters.
  - Measure per-node resource usage for kdb+, ClickHouse, and Kafka.
- **Scale up from test to production.**
  - Use linear or slightly pessimistic scaling assumptions to estimate how many nodes are needed for target volumes and headroom.
- **Validate end-to-end SLOs.**
  - Ensure ingestion latency, query latency, and replication lag remain within agreed limits under stressed tests.
- **Iterate on topology.**

  - If single-region multi-AZ cannot meet DR requirements, introduce active-passive and re-test.
  - If growth projections are aggressive, design shard layouts that can be expanded without re-partitioning everything.

- **Document assumptions.**
  - Record the load assumptions, hardware profiles, and test results that underpin your sizing.
  - These form the baseline for future reviews as volumes or strategies change.

Capacity planning is not a one-off exercise; it is a living process. But even a modest amount of structured thinking—rooted in topologies, load drivers, and headroom—will put you far ahead of purely reactive scaling.

Deployment topology and capacity planning turn abstract ingestion and reliability designs into concrete clusters that can survive real markets. By:

- Choosing topologies (multi-AZ, active-passive, or active-active) that align with your RPO/RTO and operational maturity.
- Translating business metrics into resource requirements for kdb+, ClickHouse, and Kafka/Redpanda.
- Designing sharding and partitioning to avoid hotspots.
- Building in headroom for volatility and growth.

you create a platform that not only works on quiet days, but also holds up when volumes spike and when the business inevitably grows more ambitious.

In the final section of this chapter we will connect these deployment choices to automation, upgrades, and cost management, showing how to keep such a platform reliable and financially sustainable over its full lifecycle.

7.7 Automation, Upgrades, and FinOps

By this point in the chapter, we have treated your market data platform as something largely static: you designed ingestion, backfill, interoperability, backup and DR, security, and a deployment topology with enough capacity to withstand peaks. In reality, no production platform stays still.

New asset classes are added. Schemas evolve. Operating systems and client libraries receive security patches. Hardware is retired. Cloud bills grow and are questioned. If you treat each of these as a bespoke project, you quickly end up with a fragile, expensive system that nobody wants to touch.

This section is about turning your kdb+, ClickHouse, and Kafka/Redpanda deployment into a *living* system that can change safely and remain financially sustainable. We will:

- Use automation and infrastructure-as-code to make environments reproducible.
- Introduce safe change-management patterns for schema, ingestion code, and upgrades.
- Apply FinOps practices so that storage and compute costs are visible and controllable.

Throughout, we will keep an eye on the constraints specific to trading: low latency, tight change windows, and the need for clear audit trails.

Why Automation Matters for Reliability

Automation is often sold as a way to "go faster." In trading data platforms, its most valuable property is different: *predictability*. If you can create and modify environments the same way every time, you avoid a whole class of subtle, configuration-related failures.

Think of automation at three layers:

- **Infrastructure**: machines, storage volumes, networks, and load-balancers.

- **Platform services**: Kafka/Redpanda clusters, kdb+ RDB/HDB layouts, ClickHouse clusters.
- **Data workloads**: ingestion jobs, schema definitions, and derived views.

Each of these layers should be defined as code and version-controlled.

Infrastructure-as-Code for kdb+, ClickHouse, and Kafka

Infrastructure-as-code (IaC) tools let you describe your environment declaratively:

- Which node types to provision.
- Which subnets and security groups they belong to.
- How disks are attached and mounted.

For this chapter, the key benefits are:

- **Repeatability**: dev, test, and production can be made structurally identical, differing mainly in scale.
- **Drills and DR**: standing up a fresh ClickHouse cluster in another region becomes a push-button operation, not a manual adventure.
- **Upgrade safety**: you can experiment with OS and kernel upgrades in clone environments that match production closely.

On top of IaC, configuration-management tools apply consistent settings:

- Kernel and filesystem tunings appropriate for high I/O and low latency.
- Standardized user accounts, file permissions, and monitoring agents.
- Common layouts for kdb+ HDB directories and ClickHouse data paths.

This avoids the "snowflake server" problem where each node is subtly different.

Declarative Configuration for Platform Services

The next layer is the services themselves. You should aim to:

- Capture Kafka/Redpanda topic configurations (partitions, replication, retention).
- Capture ClickHouse table schemas, storage policies, and user profiles.
- Capture kdb+ table definitions and HDB layout conventions.

in version-controlled artefacts, not just ad-hoc commands. This way:

- You can recreate a cluster from scratch with the same logical structure.
- You can review and approve changes before they are applied.
- You have a historical record of how schemas and configurations evolved.

For example, when a new topic is added to carry options quotes, or a new ClickHouse table is introduced for intraday risk metrics, these become code changes reviewed like any other.

CI/CD for Data Platforms

Continuous integration and continuous delivery (CI/CD) are often associated with application code. The same principles apply to data-platform changes, which broadly fall into three categories:

- Schema and table definitions.
- Ingestion logic (Kafka consumers, kdb+ loaders, ClickHouse materialized views).

- Operational configuration (retention settings, storage policies, partitioning).

Treating Schemas as Code

In the earlier sections, we emphasized schema versioning. CI/CD provides the machinery to manage those versions:

- Define schemas in a central repository.
- For ClickHouse, this might be a set of SQL DDL files; for kdb+, structured definitions of columns and types.
- Changes are proposed as pull requests, reviewed by both platform engineers and data owners.

Automated checks can:

- Detect potentially breaking changes (for example, dropping columns used by downstream tables).
- Verify consistency with lineage metadata and retention policies.

Once merged, a deployment process applies the changes to dev, then test, then production in a controlled order, possibly with smoke tests at each stage.

Testing Ingestion and Transformation Code

Ingestion jobs and transformation scripts—whether written in q, SQL, or general-purpose languages—are effectively the "applications" of your platform. You can:

- Run unit tests against synthetic or sampled data, verifying that transformations behave as expected.
- Run integration tests that:
- Bring up ephemeral Kafka topics, kdb+ instances, or ClickHouse tables.

- Replay a small batch of realistic messages.
- Validate that expected rows appear in the target tables with correct values.

These tests might run:

- On every commit affecting ingestion code.
- On a schedule, replaying recent real data into a staging environment.

This practice catches many bugs early, before they ever reach production volumes.

Controlled Delivery: Canary and Phased Rollouts

Given the sensitivity of trading systems to change, you rarely want to deploy a new ingestion pipeline to all traffic at once. Instead, you can:

- **Canary deploy** a new version of a consumer or transformation to a small subset of topics, symbols, or desks.
- **Shadow** a new pipeline alongside the old one:
- Both consume the same Kafka topics.
- Both write to separate target tables in ClickHouse or kdb+.
- You compare outputs over a period to ensure equivalence.

Once you build confidence, you switch traffic fully to the new path and either decommission or keep the old as a fallback during a short window.

These rollout strategies align well with the ingestion blueprints and backfill mechanisms described earlier, because you already have the ability to replay history and maintain multiple table versions.

Upgrade Strategies for Clusters and Clients

Upgrades are inevitable:

- Security patches for the OS and TLS libraries.
- New versions of Kafka/Redpanda, kdb+, and ClickHouse with performance or correctness fixes.
- Client-library updates for applications interfacing with the platform.

The challenge is to perform these without unplanned downtime or data loss.

Rolling and Blue-Green Upgrades

Two patterns are particularly useful.

Rolling upgrades.

- Upgrade one node at a time in a cluster (Kafka brokers, ClickHouse servers, kdb+ RDB hosts).
- Ensure replicas or alternate nodes continue serving traffic while one is down.

This requires:

- Enough replication or redundancy that losing a node temporarily does not overload the rest.
- Careful ordering (for example, in ClickHouse, upgrading replicas and shards in a sequence that preserves quorum).

Blue-green deployments.

- Stand up a new set of nodes or clusters (blue) with the new version.
- Switch traffic gradually from old (green) to new, typically via load-balancers, DNS, or client configuration.

This is particularly attractive for:

- ClickHouse clusters where you can mirror data to both versions for a period.
- kdb+ HDBs where you can mount the same storage from new processes.

The trade-off is higher short-term resource usage, but the benefit is a much cleaner rollback path: you can route traffic back if you find issues.

Compatibility Testing

Before rolling or blue-green upgrades, you should:

- Validate that client libraries (kdb+ gateways, ClickHouse drivers, Kafka clients) are compatible with new server versions.
- Run representative workloads against upgraded clusters in a staging environment:

- Replaying market data at or above production peak rates.
- Running typical and heavy analytical queries.
- Exercising backfill and late-data paths.

Compare:

- Latency and throughput metrics.
- Resource usage (CPU, memory, I/O).
- Correctness of query results.

Only when the new version behaves acceptably do you schedule production upgrades, ideally during agreed maintenance windows but with plans for mid-day rollbacks if something unexpected occurs.

Fast Rollback Playbooks

Despite careful testing, some upgrades will misbehave under real traffic. You should prepare:

- A documented, rehearsed rollback plan for each major component.
- Steps might include:

- Reverting to previous container images or binaries.
- Rolling back IaC changes.
- Pointing applications back at older clusters or endpoints.

Time is critical: the longer an unstable version runs, the higher the risk of data corruption or trading impact. Automated or semi-automated rollback scripts can make the difference between minutes and hours.

FinOps: Making Costs Visible and Manageable

High-performance data platforms are resource-hungry. Without active cost management, you may end up with:

- Overprovisioned clusters that are mostly idle.
- Long-term retention of data nobody uses.
- Expensive storage media holding cold history.

FinOps—financial operations for cloud and infrastructure—provides a framework to avoid this by:

- Making costs visible and attributable.
- Defining guardrails and budgets.
- Encouraging teams to optimize usage without undermining reliability or performance.

Tagging and Attribution

The first step is to tag resources in a way that maps to business structure:

- Environments: dev, test, staging, production.
- Systems: kdb+, ClickHouse, Kafka/Redpanda, ancillary services.
- Owners: trading desks, risk, surveillance, research.

Tags apply to:

- Compute instances and containers.
- Storage volumes and object storage buckets.
- Network resources, where applicable.

With tagging in place, you can build dashboards that break down:

- Monthly spend by environment and owner.
- Storage costs by dataset or table group (aligned with the storage-governance classifications from earlier).
- Compute costs associated with ingestion, analytics, and backfill workloads.

This attribution is powerful in conversations with desks and support functions: it connects technical resources to business value.

Cost Guardrails and Budgets

Next, you define guardrails, not rigid caps. Examples include:

- Expected maximum footprint for dev and test environments, beyond which a review is triggered.
- Storage budget per dataset tier (for example, Tier-1 historical orders, Tier-2 analytics, Tier-3 scratch).
- CPU-hour or query-cost expectations for certain heavy workloads.

Guardrails are most effective when paired with:

- Regular reviews where data owners see their consumption trends.
- Alerts on abnormal spikes (for example, runaway backfill jobs or forgotten development clusters).

The objective is not to block legitimate usage but to surface inefficient or unintended patterns early.

Cost-Aware Architecture Choices

Many design decisions from earlier sections have cost implications:

- **Retention policies**: keeping every tick forever on expensive storage is rarely necessary for all assets.
- **Compression and file formats**: appropriate compression can drastically reduce disk usage for tick data and derived analytics.
- **Storage tiers**: placing recent data on SSDs and older data on cheaper disks or object storage.

FinOps makes these trade-offs explicit:

- For a given dataset, you can compare the cost of an additional year of retention on fast disks with its actual usage by desks.
- You can quantify the savings from moving certain tables to colder storage at the cost of slightly higher query latency.

These discussions are easier when backed by real numbers rather than abstract claims.

Closing the Loop: Continuous Improvement

Automation, upgrades, and FinOps are most effective when they form a loop rather than isolated practices. A simple continuous-improvement cycle for your market data platform might look like this:

1. **Provision and configure via code.**
   - Use IaC and configuration management to create environments.
   - Ensure security, monitoring, and baseline tunings are baked in.
2. **Deploy and evolve workloads through CI/CD.**
   - Treat schemas, ingestion code, and operational settings as versioned artefacts.
   - Use test environments, canaries, and rollbacks.
3. **Observe performance, reliability, and cost.**
   - Collect metrics and logs across kdb+, ClickHouse, Kafka/Redpanda.
   - Monitor not only latency and errors, but also utilization and spend.
4. **Optimize and refactor.**
   - Adjust topologies, sharding, and retention based on observed usage.
   - Decommission underused datasets or scale down overprovisioned clusters.
5. **Feed learnings back into design.**
   - Update runbooks, DR plans, and capacity models.
   - Incorporate new patterns into templates so that future environments start from a better baseline.

Over time, this loop turns operations from a reactive burden into an ongoing, data-informed engineering process.

This section extended the chapter from static architecture to dynamic operation. We have seen that:

- Automation and infrastructure-as-code make kdb+, ClickHouse, and Kafka/Redpanda deployments reproducible and testable.

- CI/CD for schemas, ingestion pipelines, and configuration changes allows safe, incremental evolution of the platform.
- Carefully planned upgrade strategies and rollbacks are essential to keep up with security and performance improvements without destabilizing trading.
- FinOps practices bring cost into the conversation, ensuring that data retention, replication, and performance are balanced against financial reality.

Together with the ingestion, backfill, interoperability, DR, and security practices from earlier sections, these techniques complete the picture of a high-performance market data platform that can not only handle today's demands, but can also adapt and scale with the markets and the business in the years ahead.

Chapter 8

Applied Analytics and Architectural Patterns

This chapter turns raw ticks and order messages into trading edge. Rather than discussing features or functions in isolation, we walk through complete analytics patterns-limit order books, TCA, backtests, and real-time risk-and show how to wire kdb+ and ClickHouse into opinionated, production-ready architectures. You will see how design choices in schemas, joins, partitions, and streaming pipelines directly translate into latency, cost, and robustness at scale.

8.1 Limit Order Book Analytics

In earlier chapters we have focused on market data foundations: how ticks arrive, how to ingest them with predictable latency, and how to store them efficiently in kdb+ and ClickHouse. We now turn to one of the most demanding consumers of that infrastructure: limit order book (LOB) analytics.

A limit order book records all standing limit orders to buy and sell a given instrument. For electronic markets, the LOB is the microstructure. Trading strategies, execution algorithms, and real-time risk all depend on fast, consistent views of the book. Our goal in this section is to design an end-to-end LOB analytics stack that:

- reconstructs a consistent book from raw exchange messages,
- stores both events and snapshots in kdb+ and ClickHouse,
- uses temporal joins to align books with trades and reference data, and
- exposes pre-aggregated features with sub-second delivery for both research and live trading.

We will proceed in layers, moving from raw messages to reconstruction, then to storage design, then to temporal alignment and feature computation, and finally to pre-aggregation and serving patterns. At each step, we will contrast idiomatic kdb+ and ClickHouse approaches, so you can design architectures that use each technology where it is strongest.

From Raw Feeds to a Logical LOB Pipeline

Before diving into schemas and joins, it is helpful to have a single mental picture of the pipeline we are aiming for. Conceptually, an LOB analytics system has five stages:

- **Raw market-feed ingest**: capture order and trade messages from exchange or vendor feeds with minimal transformation.
- **Book reconstruction**: apply messages in time order to build a consistent LOB state (top-of-book or full depth).
- **Storage layouts**: persist both events and reconstructed states in kdb+ and ClickHouse, choosing schemas that fit query patterns.
- **Temporal joins and enrichment**: align orders, books, trades, and reference data into analysis-ready tables.

- **Feature and signal serving**: maintain pre-aggregated features that can be served within sub-second SLAs to strategies and dashboards.

The rest of this section unpacks each of these stages in detail.

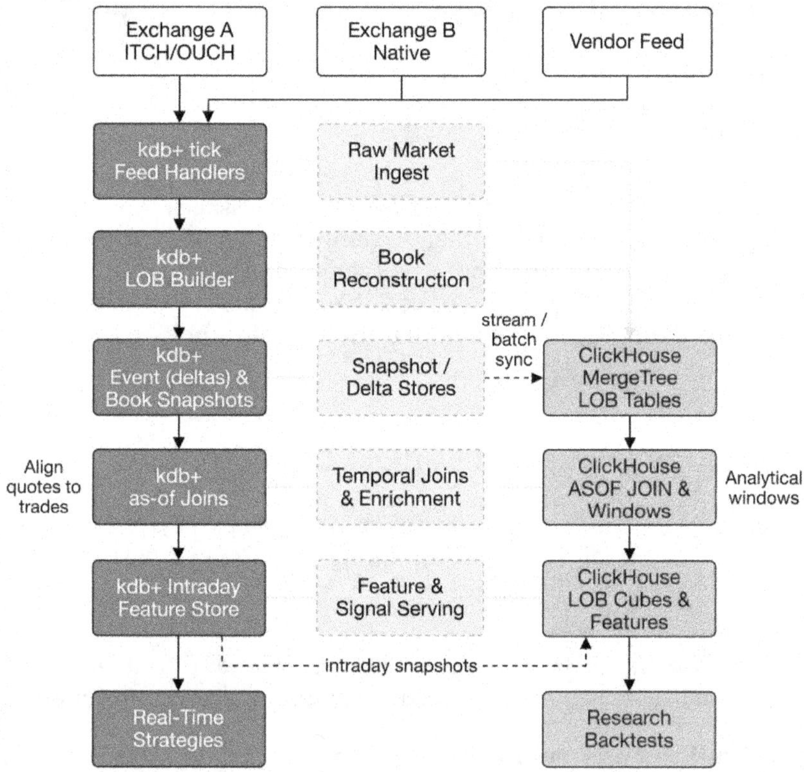

Order and Trade Message Schemas

Everything begins with the messages emitted by exchanges or vendors. While formats vary (ITCH, OUCH, FIX, native binary protocols), logically they all carry the same core ideas:

- **Order add**: a new limit order appears in the book.
- **Order modify**: an existing order changes its size or price.
- **Order cancel**: an existing order is removed.
- **Trade / execution**: two orders match and a trade occurs.
- **Administrative events**: trading halts, symbol status changes, sequence resets, and similar.

For reconstruction and analytics, it helps to think in terms of two logical tables:

- **Orders / deltas:** records every operation that changes the book. Typical columns include timestamp, symbol, side (buy or sell), price, size, order identifier, message type (add, modify, cancel, execution), and a venue sequence number if available.
- **Trades:** records completed executions. These may be derived from the order messages or reported separately by the venue. Typical fields include timestamp, symbol, price, size, aggressor side, and trade qualifiers (e.g. auction, hidden, off-book).

The exact column names and types will vary between kdb+ and ClickHouse, but the logical schema should be as consistent as possible across systems. Consistency is crucial later when you stream data from kdb+ into ClickHouse or reconcile analytics across them.

Two design choices at this stage have large downstream impact:

- **Timestamps:** Use a single, high-resolution event time column, always in a common time zone (UTC is standard). If you retain both exchange and receipt times, keep them separate so you can reason about them explicitly.
- **Identifiers:** Store stable identifiers such as order ID, symbol ID, and venue ID with enough width that you never need to renumber or re-encode after deployment. Changing identifiers midstream is one of the fastest ways to complicate book reconstruction and historical analysis.

Robust Book Reconstruction

Book reconstruction is the process of taking a stream of order events and computing the state of the LOB at each point in time. For a given symbol, the book is essentially two sorted lists:

- bids, ordered by descending price and then by time (for queue position),
- asks, ordered by ascending price and then by time.

A naive approach would simply sort all events by timestamp and apply them in order. In production, there are three complications you must address:

- **Out-of-order messages:** messages may arrive slightly out of order with respect to event time.
- **Late messages:** data may be delayed by milliseconds or seconds relative to the main stream.
- **Gaps and resets:** you may miss messages or encounter sequence resets from the exchange.

Sequence-Aware Application

Most modern feeds carry a per-venue or per-channel sequence number. When available, use it. The reconstruction logic should apply events in sequence order, not just in timestamp order. This ensures that local clock jitter or slight differences in time stamping do not corrupt the book.

When a gap in sequence is detected:

- if the gap is small and you have a backfill mechanism, pause and request the missing slice,
- if the gap is large or cannot be filled promptly, mark the book as unreliable and, if possible, resync from a full depth snapshot provided by the venue.

Handling Late and Out-of-Order Messages

Two time windows matter:

- **Reconstruction window:** how much you are willing to reorder events to restore correct sequence. For example, you might buffer a few milliseconds of data, reorder by sequence, then apply.
- **Analytics window:** how much historical state you retain in memory for downstream feature computation (such as recent depth or short-horizon volatility).

For ultra-low-latency analytics, you typically accept that extremely late messages will not be retroactively applied; instead, they correct the book for subsequent events. For historical analytics (e.g. overnight backfills), you can rebuild the book from scratch, sorting by sequence or timestamp over the full day.

Top-of-Book vs. Full-Depth

Reconstructing the full depth of book means tracking all price levels and orders. This is required for some microstructure research but is more computationally heavy. Many production analytics can be expressed in terms of:

- best bid and ask (top-of-book),
- a small number of levels nearest the touch (level-2),
- or aggregate measures such as total bid and ask volume within a price window.

In practice, a good pattern is:

- maintain a full-depth representation in memory for symbols where it is required,
- periodically derive a compact "view" (for example, the top 10 levels on each side) and store only that view for fast analytics,

- persist event deltas so that you can reconstruct full depth offline if needed.

kdb+ is well-suited to in-memory reconstruction because of its vectorized operations and tight integration with feed handlers. For example, you can maintain a per-symbol in-memory state that is updated by the real-time database (RDB) process and periodically flushed to the historical database (HDB). ClickHouse typically receives already reconstructed or partially aggregated data from kdb+, or from an external reconstruction service, and focuses on deeper retention and broader scans.

Snapshot vs. Event / Delta Storage

Once we can reconstruct the book, we must decide what to store. The two canonical representations are:

- **Event / delta format:** each row represents a change to the book (an order add, cancel, modify, or trade).
- **Snapshot format:** each row represents the entire book (or a fixed prefix of it) at a point in time, such as every millisecond or every change.

Each representation has trade-offs in write amplification, replay cost, and query latency.

Event / Delta Format

In an event table, each incoming message becomes a row. The advantages are:

- minimal write amplification: you write each event once,
- flexible replay: you can reconstruct the book at any granularity by applying events,
- compact storage: each row is small, and compression works well because many fields repeat.

The main drawback is that queries that need the state of the book at many time points must either reconstruct on the fly or rely on precomputed views.

For kdb+, event tables live naturally in the HDB, partitioned by date and often keyed by symbol. For ClickHouse, event tables are a good fit for MergeTree engines, partitioned by date and perhaps by venue or symbol range, with primary indexes ordered by (symbol, timestamp).

Snapshot Format

In snapshot tables, each row holds the state of the book at a snapshot time. A snapshot can be:

- *event-driven*: every time the top-of-book changes, store a new row with the new best bid and ask and their sizes, or
- *time-driven*: at a fixed frequency (for example, every millisecond), store the current book state.

The advantages are:

- fast query response for state-based analytics (for example, compute spread or depth at each snapshot time),
- simplified joins: you can as-of join a trade directly to the nearest snapshot.

The main drawbacks are:

- higher write amplification: many small changes can result in many snapshots,
- larger storage footprint, especially at high frequencies.

In kdb+, snapshot tables are often stored as columnar tables in the HDB, with one row per snapshot per symbol. In ClickHouse, snapshot tables also map cleanly to MergeTree, where partitioning by date and ordering by (symbol, snapshot time) enables efficient scans.

Hybrid Strategy

Most production systems use a hybrid approach:

- **Events** are stored at full fidelity for auditability and offline reconstruction.
- **Snapshots** are derived from the events and stored at a frequency and depth that balance analytics needs and storage cost.

kdb+ is often the source of truth for intraday events and near-real-time snapshots, while ClickHouse stores downsampled or aggregated snapshots for multi-year horizons. The schema design should make this flow natural: field names, symbol encodings, and time conventions should line up so that exporting from kdb+ and ingesting into ClickHouse is mechanical.

Temporal Joins: Aligning Books, Trades, and Reference Data

Having stored both events and snapshots, the next task is to line up different streams in time. A typical analytics question looks like:

> "What was the order book state one microsecond before each of my trades, and where was my order in the queue at that moment?"

This requires joining the trades table with the LOB snapshot or event-derived state based on time.

As-Of Joins in kdb+

kdb+ has a built-in concept of as-of joins: for each row in the left table, find the most recent row in the right table that shares a key (such as symbol) and has a timestamp less than or equal to the left timestamp.

In words, you can think of it as:

- walking forward through trades,
- and, for each trade, looking backwards in book snapshots until you find the last one before the trade.

This works efficiently when both tables are sorted by time and keyed by symbol. Since kdb+ stores tables column-wise and can maintain them in time order, this is a natural operation for intraday analytics.

ASOF JOIN and Window Functions in ClickHouse

ClickHouse has a similar concept called ASOF JOIN, which aligns two tables based on a key and the nearest earlier timestamp. The idea is the same: for each trade row, find the most recent LOB snapshot row not later than the trade time.

Beyond ASOF JOIN, ClickHouse offers window functions that let you express rolling metrics over time, such as moving averages or short-horizon volatility. When combined with partitioning and ordering that align with typical analytics (for example, by symbol and time), these operations can scan large volumes of data efficiently.

Reference Data Enrichment

Temporal joins are not only for books and trades. You will also want to align:

- instrument reference data (tick size, lot size, trading status),
- corporate actions (splits, symbol changes),
- and perhaps risk parameters or strategy configurations.

In both kdb+ and ClickHouse, a standard pattern is:

- Maintain slowly changing reference tables with effective-from and effective-to timestamps.

- When computing analytics, as-of join your fact data (events, snapshots, trades) to the reference tables using the symbol and timestamp.

This ensures, for example, that you always use the correct tick size and multiplier corresponding to the trade date.

Core LOB Features and How to Compute Them

With a solid temporal-join framework, you can define a library of LOB features. We will focus on a few that are widely used and that illustrate different computational patterns.

Queue Position

Queue position aims to quantify how much volume stands ahead of a given order at its price level. Intuitively, if you submit a buy order at a given price, and there are already 1000 shares resting at that price, your order will not fill until those 1000 shares move.

To estimate queue position, you need:

- a per-order view of the book when the order was entered,
- the total resting volume at that price on the same side at that time,
- and, optionally, a notion of order priority (time, pro-rata, or other).

In kdb+, one pattern is:

- During reconstruction, track total size at each price level.
- When a new limit order is added, record the current volume at that price as "queue ahead".
- As trades and cancels occur, track how much of the ahead volume has been depleted.

The key is that queue position is easiest to compute in an event-driven, stateful engine (such as kdb+ RDB during live trading) because it depends on the exact sequence of events. For historical analysis in ClickHouse, you may instead work with approximations based on snapshots and trade volumes.

Realized Spread

Realized spread measures how favorable the execution price of a trade was compared to the future mid-price. It is often defined as the difference between the trade price and the mid-price a short time later, with the sign chosen so that positive values indicate profitable trades for a liquidity provider.

To compute it, you need:

- a trades table with execution price and side,
- a snapshots table providing mid-prices at the initial time and at a later horizon (such as 5 seconds),
- temporal joins to align trades with snapshots at both times.

In kdb+, you can perform as-of joins from trades to snapshots at the trade time and at trade time plus the chosen horizon. In ClickHouse, you can either precompute snapshot times or use window functions to find the appropriate rows. Because this involves looking forward in time, it is more naturally computed in batch rather than in a live engine.

Order Book Imbalance

Order book imbalance attempts to measure the pressure in the book by comparing total bid and ask volume near the mid-price. A common definition is:

> imbalance = (bid volume near the best − ask volume near the best) divided by (bid volume near the best + ask volume near the best).

Conceptually, you:

- choose a price window around the mid-price or a fixed number of levels,
- sum bid sizes and ask sizes within that window,
- compute the ratio.

On top-of-book snapshots, an approximation would simply use the best bid and best ask volumes. On deeper snapshots, you can include multiple levels. This is a purely snapshot-based computation, which makes it an ideal candidate for pre-aggregation:

- In kdb+, you can compute imbalance whenever you write a new snapshot row.
- In ClickHouse, you can compute imbalance when building intraday or daily cubes, storing it alongside basic measures like spread and depth.

Microprice

Microprice refines the mid-price by weighting the best bid and best ask by their respective volumes. Intuitively, if there is much more volume on the bid than on the ask, the true equilibrium price may be slightly closer to the ask, suggesting upward pressure.

This is another snapshot-level feature: every time the top-of-book changes, you can recompute microprice and store it. In kdb+, it is natural to compute this in the same process that maintains the book. In ClickHouse, you can store precomputed microprice in your snapshots or compute it on the fly during analyses.

Short-Horizon Volatility

Short-horizon volatility is an important risk and execution measure. At a high level, you want to know how much the mid-price moves over a short window, such as 1 second or 10 seconds. There are many ways to define this:

- as a rolling standard deviation of price changes,
- as a realized volatility based on returns over fixed intervals,
- or as a simple high-low range over the window.

In both kdb+ and ClickHouse, this is naturally expressed as a rolling operation over snapshots, grouped by symbol. In kdb+, you may maintain short lists of recent mid-prices in memory and update volatility incrementally as new snapshots arrive. In ClickHouse, rolling-window functions over partitioned and ordered data let you compute volatility over large historical ranges.

Pre-Aggregation and Materialization Patterns

The features described above can be computed on demand, but many production systems pre-aggregate them to meet latency targets and reduce load on the underlying tick store.

Intraday LOB Cubes

An intraday LOB cube is a table that aggregates LOB measures into time buckets and symbol groupings. A typical design might store, for each symbol and 1-second interval:

- average spread, minimum spread, and maximum spread,
- average and maximum depth at the best bid and ask,
- average and maximum imbalance,
- average and maximum microprice deviation from the mid-price,
- short-horizon volatility measured over a few seconds.

For live use in kdb+:

- an RDB process consumes snapshots,
- groups them into per-symbol, per-interval statistics,

- and maintains an in-memory table with the latest few minutes or hours of cube data.

This cube table can then be queried by strategies or exported periodically to ClickHouse.

For deep historical analysis in ClickHouse:

- you ingest intraday cubes from kdb+ or recompute them in ClickHouse from raw snapshots,
- partition by date and perhaps by symbol range,
- and use them for backtests, TCA, and model training, avoiding full tick-level scans for every query.

Symbol–Venue Rollups

Modern trading often involves multiple venues or pools. Analytics frequently require:

- per-venue LOB measures, to understand local liquidity and spreads,
- aggregate, consolidated LOB measures, to understand the national or global best bid and offer.

In kdb+, a per-symbol, per-venue table can hold raw or lightly aggregated measures. A rolling consolidation process can:

- compute the best bid and ask across venues at each time,
- aggregate depth across venues,
- measure fragmentation by comparing venue-specific spreads to consolidated spreads.

These consolidated series are then materialized either as part of the intraday cube or as a separate table.

In ClickHouse, you can store per-venue and consolidated series in the same tables with flags or separate tables partitioned consistently. Grouped aggregations by venue, region, or other dimensions are cheap when data is stored column-wise and partitioned intelligently.

Time-Bucketed Feature Stores

Finally, we arrive at the feature-serving layer. Many strategies consume features at a regular cadence: for example, every 100 milliseconds or every second. A time-bucketed feature store aims to present, for each symbol and time bucket:

- precomputed LOB features (spread, depth, imbalance, microprice),
- recent-return or volatility measures,
- and possibly external signals (news, market indices) aligned in time.

In kdb+, you can maintain this feature store entirely in memory for the current trading session. Each time bucket is updated as new snapshots and trades arrive. Strategies can subscribe to updates via pub/sub, or poll the feature table directly.

In ClickHouse, a similar structure can be maintained as a table partitioned by date and ordered by symbol and time bucket. This provides:

- a clean interface for backtesting: strategies can read features as if they were live,
- a simple way to ensure that backtests and production share the same feature definitions, by generating both from the same pipelines.

Putting It Together: Sub-Second Feature Delivery

We can now summarize the architectural pattern that delivers subsecond LOB features using both kdb+ and ClickHouse:

- **Ingest:** Feed handlers ingest raw exchange or vendor messages into kdb+ tick and optionally into a ClickHouse staging area.
- **Reconstruction:** A kdb+ RDB performs sequence-aware book reconstruction, maintaining full or partial depth in memory.
- **Storage:** Events and snapshots are persisted in kdb+ HDB for intraday and recent days, and streamed or batch-exported into ClickHouse MergeTree tables for deeper history.
- **Temporal alignment:** kdb+ uses as-of joins to align trades, books, and reference data in real time; ClickHouse uses ASOF JOIN and window functions for historical alignment at scale.
- **Pre-aggregation:** kdb+ maintains intraday cubes and time-bucketed feature stores in memory for low-latency serving; ClickHouse builds larger LOB cubes and rollups for research and reporting.
- **Serving:** Strategies and dashboards consume features directly from kdb+ with sub-second latency, while backtesting, TCA, and analytics in ClickHouse use the same feature definitions applied to multi-year history.

The key to reliability and performance is consistency: shared schemas, shared definitions of features, and clear ownership boundaries between kdb+ (intraday, low-latency) and ClickHouse (historical, large-scale). With this structure in place, you can add new LOB features or strategy signals with confidence that they will behave the same in production and in research, and that the underlying data stores will keep up with both the speed and volume of modern electronic markets.

8.2 Transaction Cost Analysis Pipelines

In the previous section we focused on limit order book analytics: reconstructing the book, storing events and snapshots, and precomputing microstructure features with sub-second latency. We now move one level up the trading stack, from what *the market* is doing to what *you* are doing in that market.

Transaction Cost Analysis (TCA) asks a simple question: given a trading decision, how well did we execute it relative to realistic benchmarks? To answer that at scale, you need more than a spreadsheet. You need a pipeline that can ingest messy execution records and quotes, normalize them into a consistent structure, line them up in time, and compute a library of metrics that can be sliced by strategy, broker, venue, and client.

This section builds such a pipeline step by step, using the LOB and tick infrastructure already in place. We will:

- define a normalized schema for orders, executions, quotes, and benchmarks,
- show how to temporally align executions and quotes in kdb+ and ClickHouse,
- derive core TCA metrics (slippage and benchmark comparisons),
- and discuss architectural patterns that keep TCA scalable and maintainable.

Throughout, the emphasis remains on how kdb+ and ClickHouse support these tasks in a complementary way.

What a TCA Pipeline Needs to Do

At its core, a TCA system has four responsibilities:

- **Collect**: bring together order instructions, actual executions, and market data (quotes and trades).
- **Normalize**: map heterogeneous, often broker-specific data formats into a unified schema.
- **align***: use time-aware joins to match executions with the state of the market at relevant moments.
- **Compute**: calculate cost metrics and make them available for reporting and interactive analysis.

Conceptually, a TCA question looks like:

> "For this order that intended to buy 100,000 shares between 10:00 and 10:15, how did the prices we achieved compare to various benchmarks: the price at decision time, the volume-weighted average market price over the interval, or the mid-price trajectory after completion?"

To answer that consistently for millions of orders and executions, day after day, we must start with a clean data model.

Normalizing Orders, Executions, Quotes, and Benchmarks

Real-world TCA data is messy. Different brokers choose different field names, encodings, and time conventions. Even within a single firm, trading desks may log slightly different variations of the same concept. Without normalization, any metric becomes ambiguous and hard to reproduce.

A practical approach is to define a small set of *core tables* that everything else flows into. The exact column names will vary by organization, but the logical contents are similar.

Order Instructions

An **order** in the TCA sense is a high-level instruction, not necessarily a single exchange order. For example, "Buy 100,000 shares of XYZ today VWAP" is a TCA order, even though it may be executed via hundreds of child orders across multiple venues.

A normalized order table should include:

- a stable *order identifier* within your system,
- instrument or symbol, side (buy/sell), and notional or share quantity,
- timestamps such as decision time (when the portfolio manager decided to trade) and release time (when the algo started working the order),

- execution objective or strategy (for example, VWAP, participation, implementation shortfall),
- any client and portfolio identifiers relevant for grouping.

These fields give you the context needed to interpret costs later.

Executions

An **execution** is a fill: a completed trade that changes your position. Multiple executions belong to one order.

A normalized execution table should capture:

- the order identifier, plus a unique execution identifier,
- execution timestamp in a standard time zone,
- execution price and quantity,
- side (buy/sell) and possibly aggressor flag if known (did you cross the spread?),
- venue, broker, and route,
- flags for special conditions (auction, dark pool, alternative trading system).

If you have access to rich microstructure data, you may also want to log a reference to the underlying market trade identifier, but the basic TCA metrics can be computed without it.

Quotes and Trades

On the market side, you already have:

- **quotes** from your LOB pipeline: at minimum, best bid and best ask prices and sizes over time; ideally, deeper levels,
- **trades** from consolidated or per-venue feeds: last traded price, size, and time.

For TCA, the essential thing is that these quote and trade tables use the same instrument identifiers and timestamps as your execution tables, or can be mapped into them with a small dimension lookup.

Benchmarks

A **benchmark** is any reference price or trajectory against which you wish to compare your executions. Some benchmarks are derived directly from quotes:

- the mid-price at decision time,
- the mid-price at order release time,
- the mid-price at completion.

Others are more aggregate:

- the volume-weighted average price (VWAP) of market trades over your execution interval,
- the time-weighted average mid-price (TWAP),
- an index or fair-value reference for multi-asset or basket orders.

Rather than hard-coding benchmarks in reports, a robust pipeline will:

- create a normalized *benchmark definition* table that names each benchmark and records its recipe (for example, "VWAP over execution interval using primary exchange prints"),
- materialize benchmark values per order and per execution in a separate table, so reports can reuse them consistently.

Temporal Alignment Between Executions and Quotes

With normalized tables in place, the next challenge is to align them in time. Almost every TCA metric requires some variant of the same basic operation:

for a given execution or order, find the relevant quote or trade information "around" its timestamp.

In kdb+ and ClickHouse, this is handled through temporal joins.

As-Of Joins in kdb+ for Intraday TCA

Recall from the LOB chapter that kdb+ offers an as-of join: for each timestamp in one table (for example, executions), it finds the nearest earlier row in another table (for example, quotes) with matching keys such as symbol.

For TCA, we use as-of joins to:

- match each execution to the best bid and ask in effect at that moment,
- match each execution to the mid-price and spread at that moment,
- match decision and release timestamps to their mid-prices to create benchmark prices.

Because kdb+ typically holds the current day or recent days of quotes and trades in memory, these joins can be done interactively for intraday TCA dashboards. The same logic can later be rerun over historical data in the HDB for larger batch jobs.

ClickHouse ASOF JOIN and Window Functions for Historical TCA

For longer horizons and heavier workloads (months of executions across many clients), ClickHouse is a better fit. Its ASOF JOIN serves the same conceptual purpose as kdb+'s as-of join: for each execution, find the most recent quote at or before the execution time.

Window functions further extend this by letting you compute rolling quantities such as:

- VWAP over an interval,
- cumulative executed quantity per order as time progresses,
- reversion of prices after an execution.

A typical pattern in ClickHouse looks like:

- Partition and order data by symbol and time so that queries scan sequential runs of records.
- Use ASOF JOIN to bring mid-price and spread columns from the quotes table into the execution table.
- Use window functions grouped by order identifier to compute per-order aggregates (for example, average execution price, execution interval).

This mirrors what we do in kdb+ but operates at the scale of months or years of data with acceptable runtimes.

Practical Complications: Crossed Markets, Stale Quotes, Auctions

In theory, you could assume quotes are always clean and up to date. In practice, several issues arise:

Crossed or Locked Markets. A crossed market occurs when the best bid is higher than the best ask; a locked market occurs when they are equal. These situations are usually transient data anomalies or result from latency and routing issues. For TCA, you typically want to avoid using crossed or locked quotes as benchmarks. Two common approaches are:

- filter out quotes where the bid is greater than or equal to the ask when computing mid-prices,
- or fall back to the last "normal" quote before the execution.

Stale Quotes. In fast markets, quotes can become stale quickly. If the last quote update is far in the past relative to the execution time, it may no longer be a good representation of the market. To guard against this, you can:

- impose a freshness threshold: only use quotes whose timestamp is within a small window before the execution,

- if no fresh quote is available, mark the benchmark as missing or use a coarser benchmark (for example, last trade price instead of mid-price).

Auctions and Special Trades. Opening and closing auctions, and certain off-book trades, may not behave like continuous trading. You might choose to:

- tag executions that occur during auctions and treat them with separate benchmarks,
- exclude auction prints from VWAP calculations aimed at measuring continuous trading performance.

Both kdb+ and ClickHouse can carry these flags as additional columns and apply them during the temporal join and metric computation steps.

Core TCA Metrics and How to Compute Them

With executions and quotes aligned, we can define the key metrics that most TCA systems provide. We will describe them conceptually and focus on how the data flows, rather than on specific formulas.

Arrival Cost and Implementation Shortfall

Arrival cost compares the execution price to the market price at a key reference time, often when the trader first decided to trade (decision time) or when the order was released to the market.

Conceptually, for each execution:

- identify the relevant reference time (for example, order decision time),
- use an as-of join to find the mid-price or reference price at that time,
- compute the difference between the execution price and this reference price, adjusting the sign so that positive values represent costs for the trader.

Implementation shortfall generalizes this at the order level. It measures the difference between:

- the hypothetical return if you could have traded instantly at the decision price, and
- the actual return based on your executed prices and timing.

Computationally, this involves:

- aggregating all executions belonging to an order to compute a volume-weighted average execution price,
- comparing that to the decision price for the full notional of the order,
- optionally adjusting for price movements after the order completes.

In kdb+, this aggregate is easily computed with group-by operations over the executions table, keyed by order identifier. In ClickHouse, you can achieve the same with grouped aggregations and, if needed, window functions to track the evolution of fills over time.

VWAP and TWAP Slippage

VWAP (volume-weighted average price) measures the average price of market trades, weighted by volume, over a period. For TCA, you typically compare your execution price to the market VWAP during your execution interval.

The pipeline is:

- Define the interval: from order release time to completion time.
- Restrict market trades to that interval and the relevant venues (for example, primary exchange only or all lit markets).
- Compute VWAP using trade price and size.
- Compare your average execution price to this VWAP.

TWAP (time-weighted average price) uses quotes instead of trades: it averages mid-prices over time, not weighted by volume. TWAP slippage compares your execution price to this time average.

In kdb+, these operations are natural in a streaming context for intraday estimation, but they are often computed more comprehensively overnight across the full day. In ClickHouse, VWAP and TWAP are classic use cases for window functions and grouped aggregations, using the large historical quote and trade tables that ClickHouse is designed to scan efficiently.

Reversion and Market Impact

Reversion measures how the mid-price behaves after your execution: does it move back towards the pre-trade level or continue in the direction of your trade? This gives a sense of whether your activity temporarily pushed the price and how quickly that impact decays.

Conceptually:

- For each execution, record the mid-price just before the trade and at several points after (for example, 1 second and 5 minutes later).
- Compute the differences to see how much the price moved against or in favor of you.
- Aggregate these differences across executions, grouped by order characteristics, liquidity, or trading style.

Market-impact curves extend this across the life of the order: as you work a large order, you track how your cumulative executed volume and participation rate relate to contemporaneous price moves and spreads.

Both measures rely heavily on temporal alignment and on the ability to look *forward* in time from each execution, which is simpler in batch processing. ClickHouse is particularly effective here: once you have a table of executions enriched with pre- and post-trade mid-prices (via ASOF JOINs and window functions), you can build reversion and impact reports on top.

Architectural Patterns for Scalable TCA

So far we have discussed the logical flow of data and metrics. We now step back and examine how to structure the system so that it scales from daily reports to interactive queries over months of data.

Partitioning Around Reporting Horizons

TCA questions tend to have clear time horizons:

- daily or intraday for trading desks and clients who want fresh feedback,
- weekly or monthly for risk and oversight teams,
- multi-year for model calibration and regulatory review.

You can mirror this in your storage design:

- In kdb+, use daily partitions for orders, executions, and quotes, with RDB processes holding today's data in memory and HDB tables covering recent weeks or months.
- In ClickHouse, partition tables by date (for example, trade date or execution date) and order by keys that reflect common access patterns (such as client, strategy, and time) so that queries can prune partitions and scan efficiently.

Aligning partitioning across orders, executions, and quotes simplifies joins and batch jobs. For example, a daily TCA job for a given desk can be expressed as a set of queries over that day's partition only.

Pre-Aggregated Fact Tables

Computing TCA metrics directly from raw executions and ticks for every query is wasteful. A better approach is to materialize *fact tables* that hold metrics at the level most reports use.

Three common fact levels are:

- Execution-level facts: metrics computed per execution, such as slippage to arrival price, spread at time of trade, and local volatility. These are useful for micro-level studies and quality checks.

- Order-level facts: aggregated metrics per parent order, including implementation shortfall, VWAP slippage, and completion times. This is the primary lens for many TCA reports.
- Portfolio or basket-level facts: metrics that roll up orders by client, strategy, or portfolio per day or per period.

A typical pattern is:

- In kdb+, run intraday jobs that join executions with quotes and compute execution-level metrics into an in-memory or nearline table.
- At end of day, aggregate execution-level metrics into order-level and portfolio-level fact tables and persist them.
- Export these fact tables to ClickHouse, where they can be kept for years and queried interactively by front-ends and analysts.

Because these fact tables are already keyed at the level of interest, most TCA queries no longer need to touch tick-level data. The heavy temporal joins and window functions live in controlled batch processes, not in every dashboard query.

Reusable Query Templates

TCA reports often share a small number of core structures:

- distribution of implementation shortfall by order size and participation rate,
- VWAP slippage broken down by broker and venue,
- reversion curves aggregated by instrument liquidity.

Rather than building each report as a bespoke query, you can define *query templates* that take dimensions and filters as parameters. For example, a template might:

- select fact rows for a date range and a set of clients,

- group by a bucketed variable (such as order size deciles),
- compute summary statistics (median, percentile bands),
- and return results in a standard shape.

In kdb+, such templates may be implemented as parameterized functions over fact tables. In ClickHouse, they can be SQL views or stored queries with placeholders. The benefit is consistency: when a new report or dashboard is added, it reuses the same logic rather than re-implementing metrics from scratch.

Interactive Drill-Down Without Duplicating Logic

One of the main user demands for TCA is interactive drill-down: being able to click from a high-level chart into the underlying orders and executions that drove a metric. Architecturally, this is easiest if:

- your fact tables retain stable identifiers linking back to orders and executions,
- your query templates support both aggregated and detailed modes.

For example:

- A chart may call a template that returns bucket-level statistics for implementation shortfall.
- When the user clicks a bucket, a second query can constrain the same fact table to orders in that bucket (by identifier or by the underlying range of values) and return the raw rows or a more granular aggregation.

Because both queries draw from the same normalized and precomputed facts, they remain internally consistent. kdb+ can serve such drill-downs efficiently for recent data; ClickHouse can provide the same behavior over longer history.

Putting It Together: A Cohesive TCA Stack

We can now summarize the TCA pipeline in the same layered way we approached LOB analytics:

- **Ingest and normalize:** collect orders, executions, quotes, and trades from heterogeneous sources, and map them into unified kdb+ and ClickHouse schemas.
- **Temporal alignment:** use kdb+ as-of joins and ClickHouse ASOF JOIN to align executions with quotes at decision, release, and fill times, handling anomalies such as crossed markets and stale quotes.
- **Metric computation:** in batch or streaming jobs, compute core TCA metrics like arrival cost, implementation shortfall, VWAP and TWAP slippage, and reversion, using window functions and grouped aggregations.
- **Materialization:** store these metrics in layered fact tables (execution, order, portfolio) with stable identifiers and consistent definitions.
- **Serving and analysis:** expose fact tables via reusable query templates that can drive both static reports and interactive dashboards, while deeper studies can still return to the underlying tick and LOB data as needed.

Crucially, TCA builds directly on the structures you already established for LOB analytics: the same quotes, trades, and reference data; the same temporal-join mechanisms; and the same hybrid use of kdb+ for intraday detail and ClickHouse for long-horizon analysis. By designing TCA as another consumer of that core market-data layer, rather than a separate system, you ensure consistency across trading, risk, and oversight-an increasingly important requirement in modern electronic markets.

8.3 Historical Backtesting over Tick Data

In the earlier sections we have built upward from the raw market feed: first reconstructing limit order books, then aligning executions and quotes for Transaction Cost Analysis. Both of those topics worked primarily at intraday and single-day horizons, even if we hinted at longer history.

We now take the opposite view: imagine you want to replay years of tick data to test and refine strategies. The challenge is no longer to answer a single query quickly, but to answer many similar queries, repeatedly, over very large datasets, without unpredictable slowdowns or operational pain.

This section focuses on how to structure your kdb+ and ClickHouse storage so that multi-year, tick-level backtesting becomes routine rather than heroic. We will:

- review typical tick-level backtest access patterns,
- design kdb+ historical database (HDB) layouts that match those patterns,
- map equivalent ideas into ClickHouse partitions and primary indexes,
- outline how to build a backtest execution loop that reuses scans instead of re-reading data for every scenario,
- and discuss techniques for cache warming, pre-materialized signals, and production-backtest reconciliation.

The main theme is that storage design is not an afterthought: it is the foundation that determines whether backtests run in minutes or days.

How Backtests Actually Touch Tick Data

Before we design tables, we must make clear what backtests really do with tick data. In practice, most historical simulations involve some combination of the following patterns:

- **Sliding time windows:** strategies often look at recent history (for example, the last few seconds or minutes of trades and quotes) to form signals, then step forward in time and repeat.
- **Cross-sectional universes:** strategies rarely trade all symbols at once. They operate on specific universes (for example, a stock index, a sector, or a liquidity bucket) that may change over time.
- **Scenario batching:** researchers test many parameter sets or strategy variants on the same underlying data. The input ticks are identical; only the logic applied to them differs.
- **Non-uniform sampling:** strategies that trade at bar intervals (for example, every second or every minute) still need tick-level data to simulate intra-bar fills and slippage.

If we simply dump ticks into a generic store and scan from scratch for each run, we waste I/O and CPU and get highly variable runtimes. Instead, we want layouts that:

- read ticks in *time order* so that simulation loops can stream through them,
- prune data for symbols and dates that a given backtest does not need,
- and allow multiple strategy variants to share the same underlying scan.

kdb+ and ClickHouse, despite their differences, both work best when you cooperate with their partitioning and ordering assumptions. We now look at each in turn.

kdb+ HDB Layout for Multi-Year Ticks

kdb+ was designed from the start for time series data. The canonical layout uses a historical database (HDB) partitioned by date, with columnar tables on disk. Getting the details right can make the difference between a backtest that hums and one that stalls.

Partitioning by Date

The most common choice is to partition the HDB by trade date: each directory corresponds to a date, and within it you store tables such as:

- trades,
- quotes or LOB snapshots,
- orders or internal events.

This aligns neatly with typical backtest horizons: most runs cover a contiguous date range, and scanning day-by-day is natural. It also keeps each partition reasonably sized, which helps when mounting on multiple hosts or doing maintenance.

Symbol Organization: Wide vs. Narrow Tables

Inside each daily partition, you must decide how to organize symbols:

- **Single wide table:** one table per data type (trades, quotes) with a "symbol" column; all symbols share the same schema. This is simple and flexible.
- **Per-symbol tables or keyed structures:** each symbol, sector, or asset class has its own table or key, which can be efficient if different symbols are accessed independently.

For most backtesting use cases, a single wide table with a symbol column is the most maintainable. It works well with cross-sectional queries and avoids managing thousands of separate physical tables. You can then:

- sort each table by symbol and time,
- and use in-memory indexing or attribute hints (such as sorted/-parted) to accelerate symbol and time filtering.

If you know that some symbols are super hot (for example, index futures) and others are rarely used, you can consider separating them into different tables. But this is usually an optimization, not a starting requirement.

Time Ordering and Streaming Access

Backtest loops are most efficient when they can stream ticks in time order for a given symbol or universe. To support this, ensure:

- within each table, data is stored sorted by time (and often grouped by symbol within that),
- your queries request data in time order and then process it sequentially.

Streaming in time order has two major benefits:

- **Cache friendliness:** once a block of data is read from disk, it can be processed immediately without random seeks.
- **Natural state updates:** many strategy states (for example, moving averages, order books, or intraday P&L) can be updated incrementally as time advances.

In kdb+, this style plays directly to its vectorized operations: you pull a vector of ticks for a symbol or day, then apply your backtest logic across that vector, often in a single pass.

Balancing Granularity and Practicality

Tick-level data can be enormous. For extremely liquid instruments, you may need billions of rows per year. The HDB layout must balance:

- **Partition size:** partitions that are too large become unwieldy to back up, copy, or scan; too small, and you incur overhead handling thousands of directories.

- **Compression:** using kdb+'s on-disk compression saves space and I/O, but may increase CPU usage. The right choice depends on your hardware.

Daily partitions with compressed columnar storage are a good default. If you find that some days are exceptionally heavy (for example, volatile crisis days), you might treat them specially—for instance, by caching them on faster media or pre-warming them before large test runs.

ClickHouse Layout: Partitions, ORDER BY, and Indexes

ClickHouse is a columnar database optimized for analytical workloads over very large datasets. While kdb+ gives you fine-grained control over in-memory processing, ClickHouse shines when you want to scan trillions of rows with predictable performance.

To support backtesting, we adapt the same principles as for kdb+, but through ClickHouse's MergeTree engine:

- choose partition keys that match time-based pruning,
- define ORDER BY keys that group by symbol and time,
- and design primary indexes that let ClickHouse skip irrelevant data.

Partition by Date or Month

As with kdb+, partitioning by date is the natural choice. However, ClickHouse partitions can be coarser than daily if needed. Two common options are:

- **Daily partitions:** simple to reason about and convenient for ingest and deletions. Best for moderate data volumes or when daily maintenance is expected.
- **Monthly partitions:** fewer partitions, which can improve metadata performance and simplify retention policies, but each partition is larger.

For multi-year backtests, monthly partitions often provide a good balance: you can prune entire months when they are out of range, but still keep per-partition sizes manageable.

ORDER BY and Primary Index

Within each partition, you must define an ORDER BY expression. This controls both physical layout and how ClickHouse builds its sparse primary index. For tick and quote data, a proven pattern is:

- ORDER BY (symbol, timestamp, possibly a small sequence number).

This layout supports:

- efficient filtering by symbol and time range (common for backtests),
- sequential scanning of all ticks for a symbol within a period,
- straightforward as-of joins and window functions over time.

The primary index allows ClickHouse to skip large chunks of data that fall outside the requested symbol or time interval, leading to predictable scan volumes. This is crucial when backtests query subsets of the universe or limited date ranges.

Wide vs. Narrow Tables in ClickHouse

As in kdb+, you can choose between:

- a single table per data type (trades, quotes) with a symbol column,
- or multiple tables partitioned by instrument group.

For most backtesting, a single table per data type works best, especially when you want to write generic analysis queries that apply across all symbols. If you find that some asset classes have very different schemas, separate tables by asset class, but maintain consistent partitioning and ordering strategies across them.

Designing the Backtest Execution Loop

With storage structures in place, we now turn to the backtest engine itself. The heart of any large-scale backtesting system is the *execution loop*: the code that reads historical ticks and applies strategy logic.

From a data-system perspective, two guiding ideas make the biggest difference:

- **Stream once, simulate many:** reuse the same tick stream across many strategy variants.
- **Checkpoint and resume:** support long runs that can be paused, resumed, or branched without starting from scratch.

Streaming Once, Simulating Many

If you test 100 parameter combinations of a given strategy, it is inefficient to scan the tick data 100 times. Instead:

- design your loop so that you read ticks for a symbol and date range once,
- and at each tick, update the state of all parameter variants in parallel.

In kdb+, this might mean:

- bringing a day's ticks for a symbol into memory as vectors,
- initializing a list of strategy states, one per parameter set,
- and applying vectorized operations where possible to update all states simultaneously.

In ClickHouse, the engine itself is not a backtesting runtime, but you can emulate this idea by:

- materializing intermediate signals (such as moving averages or volatility estimates) across all ticks,
- and then applying strategy rules in a lighter-weight engine that reads those signals in batch.

The key is that heavy tick reads and basic pre-processing steps are shared, not repeated.

Checkpointing and Branching

Large backtests may run for hours or days, especially if they cover many years or a broad universe. To make them robust and flexible:

- **Checkpoint periodically:** every so often (for example, daily or weekly in simulated time), persist the state of each strategy variant: positions, open orders, P&L, and any internal variables.
- **Resume from checkpoints:** if a run fails, you can restart from the last checkpoint instead of from the beginning.
- **Branch scenarios:** you can fork new variants from an existing checkpoint to explore alternative risk limits or execution rules from that point forward.

From a storage perspective, checkpoints can be stored in either kdb+ or ClickHouse, depending on your architecture:

- kdb+ is well-suited for frequent, lightweight snapshots of in-memory state, perhaps written to the HDB as partitioned tables keyed by backtest run and date.
- ClickHouse is better for consolidating final results and a subset of checkpoints for large-scale analysis.

Checkpoint design also aids reproducibility. By capturing both the state and the code or configuration version used, you can later reconstruct exactly how a given result was produced.

Cache Warming and Resource Management

Backtests often touch the same historical periods repeatedly: for example, researchers may focus on crisis episodes or recent years. To avoid repeated cold reads from slower storage:

- consider pre-loading heavily used partitions into faster storage (such as local SSDs or memory-mapped caches),
- or running a lightweight warm-up query over the relevant date-symbol ranges before starting a large batch of backtests.

In kdb+, you can:

- keep frequently tested days or instruments on local disks of the compute nodes running backtests,
- or even pre-load critical symbol-date slices into memory before starting simulation loops.

In ClickHouse, the server's own caching, combined with thoughtful partitioning and ordering, often suffices. But you can further help by:

- clustering related backtests by date ranges, so that once a partition is warm, many runs can benefit,
- and monitoring query profiles to adjust resource allocation and partitioning strategies.

Effective cache use is less about clever algorithms and more about predictable, sequential scans and reuse of data across runs.

Pre-Materialized Factors and Signal Tables

Tick-level backtests often reuse the same underlying features:

- moving averages or other trend measures,
- volatility estimates at different horizons,

- liquidity and spread metrics,
- external factors such as index levels or macro indicators matched to time.

Rather than recomputing these for each strategy, you can build *factor tables* or *signal tables* that store them once per symbol and time bucket. These tables become intermediate layers between raw ticks and strategy-specific logic.

For example:

- using kdb+, you might maintain intraday factor tables in the HDB, computed overnight from tick and LOB data, with one row per symbol and second capturing key measures;
- in ClickHouse, similar tables can be created as part of nightly ETL pipelines, partitioned by date and ordered by symbol and time, just like raw ticks.

Strategies then read these factor tables, which are much smaller than raw ticks and more directly aligned with decision intervals. When you change a factor definition, you rebuild the factor tables once, then all backtests using those factors remain consistent.

This is the same pattern used earlier for LOB feature stores and TCA fact tables: expensive, generic computations are centralized, and strategy-specific logic builds on top.

Reconciling Backtest and Production

A recurring source of frustration in trading organizations is the "backtest-production gap": the strategy behaves well in simulation, but differently in live trading. Some differences are inevitable, but many can be reduced by aligning data and storage practices.

From a data-store perspective, three principles help:

- **Common data sources:** backtests and production should pull ticks, quotes, and LOB features from the same underlying stores, or from well-defined replicas derived by simple transformations.

- **Shared schemas and feature definitions:** if a feature is defined as a particular moving average or volatility estimate in production, the backtest should use exactly the same calculation, ideally implemented in a shared library or view.
- **Versioned inputs:** when data is corrected (for example, due to late vendor updates), you should be able to rerun backtests against both the original and the corrected datasets and see the impact.

Practically, this often leads to a design where:

- kdb+ handles intraday storage and calculation of features for live strategies,
- these features and underlying ticks are periodically exported to ClickHouse in a normalized format,
- backtests primarily run against ClickHouse's deep history but can also replay recent days from kdb+ when microsecond-level fidelity is needed,
- and a small set of reconciliation reports compares live P&L and simulated P&L over overlapping periods, using identical data slices and feature definitions.

When discrepancies are found, you can trace whether they stem from:

- differences in slippage models,
- incomplete modeling of queue position and partial fills,
- or genuine behavior changes that require strategy or infrastructure updates.

Putting It Together: Predictable, Repeatable Backtests

We can now summarize how storage structure in kdb+ and ClickHouse enables large-scale tick-level backtesting:

- **Data layout:** both systems store ticks and quotes in time-partitioned, symbol-aware tables, allowing backtests to stream in time order and to prune irrelevant data quickly.

- **Scan reuse:** strategy variants are designed to share underlying scans, either by updating multiple states in parallel (kdb+) or by consuming shared factor tables (ClickHouse).

- **Operational robustness:** checkpoints, cache warming, and resource-aware partitioning prevent large runs from becoming fragile or unpredictable.

- **Consistency with production:** shared schemas and feature definitions ensure that backtests are grounded in the same data reality as live trading and TCA.

Viewed in this light, backtesting is not an isolated activity but another consumer of the same high-performance data stores used for intraday analytics and risk. By investing in thoughtful storage and partitioning design, you gain not only speed, but also confidence that your simulations faithfully reflect the markets and trading behaviors you will encounter in production.

8.4 Real-Time Risk on Streaming Prices

The previous sections have focused on using kdb+ and ClickHouse for historical and intraday analytics: reconstructing limit order books, measuring transaction costs, and replaying years of tick data for backtests. We now turn to a closely related, but more operationally demanding, problem: computing risk *right now*, continuously, as prices and positions change during the trading day.

Real-time risk means more than a dashboard that refreshes every few minutes. For many desks, it implies:

- sub-second updates to exposures and Greeks as ticks arrive,

- immediate detection of limit breaches,

- and a reliable audit trail of what risk looked like at any point in time.

Achieving this requires a careful separation of concerns:

- a **streaming ingest path** that brings in prices, positions, and reference data,
- a **stateful in-memory risk engine** that converts these inputs into exposures and Greeks with very low latency,
- and a **durable analytical store** that archives the enriched data for later analysis, backtesting, and regulatory reporting.

kdb+ and ClickHouse play complementary roles here: kdb+ as the low-latency, stateful front end; ClickHouse as the deep, analytical back end. In this section we design such a stack step by step.

Streaming Inputs: Prices, Positions, and Reference Data

A real-time risk engine consumes several distinct but related data streams:

- **Tick prices:** quotes and trades for underlying instruments (equities, futures, FX, and so on), often at millisecond or microsecond resolution.
- **Curves and surfaces:** interest-rate curves, volatility surfaces, and other market data used for valuation and sensitivity calculations.
- **Positions:** current holdings and open trades across portfolios, updated as executions occur and as internal books are adjusted.
- **Reference data:** instrument definitions, contract multipliers, currency information, and risk configuration (such as which sensitivities to compute for which desks).

From a system perspective, the first decision is where these streams land. A typical architecture uses kdb+ tick as the primary recipient of high-frequency data:

- feed handlers write raw tick prices into a kdb+ real-time database (RDB),
- executions and position updates are streamed from order-management or trade-capture systems into kdb+ tables keyed by portfolio and instrument,
- curves and reference data are refreshed periodically and stored in smaller, slowly changing tables in kdb+ and ClickHouse.

ClickHouse may also receive near-real-time copies of these feeds, but its main role is durability and large-scale analysis; it is not the place to run per-tick risk calculations with tight latency constraints.

Separating Fast Risk Computation from Durable Storage

The central design principle for real-time risk is the clean separation between:

- a **hot path** that computes risk quickly in memory and serves live dashboards and alerts, and
- a **cold path** that writes out enriched, durable records for later analysis and reconciliation.

The hot path must be fast, predictable, and isolated from heavy disk I/O. The cold path can be slower and more flexible, as long as it does not interfere with live calculations.

Right after we introduce this separation, it is helpful to visualize the whole architecture.

In this diagram, the hot path runs through the top row: streaming ingest updates an in-memory market and position state; the risk engine transforms that into exposures and Greeks; dashboards and alerting

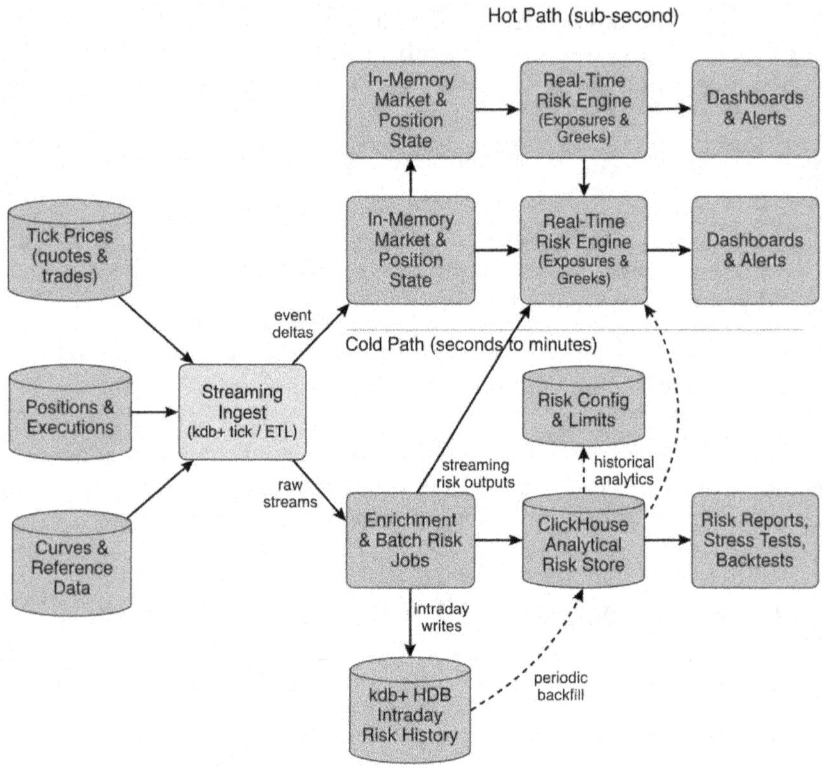

systems consume those results. The cold path flows through the bottom row: both raw streams and risk outputs are enriched and written to kdb+ and ClickHouse for deeper analysis, stress testing, and historical reporting.

The remainder of the section explains how to build each part of this architecture.

In-Memory State for Fast Risk

To compute risk metrics quickly, you must avoid recomputing everything from scratch on every tick. Instead, maintain an in-memory state that tracks:

- the latest price, curve point, or volatility surface for each risk factor (for example, equity spot prices, FX rates, interest rates),
- current positions by instrument and portfolio,
- precomputed sensitivities (for example, deltas, gammas, vegas) at the instrument or trade level, whenever possible.

Conceptually, this state behaves like a table or set of tables keyed by instrument and portfolio, with columns for positions, risk factors, and sensitivities. When a new tick arrives:

1. you identify which instruments and risk factors are affected,
2. you update their entries in the in-memory state,
3. you propagate the changes through to exposures and Greeks for the relevant portfolios.

kdb+ is especially well-suited to this style of computation:

- it can hold moderate-sized state tables entirely in memory,
- its vectorized operations allow you to update many positions or instruments in one shot when a curve or surface moves,
- its natural time-series orientation simplifies keeping track of the evolution of risk variables over the day.

The essential idea is incrementalism: each tick only triggers a small, bounded amount of work.

Expressing Risk as Incremental Updates

Risk metrics such as delta, gamma, vega, and PV01 describe how the value of a portfolio changes when underlying risk factors move. Computing them from scratch for every new market data point would be prohibitively expensive, especially for large derivative books.

Instead, we make two simplifying moves:

1. **Precompute static sensitivities:** For many products, much of the complexity lives in pricing formulas and their derivatives. You can run a heavier valuation process periodically (for example, overnight or every few minutes) to compute baseline sensitivities for each trade or netted position under a given market scenario.
2. **Treat risk factors as small shocks:** When an underlying price moves slightly, the change in portfolio value can be approximated by multiplying the movement by the corresponding sensitivity. For more complex moves, you may combine multiple sensitivities (for example, delta and gamma) or fall back to a full revaluation at lower frequency.

In real-time, the risk engine then behaves as follows:

- when a single spot price moves, update the contribution of all positions whose value depends on that price based on their precomputed deltas (and gammas if needed),
- when an interest-rate curve point shifts, apply the relevant DV01 or bucketed PV01 to positions sensitive to that curve,
- when a volatility surface node changes, update the vega contribution of the affected options.

Because this work is proportional to the number of impacted positions and sensitivities, not to the full size of the portfolio, it scales much better than full revaluation. It also aligns naturally with kdb+'s vector semantics: each event triggers a vector update over the relevant slice of the state table.

Bounding Per-Tick Work and Enforcing SLAs

Sub-second SLAs are not met by accident. You must explicitly bound the amount of work that can occur per event and design mechanisms to handle bursts of activity.

Key strategies include:

Event Batching. Rather than process every microsecond update individually, you can:

- group ticks into small batches (for example, tens of milliseconds or a fixed number of events),
- process each batch atomically, updating state and computing risk once per batch.

This reduces overhead and allows some smoothing of load during bursts, at the cost of slightly higher latency. For many desks, this is an acceptable trade-off.

Selective Updates. Not every tick matters equally. You may:

- ignore quotes that are far from the current trading range or correspond to instruments not held in any portfolio,
- coalesce multiple updates to the same instrument within a very short interval, processing only the most recent.

The engine can maintain a small queue per instrument and process the latest known state, discarding intermediate fluctuations that would not materially change risk.

Tiered Portfolios. Some books are more latency-sensitive than others. You can:

- maintain a small subset of critical portfolios in the highest-priority hot path, updated on every relevant tick,
- update less sensitive books at coarser intervals or via batch jobs that reuse the same market data.

This tiering ensures that your most important risk metrics receive the necessary resources.

Fan-Out to Dashboards and Alerts

Once exposures and Greeks are computed, they must be delivered to consumers:

- trader and risk-manager dashboards showing current and historical risk metrics,
- automated alerting systems that trigger when limits are breached,
- and possibly other internal services, such as automated hedging engines.

To preserve the isolation of the risk engine:

- avoid having dashboards query the in-memory state directly for every display refresh,
- instead, use a publish-subscribe or event-stream mechanism: the risk engine pushes updates to a bus, and consumers subscribe to the subsets they care about (for example, a specific desk or portfolio),
- maintain a lightweight read-only cache per consumer group, populated from the stream, so that display refreshes and interactive queries do not touch the core risk engine.

In kdb+, it is common to have one process responsible for core risk calculations and separate subscription servers that distribute updates. Those subscribers can write to local tables, which dashboards query. This way, a slow or misbehaving dashboard cannot stall the risk engine.

Durable Storage: Archiving Risk for Analysis

The hot path provides immediate visibility, but for governance, model validation, and research, you also need a durable record of:

- the risk metrics themselves (exposures and Greeks over time),

- the market data and positions that produced them,
- the configuration and model parameters in effect at each point.

This is where the cold path comes in.

kdb+ HDB for Intraday and Recent History

kdb+ can store intraday and recent days of risk history as regular HDB tables:

- risk metrics are written from the hot path to intraday tables partitioned by date and keyed by time, portfolio, and instrument,
- enriched ticks (such as prices with joined sensitivities or partial valuations) can be stored alongside pure market data,
- overnight, these intraday tables are rolled into the HDB, where they can be accessed for short-term backfills and sanity checks.

Because the same kdb+ cluster already holds ticks, quotes, and positions, linking risk metrics to their inputs is straightforward.

ClickHouse for Deep Analytical History

For multi-year horizons and heavy analysis-stress testing, scenario simulations, and model calibration-ClickHouse is the natural home:

- risk fact tables are ingested from kdb+ or from batch risk jobs into ClickHouse MergeTree tables,
- these tables are partitioned by date (or month) and ordered by portfolio, instrument, and time, allowing efficient queries by desk, strategy, or risk factor,
- supplementary dimension tables describe portfolios, instruments, and risk configurations, enabling rich slicing and dicing.

Because ClickHouse excels at grouped aggregations and joins, it is ideal for:

- reconstructing risk histories under alternative stress scenarios,

- computing distributional properties of exposures and Greeks (such as percentiles, tail metrics),
- comparing model versions or risk methodologies over long periods.

The key is to maintain consistent schemas and identifiers between the hot and cold paths so that a risk snapshot in the dashboard can be traced to a row in ClickHouse and to its underlying data.

Handling Late Data and Replays

In any streaming system, you must plan for imperfections: missed ticks, delayed executions, and corrections to curves or positions. A robust real-time risk stack requires clear procedures for:

- **Late ticks or trades:** updates that arrive out of order or with delay relative to real time.
- **Replay of missed intervals:** periods during which the risk engine was down or disconnected from some feeds.
- **Corrections and restatements:** changes to historical positions or market data, such as corrected trades from a clearing system.

At the architectural level, three practices help:

Idempotent Writes. Ensure that writing risk metrics and market data to kdb+ and ClickHouse is idempotent where possible:

- use stable keys (time, portfolio, instrument) so that replays overwrite prior incorrect values rather than creating duplicates,
- maintain a small set of status flags or version identifiers to distinguish original from corrected records when necessary.

Deterministic Replays. For replays:

- use the same data sources and code versions as in real time, so that risk metrics recomputed over a historical interval match the originals (absent corrections),
- structure the risk engine so that it can operate in both real-time and replay modes, reading from stored tick and position tables instead of live streams, but using the same update logic.

Because kdb+ and ClickHouse already house the full tick and position history, they are ideal replay sources.

Clear Ownership of Truth. Decide and document which system is the ultimate source of truth for:

- positions and trades (often a central trade-capture or position-keeping system, mirrored in kdb+ and ClickHouse),
- market data (usually a vendor or internal market data service, mirrored in kdb+ and ClickHouse),
- risk metrics (the risk engine, with its outputs archived).

When corrections arise, they should flow from the source of truth through the same pipelines, triggering appropriate replays and updates downstream.

Observability and Operational Monitoring

Finally, a real-time risk stack must be observable. You need to know not only the value of risk metrics, but also:

- the latency between incoming ticks and updated risk outputs,
- the rate of dropped or delayed events,
- the health of the ingestion, computation, and storage layers.

Practical measures include:

- embedding timestamps at each stage of the pipeline and computing end-to-end and component latencies,

- tracking queue depths in the ingest and risk-engine processes to detect backlogs,
- logging anomalies such as unusually large jumps in exposures or missing updates for key portfolios.

Both kdb+ and ClickHouse can participate in observability:

- kdb+ can maintain small in-memory tables of operational metrics updated in real time and periodically flushed to disk,
- ClickHouse can store longer-term logs of latencies, error counts, and throughput, enabling trend analysis and capacity planning.

With good observability in place, you can detect issues before they become crises, and you can justify architectural changes with empirical evidence.

Summary: A Cohesive Real-Time Risk Architecture

Putting all the pieces together, a robust real-time risk stack:

- ingests streaming prices, curves, positions, and reference data into kdb+ tick and supporting services,
- maintains an in-memory state of market and position data, along with precomputed sensitivities,
- expresses risk updates as incremental transformations triggered by event deltas, with carefully bounded per-tick work,
- isolates the hot path (risk engine and dashboards) from the cold path (archival storage and heavy analytics),
- archives enriched risk metrics into kdb+ HDB for recent history and into ClickHouse for deep, large-scale analysis,
- supports deterministic replays and corrections based on the same tick and position stores, ensuring consistency between real-time and historical views,

- and is instrumented with observability to monitor latency, data quality, and system health.

This architecture builds naturally on the structures developed in previous sections: the same tick and LOB stores, the same temporal joins, and the same hybrid use of kdb+ and ClickHouse. The difference is that, in real-time risk, latency and operational robustness become first-class design goals. By treating the risk engine as a specialized, stateful consumer of the market data platform-rather than a separate silo-you can deliver sub-second exposures and Greeks today, while also providing the historical depth and transparency that regulators, risk committees, and researchers demand.

8.5 Hybrid kdb+ + ClickHouse Architectures

By this point in the chapter we have treated kdb+ and ClickHouse mostly in isolation: kdb+ as an ultra-low-latency engine for limit order book analytics, intraday TCA alignment, and real-time risk; ClickHouse as a deep, scalable store for multi year tick backtests and heavy aggregations. In production, however, you almost never deploy just one or the other. You build a *hybrid* architecture in which each system does what it is best at, and where data flows between them in predictable, auditable ways.

This section develops such hybrid designs. We will:

- clarify the roles of kdb+ and ClickHouse in a modern trading stack,
- introduce a high-level topology that combines per-desk or per-region kdb+ clusters with centralized ClickHouse,
- describe interoperability patterns for streaming, snapshots, and shared schemas,
- define clear data-ownership boundaries and reconciliation workflows,

- and outline migration paths from single-technology stacks to a robust dual-database design.

The goal is not to prescribe a single "correct" architecture, but to give you patterns and vocabulary to reason about your own environment.

Clear Roles: What Each System Is For

A hybrid architecture works smoothly only when each component has a sharp, well-understood role. In broad terms:

- **kdb+ as low-latency front end**
  - primary consumer of real-time feeds (ticks, LOB events, positions),
  - engine for sub-second analytics: intraday LOB features, per-tick TCA alignment, streaming risk,
  - short-horizon historical store (intraday to a few weeks or months, depending on footprint).
- **ClickHouse as deep analytics back end**
  - repository for long-horizon tick, quote, and derived data (months to years),
  - platform for heavy aggregations and window analytics: large TCA jobs, backtesting, regulatory and management reporting,
  - integration hub for cross-desk and cross-region analysis.

Another way to say this is: kdb+ owns *intraday truth* and fast reactions; ClickHouse owns *historical truth* and broad, slower questions. Almost every design decision in a hybrid stack can be traced back to honoring this division of labor.

A High-Level Hybrid Topology

Most trading firms are not monoliths; they are collections of desks or regions, each with its own instruments, trading styles, and operational requirements. A natural topology is therefore:

- multiple kdb+ clusters, one per desk or per region,
- one or a small number of centralized ClickHouse clusters serving the whole firm.

Right after defining these roles, it is useful to look at a schematic of how they fit together.

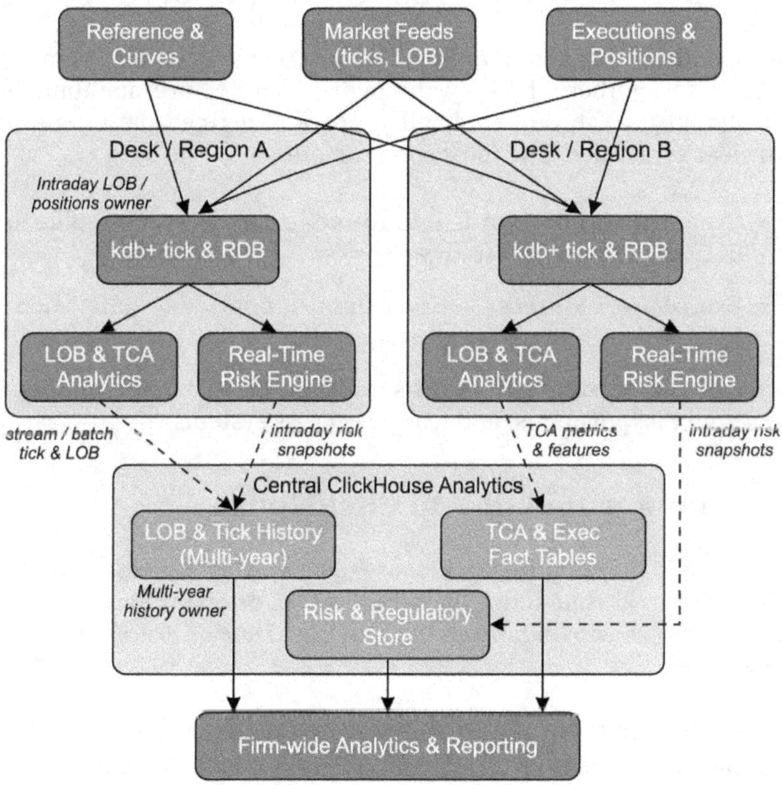

This diagram illustrates the core ideas:

- each desk or region has its own kdb+ stack tailored to its latency and product needs,
- all these stacks stream or batch-export data and derived metrics into shared ClickHouse clusters,
- ClickHouse becomes the cross-cutting analytics and reporting hub.

We now unpack how data moves between these layers.

Interoperability Patterns: Getting Data Across

Interoperability is about more than just copying bytes from one database to another. To keep the hybrid architecture maintainable, data should flow through a small set of well-defined patterns, each with clear semantics. The most common are:

- **Streaming kdb+ to ClickHouse:** near-real-time replication of ticks, quotes, or intraday metrics.
- **Snapshot exports:** periodic dumps of intraday state, such as LOB cubes or intraday risk snapshots.
- **Shared dimensions and schemas:** consistent definitions of symbols, portfolios, and features across systems.

Streaming from kdb+ to ClickHouse

For use cases that require ClickHouse to be only a few seconds or minutes behind real time (such as intraday TCA or operational monitoring), you can stream data from kdb+ to ClickHouse. Practical options include:

- a kdb+ publisher process that subscribes to tick and analytics tables and writes events into ClickHouse via an ingestion layer (for example, HTTP or a streaming connector),

- use of a message bus (such as Kafka) where kdb+ publishes events, and ClickHouse consumes them via native or connector-based ingestion.

The design principles here are:

- **Idempotence:** events should carry stable keys (symbol, time, sequence) so that replays or duplicates are harmless.
- **Decoupling:** failures or slowdowns in ClickHouse ingestion must not impact the kdb+ hot path. Buffers or queues absorb temporary backpressure.
- **Schema stability:** streaming schemas should change infrequently and in backward-compatible ways.

Typical streams include:

- normalized tick and quote data,
- LOB features (spreads, microprice, imbalance) computed in kdb+,
- intraday execution-level TCA metrics,
- real-time risk metrics at a coarser granularity (for example, every few seconds instead of every tick).

Snapshot and Batch Exports

For many analytical tasks, minute-level or end-of-day freshness is enough. In those cases, batch exports are simpler and more robust than continuous streams. Examples include:

- end-of-day LOB cubes and per-order TCA fact tables,
- daily risk summary tables by portfolio and desk,
- updated dimension tables (instrument reference data, corporate action histories).

Exports can be implemented as:

- nightly kdb+ jobs that write partitioned files (such as compressed columnar formats) to a shared storage layer, which ClickHouse then ingests,
- or direct batched inserts from kdb+ into ClickHouse, carefully sized to avoid overloading either side.

The advantage of this pattern is control: you know exactly when exports run, what volume of data they carry, and how they map to reporting cycles.

Shared Dimensions and Schema Alignment

All interoperability depends on consistent identifiers and definitions. At minimum, you should share:

- **Instrument dimensions:** symbols, exchange codes, contract details, multipliers, and currencies.
- **Portfolio and strategy dimensions:** desks, books, clients, strategies, and any hierarchy used in reporting.
- **Calendar and time conventions:** trading days, sessions, and time zones.

Practically, this means:

- keeping a small set of dimension tables under strong governance (versioned, centrally managed),
- storing them in both kdb+ and ClickHouse, using identical keys and field names where possible,
- and keeping feature names and units consistent across systems (for example, always store spreads in price terms or basis points, but not both).

With shared dimensions, you can join and reconcile data across layers without custom mappings on every query.

Data Ownership: Who Is the Source of Truth?

A hybrid system must avoid ambiguity about where "truth" lives. Without clear ownership, different teams may produce conflicting numbers, eroding trust in analytics. Ownership should be defined along two main axes:

- **Time horizon:**
  - kdb+ typically owns intraday data (ticks, LOB states, intraday features),
  - ClickHouse owns long-horizon, possibly corrected or enriched history.
- **Data domain:**
  - execution and trade records might be sourced from a central trade-capture system, mirrored in both databases,
  - risk measures may be produced by a dedicated risk engine, with kdb+ holding real-time views and ClickHouse storing archived, post-processed history.

Concretely, you might adopt rules such as:

- intraday LOB features are authoritative in kdb+; ClickHouse receives them as-is and does not recompute them,
- TCA order- and execution-level metrics are computed once (in kdb+ or in an ETL job) and exported to ClickHouse; downstream systems must not re-implement them differently,
- any corrections to tick or trade data originate from the upstream market or trade-capture system and then propagate identically into both kdb+ and ClickHouse.

Documenting these rules, and encoding them in data contracts and schemas, is as important as implementing the data flows themselves.

Reconciliation Workflows: Keeping Layers in Sync

Even with clear ownership, data can drift: exports may miss records, ingestion jobs may fail, or corrections may be applied unevenly. A hybrid architecture therefore needs explicit reconciliation workflows.

Typical reconciliation tasks include:

- **Row-count and checksum checks:** ensure that, for each partition (for example, day, symbol range), the number of ticks or executions in ClickHouse matches kdb+; optionally compare aggregates like total volume or notional.
- **Metric alignment:** compare key metrics (for example, daily VWAP, end-of-day LOB spreads, portfolio exposures) computed from kdb+ and ClickHouse representations of the same data.
- **Latency and freshness checks:** monitor the delay between intraday events in kdb+ and their appearance in ClickHouse.

These checks can themselves be implemented as periodic jobs:

- kdb+ scripts compute summary statistics over recent partitions and write them to a small reconciliation table,
- ClickHouse jobs compute the same statistics over its partitions,
- a comparison process flags mismatches beyond defined tolerances and, where possible, triggers re-ingestion or replays automatically.

Over time, reconciliation reports become crucial operational tools. They give both developers and auditors confidence that the same underlying market and trading data is consistently represented across systems.

Common Hybrid Topologies

Within the general pattern of kdb+ fronts and a ClickHouse back, there are several common variations.

Per-Desk kdb+ Clusters Feeding a Central Lake

In this topology:

- each desk (for example, equities, FX, fixed income) runs its own kdb+ cluster tuned to its products and latency needs,
- all clusters export normalized data and derived metrics into a central ClickHouse "lake",
- cross-asset analytics (such as firm-wide risk or client-level TCA) are run primarily in ClickHouse.

Advantages:

- desks can move quickly and independently on their kdb+ setups,
- central teams have a unified, queryable view without dictating intraday infrastructure.

Challenges:

- maintaining consistent schemas and dimensions across desk-specific kdb+ instances,
- ensuring that central ClickHouse has sufficient context to interpret and join desk-specific data.

Multi-Region Deployments

Global firms may deploy separate stacks by region (for example, Americas, EMEA, APAC), each close to its local markets to minimize latency. Here:

- each region has its own kdb+ clusters and often its own ClickHouse instance for regional analytics,
- a higher-level ClickHouse cluster or logical view aggregates data across regions for global reporting.

Data may flow hierarchically:

- from regional kdb+ to regional ClickHouse,
- then from regional ClickHouse to a global ClickHouse instance via periodic exports.

This arrangement reduces cross-region bandwidth usage for raw ticks, pushing heavy data movement up the hierarchy only when needed.

Cloud-Native Hybrids

In cloud environments, you can blend managed services with self-hosted components:

- kdb+ processes run close to exchange gateways or co-location facilities (on-premises or cloud edge),
- ClickHouse clusters run on scalable cloud infrastructure, possibly using object storage for cold partitions,
- data moves via managed streaming services for resilience and observability.

Cloud-native designs make it easier to:

- scale ClickHouse CPU and storage elastically for large backtests or regulatory runs,
- burst workloads to additional clusters without disturbing core production systems.

However, latency and cost considerations may still favor running kdb+ in or near traditional co-location facilities for the tightest market connectivity.

Migration Paths to a Hybrid Architecture

Few organizations start with a clean slate. More often, you have an existing single-technology stack and must introduce the second system carefully.

From kdb+-Only to Hybrid

If you currently rely solely on kdb+ for both intraday and long-horizon analytics, a sensible path is:

1. Identify heavy, long-running queries (for example, multi-year backtests, full-firm TCA) that strain kdb+ clusters.
2. Introduce ClickHouse as a secondary store for the most demanding historical tables (ticks, quotes, executions), loading from kdb+ HDB exports.
3. Redirect heavy batch workloads to ClickHouse while keeping intraday and latency-sensitive jobs in kdb+.
4. Gradually move pre-aggregated fact tables (TCA, risk history) into ClickHouse as well, following the data-ownership principles discussed earlier.

Throughout, you keep kdb+ as the primary point of contact for feeds and intraday applications, but shift the historical burden to ClickHouse.

From ClickHouse-Only to Hybrid

If you started with ClickHouse as your main data store for market and trading data, you may find its latency or stateful-processing model limiting for ultra-low-latency use cases. In that case:

1. Introduce kdb+ for new latency-sensitive applications (for example, real-time risk, very fast LOB analytics), feeding it directly from market data sources or from ClickHouse via streaming.
2. Keep ClickHouse as the central historical store, continuing to load market data and executions as before.
3. For any features or metrics that must exist in both systems, define authoritative computation in one place and export the result, rather than re-implementing logic separately.

Over time, you may migrate some intraday processing (such as TCA alignment or streaming feature generation) into kdb+ where its vectorized, in-memory model is stronger.

Choosing the Right Pattern for Your Use Case

Which hybrid pattern is appropriate depends on your constraints:

- **Latency requirements:** if you need single-digit millisecond response for per-tick analytics, kdb+ must sit on the hot path; ClickHouse stays off that path.
- **Data volume and horizon:** if you have many years of multi-asset ticks, ClickHouse should own the bulk of that history; kdb+ maintains only recent partitions needed for short-term backtests and replay.
- **Team skills and tooling:** if your quants and developers are already fluent in q and kdb+, index more workloads toward kdb+ and use ClickHouse mainly for heavy, standardized analytics. If your organization is more SQL-centric, lean more heavily on ClickHouse for new analytical surfaces, using kdb+ as a specialized engine underneath.
- **Regulatory and audit needs:** if rigorous, repeatable reporting is paramount, centralize canonical fact tables (TCA, risk, positions) in ClickHouse with strong governance, and treat kdb+ outputs as inputs to those canonical stores.

A good rule of thumb is:

> Put logic where it wants to live: low-latency, stateful analytics in kdb+; heavy, multi-year aggregations in ClickHouse. Share schemas and feature definitions so that moving data between them is mostly plumbing, not rethinking.

Hybrid kdb+ + ClickHouse architectures allow you to combine the best of two worlds:

- kdb+ delivers ultra-low-latency, intraday analytics and streaming computation, owning real-time views of LOBs, executions, and risk.
- ClickHouse provides a scalable, cost-effective platform for deep historical storage, heavy TCA and backtesting workloads, and firm-wide reporting.
- Interoperability patterns—streaming, snapshots, and shared dimensions—ensure that data flows between layers cleanly and predictably.
- Clear data-ownership boundaries and reconciliation workflows maintain consistency and trust in analytics across desks and regions.
- Migration paths let you evolve from single-technology stacks to robust dual-database designs without disrupting existing workflows.

Seen in this light, kdb+ and ClickHouse are not competitors but collaborators: each takes on the workloads it is naturally suited for, and together they form a unified data backbone for modern electronic trading and risk management.

www.ingramcontent.com/pod-product-compliance
Lightning Source LLC
LaVergne TN
LVHW010916300926
849194LV00025B/241